THE
INTERPRETATION
OF LANGUAGE

VOLUME II:
UNDERSTANDING THE UNCONSCIOUS
MEANING OF LANGUAGE

deceptive to suppose that we communicate simply on the conscious level. Beside and below the intended conscious message, there is always some "noise," the flowing back and forth of an unintentional communication on the subconscious level. Fantasies interfere with concepts; noncognitive sensations interfere with the cognitive perception. Nothing is wholly conscious or entirely unconscious. There is always an interference, one layer infiltrating into the other. The human organism implies a self-regulating mechanism, and the sound human mind has a healing capacity. This healing capacity of the conscious mind is called upon when we try to bring to the daylight elements of our language which were banished to the dream life of unconscious fantasies. Freud's dictum: "where Id was, there Ego shall be" became the foundation of psychoanalytical psychology and psychotherapy. This principle implies also the ethical attitude which once was expressed by the words: *Sapere aude!* "Dare to know!" This is also the guiding principle of the psychoanalytical interpretation of the subconscious language.

Because it is my assumption that the language we speak became shaped and transformed by repressive anxiety, it goes without saying that this anxiety accumulates around the three focal points of organic existence: one is the beginning, birth; another the end, death; and the third is the culmination in the creative act of new life, the sexual union. Human life is limited by birth and death, or, as it is said, existence is but a short interruption of the eternal nonexistence. Anxiety, the great cause of repression, dwells on the borderlines of existence and nonexistence, and on the creative act by which man transcends the limitations of his individual life. We fear things that exist, but we react to the emptiness and void of nonexistence with anxiety. Thus, by necessity, repression tends to purge from our everyday language the three topics of transcendence which are the most frightening because they imply the eternal "beyond"—birth, sex, and death. Birth, marriage, and death still remain the three events which induce man to invoke spiritual powers during his otherwise secularized life.

The transcendent experiences of organic life can be interpreted in terms of biology and physiology—such interpretation is often rejected by those who otherwise prefer the materialistic-scientific line of thinking. I do not share this kind of resistance against the understanding of human destiny in terms of its biological-materialistic limitations. In opposition to this kind of thinking, I maintain, however, that in the quest for knowledge on the metaphysical plane, the riddles of epistemology and ontology are the eternal human problems, whereas the man of the street would say: sex.

Birth, a focal point of avoidance, if questioned by the child, is not simply concerned with sex, but raises the basic ontological question: From where do I come, or what is the beginning of my and all existence?

The sexual union implies the manifestation of love; love implies both the true, intimate knowledge of the other and the search for identity.

Death, the most private event, evokes anxiety because it makes man aware of the end of his individual life, as said in the Bible: "For dust thou art, and unto dust shalt thou return" (Gen. 3:19).

Fantasies about the return to dust, implied also in unconscious fantasies about defecation, are even more prohibitive than the manifestations of love and sex. Freud described the two basic instincts: life and death. In doing so he also defined the mainsprings of verbal repression.

The following chapters were developed around these three basic motives of life. "Part I: Separation and Reunification" tries to explore the verbal fantasies that cluster around the beginning and the first years of life. "Part II: Oedipus—Identity and Knowledge" deals with the questions of existence, reality and its negation, the search for knowledge, and transcendence. "Part III: The Return—Childhood Lost" concentrates upon the topics of regression. Thus, we shall explore the regressive fantasies about the "beginnings" and creation as they became imprinted into our languages. These three events described in the three parts of the following presentation, however private and personal matters they may be, are the common experiences of all mankind.

PART ONE

SEPARATION

AND

REUNIFICATION

SEPARATION

We shall investigate by verbal means the very beginning of the individual life process. We shall try to reclaim from our language the wisdom that has been deposited in it by untold generations of past ages. How did man experience his entering in this world? In the early years of psychoanalysis Otto Rank coined the term "trauma of birth" and found in this idea the very source of anxiety.* I do not believe in the lasting effect of this physiological trauma. I prefer to see rather in the physiological process the psychological separation of the child from the mother as more important.[1] Therefore I shall deal with separation as a primary source of anxiety.

One and Two

The miraculous dividing of mother and child, who are beyond all quantitative thinking as one and two at the same time, is not necessarily identical with the moment of birth according to the fantasies recorded in our languages. Some non-Indo-European languages antedate the separation and consider the prenatal state as the definite division of the primeval unity of mother and child. For instance in Ethiopic languages "She became two souls" is the proper expression for pregnant.[2] Indo-European languages rather extend the dual unity and do not make much difference between "fetus" and

* Anxiety, anguish, and birth are closely associated in Hebrew-Biblical verbal fantasies; however, not the newborn child but the mother suffers the pangs of anxiety, for instance: "And they shall be afraid: pangs and sorrows shall take hold of them; they shall be in pain as a woman that travaileth" (Isa. 13:8), "Like as a woman with child, that draweth near the time of her delivery, is in pain, and crieth out in her pangs; so have we been in thy sight, O Lord" (Isa. 26:17). "For I have heard a voice as of a woman in travail, and the anguish as of her that bringeth forth her first child" (Jer. 4:31), or "Anguish took hold of him, and pangs as of a woman in travail" (Jer. 50:43).

15

"child." The infant, born or not, was considered rather as an object *it* than a *he* or *she* subject; hence there was an assumed legality about all the primitive customs of exposing, burning, burying, or destroying the unwanted babe as long as it was an object and had not awakened to full conscience.

The first suck, this reunification with the mother, seems to be a more important date line than the cutting of the navel cord. A linguistic examination of the available evidence will throw more light on this.

The Greek *brephos* and the Latin *partus* both mean "fetus" and "child." The same fantasies are implied in our word *child*. The Old English *cild* means "fetus" and "babe"; *cild-hama*, properly "child-cover," means "womb." The related forms in the Gothic language are *kilthei*, "womb," and *in-kiltho*, "pregnant." We may say that our word *child* properly denotes the "uterine" being, which is still one with the mother, not really "the fruit" of the womb.

The identification of the prenatal and postnatal state is expressed in Greek fantasies by the generally known representations of the child riding on a dolphin. Small infants play with dolphins; they seem to belong together like twin brothers. They are associated with one another in language, too. The *dolphin* is, for the Greek mind, a symbolic representation of the fetus. In Greek *delphus* means "womb" and *delphis* or *delphinos*, properly "uterine," means "dolphin." The word is continued also in the French *dauphin*, title of the oldest son of the King of France; hence *Dauphiné*, the name of his province. The sons of the Austrian and Hungarian nobles were also called so; their schoolbooks were written *ad usum delphini*, properly "for the use of dolphins," just as we use now the expression a "school (spelled: *schoal*) of fish." The infant and the dolphin as depicted on Greek coins belong together in their verbal representation as well as in mythical fantasies. (*cf.* p. 265.)

The question may be asked, Why was the fish perceived to be the "uterine" animal? The point in question is that the fish was perceived as "uterine" in the likeness of the fetus, and not the other way around (the fetus in the likeness of the fish). The human concept preceded the animal one. Because the fish was perceived as an embryonic being, we find an abundance of fish symbolism in myth and religion. The repressed idea of "fish" was "embryo" or "fetus"; thus the more abstract concepts of growth, generation, fertility, futurity became represented by the image of "fish." In Hebrew the word *dāgh*, "fish," carries the meaning of "prolific" also. The words of Jesus: "I will make you fishers of men" (Matt. 4:19) say more than what appears on the manifest surface of language.

The child is, according to verbal fantasies, a part of the mother; it belongs to her just as body parts belong to the wholeness of the body. What kind of fantasies were originally implied in the word *separation?* The answer to this question might be debatable if based simply on linguistic premises, but it leaves little room for doubt from the psychological viewpoint. There are two Latin verbs with similar phonemic forms: one verb is *parō, -āre,* "to make ready (*pre-pare*)," with the intransitive form *pareō, -ēre,* "to come forth (*appear*)"; the other verb is *pariō, -ere,* "to beget, bring forth, produce, create." These verbs may be disjointed linguistically, yet they are interrelated with one another by their psychological implications. It is hard to believe that the verb *partiō, -īre,* "to share, divide, distribute," or the pertinent noun *prōportio* has nothing in common with *partiō,* "bearing, bringing forth," or that the noun *pars, -tis,* "part," has no relationship with *partus,* "birth, offspring, fetus, embryo."

It can be demonstrated through many instances that in language the human body is the primary reality and the references to the body and body processes are prior to any object references. One will thus suppose that the idea of the birth process (*pariō*) was the original one; it produced, however, cover words, abstract terms that have covered up the original concrete biological content. So "birth" became disguised by the abstract terms for "division, separation"; by the same token the physiological "bring forth" was replaced by the more general "come forth," to *appear* and to be *pre-pared.* In the same way, the verb "to beget, bring forth" (*pariō*) developed the desexualized meanings of "to produce, create," just as *parturiō,* "to be in travail or labor," brought about the meaning of "to brood over, meditate." The idea of creativity is still implied. The reference to the anatomy is still transparent in the noun *pars, -tis;* it refers primarily to the parts of the body, especially to the sex organs. The word *se-parō, -āre,* "to separate," implies, in the final analysis, the idea "to be born asunder," to be severed by the birth process. All *parts* are properly "born out" in the original sense of "offspring, fetus, embryo." This illustrates the infantile fantasy that all things are *parts*, i.e., created out of the human body. Such is the primitive subjective concept of the world. It supposes that objects outside the body were originally inside.[3] The child was a "part" of the mother—this means one with her—as long as it was inside her, but being outside her, the original unity had become divided and the child became definitely one, all alone.

The normal psychological transformation of the unity of the mother into the duality of mother and child may take place during pregnancy, but it can be postponed as our languages prove, it may even never occur as some symptoms of schizophrenics indicate. It has been observed that in some cases this basic split never has been accepted either by the mother or by the child. In such cases the child remains a "part" of the mother as if the navel cord never were cut, the inside never becomes perceived as outside, thus the child emerges with a distorted or mutilated body image and utterly confused about the inside and outside of reality.[4] The birth process remains in such cases unfinished. This psychological symptom is described by the prophet in the Old Testament: "And as for thy nativity, in the day thou wast born thy navel was not cut, neither wast thou washed in water to supple thee; thou wast not salted at all, nor swaddled at all" (Ezek. 16:4).

The separation of mother and child is painful. But separation is a painful relief anyway, even in the abstract spheres of artistic creation.[5] The birth process might be perceived by the woman as the repetition of a primary separation of body products. In English Biblical language "separation" carries the meaning of "menstruation." Our languages preserved an old term for the narcissistic separation of inside from outside: The Greek term *schidzō*, "split," has its parallel Germanic forms in Gothic *skaidan,* Old English *sceadan, scitan,* equating separation with "excrements," which also meant originally, as the Latin *ex-cernere,* "to separate, discharge from the body."

The primary idea of separation is clearly expressed by the Hebrew term *bāth,* which means "separation" and "part of the body." This is to say: that which has become separated was originally a part of the body. If both concepts, separation and part of the body, were denoted by one word in Hebrew, it is hard to believe, as assumed linguistically, that they are two different words in Indo-European languages. Separation denotes, on the one hand, the verbal fantasies of "producing, creating"; on the other hand, it calls forth the two forms of anxiety, one described by "emptiness," the other by "loneliness."

Emptiness and Loneliness

The separation of the primary unity of mother and child results in the feeling of emptiness for the one, and of loneliness for the other.

Empty in the concrete sense refers once again to the sensation of the body. This feeling emerges when an inside content becomes discharged and transformed into an objective reality. The English verbs *to void* and *to waste* apply to both "emptiness" and "evacuation." The *vacuum* of Nothing, mere space without content, is not accessible to our experience of reality; it is primarily an inside sensation after the discharge of a tension; it may be the subjective experience after evacuation, postpuerperal depression, menopause or in mourning the loss of the beloved one. The pertinent expressions in our languages are not very clear, because their associations were always subject to repression, but one may recognize the outlines of bodily sensations implied. They evoke the ideas of "barren," "idle," "not working"; thus "leisure," the primary reference to procreation, can still be recognized. The idea of male impotency is suggested by those terms that equate "empty" with "loose" as in the Gothic *laus*, "empty," or Old English *leas*, "void, loose, weak," also "fake." Illustrative is the Dutch expression *"een loze noot,"* "hollow nut,[6] the nut"* the German *Mutterschraube,* properly "mother-screw," makes the underlying repressed fantasy transparent. The German word *ledig* means "empty" and "unmarried"; it connects the concept "empty" with the marital relationship. The Old Slavic languages denote "empty" (*prazdinu*) as the opposite of "pregnant" (*ne-prazdinu*).

The inside vacuum is sometimes described by neurotic patients. An example of Fischer is quoted by Binswanger and Paul Schilder:

The patient said: *"When it comes into my mind that I shall be like a room myself, everything else is connected with it. It is difficult to describe. It is quite empty, it is terrible; maybe it would be better to die."*[7]

This emptiness is sometimes verbalized also by the artist after the creative act has been completed. Hebbel the German poet wrote in his diary after he finished his tragedy *Judith:* "I feel empty like without intestines." The ineradicable loneliness of the creative mind is not simply a social condition, it is the loneliness after the separation from his creation, the inside emptiness that is the consequence of the externalization of his work.

The inside emptiness is the symbolic realization of the "existential vacuum," of the life without meaning. T. S. Eliot evoked this vision of "waste and void" with consummate poetic plasticity in his "Wasteland" and the "Hollow Men." The Creation also began with the *thōhū wach bhōhū,* the Waste, and the Void, as the opening Hebrew lines of Genesis say.

The opposite of the fantasies of the hollow cavity is the sensation of "fullness," of "filling full" or "fulfilling." Just as emptiness is the word characteristic for the detachment and estrangement from reality, the filling of the cavity is, in the same way, symbolic for the attachment and the approach to reality. "Fulfilling" is the symbolic undoing of the separation; it means to the small child the reunification with the mother by internalizing, filling himself full with the mother. The "filling full" may refer to some container or measure, yet the primary measure is man himself. The physiological body processes once more have set the pattern of verbal expressions; they may, however, appear as mere substitute gratifications for the underlying, desperate search for relatedness and unification with the one from whom one has been separated.[8]

All verbal expressions of "loneliness" emphasize the *one* as something specific emerging out of the dual unity of mother and child. Each becomes through separation a one; we can use the word *one* in English even in the plural: *ones.* This is also true of Russian. Loneliness supposes emptiness. Empty might be the space around the "one," but true loneliness supposes the inside vacuum, by which the isolation, estrangement, and separation takes place within the unity of *individuum.* The Biblical sentence: "It is not good that the man should be alone" (Gen. 2:18) has in the original Hebrew a more substantial meaning; in literal translation it says, "Not-good the-being-of (the)-man to separation his." The concept "alone" is expressed here as separation from his own self. The Hebrew *bādath*, "to divide," developed into adverbs meaning "apart," "except," "only," "beside," "alone." We shall now observe the same process of fragmentation within our Indo-European heritage.

The Scatter

What is the effect of separation anxiety upon our languages? As a ship going down in the ocean may leave small particles behind scattered on the surface of the water, in a similar way we may find many little words still floating on the surface of our languages, but in investigating these small remnants, one can still identify the central idea which disappeared from expression. Anxiety may bring about repression, but repression may result in repetitious use of the new verbal form that develops. The idea of "separation" must have been heavily loaded with repressive anxiety, because we find on the manifest surface of our languages a galaxy of scattered words pertinent in meaning and used frequently. These scattered words have a common characteristic: they lost their substantial visual content; they do not stand any longer on their own accord, but have become subservient to other words. They function as attached words, ad-jectives, ad-verbs, qualifiers, they are "syn-semantica," and must be used in connection with other words only. Having lost their linguistic independence, they developed into functional elements. We refer first to a few illustrative examples. Like "birth," such words as *awe, blood,* or *lot* evoked fantasies filled with anxiety. They referred to ideas that were tabooed and, one may expect, were avoided and their name never was used in vain. Now, though, the expression *awful* is not avoided in our colloquial language; on the contrary, it is used frequently. *Terrific* and *bloody* (the latter as used in British slang) are similar cases. The words do not evoke any longer the terror or awe which once was present (*Numen adest!*) in the original religious meanings. Some experts even suppose that such words have lost their original anxiety-ridden implication, as coins lose the impress by frequent handling. The dynamic psychological interpretation tends to prove otherwise: *the high frequency, i.e., repetitious usage, is not the reason but the consequence of the loss, or of the repression, of the original meaning.*

The process of repression and consequent repetition can be observed in all the synsemantica that crystallize around one central idea: the separation of mother and child. They are relative to the various stages of the birth process. I select a few examples:

1. The Latin adjective *seorsus, -a, -um,* "separate," and the adverb *sorsum,* "asunder, separately, apart," derive from *se-vorsus,* which is from the verb *vertō* or *vortō, -ere,* "to roll, turn around." The noun *vertex* or *vortex* denotes also the "head" as it appears first in "vertex presentation." In English *turn out* is a similar expression; it means primarily "to drive out, expel"; it refers to the outcome of labor; and in colloquial language it also means to be driven out from a place of safety and comfort by force and to a position exposed to danger and discomfort, "as to get out of bed." In Latin this "turning out" is expressive of the separation.

The genuine English term for "to separate" is *to sunder,* Old English *sundrian,* "to force apart or divide by rending, cutting." "No space of Earth shall sunder our two hates," Shakespeare says. This word perceives the forcible interference in the natural separation process such as the cutting of the navel cord. This meaning once repressed left behind many synsemantica. Such is the English *a-sunder;* in German the old adverb *sonder* developed into a preposition implying deprivation, "without." It developed also into the conjunction *sondern,* "but." Among the derivatives we find the German adjective and adverb *sonderbar,* "strange," a compound form of *sonder* and the verb *beran,* "to carry, bear." Here the feeling of strangeness emerges out of the process of separation. The newborn babe might first be strange indeed. The German equivalents of *asunder* are the adverbs *entzwei,* originally "in two," and *aus-ein-ander,* properly "out-one-other"; in this case, the "one" would be the mother, the "other" the child.

2. The preposition *except* derives from the Latin *ex-* and *cipere,* properly *capere;* thus it properly says "taken out, drawn out," a well-known operation in obstetrics. The same fantasy is present in the German preposition *aus-genommen,* "except," properly "taken out." In French *hors,* "except," is

from the Latin *foras, foris,* "outside"; thus, the French *de-hors* and *hors-mis* both mean "except," but properly say "taken out." This implication is also present in the English *but,* from *be-utan,* "to take out," akin to the Dutch *buiten,* "outside."

3. The smallness of the newborn is reflected in the conjunction *un-less.* The word *less* is the comparative degree of "little"; *un-,* originally *on-,* is a preposition indicating a position of contact. Out of this meaning developed the rather ambivalent implication of "if not." Such a consideration may emerge in the postnatal situation.

4. The English *be-side,* properly "on the side of," may denote as an adverb (*besides*) "in addition"; as a preposition, it refers to something "nearby, on the side of," but still can denote the "out of"; e.g., "beside himself" means "out of himself."

5. Before the separation, the child is *with* the mother and *in* the mother, thus *with-in.* After separation the child is still *with* the mother but *out* of the mother, thus *with-out.* The preposition *without* grasped the deprivation to which the babe is exposed.

6. The emerging of the *one* is expressed in English by the adjective and adverb *alone,* from the earlier *all-one,* thus saying the newborn child is now completely whole and one. The German equivalent *allein* (*all-ein*), also refers to the separation meaning "alone"; as a conjunction it means "but," thus "taken out." Its emphatic form is *Mutter-seelen-allein,* "mother-soul-alone." The implication of the mother into the first loneliness makes the postnatal state more evident. Another form of the "all-one" is the adjective, adverb, and conjunction *only,* Old English *an-lic,* properly "one-body." The emphasis on the otherwise obvious quality of being "one-body" indicates once more that this "one" is a specific quality. It can mean as an adjective "unique, superior, pre-eminent." As an adverb it can mean "very little"; it reveals the ambivalent attitude of the parents toward the child. If the infant senses that he can trust the mother and that the mother will not leave him *al-one,* in other words, that he is *with* though *out* of the mother, he will not develop the basic anxiety of *loneliness.*[8]

7. The postnatal state is exhibited by the correspond-

24

ing German term *bloss* which means "nakedly." In related languages *bloss* can denote "soft, tender," also "wet" and "only." The same holds true for the corresponding English adverb *bare-ly,* meaning literally "naked-body." The implication of nakedness in this whole complex makes it once more probable that the primary reference of all these synsemantic elements is the human body and the body process of separation from the mother. Nakedness is the attribute of the newborn child, as expressed by these famous Biblical words: "Naked came I out of my mother's womb, and naked shall I return thither" (Job 1:21). The Greek *choris,* "except, apart, only," reveals another aspect of "nakedness." It is a derivative of the verb *choridzein,* "to separate"; *chatos* means "to be deprived of (as stripped of), be forsaken"; *cheros,* "to be deprived, forsaken." The hardship of early infancy is pointed out by these words.

8. The English preposition and conjunction *save* and the French *sauf,* "except," display the happy state of affairs. They originate from the Latin *salvus,* "healthy." What else could be "taken out" and be "healthy" at the same time if not the separated child? Again, different is the attitude revealed by the German *nur,* "only," originally *ni wāri, ne waere,* meaning literally "would not be" and implying "it would be better if it would not be." In this case a whole meaningful sentence has been wiped out by repression and reduced to an adverb— which is an indication that the meaning was objectionable, indeed.

Perhaps all these adverbs, prepositions, and conjunctions can be considered as separate, as individual words; yet as a whole group, one cannot avoid the inference that there is a common motive operative in all these words. They hang together by unconscious fantasies. These fantasies reveal that something has been separated, forcibly taken out of one-another, beside it, with it, and out of it, one-body, very little deprived, sound, naked, healthy, mother-soul-alone, and perhaps would-not-be. The meaning implied must have been a highly delicate one, because all these words have lost their independent existence. For this reason, however, they rank high in frequency. As functional elements, they are used more frequently because they can be attached to any independent word. They refer to one idea loaded with awe: this is the separation, to be born out into singularity and loneliness.

The Holy

Beside the debris left behind in synsemantic words, the central idea of separation developed into religious images and rituals. The inspection of the newborn after birth, deciding whether it was a healthy child or a crippled one (the latter called in Latin *prodigium,* "monster, prodigy"), was an important moment of birth rituals. For the infant it meant life or death. Some early cultures required by law the destruction of infants who were not born "whole" and "healthy," but before they were destroyed they had to be shown to the elders or neighbors. For such reason one will understand the emphasis on the "one-ness" and "health" in the first perception of the infant. These expected qualities of the newborn became the constituent characteristics of holiness. The Lord is called "the Holy *One* of Israel" in the Old Testament.

The terms *holy, holiness* derive from the Old English *hālic, hāl,* meaning "sound and well"; this is still the meaning of our *hale* or *hails.* The Gothic *hails* positively means "healthy." The first appraisal of the newborn is in terms of his "wholeness" and "health." Both words, *wholeness* and *health,* are derivatives of the Old English *hāl,* "healthy"; *whole* means in our language "being in good condition, unhurt, or without signs of injury; not broken or damaged." "Whole as a fish" still recalls the fetus. Some experts wonder about how the idea of "holiness" developed out of the concept of "health." Their answer, however, stating that holiness brings "well-being or health," health is powerful, and power leads to the supernatural, is mere speculation. The primary reference is also, in this case, the human body. Only the human body can be healthy and holy. The primary state of the newborn child is both at the same time. The Greek *hagis,* "holy," and the Latin *sacer,* "holy," mean also the "cursed." How can "holy," "healthy," and "cursed" refer to the same object? Very simply, these words describe the ambivalent feelings of the parents toward their offspring.

The Greek term *sōs,* from the earlier form *sav-os,* means "safe and sound, alive and well." Zeus is sometimes called *sōtēr,* "savior." The linguistically corresponding Latin word is *salvus,* "healthy, hale, well-preserved, unhurt, uninjured, all is well"; thus *salvator* is used for translation of the Greek *sōtēr* as "savior." The Latin verb *salveō* means "to be well" or "to be in good health." The reference to the body cannot be denied in these cases. In German the Savior either is called *Heiland,* properly "the Healing One," or is named with the more complicated term *Erlöser,* "the Looser." The "Healing One" has obvious bodily references, but why the term "Looser"? I think Christ is called "Looser" because the birth process is also perceived as *Ent-bindung,* properly "un-tieing, un-binding." The separation is, in this case, considered as the liberation from the compacted situation in the womb. Our terms *delivery* and *deliverer* are most expressive in this connection. They derive from the Latin *de-* and *liberāre,* "to set free," and thereby equate "parturition" with "liberation."

It might be discussed: Who is delivered through the act of separation? While people today think first of the mother, the verbal fantasies seem to indicate that the child is the liberated one. The Healer is the Liberator. "Deliver us from evil" is the prayer for salvation. The paralyzing effect of anxiety has been figuratively depicted in myth as a magic "binding" or "tying down" as expressed in the term *spellbound.* Anxiety ties down as with a rope, therefore, the wicked "shall be holden with the cords of his sins" (Prov. 5:22). Accordingly, in the New Testament, the Apostles have the power "to bind on earth" and "to loose on earth" (Matt. 16:19, 18:18). The Homeric gods also have this power. The evil is like a rope and the gods can deliver man from evil by untying this rope.*

The Hebrew language is in some respects more transparent in denoting "holiness." In Hebrew "holiness" is *kadhesh* and "holy" is termed *kadhosh;* both words are connected with the verb *kadhash,* which means "to cut off, separate." It is rather interesting to observe how otherwise excellent Bible scholars do not understand this strange connection between the term *holy* and the underlying meaning "separation." I quote as an instance the following statement of an expert:

> The efforts to trace the origin of the idea from the etymology have not been satisfactory. It has been connected (by Feisher, Delitsch, and Baudissin) with the root *kaddadh,* "to cut off, to separate," and so appears to have a purely negative connotation. But the word itself does not

* *cf.* p. 237.

tell from what, or for what the separation takes place leaving more exact definition to be made by the limiting expressions.[9]

It does not come to the mind of the expert that unconscious fantasies refer first of all to body processes and that the idea of holiness may transfer the love of one's own body to that substance which has been separated from it. "Separation" is not a purely negative definition, because the separated one is loved by the mother as a "part" born out of her own self.

What, then, is the meaning of "holiness"? Our languages store and transmit the deposits of untold generations, and this fact should not be confused with the correct interpretation of an etymology. There can be no doubt that "holiness" in the Old Testament language derives its primary emotional implications from "separation." The Hebrew language shows what the Old Testament people understood by the term *holy,* and not what *we* would like to understand. *Our* understanding of this idea is different. It has received its phenomenological description in the classic of Rudolf Otto.[10] One can well observe in his analysis how the original body reference became sublimated and transformed into abstract terms. The fascination that the believer experiences when he is confronted with the *mysterium tremendum* arouses, according to Otto, the feeling of dependency and the "creature feeling," but the "holy" is primarily perceived as "wholly-other." This is but the spiritualized translation of the concept of "separation." Concerning the "bliss unspeakable," which also may enter this fascination, it should be noted that the words *blessing* and *bliss* refer to the conception. The "bliss unspeakable" properly refers to the fantasies about the clotting of the blood, which is, according to primitive birth theories, indicative of the conception.

Buddhist mysticism does not approach the sphere of numinous holiness by "separation," but by the *sunyam* and *sunyata,* the "void" and "emptiness." This is, says Otto, "a numinous ideogram of the Wholly-Other." Chinese art, especially painting, seems to be dedicated to depicting this void and emptiness. "The void itself is depicted as a subject, is indeed the main subject of the picture."[11]

The New Testament religion supposes a radical change

in the perception of the "holy." It is no longer the Old Testament "separation" as from the "wholly-other," nor the Eastern fascination with empty space, the void, but the New Testament which perceives the presence of the *numen* as the opposite of separation, as fullness and fulfillment.

The New Testament Greek term for "fullness" is *plē-rōma,* from the verb *pleroō,* "to fill." The presence of the Lord means the "fulness of him that filleth all in all" (Eph. 1:23); "in him dwelleth all the fulness of the Godhead bodily" (Col. 2:9) and "of his fulness have all we received" (John 1:16). This "fullness" is the reaction against the void and emptiness which is the consequence of separation. This "fullness" is symbolic for the reunification after separation.

The Latin equivalent term is *pleō, -ēre,* "to fill," and *complētus* means "to be filled up." The "sanctification," i.e., making holy, is in New Testament Greek *teleioō,* "to make perfect, complete." A container or a cup can be filled up and completed. The German word for "completion" is *Voll-endung,* properly "full-ending." The verb *accomplish* derives from *ad-,* "to," and *complēre,* "to fill up."

The last gestures of Christ are mostly misunderstood by our generation, which has lost the understanding of verbal fantasies. In the record, according to John, it is said: "After this, Jesus knowing that all things were now accomplished, that the scripture might be fulfilled, saith, I thirst" (John 19:28).

The desperate outcry of Christ: "I thirst" is the climax of his earthly life. The commentators of this critical passage unanimously suppose that this outcry expresses an actual bodily need. They also assert, by the same token, that the saying of Christ: "He that believeth on me shall never thirst" (John 6:35) refers to the physiological desire for liquid. They interpret accordingly the last outcry—the climax—like this:

> . . . but now all has been accomplished, the moment of His departure is at hand and He seeks relief from the physical agony of the thirst caused by his wounds. . . . This saying of our Lord, I thirst! makes plain that the body has its rights. . . . It is a moving cry to come from one who claimed that he who believes in me shall never thirst.[12]

In contradiction to such common-sense platitudes, I suppose that the saying, "He who believes in me shall never thirst," evokes the primary mother-child unity, and translating this symbolic pronouncement into the terms of the (pre-Oedipal) mother, it says: the child who *de-pends* upon me never will remain without milk. In the language of Christ *thirst* means, as for the small child, "emptiness," "loneliness," and "separation."* The "fullness" is symbolic of the reunification, the atonement, properly *at-one-ment*. "When Jesus therefore had received the vinegar, he said, It is finished; and he bowed his head, and gave up the ghost" (John 19:30).

The rendering "It is finished" once again destroys the verbal fantasies. The Greek text says *tetelestai,* "It is completed; it is filled full, or fulfilled!" The idea of *com-plete,* this "filling full" became adequately expressed in French (*tout est*) *accompli,* in Italian (*ogni cosa*) *è compiuta,* and in Spanish *cumplitudo está.* In Latin these last words are more explicit, *consummatum est,* which means, "it is consumed." In German, *es ist vollbracht,* means "it is brought full."

Separation is, of course, perhaps the greatest revolution of life in the biological sense, this transition from the intra-uterine conditions to the postnatal extra-uterine state, from the life under the amniotic fluid to the first intake of air through the lungs, from darkness and warmth to the light and cool open air. The birth process itself, the narrow exit out of the mother, is surely painful.

The child, if not doped, enters into the world with the "birth cry"; his first vocal manifestation expresses pain and discomfort. However, we may suppose that many of the birth rituals and ceremonials as practiced in various parts of the world made it even more difficult for the newborn babe to adjusts to its new existence in the outside world.

It belongs to the psychological wisdom of myth that many of its favorite heroes are foundlings, exposed children, sometimes nurtured by a wild animal, as by a she-wolf, as in the case of Romulus and Remus. This hardship of the helpless and exposed babe illustrates with great emphasis the transition from the peaceful bliss of intra-uterine dreaming life to the

* *cf.* p. 275.

dangers and frustrations of the outside reality. As soon as the basic polarity between inside and outside emerges, the outside world is felt to be harsh and hostile. The naming of the grammatical category of the outside world is in this respect significant. This is the world of *objects,* the objective reality, which presents itself in opposition to the inside subject. The word derives from *ob-jicere* which is from (Latin) *ob-jacere,* "to throw against." The "object" thrown against the subject hurts. In German the object is called *Gegen-stand,* the twin word of *Wider-stand,* "resistance." In the temporal category the object is "presence," in German *Gegen-wart,* properly "that which is turned against"; its twin word is *wider-wärtig,* meaning "disgusting."

The objective reality that the newborn babe has entered is first perceived as frustrating. As if the birth in itself were not frustrating enough, there are birth cere-monials, e.g., the submerging of the newly born babe in the cold water of a well, or rubbing its fine sensitive skin with salt, etc., as still practiced in folklore. The swaddling in itself, a general ancient practice of putting the newborn into the straitjacket of swaddling cloth, thus "un-doing" the "de-livery," increases the state of hopeless helplessness and the resentment felt against the world. The circumcision on the eighth day, as widely practiced on religious grounds, is one more of the painful experiences in the first days of life.

The ambivalent sentiments of those upon whom the life of the babe depends is attested by the various ways and methods used for disposing of the unwanted children. Girl children were most liable to this danger. The idea that the child is sexless is one of the fallacies of the Victorian puritanism, Freud said. It is not quite so. The testimony of all our languages shows that the babe was considered to be more an object not having the attributes of all higher living organisms than to be either masculine or feminine. One dealt with it, disposed of it, as with any other object.

The object-character of the child is pointed out by such denotations as *infant,* from Latin *infans,* "speechless," a derivative of the verb *fāri,* "to speak." Slavic words, such as the Polish *niemowle,* express the same notion of "speechless." The Greek *nēpios,* "child, infant," also contains the negative particle *ne,* and perceived the infant as not having mind or reason, thus "silly." Or it considers the infant simply as the result of the generative act, so *teknon,* "child," properly that which has been generated from the verb *tiktō,* "to generate." The German *Kind,* "child," belongs to this category. The general term for "child" in Germanic languages refers to the object-character by denoting it as that which is carried; so Old English *bearn,* Old High German *barn,* Gothic *barn,* etc., all from the verb *beran,* which is continued in our *bear, bore, born,* the original meaning of which was "to carry," presumably in the womb.

The linguistic characteristic of these words is the neuter gender, as Greek *teknon,* Old English *bearn,* German *das Kind,* and in English the personal pronoun referring to the infant as *it.* There is little doubt as to the category of sex to which the newly born babe belongs, but *it* became classified as an object proving that it was not considered to be a *he* or *she* person.

The idea of motherhood is heavily charged with emotions and fantasies. Its symbolism shows various aspects, one being as significant as the other. The "expectant mother," who is "great with child," represents an archetype of human experience, just as the "nursing mother," then again the "Mater Dolorosa"; all have found their most sublime representations in myth, religion, and art. Moreover, myth knows about the "Terrible Mother," who is also a true personification of motherhood in infantile fantasies. In the Biblical account, the pangs of childbirth are evoked by the words: "In sorrow thou shalt bring forth children" (Gen. 3:16), and these words are set beside the toil of man: "In the sweat of thy face shalt thou eat bread" (Gen. 3:19). The verbal instances also display the conspicuous connection of the idea of childbirth with *labor,* meaning originally "hardship" and "pain"; and of *travail,* through French from the Latin *tripālium,* an instrument of torture. There is in Old English *swingan, swang, swong, swungan,* "to scourge, afflict" and "to labor"; the word *swong* means, on the one hand, "scourged, labored"; on the other, "idle, lazy"—a striking difference in the meaning, which, however, can be well understood in reference to pregnancy. English *swink,* "to labor, toil," and German *schwanger,* "pregnant," also belong to this word cluster. It seems to be a very old idea that childbirth is the woman's part, which equals the labor, toil, travail, and hardship of work which is the fate of manhood.

REUNIFICATION

The painful separation from the mother is followed by the blissful reunification with her in the sucking situation. The breast and the lap of the mother are for the child the first and foremost substitutes of the womb. The outside cavity now fulfills functions similar to those which were before performed by the inside cavity; it is again a place of warmth, food, and security, a place of hiding and protection against the frustrations of the extra-uterine life. The Psalmist says: "But thou art he that took me out of the womb: thou didst make me hope when I was upon my mother's breasts" (Ps. 22:9). The significance of the breast for the protector and the protected ones is not yet clearly distinguished in Hebrew, in which *chābab* means "to hide" and "to cherish," hence *chōb*, "cherisher" and "bosom," and *chābā* and *chebyōm*, "concealment, secret." It makes no difference for unconscious fantasies whether something is concave or convex: "breast" and "lap" are blended in the fantasy of "bosom." In the same way, "belly" is blended with "stomach" and "womb," but "womb" and "bosom" are also overlapping ideas. Latin *sīnus, -us* means the "curve, concavity" in which the child is carried, but it also covers the meanings of "belly," "womb," "bosom," and "lap," and the "innermost part," and "hiding place"; thus *in sīnu gestāre* means "to carry the child in the lap" as well as "to carry in the womb." *In-sinuāre, -ātum,* from which the English *insinuate* is derived, means "to penetrate" into these intimate regions. The derivative Italian and Spanish *seno* denotes the "bosom," while French *sein* refers to "bosom" and "womb." All these words indicate that the "lap" of the mother is a substitute for the "womb."

The breast of the mother is the first reality object perceived by the babe. Greek *mammē* and Latin *mamma* mean both "breast" and "mother." Both meanings are fused into one experience by which the mother exists for the babe. The Late Latin *mamilla* means "nipple"; *mammula*, "breast";

mammāre, "suckle"; *mamma*, "mother"; all these different notions mean basically the same for the infant. The pertinent words in Romance languages have developed accordingly, fusing the idea of "breast" and "mother" into one sensation. This is but the linguistic corroboration of the fact Freud disclosed through analytical technique: "A child's first erotic object is the mother's breast, . . . and this first object subsequently becomes complete as the whole person of the child's mother."[13]

The Late Latin *puppa* also means "nipple"; this word became completed not in the direction of the mother but in that of the "child" and "doll." We may suppose that in this earliest state of life the subject and object poles are not yet clearly differentiated. The babe may feel that the breast of the mother is a part of himself. He may still be fused by the biological unity with the mother in whom he existed before.

The reunification of mother and child by sucking is a happy state enjoyed by both, also indicated by the fact that under primitive uncontrolled conditions it is a long protracted process, maintained for pleasure and not by necessity. In Old Testament times the sucking lasted for two or three years; there are pictures of people in Melanesia in which a lad while sucking is holding a cigarette, smoking and sucking alternatingly. This pleasure sucking may perhaps be the reason that the Late Latin *mamma* developed also the meaning of "grandmother," as Italian *mammina, mammadonna,* etc. It is known that the grandmother also participated sometimes in the suckling of the babe (serotine lactation).

The suckling situation represents at all times the picture of bliss and satisfaction of both mother and child, their happy reunification after the trauma of birth. One can observe in our languages the outgrowth of luxuriant illustrations referring to the unity of mother and child. We take an example from Latin interrelated words: *fē-lō, -āre,* "to suck"; *fēmina,* "woman who suckles"; *fētō, -āre,* "to fertilize"; *fē-ta,* "pregnant" or "woman who was borne"; *fē-tus,-ūs,* "birth, generation"; *filius,* from *fē-lius,* "son who is sucking"; *fēcundus,* "fruitful"; *fē-lix* is the mother who is suckling, then "fruitful" and "happy," etc. The word *fe-male,* from *fēmella,* the diminutive of *fē-mina,* indicates that the "suckling" has been considered as the main characteristic of the female sex.

The same holds true for the Greek in which the phonemic equivalent of Latin *fē-* is *thē-;* thus *thē-sthai,* "to milk"; *thē-satō* (past), "suckled"; *thē-lē,* "nipple, teat"; *thē-lamon,* "nurse"; *the-ladzō,* "to suckle"; *thē-nion,* "milk"; *gala-thē-nos,* "sucking milk, young"; and especially *thē-lus,* "female, of female sex," etc. This is an old word complex deeply rooted in our languages; thus we may interpret it as being highly significant for emotional development. "Can a woman forget her sucking child, that she should not have compassion on the son of her womb?" (Isa. 49:15). Suckling is as well a gratification of motherly sentiments as sucking is for the babe.

The meaning of sucking also can be approached from the phonemic angle. It can be shown by a mere formal analysis of the sound patterns of pertinent words that the breast of the mother, *mamma,* is a primary concept in the development of the child's mind.[14]

It goes without saying that the mouth of the babe first comes under his control; the muscles of the mouth and their innervation, which is necessary for sucking, have a preference in development. The "oral" stage is necessarily the first period of the infant's language development. Translating this fact into the terminology of phonemics, it means that the so-called "labial" sounds, *m, p, b,* produced with the lips, will develop first. The labial sounds also have another advantage: their articulation by the lips is not only heard but can be seen (lip reading). It is perhaps a sign of infantile notion-picture formation that some languages, e.g., Hebrew, denote the idea of "language" by "lips," while we do it in reference to the "tongue." In German "dialect" is called *Mundart,* properly "way of mouth." In our thinking the lips in relation to speech signify rather the outwardly display (lip service) as opposed to the inside invisible "tongue" or "language." But for the infant this outward display counts first. Consequently in the range of consonants the labials *m, b, p,* formed with the lips, appear first in babbling. Next follow the "dentals," *n, d, t,* formed with the teeth, which are, though not articulated as visibly as the labials, produced in the front part of the mouth. Relatively difficult to learn only by hearing are the "palatals," produced by the back of the tongue; their articulation cannot be seen.

The same holds true for the vowels, among which the

a and *e*, produced with the front and center part of the tongue, have preference over *o* and *u*, produced by the back of the tongue. The most simple combination of consonants and vowels is achieved by simple repetition. Repetition is the most elementary structure of production. Summing up these phonetic observations, we come to the conclusion that the most primitive, most infantile among all possible phonemic patterns is *ma-ma*, the name of the breast, the first reality object of the infantile world.

Elaborating further the phonemic approach to the infantile world, we can draft a chart of emotional values according to the range of phonemic preference.

		1 *m*	2 *b*	3 *p*	4 *n*	5 *d*	6 *t*	7 *g*	8 *k*	9 *h*
1	*a*	ma-ma	ba-ba	pa-pa	nana	dada	tata	gaga	kaka	haha
		ama	aba	apa	ana	ada	ata	aga	aka	aha
		mam	bab	pap	nan	dad	tat	gag	kak	hah
2	*e*	mi-mi	bibi	pipi	nini	didi	titi	gigi	kiki	hihi
	i	imi	ibi	ipi	ini	idi	iti	igi	iki	ihi
		mim	bib	pip	nin	did	tit	gig	kik	hih
3	*o*	mu-mu	bubu	pupu	nunu	dudu	tutu	gugu	kuku	huhu
	u	umu	ubu	upu	unu	udu	utu	ugu	uku	uhu
		mum	bub	pup	nun	dud	tut	gug	kuk	huh

The peculiarity of these sound patterns consists in their generality. They are found in the most distant, unrelated languages, proving that in this case there exists once more a secret relationship between sound and meaning which breaks through in various language communities. Multiplying the numbers of the table, the following range of emotionally important things can be established (I omit the generally known words of English adult baby talk). The group (1 × 1) primarily refers to "breast," "mother," sometimes also to "grandmother" and to the suckling wet nurse, or "midwife." In the Slavic languages *baba* (1 × 2) means "old woman," and the same with medieval German *Babe*. The English *babe*, *baby*, corresponds with this idea in a similar way, as if the child is called "little grandfather," a name that can be interpreted in reference to the family. The notion of "father" also sometimes enters this group (1 × 2), for example, Aramaic *abba,* Greek *abbas,* Late Latin *babbus.* However, the "father" is mostly denoted by (1 × 3) or (1 × 5 or 6): Greek *pappas,* Latin *papa,* continued in English *pope,* etc.

In the group (1 × 4) the leading notion is "suckling nurse" with names as *Anna, nanny,* also called *dada* (1 × 5). The "father" is called in group (1 × 6) in the Homeric, *atta,* in Latin *atta;* the Gothic name *Attila,* from *atta-ila,* meaning "little father," is also a name for the king. The Russian czars were called so (*atyuska*). In (2 × 1) the notion of "milk" is in the foreground, perhaps as adult baby talk in reference to milk. The groups (2 × 5) and (2 × 6) are mostly used for denoting the "nipple," as *tit,* Late Latin *titta,* then for *titillation.* The group (1 × 8) refers mostly to elimination, as does the Greek *kakkē* and *kakos,* "bad."

Many of these words belong not to the child but to the mother in adjusting her speech to the understanding of the infant (adult baby talk); yet these phonemic patterns are so general in otherwise unrelated languages that their psychological relevance cannot be doubted. They describe the primary narrow world of the infant centering around "nipple," "mother," "nurse," "father," "intake of milk," and "elimination."

It has been demonstrated rather conclusively by dream analysis without any reference to the pertinent verbal expressions that adults revert to the "oceanic feeling," to this primary state of happiness, while falling asleep and while dreaming. There are blank dreams when the dreamer perceives just the blank background and no dream pictures. Such dreams represent the return to the primary happiness: falling asleep at the mother's breast after nursing. The blank white screen upon which the dream pictures appear is the breast of the mother as the suckling perceived it, flattened out, white and soft.

Otto Isakower has given a classic description of this regression to the sucking state.

A patient said that she feels in this state as if "childhood was coming back." Another patient feels: "I am all mouth," and then there is also the sensation of "falling down" because in English we "fall" asleep. To be ful-filled as mentioned previously is experienced by the suckling before falling asleep. This has set the pattern of experiencing pleasure, bliss, and happiness.[15]

Another association of "pleasure, happiness" can be observed in the Latin *laetus*, "happy," and *laetitia*, "happiness," and also in the name *Letitia*. The primary meaning was "prolific, fertile," as in *fē-cundus*, but its implication can be seen in the words *laetamen*, "dung, excrements," and *laetāre*, "fertilize with manure." In this case "pleasure" is again expressed by a reference to the alimentary process. Some transitory meanings have been offered to bridge the gap between "pleasure" and "dung" in the agricultural realm, but in this case, as in the former one, the fantasies involved even in the naming of agricultural fertilization refer once more to the "bosom" of Mother Earth. The fantasies start neither from the ocean nor from the earth, but from the sensations and functions of one's own body. We shall come across other terms for "pleasure" and "happiness"; the alimentary function, this first and most important pleasure of the infant, will appear as their decisive characteristic.

If we generalize this preliminary observation, we will understand that the suckling feels and thinks in terms of its alimentary function. Its philosophy of the stomach will remain the foundation of the subsequent development. Its fantasies concerning the inside contents of the body are primarily occupied with the intake of food and digestion.

There exists an over-all diffuse concept of *entrails* (from the Latin *internea*), "guts and bowels" which can be seen from outside like a pot-belly; this is also called *paunch*, from the Latin *pantex, pantices*, "entrails, bowels," thus referring to the inside aspect. The interest in the breast becomes in this way expanded upon the whole body of the mother, especially if she is pregnant. The observation of the mother resulted in the over-all notion of "belly" and "womb" in a diffuse connection. Even the whole body of the mother, the "mother-body," became identified with this "womb-belly" concept, for instance, in German *Mutter-leib*, properly "mother-body," or *Gebär-mutter*, properly "bearing-mother." In other languages "mother" and "womb" are simply equated with one another, as in the case of Italian *modre*, Russian *matka*, "uterus, female, broodmare, queen," and so on. That the child's fantasies explore the inside of the mother (especially the *hustera*, meaning "the behind," the back part of the mother) can be best observed in Latin *mātrix*, "womb," a word which is a blending of *māter* and *nutrix*, "nourishing," and thus a condensation of the nourishing mother herself. The adjectival form of *mātrix* is *mātricalis*, properly "pertaining to the *mātrix*-womb," hence "uterine." This word developed in Italian to denote the "hystery" (*medregal*), but we also find this word as a term used to denote a form of poetry, the *madrigal*, a word whose repressed meaning never could be properly understood by its lexical definition.

The child observes that the mother is taking in food; therefore the intestines and the stomach are also implicated in these inside fantasies. The idea of "stomach," "belly," "womb" is blended in one in the Greek term *gastēr*, and the stomach is sometimes specified as "rear stomach," *hystros gastēr*. The outside and the inside aspects are fused with one another in this case again: The inside invisible stomach is called *gastēr*, and its outward appearance is represented by the "belly" of the jug called *gastra*. Similarly, the word for "mother," *mētēr*, also became supplanted in Late Greek by *mētra*, the current term for "womb." The same stomach-womb identification is present in the Greek *koilia*, in the Latin *uterus*, in many Germanic and Slavic terms, so we must suppose this is a most general spontaneously developing fantasy. The stomach is thought to be as characteristic for the mother as the breast and the womb. In Greek *stoma* means "mouth" and *stomachos* is properly the "little mouth"; thus we interpret the stomach-womb as being the inside, invisible imaginary "doll-mouth" which can be seen in the outside world by the real mouth.

We shall understand on these premises the mythical idea of the "Devouring" or "Consuming Mother." She is the "Terrible Mother," the bad one who is also an archetype of infantile fantasies. Her mouth with the teeth is her characteristic feature. The image of this terrible mother has been often recovered behind the screen of anxiety in children. While she is feeding the babe with milk, she herself eats meat. The polarization of "milk" and "meat" makes the difference between "child" and "adult" even greater. This distinction is also current in Biblical language. "For every one that useth milk is unskilful in the word of righteousness: for he is a babe.

But strong meat belongeth to them that are of full age," Paul says (Heb. 5:13–14). The Mother Earth, this mythical projection of the mother image, is also conceived, on the one hand, as the fruitful, fertile, nourishing one, and, on the other hand, as the "swallowing womb," as Shakespeare said. So in the Greek myth the female deities of fertility and fruitfulness are by the same token rulers in the underworld among the dead. Characteristic is, in this respect, the word *sarcophag*, from the Greek *sarko-phagos*, properly "flesh-eater." This word seems to refer to the return into the "swallowing womb" of the mother, who is in Greek fantasies sometimes depicted as having teeth. The *Terra Māter*, Mother Earth, in Greek *Dē-mētēr* (from *gē-mētēr; gē* meaning "earth"), is a universal mythical concept. An old German folk song says about her: "She is a fine mother, She feeds many thousands of children. She is so rich, No one equals with her. She nourishes all with her rays, Then devours them all together."*

Dependence

By calling the relationship of the child to the mother *de-pendence*, we say properly "hanging down," from *de-*, "down," and *pendō, -ere*, "to hang," *pendeō, -ēre*, "to be suspended." The question is again: What or who is hanging down? The expression is generally understood in reference to the fruit, mostly to the "apple" hanging down from the tree. We prefer once more the human interpretation which starts with man and not with the tree. This equation seems to prove that the "hanging down" of the apple from the tree has set the primary pattern by which the "hanging down" of the breast with the suckling was perceived. The closer inspection of the idea of "apple," however, shows that the bodily fantasies were first. Thus the "apple" has in English "flesh" and "skin." In Greek the "stalk" on which the fruit is hanging down is called *omphalos*, "navel," like our "navel oranges"; even the "sap" of the tree and fruit is called *haima*, "blood," etc. There can be

---

* "Es ist eine Mutter fein,/ Sie nährt viel tausend Kinderlein,/ Sie ist so reich,/ Kein Mensch ihr gleich,/ Sie nährt sie all mit ihrem Strahl,/ Verzehrt sie wieder allzumal." This is the motto of Albrecht Dieterich, *Mutter Erde. Ein Versuch über Volksreligion*. Stuttgart: Teubner, 1905.

little doubt as to which has been perceived first—the apple or the "fruit of the womb."

The reference to the fruit and the tree is indicative of the dual unity of breast and child. The "apple" became symbolic of the "breast" as well as of the "fruit" of the womb; they are still one, but the healthy differentiation took place: the "apple" is not anymore the same as the "tree."

The primary symbol of unity and dependence as indicated by the Greek term for the "stalk," *omphalos,* is the "navel." The idea and its phonemic pattern both belong to our Indo-European heritage; their genuine antiquity proves their emotional significance. This is also apparent in the ancient Greek religious worship and representations centering around the Delphic *Omphalos,* the "navel," as the center of the world. Buddha is "navel gazing," because the navel is the symbol of eternity, connecting mother and child since immemorial ages.

The meaning of "dependence" as we use the word in reference to the child-mother relationship may be figurative in the present usage, but it depicts well the primary situation conceiving together the breast and the suckling as an appendix "hanging down."

In the preface of the Authorized Version of the Bible (1611) the translators say:

> And lastly, . . . that those mothers are holder to be lesse cruell, that kill their children as soone as they are borne, then those nursing fathers and mothers wheresoever they be that withdraw from them who *hang upon their breasts* (and *upon whose breasts againe themselves doe hange* to receive the spirits all and sincere milke of the word) livelyhood and support fit for their estates. [Italics supplied.]

The idea of "depend" developed into the notion "to think." Originally in Latin the verb *cogitō, -āre* (from *co-agitō, -āre,* "to set in motion, shake") was the proper term for the act of thinking. This standard word of the classic language became almost replaced in the Late Latin by the verb *pensō, -āre,* "to think." This word must have carried a stronger emotional stress, otherwise it could not outmode the standard expression. This shows the psychological value of the Late

Latin continued in French, Italian, and Spanish in that it shows the driving and repressed forces beneath the conscious standard language shaped partly by the authority of an educational or social language Superego. The Latin *pensō, -āre* is a derivative verb of the Latin *pendeō, -ēre,* "to hang on something," and of the alternate form *pendō, -ere,* meaning "to hang, swing, rock," as the derivative *pendulum* makes very clear. A secondary meaning is, as in the English *ponder,* "to weigh," which developed into the notion "to think." Another form of the verb *pensō, -āre* developed into *pēsō, -āre,* "to worry"; this "pressing" seems to be just another way of measuring the weight. We would be completely satisfied by explaining all these related terms of "hanging on," "measuring the weight," "pressing," "pondering," "swinging" as a primary reference to the balance; however, by closer inspection we shall find within this word cluster denotations of actions which hardly can be attributed to the idea of "balance." German *die Wiege* means "cradle"; *die Wage,* "the balance"; the verb *wiegen,* "to cradle" and "to weigh"; and *er-wägen,* "to ponder." The Late Latin implies beyond the verb *pensō, -āre* the meaning also of "nursing, feeding, fostering, taking care." By the same token the French verb *penser,* "to think," developed *panser,* "to care, to dress" a wound. We may surmise that the "rocking," "swinging," "feeding," "nursing," "fostering" referred primarily not to the balance but to the Alma Mater, "Nourishing Mother," an archetype of infantile fantasies. This primary reference to dependence upon the mother may also be the reason why the Late Latin *pensāre,* as continued in French *penser,* has crowded out the original classic verb *cogitō, -āre.*

The primary reality object, the breast of the mother, seems to be implied in the child's fundamental experience of truth. This association is the more probable because the French verb *savoir,* "to know," from Latin *sapiō, -ere,* "to taste," also refers to the internalized image of the "Nursing Mother." The phonemically related Old English *sefa* means "insight." The French *savoir,* which is a related form of English *savor,* has outmoded the classic Latin term *sciō, -īre,* "to know," just as *pensō, -āre* succeeded in replacing the original term *cogitō, -āre.* It seems to be very probable that for the same reasons the Late Latin *materna lingua,* "mother tongue," has defeated and repressed the classic *sermō patrius,* "paternal language."[16] In Biblical language the "word" is closely associated with the notion of "milk," for instance in the words of Paul: "As newborn babes, desire the sincere milk of the word, that ye may grow thereby" (I Pet. 2:2). The "fluency" of speech still reminds us of the liquid character of the milk.

The clinging to the mother and the equilibrium of the stabilized Ego may indeed have some special relationship with the dependency upon the mother and the gradual separation from the breast. The "balance" would be in this aspect the symbol of the Ego, which after much swinging finds its true self-identity, equilibrium, and stability.

PART TWO

OEDIPUS—

IDENTITY AND

KNOWLEDGE

OEDIPUS—
IDENTITY AND
KNOWLEDGE

The biological separation is followed by a stage of reunification that is not just simply a biological process but a cultural transmission forging a link between the past and the present, shaping the newborn child into the mold of an already existing reality. The small child experiences the reality of the world primarily as the reality of the mother, father, brothers, sisters and of the whole family setting. Our understanding of man would remain fragmentary, indeed, if we did not consider this closest and most concrete relationship between the individual and the world. Just as figure and ground are inseparable in our perception, the perception of the child's self-identity develops within the frame of a given family setting. By "family" we denote not the legal nor the biological entity but we mean rather the body of persons who attend the child, and the personal relationships forming the intimate and close elementary community, the household world with which the child will become "familiar" and grow together.

It is to the credit of Freud that he turned attention toward the psychological constellation of the family into which the child is born. He demonstrated the thesis that if we want to understand man as a unique individual with his specific characteristics, we must go back and observe how he has grown up as a small child within his family. No man has grown up alone, without having accepted a cultural heritage. His relationship to those who have attended him during the Golden Age of dependency has shaped his basic character traits. The way he speaks, how he handles his mother tongue, reflects the specific kind of idiom used in his home. We never can properly separate the character traits that were transmitted through biological inheritance from those that were imprinted into the small child through the cultural continuity. Language is the primary carrier of this continuity.

45

The Thumb

The infant experiences his own independence first in a positive form by sucking his thumb and fingers. Thumb-sucking has been interpreted (as the verbal expressions suggest) to be basically "sucking," but in one respect it is not that. Freud hit upon this very point in his classic analysis by stating that "the child thus makes himself independent of the outer world which he cannot control."[1] This is the basic difference in principle between the sucking of the breast of the mother and the sucking of the child's own thumb and fingers. The thumb is not only an outside object like the breast but is felt also from within: it is an outside *and* inside reality at the same time. There is no greater reality for him than this "first hand" experience with his thumbs and fingers. Their reality is verified by the coincidence of the outside experience with the true reality of the inside experience. By sucking the thumb the infant achieves a more perfect unity of subject and object than by sucking the breast of the mother, even though the pleasure might be reduced. In doing it repeatedly, the repetition of this experience, the sameness of subject and object, gives him the sensation of being always the same—the primary experience of self-identity. Long before the adequate verbal expression could develop, the thumb-sucking infant experiences the "I am," his own existence. In the blissful satisfaction of being absorbed by one's own existence, of being *on-ly* and *al-one*, there is also found the primary form of the feeling which has been called by self-conscious philosophy the "shut-upness" of individual existence (Kierkegaard's term is *indeslutedhet*). A description of the subjective sensations of thumb-sucking is difficult to obtain from children, but such phenomenological description,[2] if revealed at all, can approach a high perfection of that state which is generally termed "existential experience." By introjecting various objects at hand the small child wants to find out whether various objects are as real an existence as its own thumb.

The thumb and the fingers are the first playthings of the infant. The thumb is the only finger that has a distinct name; this means it is the most individualized finger. It can make grasping movements in an opposite direction to the other fingers, an anatomical characteristic of the thumb (not of the big toe) which man shares only with the ape. The Greek language grasped this anatomical quality of the thumb and called it *anti-cheir*, properly "anti-hand."

The closer inspection of the fantasies concerning the mythological or legendary Thumb may disclose a fuller understanding of the thumb-sucking infant.

There can be little doubt concerning our *thumb* or the Latin *pollex*, that these words refer to the mythological Thumb of fantasies and not to the anatomical thumb. The idea of "swelling" is implied in the English word, as can be seen by its relationship to the Latin verb *tumeō, -ēre,* "to swell." The Latin term refers to the verb *polleō, -ēre,* "to be strong, powerful, potent, to be able." Yet, behind these manifest meanings again the idea of "swelling" becomes transparent in other related forms such as the Greek *phallos*. Why should the capacity of strength, power, and swelling be attributed to the thumb? In answering this question related to "swelling" the Biblical saying, "My little finger shall be thicker than my father's loins" (I Kings 12:10), will be understood in this context—the "loins" being a euphemism for "genitals." The fantasy Thumb has absorbed some qualities that belong to the male. In fact, thumb-sucking has always been interpreted rightly or wrongly as an autoerotic manipulation. It is generally known that the interest in the thumb, which is a characteristic of the first two years of life, expands upon the genital zone during the following years; consequently the thumb in fantasies assumed phallic attributes such as the capacity of swelling and of growing stout and strong.

This linguistic explanation will become more convincing if the mythical representations of the imaginary Thumb are also taken into consideration. The Greek myth knows a special type of imaginary beings called *Daktuloi*, properly "Fingers." In Greek the thumb is called generally *megas daktulos*, "big finger," and therefore the mythical name refers in general to the "fingers," not specifically to the thumb. Almost the same fantasies are called in Germanic folklore by the word *thumb*, so in German we have *Däumlinge*, properly "Thumblings." In English *Tom Thumb* of folklore is a typical representative of the whole species of fantasies. These popular figures of the folk tales, however, represent the more recent layer of fantasies which derive from the prehistory of Germanic mythology. In the Germanic myth something uncanny must have been implied in these imaginary "Thumblings" or "Fingers," because people preferred to avoid their names, and to use a common noun instead of the personal names so we may surmise that some risk, anxiety, or fear is involved in mentioning the names. The Germanic languages generally refer to an imaginary being by the common noun meaning "thing"; for example, instead of calling it "the thumb," they prefer to say simply "the thing." The corresponding English term is *wight*, "a creature, a living being," mostly an unearthly being, now applied humorously to human persons. The jocose and archaic character shows the aftereffect of the formerly feared implication which lost its taboo character. In Old Saxon the singular *wiht* means "thing, creature," and in the plural it means those demonic uncanny "beings." The feared mythical character became transmitted in the course of history into a more human "goblin, villain," but it is still basically the "bad child" which appears in their shape. The Gothic feminine of the word (*vaihteis ubilōs*) translates the same as the authorized version of the Bible does by "appearance of evil" (I Thess. 5:22). This connotation remained preserved in the veiled form of the German compound word *der Böse-wicht* meaning "naughty boy, villain," but the medieval German uses rather *unreinez wiht*, "unclean wight," making more explicit the fault in the naughtiness of the small child. The implication of "evil" and "anxiety" proves that the feeling of guilt became associated, we may assume, not with the thumb but with the fantasies implied.

The *wights* appear mostly as a group; grammatically the noun is used mostly in the plural. Greek *Daktuloi* and German *Däumlinge* are plurals, Old Saxon *wiht* denotes in the plural only the imaginary beings; in the singular it means simply "thing." The question may be asked, What is the reason for this plurality? The obvious answer will refer to the idea of "fingers," which represent a plurality of ten. This may be the reason why the *Daktuloi* did not reach the unique personal qualities of the other gods of Olympus. They are still on a stage that preceded the development of personal characteristics. Children are more alike than adults. The "wights" are projected by the infantile mind before the maturation of the adult personality traits represented in gods and goddesses.

Another infantile characteristic of the *Daktuloi* is their smallness. They all appear as dwarfs, heroes of the small child.
However, their smallness is deceptive. They can do great
things. Sometimes they appear as giants. In the German folk
tales *der grobe Wicht*, "the rude wight," is also a giant. The
English verb *to dwarf* can mean either "to stunt in growth, to
keep small," or "to tower over, to make the other to appear
small (so as to make the subject appear very big)." Despite
their seeming smallness the wights represent great strength.
"Smaller than small, bigger than big" is their permanent
attribute in the folk tales. This may be interpreted again as the
outgrowing of infantile fantasies. Being aware of its physical
inferiority, the infant compensates by dreaming wishfully of
the strength of a giant hidden in a weak body frame. The
attributes of swelling, growing stout and thick, being able to
do, are meaningful for the infant's whole personality.

A rather specific characteristic of the *Daktuloi* is their
skill in mining; this means they work under the surface of the
earth, hidden from human sight. Their imaginary character is
pointed out in this way, projecting their work into the inside
of the Mother Earth. The mining of metals, especially the
production of iron, was heavily charged with inside fantasies
in the Greek myth; it was attributed to Phrygian magicians
dwelling on Mount Ida. The idea of wrongdoing, the indication of a bad conscience, affected this realm of associations
also. The *Daktuloi* are the helpers of Hephaestus, the divine
forger of iron, keeper of the fire. His limping gait seems to be
a psychosomatic trait indicating that he did something wrong
relative to his father Zeus and his mother Hera. How consistent these forgotten fantasies are can be shown by our
words to *forge, forger, forgery*, which still carry beside the
professional skill the idea of wrongdoing. These words refer,
on the one hand, "to shape by hammering, as hot metal" and,
on the other hand, "to imitate fraudulently; to make or devise
something which is not genuine, to fabricate, to counterfeit."
The *Daktuloi* participate in the work of the divine forger.

The mining profession may serve once more for the
realistic explanation of their conspicuous outfit: they carry
generally a lantern, or some kind of lamp indicating that they
work in darkness under the earth. They then have a sledge
hammer, which is, of course, an attribute of the blacksmith

and forger. A special feature is the hood covering their heads. One may think this belongs also simply to the miner's outfit. The verbal forms, however, point to a deeper layer of associations. The characteristic of the hood is not only its conical form, but the making of it. It is made out of one piece of material together with the cloak, gown, or garment. We must suppose that this material was originally—preceding weaving —an animal hide. The analysis of dreams has found that the idea of "hat" is a recurrent symbol for "male," but verbal forms relative to the "hood" make this symbolism more transparent. The Latin term for "hood" is *cucullus;* this word, however, has significant variants such as *cucūtium* and *capū-tium*. This *cucūtium* seems to be a condensation of *cucullus* and *cutis* meaning "skin, foreskin, hide." The *capūtium* is a blending of Latin *cappa,* "cap" or "cape," and the word contained also in *prae-pūtium,* "prepuce, foreskin." The latter word cannot be separated on formal grounds from the noun *putus,* meaning "little boy."[3] We meet this imaginary inside child also in connection with the *pupil* of the eye. This may serve as the linguistic answer to the question as to why the wights appear wearing a "hood." The medieval German is very expressive in this respect. It says *zumpfen-huetilīn,* properly "little hat of the penis," meaning the "foreskin." In English the word *hood,* a phonetic equivalent of the Latin *cutis,* "skin, foreskin, hide," also suggests that this covering of the head was originally made of skin. The word is related to *hide, hat, head,* and *heed,* also to German *Hut,* "hat" and "protection." The linguistic point in the history of these nouns is that they developed into the suffix *-hood* which appears in the older English language as *-head,* preserved in *god-head.* The original independent meaning must have been charged with fear and anxiety, consequently repressed and wiped out as a noun: this was the Old English *had,* of which the primary meaning was "sex, person, form," thus *man-had,* "manhood"; *wif-had,* "womanhood"; *cild-had,* "childhood"; *brother-had,* "brotherhood"; *preost-had,* "priesthood"; and so on. Why should the noun *hood* have lost its significant meaning if not for the reason that anxiety repressed it for its connotation? The same association which blended *cucūtium, capūtium,* and *praepūtium* in Latin transformed the English word into a repetitiously used formative element.

SELF-IDENTITY

The sucking of the thumb, and often of the index finger, is the first positive step in discovering the secrets of one's own body, an activity which later on becomes expanded upon the genital zone. It is associated with the sensation of pleasure, and this sensation shapes the first framework for the subsequent development of the Ego-consciousness. The gradual perception of the body-self and its functions is the solid foundation upon which is based the healthy development of personality and the perception of the outside reality.[4] By way of contrast the distinctive feature of the diseased mind manifests itself in a distorted perception of the body-self and in a misconception of its functions.

The classic command "know thyself" can hardly be separated from its autoerotic implication. In fact, the Greek *Gnōthi Seauton* is of pre-Socratic origin; it was an axiom of the Delphic priesthood. The tradition holds that the seven wise men paid a visit to Delphi and offered the first fruits of their wisdom, the two maxims that were then inscribed upon the porch of the temple of Delphi. One maxim says *Gnōthi Seauton,* "know thyself"; the other says *Meden Agan,* "nothing too much."[5] The inscriptions are complementary to one another and indicate that some restraint must be imposed upon the exploration of one's own self. Putting this wisdom into more explicit terms, the two inscriptions say: "Do not explore in excess from the outside what you know anyhow better from inside experience." This wisdom persists in religious experience.

But such subject-objects are also one's own body and the body of the mother. The body-self and the body of the mother became just as taboo as divine beings. The body of the brother or sister is also included in this circle of prohibitions. Masturbation has been considered for these reasons to be a fornication much like incest with those with whom one has shared the same womb, with "brother" and "sister," expressed

51

in Greek by *a-delphos* and *a-delphē*, properly meaning "out of (the same) womb." The Latin term *māsturbō, -āre,* which is not very transparent in its first part (and can be found also in *mas-culīnus*), has a synonym parallel in the noun *mās-carpiō, -iōnis,* "masturbator." The second part of this latter word belongs to *carpō, -ere,* "to pull out" (as a *carpet,* from *carpita,* means something "pulled out"), and it denotes also "to pluck." In the Greek *karpos* means "something plucked," and "fruit plucked from the tree," while *fruit,* from *fructus,* from *fruor, -ere,* means also primarily something "enjoyed." The "plucking" of the fruit from the tree seems to be symbolic of the autoerotic pleasure, just as in the case of the Biblical plucking of the apple from the tree of knowledge. In vulgar German *abreissen,* "to pluck," carries also the same meaning as the Latin *mās-carpiō.* Freud has found in complete independence from any linguistic considerations that in the symbolism of dream language "to pull out" as a tooth or "to pluck" stands for the same meaning we have found implicated in the Latin *mās-carpiō.*

We come across the autoerotic exploration of the body-self and of bodily functions in connection with the beginning of infantile speech called echolalia. The hearing of one's own voice is, just as the sucking of one's own thumb or exploring one's own body, a primary pleasure implied in discovering self-identity. A boy of eight is reported to have called his masturbation "he felt himself."[6] The disturbance of this feeling of "himself" becomes most distinctly exhibited in the case of twins when one twin has lost his identity in the other.

The ideas in the expressions "We are only halves of the same body" and "one leg of the same body" are expressed in "shoe-symbolism": A man (Jack) married the girl friend of his twin (Sam). Jack said: "The shoe could have been on the other foot." "I am a living corpse," said one of the identical twins.

"I am a living corpse who lives within his coffin" ("Je suis un mort pensif qui vit dans son cercueil"), said the "Man with the Iron Mask," the accursed twin without identity in Victor Hugo's Les Jumeaux *(The Twins).[7]*

The writings of Samuel Clemens disclose the fascination of the mistaken identity of twins. Even the chosen pen name Twain *suggests a neurosis of identity.*

The story of Oedipus represents the classic exposition of the loss of the self-identity. The verbal expression of the self-identity is the personal pronoun *I*, German *ich*, Latin *ego*, Greek *egō*, Sanskrit *aham*, etc., all phonemically related forms belonging to the oldest stock of the Indo-European language community. This pronoun is a unique phenomenon in our whole vocabulary: it has no gender; no cases, because the *I* is always the subject and never an object; no plural, because the plural (as in the case of twins as shown above) would lead to the essential disturbance in the feeling of self-identity. The emphatic form *I my-self* properly means "I my self identity."

This basic experience of self-sameness can, however, be expanded by identification. The first step in this expansion is implied in the *I-thou* relationship. The use of the *thou* is reserved as referring to those with whom the *I* can identify itself, as this is most clearly expressed, e.g., in the German *ich-du* relationship. Therefore it is logical that in our language the *thou* has no genders (it has masculine and feminine in Hebrew); it has, though, developed an object form in the singular, *thee*, but not in the plural. The mother-child relationship has set the primary pattern of the *I-thou* identification. The plural *we* is another, though even larger, expression of this collective unity (by forming a group identification). The third person of the personal pronoun refers to those persons with whom or things with which we do *not* identify ourselves.

The *I* represents the subjective foundation of identity. The objective aspect of the *I* is denoted by an altogether different word, which means that the inside experience of the *I* is also different from the outside aspect called *me*. The *I* experiences its sameness first by exploiting the environment, by declaring—often shouting—its primary wants, needs, or urges; thus the vocative became the primary nominal, the imperative the primary verbal form in grammar. The *I* appears first as a self-centered, autistic agency with no respect how as a *me* it may affect others. During the process of maturation, however, the *me* and, at the same time, the *we* are growing in their importance; they may even outgrow the *I*. This means that the appearance, the mask, the social role and outward display may absorb the inner truth. Identity develops through the *we* by identification with others. The *I* experiences its own being not in the empty space of loneliness but in the interplay with others, how it is understood, reflected, and appreciated in the mirror of the other person. The self-sameness of the *I* becomes conscious if it can predict the *me,* the impression it makes upon other people, and is able to integrate this outside appearance with the inside essence. The desire for intimacy with the other, in which the man of the street will see nothing but sex, is primarily the search of the *I* for its *me,* its true mirror image through the intimate identification with the other. The *me* is called in grammar *accusative,* the case of accusation and guilt. The Latin *intercursus,* "intercourse," properly means this intimate *I-thou* relationship: "a running between, intervention," the mutual exchange; it means in English the verbal exchange, not simply the sexual connection.

The sexual union, however, remains the peak experience of the subject in the search for its objective image. The *I* may even vanish in the other and emerge again in the fully experienced reality. A special form of identification appears in the narcissistic identification with the introject. This may be the case in melancholia, when—as Freud expressed it—"the shadow of the object fell upon the ego";[8] and this might be the case of sexual union. The Old Testament language expressed it plastically: man and woman "they shall be one flesh" (Gen. 2:24). The Greek mythological fantasies created the image of the *Androgynos* and called the "matrimony" *androgunon,* the perfect union of man and woman.

I quote as a clinical illustration the dream of a female patient, a borderline case:

A woman dreamt about her sexual union with a man. The elements of her dream are: she saw the act on film (complete depersonalization); the picture "melted down" and they "melted together"; she saw a "house of cards" (the feeling her ego will collapse); she experienced a "sense of sinking" (to lose the ego control like by falling *asleep); a* "loss of identity"; *the man lost his identity, too; they became a "fluid together" (the mixing of fluids is called in English adultery); the "house of cards" finally collapsed; the man was in her.*[9]

DOLLS AND MASKS

Puppets, dolls, and masks are the tools that guide the children in the development of self-identity and help them in looking objectively upon themselves. Before children learn to overcome their autistic fixation and become aware of the difference between the subject *I* and the object *me,* they project their subjectively experienced identity into the outside reality through puppets and dolls. These tools replace the objective self-perception in the child's world; they are therefore in some respect felt as more real, more positively existing than the objects of reality. They represent the imaginary alter-ego with which the small child can identify itself. The outside *me,* which the others perceive, appears first as a mask covering up the inside true identity. The true reality for the small child is the *inside* reality; true knowledge means the inside knowledge—thus *in-sight,* revealing what is hidden behind the mask. Children like to explore everything that is "inside," even inside their dolls. They like to cover their faces with masks as all primitive people do, or as did the actors of the Greek tragedies. In regressive states the dolls and masks, like the masks of Greek actors, become once again important representations; they may serve as protection against the accusative environment or conscience. The small child has a special understanding of the "clown" who is distinguished by his whole outfit as not belonging to physical reality, who acts as a living puppet or marionette on an imaginary playground.

The English *doll* is a diminutive pet name of *Dorothy,* just as *marionette* is the French pet name of *Marion.* When personal names are used as common nouns, they usually cover up a delicate meaning. These nouns as diminutives refer to little things, but their smallness indicates also that they represent imaginary inside realities, which no eye can see. They are imaginary diminutives.

The words referring to "mask" indicate that the holes of the mask, permitting an *in-sight* into the true identity—the

55

openings of the mouth and the eyes—appear as the characteristic features of the object "mask." Our languages distinguish
two kinds of masks: the oral mask and the ocular mask, and
also accordingly two kinds of puppets, i.e., two kinds of
imaginary infants or fetuses: the oral puppet-child and the
ocular one. One can observe as a third variety the anal child
as a product of early birth fantasies.

On the oral level of development the mouth is considered to be the aperture through which one can look behind
the mask and gain an insight into the invisible puppet-child.
In Greek *stoma* means "mouth," thus *stomachos* denotes "the
inside mouth, throat, gullet, stomach," and the diminutive
stomation, properly "the little mouth," denotes the "puppet."
The same holds true for the Latin *ōs, ōris,* which means both
"mouth" and "mask." If the word *per-sōna* is of Latin provenience, it also refers to the oral mask which permits "per-
sound" to find out the true identity of the actor hidden behind
the mask. The compound noun *ori-ficium* expressed properly
the idea of "making the mouth," while the diminutive *os-
culum,* "little mouth," assumed the meaning of "kiss." Another form of the diminutive, *os-cillum,* "little mouth," means
"mask." This word, however, is found also with the meaning
"pendulum," and the verb *os-cillāre* means "swing." The
latter two meanings apparently inject into the whole complex,
as our best vocabularies show, a bewildering discrepancy that
is expressed by the same phonemic pattern. An obstacle,
indeed, are such disparate meanings for interpreters who want
to find out some transitory connections not in the realm of
dreams and fantasies but on the level of objective realities.
Difficult it is in this case to figure out the connecting link
between "little mouth-doll-mask" and "pendulum."

A welcome help for these interpreters[10] is found in
Virgil (*Georgica* 2:387), who speaks about the *oscilla,*
"masks," which people used in feasting the *Liberalia* in
veneration of Bacchus-Dionysus. On such occasions they used
to hang *ōscillae* in the vineyards, thus honoring Dionysus,
who was the "god of masks" and of the theater as well. The
Greek Dionysus became equated with the Latin god *Liber;* the
female partner of Dionysus, *korē,* meaning "girl," became
accordingly equated with *Libera.* Their names were also used
in the plural *liberi,* denoting "children." There is, of course, a
hidden interdependence of the meanings involved, namely that

the suspended masks of the Liberalia were necessarily swinging, thus giving the name to the "pendulum." *Swing* and *wing* are inseparable in phonetics and in meaning, both characteristic attributes of the puppet-child. The connection between "mask," "doll," "puppet," and "pendulum" cannot be found on the manifest surface of language, because these words hang together by repressed unconscious fantasies.

The ocular mask derives its name from the eyeholes. The Greek *opē* means "opening, hole"; *omma,* from *op-ma,* means "eye"; *pros-ōpon* means "face, visage, countenance"; and *pros-ōpeion* means "mask." It is a conspicuous phenomenon of many languages that they denote the "face" with reference to "seeing" or "eye." So the Greek *ōps* means "eye, face, countenance"; the same holds true for the German *Gesicht* or for the French *visage,* and so on. The psychological reason for this identification of "face" and "seeing," however, is not, as generally supposed, that the "look" is most characteristic of the "face," but that the face is considered to be a living ocular mask, as suggested also by the above Greek instances. Even the word *face,* from the Latin *faciēs,* refers to the artificial "making up," from the verb *faciō, -ere,* "to make." Much like the Greek *pros-ōpon* or the Latin *superficies,* "surface," it refers to the outer *sur-face* in contradistinction to the inside essence. Some people dream that they have lost their face.[11] The "loss of face" refers primarily to the loss of the hiding mask and being exposed, unmasked; it brings about the feeling of shame and the desire to hide in invisibility.

The ocular puppet-child is represented in Greek by *korē,* meaning "girl, puppet, doll," and the "pupil of the eye." This is also the name of *korē,* by which the divine daughter of Demeter, i.e., Persephone, was worshiped. This mythical representation of *korē,* "girl," is a clear indication that this inside "puppet" or "child" should not be searched for among object realities because it is a reality of inside fantasies. Sometimes a "little man" or a "little boy" is represented by a doll. In fact the Hebrew *ēyshōne* properly means "little man" and is translated as "apple of the eye" in the Bible. In Latin *pupillus* means "little boy"; *pupulus* "little boy," "puppet," and "pupil of the eye"; *pupula,* "little girl," "puppet," and "pupil of the eye." Summing up the fantasies implied in these verbal instances, one may say that there are "little men," boys, and girls present inside the body and that they can be seen behind the eyes. They are represented outside the body by dolls and puppets. As a clinical description of this fantasy I quote a passage from Schreber's *Mémoires of My Nervous Illness:*

> During my first months here the miracles on my eyes were performed by "little men" very similar to those I mentioned when describing the miracle directed against my spinal cord. These "little men" were one of the most remarkable and even to me most mysterious phenomena; but I have no doubt whatever in the objective reality of these happenings as I saw these "little men" innumerable times with my mind's eye and heard their voices. The remarkable thing about it was that souls or their single nerves could in certain conditions and for particular purposes assume the tiny human shapes (as mentioned earlier only of a few millimeters in size) and as such made mischief on all parts of my body, both inside and on the surface. Those occupied with the opening and closing of the eyes stood above the eyes in the eyebrows and there pulled the eyelids up or down as they pleased with fine filaments like cobwebs. . . .[12]

The "little men" appear also in a special kind of recurrent dream, so they must refer to a very constant element of psychic life. The "Gulliver Phantasies" were interpreted as the projection of infantile elements, especially if the dreamer harbors doubts about his sexual capacity, which might have been the case of Swift's Gulliver.[13]

In Late Latin one can find a variety of expressions all connecting the "pupil of the eye" with "child" and "doll," and also in accordance with our previous observation of "swing" and "pendulum." Thus the Late Latin *baba* means "little child" in the derivative *vava,* and "pupil of the eye" in *vavaredda.* The Italian *bambino* means "child" and "pupil of the eye"; *bambolo,* "doll"; and *bamba,* "swing." The Italian *ninna* means "little child." The Spanish *niña* "pupil of the eye"; *ninna-nanna,* "lullaby"; and *ninnolo,* "doll, plaything," and so on. In view of these words we shall discover an elementary coherence that is present in the Latin mind between the "swing of the pendulum" as found in the swinging of the suspended masks in the feast of Liberalia, on the one hand, and of the "little mouth-mask-girl," on the other.

Fantasies about the anal birth and the anal child

became fully expounded by child analysis.[14] The dwarfs appear in dreams in the role of the anal child.

A patient commented that a dwarf is residing in his rectum like Alberich of the Nibelungen. He identified his bowels with the cave of the tale, filled with gold and treasures, and thus referred to the unconscious equation of "gold, treasure" and "excrements." He also said that "nobody knows" about this dwarf "but me," which is the confirmation of the fact that this inside "little man" is a subjective reality.[15]

Another patient attributed each bowel movement to an indwelling little "demon."[16] *Here again a linguistic interpretation is in order because the patient, a paranoiac, reproduced long-forgotten fantasies. The word* demon *refers to the alimentary process; it is a derivative of the verbs* daiomai *and* daidzō, *which mean "to slay, rend, divide, or tear asunder," in reference to mastication. Some people feel the "digestive bite," which is also implied in the word* stomach, *from the Greek* stomachos, *properly "little mouth." Fantasies about demons are ambivalent according to the benevolent or aggressive components of digestion.*

A little girl liked to play while moving her bowels: "Mary is coming out." It pained her because she was so big. "Freddy" has a bad smell because he was so long inside her.[17] *Anal-birth fantasies were implied. In American English "John" became a common noun.*

Late Latin "children" are called "excrements"; thus *ecrême* denotes the newborn "babe." The Latin *merda*, "excrement," developed in French *merdeux*, "little child"; in the same way French *ma crotte* is a pet name for the child. These words are all derisive or derogatory pet names, expressing the ambivalent feelings of the mother concerning her child.[18]

The word *mask*, from Late Latin *masca*, has its origin in the Arabic *mas-chara*, denoting the masked person, like a clown or buffoon—thus a live doll. This Arabic loan word was not understood properly by the Roman people, who adopted it as *masca*, and we may surmise that they assimilated the foreign word to their own verbal resources. At least the first part of the compound sounded familiar to the Roman ear. The Latin *mās* or *mus, maris* properly denotes the "little man" with special reference to his procreative capacity. The diminutive idea implied gave rise to a further diminutive form: *mas-culus* referring once more to the "virile, male" qualities, hence the word *mas-culīnus* as having the qualities of the *mas-culus*. It is remarkable that these words had some objectionable connotation for the Romans; they provoked the moral resentment of the grammarians and became under protest, perhaps just because of their opprobrious meaning, repressed grammatical terms. The indignation provoked by these words seems to be more indicative than the vocabularies stating that the etymology of the words is unknown, or, at least, is dubious. It is not so; it is only repulsive. *Mās, maris* means beyond doubt "little man," hence "doll," and "puppet"; as an adjective it denotes "male." The second part of the compound seems to have received its indecorous meaning from *cūlus, -i,* the classic term for "anus"; thus *mas-culīnus* denotes the "little man" pertaining to the anus, the anal child. It was, for this reason, not a proper term in Latin (*bona fēmina et malus masculus*); as such it was used in *masculo-fēmina,* a "man-woman." Freud demonstrated the identity of "child-penis-excrements" in unconscious fantasies. These fantasies became condensed in the image of the anal child.

In the German language one also can detect some very veiled references to the fantasies of an anal child. The word *mas* appears also in German, always in a veiled compound form. It meant originally "chewed food"; thus the German *Mast-darm,* from former *Mas-darm* (using the additional *t* for the sake of covering up), denotes the rectum. This word, however, again covers up the older, original name which was *Ars-darm.* Now this German *Mas,* which must contain the same implications as *Ars-,* appears also in such tender flower names as *Mas-liebchen,* "Bellis perennia." The original meaning must be spelled out as "arse-darling," uniting, like the Latin and French terms, the ideas of excrement and child. There exists also a quite old name *pumpernickel,* which entered the English language, too. The word denotes "a coarse, dark, sour bread made of unsifted rye." It is a quality of this dark-brown bread that it produces, like the beans which were taboo for the Pythagoreans, flatulence. The first part of the German compound, *pumpern,* means "to pass wind"; the second part, *Nickel,* "a goblin"; this is a diminutive of *Nick,* the pet form of *Nicholas.* The original English term for this kind of unsifted rye bread was *booby,* meaning also a "stupid little fellow." Behind all these veiled verbal expressions the idea of the anal child is the primary reference.

REALITY

Verbal forms are relevant to the acceptance and rejection of reality.[19] Some light should be shed upon unconscious fantasies in which the early development of the Ego is reflected.

The *thing* appears in our languages in the same twilight as the thumb: it is not simply a physical object, but rather a numen, in the sense in which Heraclitus said: "All things are full of god." The word occurs first in the name of a Germanic divinity, *Mars Thingsus*.[20] Whatever may have been its proper meaning, it was the attribute of one of the supreme Germanic gods and denoted something which can be attributed also to man. We know little about this *Mars Thingsus,* to whom the Roman-German altar was dedicated, but he must have been an important god, because he was able to supersede in Germanic religion even the Teuton Jupiter whose name remained preserved in Old English *Tiwes-day,* our *Tues-day*. The German language replaced his name with *dinges-tac,* i.e., *Dienstag,* meaning properly "Thing's day." The Roman *Mars,* with whom this Germanic god became blended, is generally considered as the god of war, but there are strong indications that he became also one of the gods of fertility and procreation in time of peace (like the Hebrew *Jahvē*). In his veneration the animal sacrifices called *suovet-aurilia* were performed. One may surmise that the Germanic *Thingsus* referred to the procreative power of Mars. It is consistent with this quality of the Germanic god that the great convocation of people took place on the day that was called in the Roman calendar *Martis dies,* continued in the French *Mardi*, in English *Tuesday*, in German *Diens-tag*.

In Old English *thing* denoted primarily the convocation of the people. This was sacral in character. Cultic and legal proceedings were performed on such occasions; also the great sacrifices of human life were offered upon the holy ground dedicated to the divinity *Thing,* who was symbolically represented there, like the god Frey, in the form of a huge phallus. This *ingentis priapus* has been described by the missionary Adam of Bremen. We may thus understand that this powerful god was virtually present in the sacral lawsuit; he stood for the substantial truth that was to be brought forth through the deliberations and, we may add, was of phallic nature. *Thing* was a numen, a venerated taboo, a symbol of fertility and of the lawful order of nature and society. Thus the word *thing,* which primarily referred to a god, came to denote the people's convocation dedicated to his veneration; then as the sacral truth brought to light in the religious and legal proceedings, it meant the substantial truth. The *thing* was thus a numinous object of great religious importance, the object which really "mattered" in the people's convocation. It denoted in the Old English also an affair of dispute which has to be decided by the numen. A similar implication can be found in the Latin *causa,* continued in the French *chose,* "thing," Italian *cosa,* "thing," among others. Not a trifle but a very important "thing" was meant also by the Old English *sacu,* continued in our *sake,* related to German *Sache,* "thing"; this word also referred originally to "strife," to the effect of an object arousing antagonistic emotions. The word *thing,* however, must have been charged with stronger emotions than these other words for legal affairs, because its taboo content became repressed to such an extent that it has changed into a formative element used repetitiously, meaning *some-thing, every-thing, any-thing, no-thing.* The linguistic peculiarity of this transformation consists in the strange reversal of the meaning. Originally its meaning equaled "phallus," but this tabooed meaning became repressed until the word, being void of meaning, could be used repetitiously as a most general term for any object. Having reached, however, this low state of repression, it became used again as a euphemism in its original sense, a verbal "return of the repressed." The "little thing," especially in the nursery language, does not mean simply a trifle, but a very important taboo object, the "penis" of the child. The same holds true for the parallel word *wight.* It meant a fantasy, the imaginary divine child with phallic attributes, on the one hand, and some unimportant trifle, on the other.

It seems to be a strange phenomenon that the important, essential truth became equated in the fantasies of the

Germanic people with the idea of "phallus." However, parallel associations which point to the same direction are generally known. The *testicles,* from the Latin *testis,* "witness," are called "little witnesses." This is a derivative of a former *ter-stis,* referring to the "third one" present. We cannot elaborate this fantasy otherwise than supposing that the testicles are the witnesses of the hidden "truth."

The fantasy of a five-year-old girl indicating that her father has "three" sex organs became verbalized by her direct questioning of the father.[21]

Freud observed correctly that the shamrock, also an emblem of Ireland, is symbolic of the male. He did not refer to linguistic evidences of such associations as, e.g., the Hungarian ló-*here, "shamrock," properly means "horse-testicle."*

The genitals appear in language as the very first reality after the thumb and fingers. They are real not by simply "being there" as said in the German *Da-sein,* or *Vor-handen-sein,* properly "being at hand," but by their true *ex-sistence,* properly "made to be standing out," from *ex-,* "out," and *stō, stāre,* "to stand," by being "out-standing." This means, in other words, that they are the very organs by which the identity of the outside-inside reality is first experienced. The French *main-tenant,* "now," from Latin *manu-tenere,* "hold-in-the-hand," conceives the present moment in such factual reality.

In the Old Testament age the oath had to be taken with "the hands under the thigh," i.e., holding the genitals of those before whom the oath is spoken. Abraham said to his servant: "Put, I pray thee, thy hand under my thigh: And I will make thee swear by the Lord. . . . And the servant put his hand under the thigh of Abraham his master, and swore to him concerning that matter" (Gen. 24:2–3, 9). The truth is in this instance of genital nature. The essential truth was according to these people the genital truth. It is an Old Testament term *mille yādh,* "to fill the hand," which means also "consecration" (Exod. 28:41; 29:9). On account of these linguistic data I do not think that reality as it appears in conscious and unconscious fantasies is of feminine genital nature as this is generally supposed in psychoanalytic literature. It is essential for the proper understanding of these verbal instances that the female does not see her organs except in a mirror, while the organ of the male is *outstanding*. There are many clinical illustrations of the French *main-tenant;* in dreams holding the male organ gives the dreamer the feeling of stark reality.[22]

The early seduction of the female, as this has been observed, may result in arresting the luxuriant fantasies which flourished before the girl experienced the reality of the sexual encounter. Premature sexual overstimulation may even lead to later frigidity, apathy, and boredom. The complete loss of illusions, this quality of the reality principle which appears in boredom, is difficult to separate from the verbal expression used for it in English. *To bore, to be bored, boring* seem to refer according to the suggestions of our good dictionaries to a monotonous wearing activity, but this idea fits only the boring instruments of our highly developed machine age; yet the verbal expressions are of earlier date. The word itself is of Indo-European origin. The equivalent Latin verb is *forō, -āre,* "to bore," known in the form of *per-forāre*. The verb appears, if we would extend gender to verbs, to be of feminine gender: the male is "boring" and the female the "bored" one. This is the denotation of "female" in many languages; the verb preserves this sexual meaning even in the English slang. I quote a college girl, twenty years of age:

> I believed in my mind and had plans for a brilliant future for myself. I was forever growing in every way. . . . After I was raped, however, I found I had an experience that seemed *to fit in* nowhere and that never would. . . . And now that my future and purposes have disintegrated, life has become static. My life has become an *eternal present* of a life I no longer dare examine. . . . In my case, a deformed and lonely person has emerged with no fantasies but a defeatist attitude that has caused her to withdraw from people. . . . My trust in my mind has vanished and the weak voice that crawls out of my mouth speaks for none of the many things I know. . . . You see somewhere in my development I was deprived of a future. For that reason I would rather sleep with a boy than wait for love. . . . *I was bored* with the curriculum my sophomore year. . . .

The *thing* is the most general term for any reality object; it can stand for any object noun. In German when something is on the tip of the tongue they say *dings* or *dingsda*, a filling word for everything repressed. The same is true with the Latin *causa;* hence French *chose* has assumed this function; in Italian *cosare* is used in this function for denoting anything for which one does not find the proper word. Our languages reveal thus in a remarkable way that this "Rumpelstiltskin" *thing* refers to a reality that though existing in fact has a name that has been rejected, and consequently repressed.

NEGATION

We shall investigate some verbal expressions that are called in grammar "negation"; they refer to the rejection of reality. "Negation is a way of taking cognizance of what is repressed," Freud said in a comprehensive paradoxical statement.[23] This means, in other words, that we may become aware that something is not admitted by our sound judgment objectively, yet subjectively it exists, nevertheless, somewhere in our mind. Negativism is the verbal parallel of destructiveness as it appears in extreme cases in psychosis; it is the verbal way of expulsing waste that cannot be integrated into our ego-system.* For instance, say "it is there" and "it is not there." The word *not* contains the meaning of negation. From where did this word draw the almost magic power to make subjective realities into objectively nonexistent entities? This word fulfills now only the grammatical function of undoing and destruction, but investigating into its background we shall discover that it once contained a fullness of meaning which left behind the emotional power of negation.

We described previously the various attributes of the *wights,* and it became abundantly clear that these imaginary representatives of the small child are of phallic character—the hood with which they are covered being the imaginary equivalent of the prepuce. The various terms for the *wights* reveal a further grammatical quality not mentioned previously: these words may belong either to the masculine or to the feminine

---

* An element of anal aggression is implied. This is indicated by the fact that the old negative *ne,* an interjection of disgust, could be accompanied or substituted by an expressive gesture of the nose. This negative attitude is called in German, *die Nase rümpfen,* in French, *foncer les narines,* while the corresponding English phrase, *to screw up one's nose* is not so expressive. The negatives begin with a nasal consonant in many other related and unrelated languages. See Otto Jespersen: "Negation in English and other Languages," *Selected Writings.* (London: G. Allen and Unwin, 1962), pp. 3–150.

or to the neuter categories. They are masculine in the German *der Wicht,* feminine in the Gothic and Scandinavian languages; they are also sometimes neuter. They appear in fantasies not always as boys, they may be sometimes girls, or they may even change their sex. Behind this strange grammatical phenomenon one may recognize the verbal expression of one of the great events in the emotional development of the small child, generally termed as sex recognition. This event of early life when the anatomy of the other sex becomes first clearly recognized is mostly a memory deeply buried during adult life because it is fraught with feelings of anxiety and guilt. Nevertheless, it is a recognition that man shares even with the lower scale of animal life. If animals recognize so instinctively whether the other is a male or female representative of the same species, it would be surely a mistake to minimize the importance of this discovery of the other sex for infantile human life. We will understand in the light of such considerations that the obviously phallic wights possess the strange capacity of making themselves invisible. They might be seen or might not be, so it amounts to the same thing whether there are sometimes wights or there are no wights. Putting it in other words: there is sometimes the little penis present, sometimes it is missing. This reflects the observation of the small boy when he becomes first aware that girls are anatomically different than he is. This "being-there" and "not-being-there" corresponds to the early fantasies of the boy observing the opposite sex. Freud was relying exclusively on psychological observation when he wrote:

> We know how they [the boys] react to their first perception of the absence of the penis. They deny its absence and believe they do see the penis all the same. Gradually they come to the conclusion so fraught with emotion that at least it had been there and had at some time been taken away.[24]

This event in the development of a small boy, the recognition of the opposite sex, has set the pattern of fantasies for the verbal negation. If the *wight* is there, the verbal expression says *aught,* from Old English *ā-wiht,* "ever-wight." This word came to denote the goblin of mathematics, the

68

cipher zero. But *aught* means the same as *naught*.* This *naught* comes from Old English *ne-ā-wiht*, "not-ever-wight." In English this word is significantly used as the adjective *naughty*, now chiefly applied to children as, e.g., *naughty boy*. This "not-ever-wight" became continued in the English *nought*, "a nothing," and resulted finally in the word *not*, the grammatical function of which is to negate. That the name of a numinous being became changed into a functional element of grammar, is in this case, too, the outcome of strong repression. The German language developed in the same way its negative particle *ne-ā-wiht*, "not-always-wight"; this became *neo-wiht*, *nī-wiht*, and finally *nicht*, "not." The synonymous *thing* shows almost parallel forms in *no-thing, any-thing, some-thing;* the same holds true also for the taboo word *body* in *no-body, any-body, some-body*. The *wight*, the *thing*, and the *body* are connected with one another by a primary association.

All these instances show once more the process by which nouns reappear in a repetitive function after their substantial meaning has been repressed. The same can be observed in the change of the Latin *rēs, rem* into the French *rien*, meaning "something" and "nothing"; in other languages the particles for "no" and "nothing" assumed the meaning of "something" or "someone." All such words can be explained and have been explained on purely formal grounds, and present-day linguistics seems to prefer such interpretation. Then it must be assumed that these words have just "absorbed" the negative meaning, because they have been often used in such context. It is, however, obvious that there must be inherent in all these words a psychological reason that makes them capable of assuming the positive and the negative sense as well—"to be there" and "not to be there" at the same time. In English and German these words *wight, thing, body, one* leave little doubt concerning the very positive reality that can assume the positive aspect and the negative one as well. In German the word *man* makes the implication even more expressive; it can mean *Mann*, "man" and *ne-iō-man*, "not-ever-man," i.e., *niemand*, "no one."

The discovery of the autoerotic secrets of the self

* "All Cambridge scholars call the cipher *aught*, and all Oxford scholars call it *naught*." (NED *s.v. aught*.)

coincides with the time of sex recognition; these two moments, therefore, are closely associated with one another. The feeling of anxiety and guilt which pervades the one permeates the other too. The frustration inherent in sex in all higher culture enters the infant at an early age. In a more explicit expression: *Masturbation and sex recognition are both inherently associated with castration fantasies.*

The *wight,* the representative of the small boy in the "phallic" period (i.e., the period preceding sex recognition), denotes in the medieval language also the "puppet," "doll," the imaginary equivalent of the small child. We refer as an instructive example to a medieval German marionette called *Wichtel-spil,* "wight-play." The *wight* means in this case the puppet or marionette, whose strings are pulled by the child's own ego to project the inside fantasies of the child into a doll house. Once Plato referred (in Book VII of the *Republic*) to such marionettes representing the Ego: "like the screen which marionette players have in front of them over which they show the puppets." The medieval German play expresses clearly of what this puppet play of the small boy consists: "Whoso knows, yet will not know, smites himself with his own hand, His wisdom I value no more than a play that they call the little wights."* The boy who "knows yet will not know" is confronted with a fact but does not believe and will not believe his own eyes at the first glance upon the opposite sex, but at the same time "he smites himself with his own hand"; thus he is a *naughty* boy beset with fear and anxiety.

While the "thing" and the "wight" are of a phallic-masculine nature, the *not* and the *no-thing* appear in the female form in unconscious fantasies. This means, in other words, that the "nothing" is not just the negative aspect of "thing"; it is also different in kind, a very concrete aspect of the female genitals connected with the notion that there is something missing. Why is it missing? The answer is at hand: it has been taken away for some reason. The fantasy may arrive in this way to the idea of castration. While ignorant

---

* "Swer weiz und doch nieht wizzen will/ Der slact sich mit sīn selbes hand,/ Des wisheit aht ich zeime spil daz man diu wihtel hat genannt." Jakob Grimm, *Teutonic Mythology* (London: Sonnenschein and Allen, 1880), 2:441.

parents often implant the threat of castration in order to prevent autoerotic manipulations, the small child himself may develop castration fantasies simply by observing the female sex.

Existentialist philosophers, such as Kierkegaard and Heidegger, developed the metaphysics of "Nothingness," which was anticipated by the early Greek philosophers and in religious language by the Genesis of the Old Testament. Reality and existence much like the figure become meaningful if held against the ground. The ground of existence is the nonexistence, the Nothingness. Heidegger even said that the "thing" has to be put into the "No-thing" in order to disclose the fullness of its meaning.[25] Kierkegaard explained that man reacts to the reality of existing things with sense perception, but what is man's reaction to "things" which do not exist? We love, hate, desire, fear existing things, but what describes the human awareness of the nonexistent, No-thingness? Man's response to Nothingness is anxiety. Man fears real, physical dangers but suffers the basic, existential anxiety if confronted with the beyond-physics, that is meta-physics. Hegel observed that people run away from metaphysics as from the plague.[26] It is my contention that the metaphysical interpretation of anxiety by philosophers is not very different from the meta-psychological interpretation of Freud.

Freud with advancing age and progressing search for the sources of anxiety came to the conclusion that anxiety does not result from repression; on the contrary, it is prior to repression, the chief driving force which produces repression. But what might be the source of anxiety if it is not something repressed? Anxiety, so Freud thought, must derive from the fear of a very real danger, and this very real threat in the fantasies of the small child is the fear of castration.[27] Such fantasies may grow up in the small boy by simply observing the other sex and becoming aware that there is no "thing." The No-thingness of the philosophers is the abstract elaboration of the "no-thing" as perceived in the infantile sex recognition. The Nothing's nature is, Heidegger said, to "repel" but also to arouse "wondering." This wondering is the revelation of the No-thing. This wondering is manifested in the riddle questions: Whence? Where? Why? It appears with compelling force in the small child just as it springs to the lips of the philosopher of existence. Heidegger asks: "Where shall we seek Nothing? Where shall we find Nothing? In order to find something, must we not know beforehand that it is there? Indeed we must! First and foremost we can only look if we have presupposed the presence of a thing to be looked for."[28] This is exactly the same experience that Freud described first as the wondering disbelief of the small boy when he is confronted with the no-thing of the female. The difference between Heidegger's and Freud's conceptions is that Heidegger maintained the priority of the Nothing—this means that the negation derived its negative power from the Nothing—while Freud said that negation draws its repressive power of denial from the reality fear of castration. Their final conclusion is almost the same. Both, however, have missed one point, and this is the understanding of the verbal expression of *No-thingness*. Their thinking, though different in kind, followed the same pathways of unconscious verbal fantasies.

KNOWLEDGE

Knowledge supposes in the further development of the Ego the polarization between the subject child and the object reality, also the intentional act of grasping, taking hold, and internalizing the outside object distinct from the inside Ego. Our languages show three different ways of the grasping of the knowledge-object: through the mouth, through the genitals, and through the eyes. In accordance with the former observations made on masks and dolls, we distinguish oral knowledge, genital knowledge, and ocular knowledge.

The mouth is the primary organ of knowledge for the sucking infant. The infant displays the impulse to introject everything it wants to know. It gives the babe the first orientation to the outside reality.[29] For this reason "taste" is often blended with the tactile perception. The English verb *to taste* and the according German verb *tasten,* "to touch," from the Latin *taxō, -āre,* "to touch," illustrate well this fusion of taste and touch. By the same token the Latin *libō, -āre* and *degustō, -āre* mean "to taste" and "to touch slightly." To taste something presupposes, of course, to touch it first not simply with the hands but with the mouth. While touch refers only to the sensation of the surface, taste reveals an intrinsic quality. The Biblical words about the prohibited apple make this difference between the internal and external contact very clear by saying: "Ye shall not eat of it, neither shall ye touch it" (Gen. 3:3).

The suckling infant tastes and smells the mother, feels the smoothness and temperature of the skin, feels the nipple by touching it with the mouth, tasting the milk and smelling it at the same time. No wonder that these sense perceptions of taste, smell, touch, smoothness, and warmth became fused and charged with emotions and, in the course of cultural development, drifted a long way from their primary concrete reference toward highly abstract and spiritual concepts.

Our term *sweet* is related to the Greek phonetic

equivalent *hēdus* and to the Latin *suāvis*, from former *suadwis;* the Greek term is a derivative of the verb *hēdomai,* "to enjoy oneself, take delight, take one's pleasure"; the according noun *hēdonē* means "delight, enjoyment, pleasure." These words do not refer specifically to taste but denote the fused over-all sensation of pleasure. For infantile perception "sweet" and "pleasure" seem to be inseparable. The kind of pleasure referred to seems to be a tactile one, the feeling of "smoothness" of the breast of the mother. In the more abstract sense the English *suave,* from the Latin *suāvis,* "sweet," suggests the smoothness in social intercourse. The Latin *suāvior* means "to kiss"; *suāvium,* "a mouth puckered up to be kissed" and "kiss." The infantile experience of "sweet" is still active in such words as *sweet-heart* and is represented extensively by the word *sweet* in various slang expressions.

Tasting, touching, enjoying the good taste and rejecting the bad one are primary functions which man and animal practice alike. It is a characteristic feature of the words of taste that their meaning is often blended with the idea of "to try" or "to choose." The same word which is used in one language for denoting "taste," as the German *kosten,* developed also the meaning of "to enjoy," obviously the good taste, in other languages. Thus the Latin *gustō, -āre* and all its Romance derivatives, such as the French *goûter,* the Italian *gustare,* mean "to enjoy." The same phonemic pattern, however, also developed the meaning of "to make a trial, to try," as the Old English *costian,* the Old High German *kostōn,* the Gothic *kiusan;* or "to select, to choose," as the German *kiesen,* the English *choose,* the French *choisir;* or even to love or to enjoy the chosen one, "to love." And "to love" is the meaning in Sanskrit, much like the German idiom *er findet Geschmack an ihr,* "he finds taste in her," which means "he likes her." It seems to be, as reflected by these words, a primary pattern of experience to sniffle around, to put something in the mouth, to taste it, to try to eat it, to choose and enjoy the "good" taste and reject the "bad"—and all this is perceived to be essentially one act.

The essential motive of psychological importance is the elementary fact in the implication of the judgment used in choosing and accepting that which is useful as "good," rejecting that which is harmful as "bad." This selective activity set the pattern of all subsequent knowledge on a higher level of mental development. The progress from taste to intellectual decisions can be traced in the verbal expressions. The Latin *gustō, -āre* is used to denote "to become acquainted with," and the Latin verb *sapiō, -ere* means besides "to taste" and "to smell" also "to have insight of," "to understand." The noun *sapientia* originally referred to taste and smell, then developed the meaning of the highest level of insight, which we call "wisdom." This word was charged with the emotions implied in the earliest oral knowledge; therefore it was able to replace in the Romance languages the old verb *sciō*, "to know"; thus the French *savoir*, the Italian *sapere*, the Spanish *saber* have all developed from the Late Latin *sapere*, this from the classic *sapiō, -ere*, "to taste, to smell." The Hebrew *tā'am* means "to taste, to perceive," the according noun *ta'am* means "taste, perception," also "intelligence, a judicial sentence." The related noun *tē'em* means "flavor," on the one hand, "judgment," on the other. All these instances show that knowledge developed in its rudimentary form on the oral level; therefore we call it oral knowledge.

Genital knowledge is different in kind. It is called in legal language "the carnal knowledge of the woman." It is considered according to the confessions of our languages to be the most intimate, true knowledge of another person, therefore called as in Greek *homileō*, "to be intimate with," or as in German *bei-schlafen*, "to sleep with," or as in Latin *co-habitāre*, "to dwell with," or simply *co-īre*, "to walk with," and so on. The characteristic feature of all these terms is that they imply the "together" of intimacy. This intimacy supposes that the one learns to know the other and by this very act both subject and object of knowledge become changed. The Biblical formula "to go in unto her" means the entering of the innermost privacy of the female personality. The Latin language uses with the same meaning *cogere aliquem intra suam cutem*, properly "to know within the skin."

The impulse that appeared on the oral level as introjection into the mouth becomes differentiated on the genital level of maturation: in the male it develops into the aggressive impulse to penetrate, to enter into the female; in the female it changes into a new form of introjection, the desire to internalize the male. The Biblical "And they shall be one flesh" means that man and woman shall learn to know one another from inside and outside through identification just as each of them knows himself or herself. "So ought men to love their wives as their own bodies. He that loveth his wife loveth himself" (Eph. 5:28). While the object of oral knowledge was described by the "good taste" of the mother, the objects of genital desires developed out of this background as the mother, one's own body, and the loved person. Man learned to know primarily that which he loved; knowledge gradually became expanded to ever wider circles, to other persons and other objects which are not loved, but such knowledge which is not love as well "puffeth up," Paul said (I Cor. 8:1).

The significant characteristic of all these terms referring to intimacy is their tendency to develop into the concept of knowledge. The psychological point of this change of meaning should not be overlooked because it reveals the essential truth that says that the genital act has been perceived primarily as a cognitive act since prehistoric ages. It can still be observed in social and clinical situations that the sexual union does not spring simply from the primary process of seeking tension reduction; it is not the outcome of a physiological-hedonistic pleasure-seeking, but rather the result—often the tragic fulfillment of the desire to know, to discover, even to extort by inflicting pain, the very secret of the other person. That knowledge has been perceived as a genital act can be demonstrated through the Greek, Latin, Sanskrit, Germanic, Slavic terms dating back to Indo-European prehistory, through a whole family of languages which say in their own wording the same as does the Hebrew, "Adam knew Eve his wife; and she conceived" (Gen. 4:1). One should accept the testimony of the coherent verbal forms that were developed by the common ancestry countless generations ago during prehistoric ages. It is also a common grammatical characteristic of these verbs meaning "to know" that they tend to become defective, an indication of repression that blocked out forms. But why should the idea "to know" become repressed if not for the reason that it referred primarily to genital knowledge?

The tabooed idea once repressed developed an abundance of words devoid of the primary meaning: in Greek the basic meaning became transformed into *gi-gno-mai,* "be born, come into existence, to become"; *gen-naō,* "beget" said of the father, "bring forth" of the mother; also many other terms referring to birth as *gen-esis,* "origin" and "consanguinity," etc. The same phonemic pattern that developed, on the one hand, the ideas of procreation and birth is found, on the other hand, as *gi-gno-skō,* meaning "to be familiar with, to know carnally, to learn to know and to perceive." Because the phonemic forms are inseparable from one another, one must suppose that the meanings hang together, too. In Greek *gnō-tos* means "parents" and "well known"; also, *gnō-sis* means the "search for knowledge, inquiry, carnal knowledge, higher knowledge." The whole Oedipus story revolves around these concepts.

The related Latin terms reflect in the same way the double aspect of genital knowledge. One aspect is present in *gi-gn-ere,* "beget"; *na-scō,* from *gna-scō,* "to be born"; *nā-tus,* from *gnā-tus,* "born," etc.; the other aspect leads to the group of words like *nō-scō,* from *gnō-scō,* "to know." Some interpreters, when confronted with this identical word cluster as found in almost all Indo-European languages, either say the whole coincidence is mere chance, which is in any case possible; or they state that "beget" implies to be physically "capable," while "to know" means to be mentally "capable"; thus "capability" may have been the original idea out of which two so different meanings emerged. The meaning of "potency," i.e., "capability," is, in fact, implied but not as a transitory connecting link of disparate meanings.

The English and the related Germanic languages developed this word cluster in a way which cannot be attributed to chance. The Old English *cen-nan* refers in the general sense to "procreation," "giving birth"; *cen-ning* means "birth" as in *cenning tide,* "the time of her travail" (Gen. 38:27); derivatives of this old verb are the nouns *kind, kindness, kin,* the adjective *kind,* and the German noun *Kind,* "child." The other side of the same phonemic form can be found with the meaning of English *know-knew;* in German *können, konnte,* like the English *can,* "be able, to know how"; the German *kennen, kannte,* "to know, be familiar with"; the German *kund,* "to be known," etc. The same meaning complex can be found in almost all the other Indo-European languages, which should be accepted as proving that the perception of knowledge as a genital act is an old and genuine part of our ancestral heritage.

The words which denote the mental acts of knowledge still keep a slight reference to the male or to the female, one in the dimension of aggressive penetration, the other in the dimension of introjection. The English verb *to grasp* means "to take hold of firmly, as with the hand"; it indicates also that this taking hold was made "eagerly and greedily." It denoted at the same time "to take hold mentally." The noun means "absolute control and possession." The German *be-greifen,* "to understand, grasp," shifted the original idea "to grasp with the hands" into "fondle, caress," especially in the sense "to pet." To *perceive* and to *conceive* both denote the mental acts of grasping and understanding. The Latin verb *per-cipere* contains in its second part the idea again of "taking hold, grasping," from *capere,* "to take," but this taking is modified by the prefix *per-,* "through," i.e., taking hold "through" a hole, an opening, because the primary reference of "through" always refers to a hole. In distinction to this "grasping through" the verb *con-cipere* refers to the together-ness of the act—*con* meaning "together." The *percept* suggests by its connotation the male, whereas the *concept* suggests the female *conception* in the mental operation. The Latin verb *prehendō, -ere* implies in the same way as *apprehend* through the prefix *ad-,* "to," the physical nearness in the act of "grasping," while *comprehend,* from *com-prehendō,* expresses again the "together" implied in it. The Greek *sul-lambanō,* a term used for the sexual encounter, properly means "to catch together."

Even though our languages emphasize the "together" in the sexual encounter, calling it "grasp together," "linked together," "sleep together," "lie together," "dwell together" as in Old English *haeman,* "walk together," and many other similar terms, the "together" is not always achieved, not even in perfect marriage. This "together" of mutual intimacy is not implied in the Biblical saying: "Adam knew Eve his wife and she conceived." It rather leaves behind the question: Did the wife also know her husband? The primitive conception theories suppose that the true father is the spiritual agency that animated the child while the mortal father who begot the child appears more or less in a marginal position as the foster parent. This means that from the female viewpoint the woman never can be sure who is really the father of her child, who it is who entered her: the spirit or her husband. A moment of doubt and insecurity must arise in the woman who loves and does not "know" for sure who is the father of her child. The Greek mythology is replete with stories in which an Olympian god in disguise of a husband deceives the faithful wife, thus begetting through this mortal mother a demigod. Zeus, the Father god himself, liked such excursions into the realm of mortal men. Heracles was begotten in this way by Zeus in human disguise with the woman Alkmene. The psychological truth of such stories is that the male, desiring to "know" all the secrets of the woman, wants to remain a mystery in the darkness of the night. One will recall in this context the lovers who, like Lohengrin, want to remain anonymous and tell the bride: "Never ask my name"; or as the Greek Eros said to his Psychē: "Never want to see my face. If you do so, I am gone for good." Under present social conditions one can observe husbands who want to "know" thoroughly their wife and at the same time preserve the charming ignorance of naïveté in the woman, yet for themselves claim the mystery of privacy in social affairs, professional life, and financial dealings. Mutual intimacy supposes "to know together" one another. There are women who reject the idea of mating with an illusion; they also want "to know" the husband in the daylight of realities, even with the risk of losing him forever. Perhaps the daylight will reveal that he is not an Olympian but a monster.

Freud also pointed out in interpreting the compulsion to doubt that love ought to be "the most certain thing" in the whole mind and quoted Hamlet saying: "Doubt truth to be a liar, But never doubt I love." This is in accord with the verbal forms that understand the sexual union in its epistemological function. Because the genital knowledge of the woman excludes any doubt of identity, the "unknown" assumed the meaning of "virginity." The Hebrew *bethūlāh,* "virgin," properly means the "separated"; the Polish *nie-wasta* denotes properly the "unknown." It is an age-old custom of many, many races which requires that the "bride" shall appear "veiled" or "hidden" before the bridegroom. This custom is generally recalled in linguistic literature as an explanation of the conspicuous coherence that exists between such words as, on the one hand, the Latin *nūbes,* "cloud"; *ob-nūbō, -ere,* "to cover"; and, on the other hand, *nūbō, -ere,* "to marry," originally used only for women; *co-nūbium,* "marriage"; and also the relative Greek *numphē,* "bride, virgin." The difficulty of this equation, so our good dictionaries say, lies in its prehistoric antiquity and in the completely lost connection of the two meanings in historical ages. Not supposed, however, is that the "bride" or "virgin" had been called "covered" because it was customary to cover her by a veil, but, on the contrary, that the bride was veiled and also so named because the "virgin" is the "unknown," the opposite of genital knowledge since prehistoric ages. The Hebrew *alām,* "to veil from sight," also developed the meaning of *almāh,* "maid, virgin." The more abstract ocular knowledge, as shall be demonstrated, connects the "unknown" with the "invisible"; genital knowledge identifies it simply with "virginity." However, I shall not develop in this context the reasons why the exploration of the "unknown" or the "naked" truth is perceived to be an *adventure,* properly "on-coming," from the Latin *ad-venīre,* an idea which has kept its connotation of exploring the "unknown" up until the present modern usage of the term.

Genital knowledge may "discover" the "naked truth" in a new dimension. It becomes evident through this knowledge that reality means more than simply "being there" or "being at hand," as said in the German *vor-handen-sein:* there might be something hidden in it which has not yet become real but is implied and can enter reality at any moment. The creative capacity within the person is called *potentiality;* the primary meaning, however, refers to *potency.* The semen and the ovum have been considered since Aristotle as the paradigm of this latent state when something is more than what it factually represents; it is not yet full reality though much closer to realization than that which is termed to be unreal or impossible. The overvaluation of intrinsic individual capacities, the "omnipotence of thoughts," makes it very clear that reality has been perceived in a new dimension through the genitals. We have in our languages an abundance of words that prove that *can* originally referred to "sexual potency"; *can* originates from the aforementioned verb of genital knowledge *cen-nan, can,* "beget." The same is true with the German *kennen,* "be familiar with," and *können, kann,* "can." Another term for potency is *may, might,* German *mögen, mag;* the nominal forms are the English *might,* the German *Macht,* "might," and *Ge-mächte,* which is the obsolete term for "genitals." The German *ich mag es* means "I can, I am able to," and "I like it" or "I love it"; this usage shows once more that this is the genital "know how," which means "love" as well.

The word *power* originates from the defective Latin verb *potis sum,* which developed into *possum,* "to be able, I can." This word is implicated in many symbolic representations, among them the Greek *posis,* from *potis,* meaning "husband," or the Greek *des-potēs,* "lord, master of the house," or the Gothic *brūth-faths,* "bride-groom," etc. The most significant of these denotations, however, referring to the genital power seems to be the meaning of the "own self," the symbol and the very core of self-identity, so expressed in the Latin *ut pote.* The Lithuanian *pats* means "self" and "husband," while *pati* means "self" and "wife"; even in the ancient Hittite *-pat* meant "the self." In Hungarian "myself," "thyself," and "himself" are expressed by "my seed," "thy seed," and "his seed," *magam, magad, maga.* The self-identity is perceived on the genital level by one's own semen. The truth has to be "dis-covered." The Greek term denoting "truth, reality" is *a-lētheia;* it properly means the "uncovered." It derives from the verb *lanthanō,* "to be hidden, forgotten." It is the hidden nakedness which can be uncovered. Thus the Old Testament law formulates the crime of Oedipus in terms of knowledge and "discovery": "The nakedness of thy father, or the nakedness of thy mother, shalt thou not uncover: she is thy mother; thou shalt not uncover her nakedness" (Lev. 18:7).

Ocular knowledge is distinct from the oral as well as from the genital knowledge. The above-quoted prohibition of incest in terms of genital knowledge and "dis-covery" of the "naked truth" is worded by the Old Testament law in terms of ocular knowledge: "Cursed be he that setteth light by his father or his mother. And all the people shall say, Amen" (Deut. 27:16). The "light" has been perceived since prehistoric ages to be symbolic of the consistent, conscious reasoning, while darkness and night became the cover of dreams and ignorance. The age of enlightenment supposes the effects of the plain daylight in distinction of the dark ages that preceded it. One must be aware of the fact which proves that man is a visual being, that he does not live by the trial and error of indiscriminate tasting but by sight, insight and foresight, and perceives the world primarily through the eyes.

Freud formulated his opinion in stating that knowledge corresponds, on the one hand, to acquisition and, on the other hand, to inquisitiveness; the energy with which knowledge works comes from the looking impulse.[30] The observation of children left no doubt concerning the scoptophilic interests of early childhood which the prophet of the Old Testament formulated as Jerusalem's sin: "In thee have they set light by father and mother" (Ezek. 22:7). This "looking impulse" is restricted to the perception of the surface form, shape, and color, therefore it is not as convincing as is the oral and genital introjection. It developed instead the idea of the "inner eye." If there exists a "little man" or a "little girl," *korē-pupilla*, behind the eye, then there exists also in accordance with this mirror logic an inner room seen by the inner eye. The Greek *oph-thalmos*, "eye," denotes properly the "eye-room," the "eye socket" as mostly interpreted; the reference is to the imaginary inside aspect that is also described by the *insight*. The Old English *in-vit* means "conscience" and "understanding."

Ocular knowledge is the world of Apollo. It perceives reality at a distance in distinction to the other kinds of knowledge which suppose the immediate contact. In Hungarian the "world" is this Apollonian world equated with "light" (*világ*).* It is the visual world that Schopenhauer called the world of "appearance." The "appearance" never can stand for the truth of the "together" and intimacy but develops in a new sense the idea of "seeing together." One will ask: "Together with whom?"—since no carnal partner exists in the case of the ocular cognizance always present in genital sharing: like two mirrors, reflecting one another mutually. Ocular knowledge can be extended to various objects and it can be one-sided; however, following the pattern of togetherness, it developed the idea of an imaginary partner. This may be the internalized Superego, an idea born out of the child-

* *cf.* p. 162.

parent relationship. "To see together," and accordingly "to know together," thus means to see with the outside eye together with the "inner eye"; the outside eye means the sense perception, whereas the "inner eye" is the organ of true understanding. Real understanding supposes on the level of ocular knowledge this "seeing together" of the outside and inside eye. If this togetherness is missing, there will accordingly be a case as in the Biblical words "That seeing they may see, and not perceive" (Mark 4:12). In our psychological terminology this means: Sensation in itself is not enough for the perception of an object if the subjective element, the "inner eye," is missing.

The deep-rooted difference between genital and ocular knowledge can be demonstrated best by those languages which have preserved this separation until the present day as the German *kennen* versus *wissen*, and in the same way as the English *know, knew* versus the obsolete *wit, wot*. The German *kennen*, "to know, be familiar with," and *können*, "can, to know how," developed their meanings from the primary notion of "to beget," whereas the German *wissen*, "to know," is related to Latin *videō, -ēre*, "to see." The same holds true for the English *know, knew* and *can*, both referring primarily to the genital act, on the one hand, while *wit, wot* is "to know" as in *to wit-ness* (eye-witness); *witting* developed the notion of "to know" from "to see."

All such verbs as the English *can, may, wit*, or the German *können, mögen, wissen*, etc., display a peculiar feature reaching back into pre-Germanic times: they are all defective verbs. This means in the dynamic interpretation that the forms missing did not just "die out" or fade away as mostly supposed, but that these forms were blocked out by some force; i.e., they became repressed because of their association with unconscious fantasies that evoked anxiety. This defectiveness is a telling symptom of the repressed fantasies implied in them.

OEDIPUS

Freud discovered that the Greek myth projected in gigantic proportion the decisive moment of the small child's emotional life after it had passed through the state of sex recognition: this is the conflict through which every child has to grow when its interests expand beyond its personal self-centered Ego. The child has to establish the primary interpersonal relationship with those upon whom its life depends: these are its own parents. Freud rediscovered the psychological wisdom that is implied in the Greek story of King Oedipus. In it he found illustrated the "nucleus" of the character development, and therefore he termed this great event of the child's emotional development the "Oedipus complex."[31] We shall re-examine now this classic cornerstone of analytic psychology in the light of the premises we have explored in the previous sections. In the vestiges of repressed word contents we may discover thought fragments still in their primary form while the mythical account displays only their secondary rationalization. The account of the Oedipus story as given by Sophocles is just an illustration exhibiting the forlornness of the infant as his entanglement with reality unravels on the dramatic scene.[32]

The mythical motivation of the Greek name *Oidipous,* meaning "swollen-footed," is an example of a typical secondary rationalization. Sophocles, the narrator of the myth, does not understand why Oedipus has been called by this name. He feels that there is a need for explanation; thus he resorts to plain common sense and says that when the babe was exposed on the slope of the mountain he was found tied up, his ankles bound so fast that lasting injury resulted. So the nameless foundling babe was called "swollen-footed." It is the specific mark by which the identity of King Oedipus and of the foundling babe will be discovered. This interpretation of the name is not a true folk-etymology but is rather a learned common-sense reasoning we meet so often in literature. The verbal associations suggesting it can be found in the age-old connection between Greek *pous, podos,* "foot," and the relative *pedē,* "fetter, anklet," and the verb *pedaō,* "to bind with fetter, to bind fast." The same association is present in the Latin *pēs, pedis,* "foot," and in *im-pedīre,* from which English *impede* has derived. The reason that the "swollen-foot" resulted from "binding fast the ankles" came to Sophocles' mind, we may surmise, by this verbal association of "foot," "bind fast," and "fetter," much like English *foot-fetter* or German *Fuss-Fessel,* meaning "foot-fetter."

The swollen foot may be characteristic for Oedipus in another way, understood by its implication of forgotten fantasies. The idea "to swell, to become swollen" does not originate in this context simply from an accidental injury, but it can well refer to the tumescence of the male organ as well as of the pregnancy of the female. These primary objects of reference by which "tumescence" has been perceived, now forgotten and repressed, may be the reason why English *swell* is repetitiously used in slang. In Greek *oidma,* "swell," means also "sea"; the ripening of the fruit is called "swelling." Another term denoting "to swell," *kueō,* is descriptive for *kuma,* "fetus," also the "waves" of the sea, and for *kuos,* meaning "pregnant," while the term *tulos,* "swell, swelling," means expressively "penis." It seems significant that the German language developed the equivalent of Oedipus into *Dollfuss,* "swollen-foot."

The question may be asked whether the Greek *Oidipous* and the German *Dollfuss* refer simply to a physical deformity or are understood to refer to a psychosomatically symbolic character trait. Freud has pointed out that a neurotic inhibition may develop when walking is perceived to be "the symbolic substitute of stamping upon the Mother Earth"; thus the impediment in walking will occur "because it is as though forbidden sexual behavior were thereby indulged in." This interpretation may sound strange to our understanding, but it would not be so for the Greek mind, because in Greek *pedza,* "foot"; *pedilon,* "sandal"; *pedon,* "ground, earth"; *pedion,* "a plain, cultivated field" as well as "female genitals"; and *pedaō,* "to constrain, trammel, shackle" were so closely associated in their meaning with one another that they all developed from the same phonemic pattern.

The attribute of "swollen-footed" should not be understood simply as referring to the physiological "tumescence." It is symbolically expressive for the very core of Oedipus' personality. The Greek verb *oidaō*, "to swell, to become swollen," refers also to the specific character trait "to be inflated," "to ferment," "to be troublesome." In Latin besides the bodily *tumor* there is also a *tumor rērum*, an expression used for a fermenting, critical situation. The world around Oedipus is in such fermentation. The Greek synonymous terms *kuein* and *phlegmanō* are also used in such characterological meaning. To "swell" or to be "swollen" is the bodily expression for the boasting, bragging man, for the "braggart." In the colloquial language the *swell-head* means the "egotistic, conceited person, a conceit." The Greek language attributed the conceitedness to the foot; the English language perceived it in the head. The man whose pride has no foundation in reality is depicted by unconscious fantasies as inflated.

Oedipus, the solver of riddles, is inflated and infatuated by his "knowledge," but such knowledge "puffeth up," Paul said (I Cor. 8:1). A Sudanese proverb says: "A man who thinks he knows everything will finally marry his own mother."[33] The logical consequence is infatuation and error. Augustine says in his *Confessions*, " . . . for thou humblest the proud like one that is wounded, and through my own swelling I was separated from thee; yea, my pride-swollen face closed up mine eyes."[34] Here the "swelling" of the face became the symbolic expression of the infatuation.

Sophocles did not comment on the name of King Laius, though the name may have a similar psychosomatic implication as does the name of Oedipus. The Greek *laios* means "left" and is descriptive of the left-handed person. It is a twin word of *skaios*, "left, unlucky, ill-omened, left-handed, awkward, clumsy." The same interrelationship is present in the Latin *laevus* and *scaevus,* both meaning "left, awkward, perverse, foolish, silly," *laeva* and *scaeva* also denoting the "left-handed," and "ill-omened person." These words are again connected with one another by their meaning as well as by their phonemic form in Greek and in Latin; they obviously hang together by a very old complex that has grown out of the psychosomatic fantasy supposing that the *laios*, "left-handed," person is at the same time awkward, perverse, foolish, and clumsy. It was a fatal happening, indeed, when the swollen-footed son Oedipus met his left-handed father Laius at the crossroads and killed him. The "crossroad," in Greek *hodos schistē,* is in itself significant: the three lines meeting at one point are the age-old pictogram of "man,"* the answer to the riddle of the Sphinx.[35]

Various Greek sources intimate that King Laius had been the person responsible for introducing pederasty into Greece. He is charged with the crime of homosexual seduction and rape of a minor. The victim of his violence was Chrysippus, son of King Pelops. It was the curse of King Pelops laid upon Laius that his own son should kill him and marry his mother.[36] The Oedipus tragedy is the outcome of the fate of the left-handed father. The clinical wisdom of the Greek story thus says that the trouble of the child is rooted in the personality of the parents.

The Sphinx is the focal point of the tragedy. It seems to be the deficiency of Freud's interpretation and of the subsequent psychoanalytical literature that it almost dismissed the Sphinx from the story and described the tragedy simply as a case of a son who killed his father and married his mother. In such interpretation there is no need for the Sphinx. We do not understand by this simplified version why Oedipus had first to solve the riddle of the Sphinx before marrying his mother. The Sphinx is the pictogram of the riddle and the riddle is a problem of knowledge. If we understand the Oedipus story in the light of our previous considerations as the tragedy of self-identity and knowledge, the riddle of the Sphinx will become of primary importance, the more so because the riddle question and its answer is properly: "What is man?" the essence and summary of all psychology. It would be strange, indeed, if we would not see in the riddle question the central motive upon which the tragedy, not of incest but of knowledge and self-identity, hinges.

The name *Sphinx* has kept the connotation of the mysterious "Unknown" or "Unknowable" until its present usage.[37] The Sphinx is the personified "riddle," which means,

* This seems to be the primary reason why the Latin *tri-via,* the "three-roads" which meet at one place, became the symbol of the most general, "commonplace," "ob-vious," and *trivial.*

as found before, virginity on the genital level, the invisible on the ocular level. The mythical Sphinx is the daughter of Chimaera. The Greek *chimaira* is the term for "she-goat," a symbol of boundless sexual promiscuity; this may be a hint that the Unknown has to be referred to the sexual sphere. The name *Sphinx* itself is a derivative of the Greek verb *sphingō*, meaning "to bind tight, bind fast," but this binding does not refer, as does the above-mentioned Greek *pedaō*, to "fetter" or "anklet," but implies the more general sense of close pressure, "constriction." The synonymous term in Greek is *angchō*, "to press tight, to strangle, to throttle"; its Latin equivalent is *angō, -ere,* with the same meaning. Derivatives are *angor*, "strangling" and "anxiety," *angustus* and *angustiae,* referring to the "choking" tightness, but at the same time it is the term for an emotional state of distress, as in the derivative English *anxiety, anguish, anger,* the German *Angst,* the French *angoisse,* etc. We may venture to say that the very being of the Sphinx not only consists in the mysterious Unknown which is of sexual nature and implies the opposite of genital knowledge, but represents also the emotional state of anxiety and anguish. The "strangling" attribute of the Sphinx is mostly understood to be characteristic of a demon of death, but this generally adopted explanation has no more evidence in our languages than the interpretation that refers anxiety to the narrow exit out of the mother. The *Sphinx* is a descriptive name for the psychosomatic effect felt as the "binding fast, suffocating, strangling" pressure of the agony of anxiety. This anxiety is evoked in the fantasy of the small child by the sexual riddle. The original question of the Sphinx was not the riddle inserted in Sophocles' play, but the great question of the infantile fantasy: Where do we come from? The true riddle is the philosophical riddle: "What is man?"

The distinctive quality of the Sphinx, propounder of the riddles of existence, is the female upper body, characterized by the head and the breasts, combined with the animal lower body, mostly that of a lion with a conspicuous tail. Wings are often added as a third attribute. The infantile character of these fantasies is obvious. The small child is familiar with the head and the breasts of the mother, but the lower body, always kept covered, represents the mystery of the Unknown. It is in the line of infantile fantasies to "uncover the nakedness," as said in Biblical language, of the father as well as of the mother, but this being forbidden and repressed, the scoptophilic interests of the child became charged with guilt. For this reason the early sex recognition substitutes for the lower human body an animal one that can be observed and represented in its nakedness without guilt and shame. The huge tail, always characteristic of the monster, is symbolic in all our languages for the male organ. Still not knowing the anatomical differences between the sexes, infantile fantasies perceive the father and the mother as being one undifferentiated body in a bisexual unity. The wings, which are added, point to the egg, the best-known embryonic representation of the beginning of life. Our language displays a phonemic interrelationship between *swing* and *wing.* We found previously in connection with the masks that "swing" contains a reference to the inside imaginary-child fetus; the German *schwanger,* "pregnant," and *Schwanz,* "tail," developed from the same phonemic pattern. "Their glory shall fly away like a bird, from the birth, and from the womb, and from the conception," the prophet says (Hos. 9:11). In *Oedipus King* it is said by the chorus: "See how lives like birds take wing like sparks that fly when a fire soars to the shore of the god of evening" (168–174).

It is a specific characteristic of the Sphinx of Giza that it shows only the head of the monster. The question may be properly asked, Why just the head? What is the reason for this strange representation of the otherwise generally known mythological image? The Sphinx of Gizâ displays just as much of the monster's body as the small child may observe of the uncovered adult body: the head. Below the neck the body is covered by cloth and its nakedness must be constructed by fantasies.

How this body is posited may also be revealing for the whole mythical representation. The Sphinx is mostly pictured as sitting on a rock or mountain, or lying heavily upon the ground as if it were the guardian of a treasure. The monstrous head of the Sphinx of Giza—monstrous because it looks human even to those people who know that the invisible body is animal—emerging in immense proportions out of the earth suggests that the solid ground upon which the whole body rests must be hidden deeply under the surface of the earth. The idea of "possess" is often expressed by the pictograms of verbal fantasies as "sit upon": in the Latin *pos-sidere*, from *potis sedere*, the German *be-sitzen*, and the Old English *be-sittan*, and in the Slavic languages as well. If this suggestion implied by our languages is correct, then the Sphinx is one of those mythical monsters that hide their fabulous treasures by *pos-sessing*, i.e., by sitting upon them, guarding that which is hidden deep under the earth. Fantasies concerning the inside of the earth are indicative for the infantile fantasies about the inside of the mother.

It seems to be inconceivable, considering the manifest surface of language, that the idea of "gold" has anything in common with the idea of "excrements." These concepts are, indeed, distant from one another and realistic-minded interpreters of language never could perceive or admit that such interrelationship exists at all. Yet Freud has discovered through the analysis of dreams that "gold" and "treasure" are expressive of the fantasies about the inside content of the body, notably of "excrements." A large quantity of clinical and anthropological evidence—contributed by Abraham, Ferenczi, Róheim, Alexander, and others—has turned this finding into one of the best-proven facts of psychoanalytical interpretation. Our languages have not been consulted on this point, though one could find many instances that can be understood only in this context, e.g., the Old English *gold-hord-hūs*, properly "gold-hoard-house," meaning "privy, latrine," etc.*

We shall apply this interpretation for the clarification of a word that has been repeatedly declared by the best authorities to be inexplicable: the word *treasure*, a derivative through Latin mediation from the Greek *thēsauros*, meaning "a store laid up, treasure, a storehouse, treasure house." This Greek word seems to be inexplicable indeed if we take for granted that language must refer to object realities. But verbal expressions may create fantastic pictograms that have no correspondence with object realities, as the picture of the Sphinx represents just such an inside reality. The Greek word can be well understood if we consider it to be a compound of

* *cf.* p. 179.

thē-sauros. The first part is the well-known word referring to "suck," "breast," and "nipple"; this word is used to point out the characteristic feature of the notion "female" in the Greek *thē-lus* and the Latin *fē-mina.* In distinction to this "female" part of the compound word, the second part, *-sauros,* points to the distinctive feature of the "male." The Greek *sauros* is the general term for "lizard," well known as the second part of such compounds as *ichthuo-sauros, dino-sauros.* The primary meaning of this *sauros* is "membrum virile"; this meaning became applied to "lizard" in reference to the huge tail of reptiles. The diminutive *sauridion* is used especially for the "penis of children." That "membrum virile," and not "lizard," was the primary meaning can be demonstrated by the words *sauro-tēr,* "a ferule or spike at the butt end of a spear, by which it was stuck into the ground," i.e., a "little cylindrical tube"; *sauroō,* "provide with a tube"; *saunion,* "javelin" and "penis." There must be a common denominator for "lizard," "little tube," "little spear," "javelin," and this common element must fit all three concepts. The synonymous *crocodile,* from the Greek *kroko-drilos,* contains in its second part the same reference, *drilos,* covering almost the same meaning as *sauros.*[38]

Thus the word *thē-sauros* is a strict verbal parallel to the Sphinx: in the first part it points to the nursing female, in its second part to the saurian character with the huge tail, descriptive of the male. The blending of male and female attributes, this distinctive feature of the Sphinx, is inherent in these words; therefore they appear as masculine and feminine, as the Greek *sauros* and *saura* or the Latin *lacertus* and *lacerta,* both with identical meaning.

Formally, this compound *thē-sauros* seemed transparent; however, the very stumbling block is its meaning. It must appear, indeed, as an absurdity for realistic-minded thinking that this monster "female-sauros" is used for denoting a "store or deposit of treasures." In fact, the mythical saurian monsters are for some good reason brought in close connection with the hidden underground treasures they "possess." In the North Germanic Nibelungen myth the dragon Fafnir is the possessor and custodian of the gold treasures and is depicted as a huge saurian reptile. The same holds true for the Old English Beowulf epic: it even gives a detailed description of the fabulous gold treasures found in the cavern in which the dragon was killed.[39] In this case, too, a monstrous paleozoological reptile appears to be the keeper of the underground treasures. Despite these and many other examples, it seems strange that the gold is called *thē-sauros,* "femalelizard," a name which would better fit the dragon than the treasure. The dragon and the treasure are one. This conspicuous shift in the meaning from the "dragon" to the "treasure" will become more plausible by considering the Germanic terms for "treasure"; these are the German *Hort,* the Gothic *huzd,* the Old English *hord,* continued in *hoard,* and others. The phonemic equivalent of these Germanic terms is in the Latin *cust-os,* meaning "custodian, guardian," and also "container." The dragon Fafnir is indeed the custodian of the *Nibelungen-hort,* "Nibelungen treasure," ever since detrimental to man. We can observe by this implication that the name of *cust-os,* the guardian, has been used to denote the hoarded treasure. The primary meaning of this word may become manifest in Greek: the phonemic equivalent means in this language "vulva," *kusthos;* the pertinent verbal form is *keuthō,* "to contain, to conceal, to cherish, to keep secret from, to be concealed, to lie hidden." The noun *keuth-mōn* means "hiding place, hole, hollow, the deep dark vault (of the Netherworld)," and also "the most holy place, sanctuary." In this case we refer especially to the Sanskrit in which the phonemic equivalent is the word *kōsthah,* which means "container, abdomen, treasure house, storeroom." We refer also to the Irish language, in which the equivalent word *owthr* means "abdomen, large intestine, vulva." All these words positively evoke the feminine idea. We shall understand the Latin *custos* by observing that this "guard, watch, preserver, keeper, overseer," etc., is often a eunuch, the "attendant of women"; he is the faithful servant used for the most confidential duties such as "the man who took charge of the vessel into which voting tablets were put." He can be used also as "watch, spy, jailer," but his real nature is revealed by the association by which *custos* is also used for "the stump of an amputated vine branch." Castration fantasies evoke always the effeminated character. Thus *custos* means also in the feminine sense "receptacles, safes, a quiver, incense box," all symbolic for the Greek *kusthos,* "vulva."

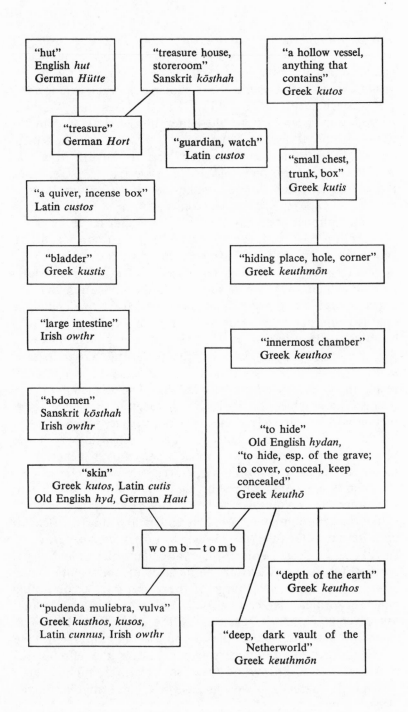

Another Germanic term for "treasure" is the German *Schatz*. In the Old Nordic *Niflunga skattr* is the name of the mythic treasure; the Old English *skatt* denotes "coin" or "property." The history of these terms shows how the original grandiose mythical proportions were reduced to small human realities: the Germanic term developed into the Late Latin *scatula*, the Italian *scatola,* and the German *Schatulle,* all meaning "treasure box," but the German derivatives, formerly *Schatel* and later *Schachtel,* assumed also the original meaning "womb."

In summing up the whole meaning complex, we find that the farther we follow the implications of this word cluster the more it becomes evident that the female genitals are the primary object of reference and of the various meanings—such as "container, innermost cavity, dark vault, storeroom, sanctuary, custodian, guardian, hidden treasure." All are figurative expressions for the same idea; they all have grown out from infantile fantasies about the inside of the mother. They display the unconscious fantasies of the small child when he is still in the phallic state of development or is just becoming dimly aware of the anatomical differences of sexes, and thus perceives a knowledge which after all is present even on the low scale of animal life. The large intestines and the excrements are brought into this context of associations because the laying of eggs and the anal birth are in accordance with these early fantasies.

The Sphinx with a "female-male" winged body belongs to the same stock of imagination as do the other mythical monsters that are guardians of hidden treasures; however, the Sphinx appears to be a unique variant, comparable only to the fiery Archangel with the sword guarding the Tree of Life, which is in Paradise beside the Tree of Knowledge. The hidden treasures of the monster are not of gold. The fabulous treasure is in this special case an intellectual one: knowledge. The hidden and closely guarded secret is the Unknown of the sexual riddle. While the dragon must be killed in the other stories in order that the treasure may become the possession of man, the Sphinx significantly kills herself when her secret is broken in time of maturation. Oedipus, the swollen-footed hero, does not kill the monster by physical force but defeats her through insight and knowledge. The primary anxiety, connected with the sexual riddle, shapes the pattern of all subsequent anxiety arising from the Unknown, especially if one is confronted with the riddle of existence and nonexistence. The dragon killer is a hero if he is the victor in the struggle with his own monster—with the feeling of anxiety and guilt that lies hidden in his unconscious fantasies. The psychological wisdom of these mythical fantasies consists in the insight that the unveiling of the riddle as well as the acquisition of the hidden treasure is, in the final analysis, detrimental for man. A curse lies upon this knowledge which is derived in one part from acquisitiveness, in the other part from inquisitiveness. This curse is stronger than the victorious hero. All dragon-killer heroes become finally the victims of their victory over unconscious fantasies. Oedipus, just because he has defeated the monster* of the Unknown, personifies, we shall see, the greatest blunder, the final defeat of the conscious self-evident thinking and the victory of the Sphinx, i.e., of the psychic forces which are hidden in the Unconscious and the Unknown of the own self. He is the victim of his infatuation.

The Error

It has been pointed out—in contradiction to Freud—that Oedipus had no Oedipus complex, because he killed his father without hatred, married his mother without love, thus acting blindfolded and not intentionally. The motives of his doings are not only totally unconscious but also completely rejected by his conscious mind. The unintentional character of the evil deeds is just the point in Oedipus's story. In fact, intentional ethics, as brought about by Christianity, were absent from the Greek mind. He did with purpose everything to avoid these evils.

It seems to be significant that the Greek idea of "guilt," "sin," or "evil" became denoted by words that mean in our language simply "error," i.e., unintentional "mis-take," especially the stumbling of someone who is like Oedipus, inhibited in walking. The clinical representation of guilt may also produce the picture of "falling," a stereotype of anxiety

---

* The Latin *monstrum*, from the verb *mōneō*, *-ere*, "to remind, admonish, warn," originally meant a "divine omen indicating misfortune, an evil omen." Anxiety attacks send warning signals to the Ego.

dreams. We "fall" asleep but speak also about a "fallen woman."[40]

The Greek *hamartia*, "sin," originally meant "fault, failure, error"; it is a derivative of the verb *hamartano*, "to fail, to miss the mark, to err." Another term for "guilt" and "sin" is *sphalma*, which refers specifically to the error in walking, much like our *fall*. *Sphalma*, whose original meaning is "trip, false step," is derived from the verb *sphallo*, meaning properly "to cause to fall by tripping." From the same phonemic pattern developed also the Latin *fallo, -ere*, "to deceive," and the English *to fall* and *to fail*. The Latin word for "sin," *peccatum*, is a derivative of the verb *pecco, -āre*, "to make a mistake, to err." This verb developed from a former *pedi-cāre*, "stumble," containing as the primary notion *pēs, pedis*, "foot," and *pēdica*, "fetter." The Greek verb *ptaio*, "to stumble," also developed in New Testament Greek into the religious-moral sense of "sin" and "guilt." The unintentional character is present in all these terms denoting in our languages the knowingly and willfully committed "sin," just as our *to err*, from the Latin *error*, developed out of the primary meaning "to fall in error, to go astray," into the moral implication of "to do wrong, to sin."

Even more revealing for the swollen-footed hero who stumbled are the terms for "error." These words refer mostly to "wander about" and more specifically to "go astray." The Greek term for "error, mistake," *plane*, means properly "wandering, roaming, straying, traveling, going astray"; the according verb *planao* means "to make to wander, roam about" and the according noun *planes* means "one who wanders" or "roamer, vagabond"; so do the *planet* stars. The same implications are present in Latin *erro, -āre*, "to wander up and down, go astray"; *error* means "wandering"; *via errāre* means "to deviate from the right way." In New Testament Greek this "going astray" became symbolic for the "straying from the Way and the Truth." An error is an unintentional mistake.

We can better understand through these words why the swollen-footed Oedipus was such a lonely roamer arriving at the crossroads when he met his father by chance. He had chosen the wrong way. Even the English word *blunder*, related to *blind* and *blend*, meant primarily "to move awkwardly, stumble, make a stupid mistake." This is the essence of the Oedipus story. In this situation, again, the involuntary quality of his doing is pointed out, but considering this unintentional stumbling, tripping, falling, or going astray, we must ask: Is all this really done without purpose or is there an unconscious motivation in these involuntary errors?* Sophocles followed the psychological wisdom of the Greek language when he considered the very source of the evil deed not in the purposive overt actions but in the involuntary and unknowingly committed crime by error and mistake, since such a crime reveals the very nature of the otherwise hidden inside of man. Paul also realized that behind the actual and manifest human will an unconscious imperative may pull the strings of our overt actions: "For that which I do I allow not: for what I would, do I not; but what I hate, that do I" (Rom. 7:15). Oedipus did what he hated most.[41]

The return to the mother as sexual object is Oedipus' great mistake. The solver of the riddle made the worst *error in persona,* the greatest blunder ever made: he married his own mother. He did not know what he should know best from inside experience: his own body-self, his own mother, and his own wife. He prevailed upon the Sphinx but did not understand his own inside riddle: the self-identity of his person, the identity of mother and wife. He personifies the unity of the distinct meanings "to be born" (*gi-gno-mai*) and not "to learn to know" (*gi-gno-skō*) his parents, "to beget" (*gen-naō*) children and not "to perceive" (*gi-gno-skō*) who was his wife. In Greek *gnōtos* means "parents" and "well-known," yet in this tragic case the parents were not well known to the child. The Greek *gnosis* means the "seeking to know, inquiry, higher knowledge," and also "carnal knowledge." Oedipus had all carnal knowledge, and he was "seeking to know," but he did not perceive that his "genital knowledge" was not "higher knowledge" as well.

The "inner eye" of ocular knowledge is paramount in Oedipus' tragedy. It is represented by the "seer" Teiresias, who is blind and sees and knows the whole truth hidden from the outside eyes. While Oedipus has the genital certainty but

---

* *To stammer* and *to stumble,* original *stumelen,* are twin words. The use of the one and the same phonemic pattern for denoting these two different meanings is found in other languages too. Stammering and stuttering are perceived as speech *im-pedi-ments.*

has no "insight," Teiresias displays the reverse case: he has no experience with the carnal eyes, yet he "sees" with the inner eyes. The inner eyes of Oedipus and Jocasta were blindfolded. Their crime was a crime of conscience. Oedipus, when mocking the blindness of the seer, was rebuked by these words of Teiresias: "But I say that you with both your eyes are blind." The tragedy comes to its climax when Oedipus realizes: "I am not sure the blind man can not see."

One must understand this "inner blindness" on the ground of the underlying Greek verbal fantasies; in Greek *idein* means "to see," and the past form *oida,* "I saw," means at the same time, as a defective present, "I know." However, it must be asked why the past tense of "to see" had to be used also as the present tense "I know." Obviously, we may surmise that this verb for ocular knowledge had to supplant a verb that had been repressed, i.e., forgotten, because it referred to genital knowledge. Thus *sun-idein* means "to see together" and its past *sun-oida* means "saw together" as well as "to know together" outwardly and inwardly; this covers exactly the Latin *con-sciens,* a notion that hardly can be expressed adequately in English.

Oedipus blinds himself. Freud has pointed out that this blinding stands for the only logical self-punishment, castration. The eyes are as precious to man as are the genitals. One may expand this interpretation by stating that Oedipus retaliates upon the eyes not only the epistemological mistake in genitalia (both being organs of knowledge), but he avenges also on the outside eye the blindness of the inner eye. What was the sense of those carnal eyes when they saw and did not perceive? This is what Oedipus says in blinding himself: "You were too long blind for those I was looking for." The same implication is present in the words of Christ stating that adultery can be committed not only by the genitals but also by the eyes; consequently to pluck out the eyes is tantamount to castration.

CASTRATION

Introduction

The castration complex has not found the same general recognition as the Oedipus complex, which has been accepted by and large even by those who disagree with psychoanalysis on principal ground. Freud, however, with advancing age, stressed more and more the fundamental significance of castration fantasies for the development of personality.[42]

Relying primarily on verbal evidences, we also came to the conclusion that the castration fear is rooted in another layer of the mind than the Oedipus conflict. The regression which leads to the Oedipal feelings (and which can be tested by hypnosis) supposes a longer and deeper regression to a more faraway past than do the castration fantasies, for the castration fantasies seem to be somehow nearer to the surface; they can be verified more easily. If we can through hypnotic experimentation distinguish some layers of regression, we would say that the Oedipus complex can be re-experienced through the total regression proper, while the castration complex can be reached through a partial regression, sometimes called "regression in the service of the Ego."

We may call the fantasies to which castration refers, the world of the pastorale. This regression to the idyllic rural life is generally known through literature, music, and art. We know that the court of Versailles of Louis XIV liked to dress in the costumes of shepherds and indulge in a fictitious simplicity of the rural life. They were well aware that all their pastorale was nothing but a play—an enjoyable play amidst a reality of baroque formalism. I do not want to go in this context into the details of this partial regression. I mention only as a representation of the total situation the idea of the *husband*. We know that he is properly the tiller of the soil, but when we describe the man so in his specific relationship to his wife, we understand that this name is only a costume disguis-

98

ing him as a rural tiller and sower, for we know that he is then properly the "tiller" of his wife. He is *cultivating* his wife as the farmer is plowing, fertilizing, and sowing his field. The castration fantasies suppose in our world the partial regression to the animal *husbandry*.

Castration of Animals

Castration is an everyday occurrence on the farm, yet its practical usefulness alone does not prove that just this practical motive was also its original meaning. One must keep in mind that most taboo prohibitions or rituals became rationalized in such secondary ways by explaining that they were useful, sanitary devices. It would be, however, a great mistake to suppose that they really developed out of such realistic considerations. This holds true for the incest taboo, for the various religious prohibitions of certain foods, as well as for circumcision. It is quite possible that the castration of animals may have originated from some primary religious ritual that later on, when it became superseded by the cultural development and lost its original religious implications, became realistically excused and explained by simply stating that it was after all useful. Such suppositions seem to be the more probable because cattle, sheep, and swine were not only the classic *castral* animals but also the classic *sacral* ones. They were *sacrificed*. This word means "made sacred, made fit for the religious purpose." The Latin term *su-ove-taurilia,* properly "swine-sheep-cattle," denotes the offering to Mars and refers patently to these three kinds of animals. It may be argued that these domesticated animals were selected for blood sacrifice just for the reason that they represented the most valuable food of man, therefore they were offered as food to the gods; their sacral character was in this way a secondary matter, a consequence of breeding. This argument, however, is not very probable; moreover, it does not apply to man, only to the cattle. It supposes that the castration of animals first developed as a breeding device; therefore it came about by motives different from those for the castration of men, which also has been practiced for ages. The basic assumption of all the above quoted instances points to the opposite by making it very probable that the primitive mind did not know such categorical differences between plant, animal, and man. It did not distinguish either between the truncation of the tree, the castration of the animal, and the castration of man.

Tree and Man

We shall first consider some terms relative to the tree "nursery" and "surgery," in order to demonstrate that unconscious castration fantasies were implied in these terms. We can show in particular that the truncated (this is the castrated) tree is the "good" or sacral one, fit for religious purpose—in distinction to the tree not made so. An outstanding example of the "good" or sacral tree is the Greek *a-kakia*, "acacia," the word properly meaning "without badness," free from depravity; it is denoted as the Hebrew *shittah* tree, which was sacral and used for the building of the tabernacle. In Latin the verb *putō, -āre* means "to chip off" in reference to the tree as well as to the human body; it is used so in *am-putō, -āre*, "to amputate." The word, however, came to denote also "to clear, cleanse, make clear." One will ask: What part of the body is referred to as being made clean by "chopping off"? The answer to this question will be found in the word *prae-putium*, "prepuce, foreskin." (There are a few other words that belong to the same phonetic pattern, but their meaning puzzled the interpreters.) Such a word is the Latin *putō*, "penis"; *putus*, "little boy"; the emphatic form being *puttus*, "child." Putting these data together, one may surmise that the twig of the tree and the penis of the small boy are equally referred to by "chopping off," also "cleared" by this operation, made clean as if this part that is cut off would be the seat of uncleanliness. The word refers to the "little boy" or to some other pet name; the words are used interchangeably. They carry the connotation of being "chopped off," a *putus*, which is a veiled threat of castration even if applied as a jocose pet name. In further elaboration the "little boy" is also called "girl," "cunnus," and, as such, also a "prostitute." The word absorbed in this meaning all the defamatory implications of the effeminated man. Thus the Spanish and the Portuguese *puto* is used with the meaning of "homosexual," while the Italian *puttana* and the French *putain* mean "prostitute." The fantasy of chopping off is implied in all these terms.

In accordance with these fantasies the male organ became denoted in almost all our languages by a reference to a "twig" cut from the tree. On the conscious level the "rod, twig, piece of wood" is named but it is by the unconscious fantasies that the male organ is understood. Such examples are the Greek *hrapis*, "rod," and its Latin equivalent *verpa*, meaning "membrum virile" (feminine!), *verpus*, "circumcised man." The Latin *virga* means "twig" and "penis" (feminine!); the derivative French *verge* also covers both meanings. So does the German *Rute*, "rod" (feminine!). The English *rod* also has this double reference to man and tree; in the United States slang it also denotes "pistol."

The same holds true for the English *yard*, Old English *gierd*, "rod," which is in Chaucer's language the usual word for "penis." These instances show that a straight, slender stick cut from the tree appeared as the symbolic representation of the male organ and was often used denoting it.

The identification of tree and man is not always as obvious. It might be repressed to such an extent that no connecting link can be found. This is the case with the Old Nordic *bulr* or *bolr*, meaning "tree stump," and the related *boli*, meaning "bull," both words corresponding phonemically to the Greek *phallos*. We gather from these words that the truncated tree became the symbolic representation of the bull.

A similar relationship exists between the Latin noun *cauda, cōda*, "tail, membrum virile" (feminine!), and *caudex, codex*, "tree stump." Both words are nominal forms that pertain to the verb *cūdō, -ere*, "to cut off." It seems to be rather strange to our understanding that a tree stump evokes the fantasy of the male organ or vice versa. Castration fantasies seem to be implied in this association. An outstanding example of these fantasies is the religious veneration of tree stumps. For instance the Germanic people venerated a pole called *Irmin-sūl*, which was described as a "stump of a tree" (*truncam quoque ligni*) and worshiped as "the pillar of the world" (*universalis columna*).[43] It seems to be obvious that the stump of a tree can be considered as the universal pillar upholding the world only in the language of delusions and fantasies. The simple reference to the object reality "tree stump" could hardly justify its overcharged emotional significance. The religious veneration reveals the fantasies that dwell upon the tree having been truncated, perhaps through lightning, by the Germanic father-god himself; being "chopped off" it has been made sacral, fit for religious service. The Latin *truncus* denotes the "trunk" of the tree and of the human body as well; the original meaning of the word was "mutilated."

An objection might be raised against this interpretation because the latter applies perhaps to one special tree stump or another that was an object of religious veneration, but one should not generalize such singular cases; language, however, refers to the general and not to the singular. Every tree stump could not evoke castration fantasies. These objections appeal to common sense; assuredly, one must keep in mind that modern man has lost the whole primitive identification of tree and man. We have forgotten the cultic veneration of trees; therefore we can no longer understand the religious rituals that were performed whenever a tree was cut down. The rituals connected with the veneration of trees are as archaic as general in our language communities and all over the world; therefore the ever-same human nature must be considered as their world-wide motivation. The verbal connection between the Latin *cauda* and *caudex,* "penis" and "tree stump" respectively, is just one of the instances among many others.

In this case an illustration of the fantasies is the ritual of the Greek-Roman spring festival centering around the god Attis. This venerated divinity, it is said, emasculated himself "under a pine tree" in love for the Mother Goddess Cybele. On March 22 (the day called in Latin *Arbor Intrat,* "the tree entered") the *dendro-phoroi* (Greek for "tree bearers") brought a chopped-off pine tree to the sanctuary of Cybele. The trunk of the tree "was swathed, like a corpse with woolen bands, the trunk was covered by a wreath of violets." These flowers were called in Greek *priapoi* because it was held that they sprang from the blood of Attis when he emasculated himself. "On the third day of the festival, March 24, called 'the Day of Blood' (Latin *Sanguen*), the tree trunk was sprinkled with human blood. On this day the novices sacrificed their virility. . . . They dashed the severed portions of themselves against the image of the cruel goddess. These broken instruments of fertility were afterwards reverently wrapped up and buried in the earth or in subterranean chambers sacred to Cybele."[44] If the imaginary identification of the truncated tree and human castration has come to such religious ritualistic elaboration requiring a great personal sacrifice, it will not be considered as nonsense if one meets the same fantasies in the verbal expressions as in *cauda* and *caudex*.

Castration of Men

The words referring to castration are used indiscriminately for animal and man. It makes no difference whether the technique of "cutting," "extracting," "crushing," "splitting," "striking," or "cauterizing" is specified by this operation, inasmuch as all these various techniques were not only used for the castration of animals but also, as attested to, were applied to man. "Let Indra with the two pressing stones split his testicles," the Sanskrit religious text said (*Atharva Veda* 6.138:2). To crush the testicles in hot water was a technique practiced with the small child; thus the child after castration was called in Greek *thlibo* or properly *thlasiae* ("crushed"), from the Greek verb *thlaō*, "to crush." Cauterizing the wound inflicted, thus "healing with iron and fire," was in accordance with the general practice of ancient surgery. The Greek *ektomias*, or *tomias*, properly denotes the animal as well as man. The Greek *spadō*, also the Latin *spadō*, was used in the same way, meaning the "extracted ones"—the word being a derivative of the Greek verb *spa-ō*, "to extract."

The Romans taught all Europe the castration of the cock; the pertinent words, however, are of Greek origin. The Greek *galloi* denoted originally the castrated priests of Cybele and Attis; these priests were called in Latin *galli*. The name of the priest, *gallus, -i,* is thus identical with the name of the "cock," which became also generally castrated. The question arises as to who was named first so, the priest or the cock? We want to leave this question undecided and simply accept as a matter of fact that the cock and the priest were both called by the same name. The cock became castrated within the Roman civilization, but it should not be overlooked that it also became a favorite sacral animal at the same time. "I owe a cock to Asclepius," were already the final words of Socrates. The cock played an even more important part in Roman religious rituals. The castration of priests and of cocks, both served the same religious end, both were sacred to the divinity.

Inquiring further into the original meaning of castration, we suppose that the religious rituals have preserved best, besides language, in this case like in many others, the basic psychological truth.

The deed of Attis which was repeated by his priests, the *galli*, leaves little doubt about the sacral origin of this ritual. The priests made themselves sacred in the original sense of the word *sacri-ficium*, "making sacred." This operation was the condition of becoming a *sacer-dos*, "priest," the word properly meaning "set sacred"; thus the priest had to be rendered sacred.

It is no surprise to find among the pertinent terms of castration such notions expressed as to make "gentle, docile, clean, tame," which are all priestly qualities.

These religious implications may explain the seemingly paradoxical fact, which can never be understood on the level of object realities, that "castration" is called in Latin *sanō, -āre,* "to heal." With this meaning the word became general in the Romance languages. By the same token the Old English *haelan,* meaning *"to* heal," and the German *heilen,* "heal," carried also the specific meaning "to castrate." Thus the word *health,* a derivative of the Old English *hal,* "hale, sound, whole," means properly "a state of being sound and vigorous in body, mind"; to *heal* means "to restore to health." The affiliated English words are *whole, holy,* and *holiness.* In the light of these words castration appears not as a bodily mutilation but as a healer of spirit. It means the spiritual restoration of the soul to its complete health. The same idea is also in accordance with the Greek term *hieros,* which means, on the one hand, "strong, powerful" and, on the other, "holy, sacred." Holiness implied the idea of spiritual power. Castration is thus understood as the delivery from the evil of sexuality; it is the means to the end of *salvation,* to cleansing man of his passions that are the source of sin.

The following clinical materials help elucidate the above points:

It has been pointed out, that self-castration fantasies which may emerge in schizophrenia do not simply derive out of guilt feelings and self-punitive tendencies. These fan-

tasies may have also a source in passive, masochistic and submissive desires to be [transformed into] a woman, and act like one in sexual fantasies.[45]

A boy of eight before the operation on testes dispensed his anxiety and asked the therapist: "Could he's be made into she's?"[46]

The cosmogonic delusions of the paranoiac Schreber might be influenced by the Biblical account of the creation of man, yet they may also have grown up spontaneously. He writes:

> Now, however, I became clearly aware that the order of things imperatively demanded my emasculation, whether I personally liked it or not, and that no reasonable course lay open to me but to reconcile myself to the thought of being transformed into a woman. The further consequence of my emasculation could, of course, only be my impregnation by divine rays to the end that a new race of men might be created.[47]

"Salvation" is called in German *Heil.* This word referred primarily to the uninjured state of the skin; hence the German formula *mit heiler Haut,* properly "with uninjured skin," means "safe." The noun *Heil* refers to the saving of the soul and the verb *heilen* means "to heal" and "to castrate."*

The generally accepted interpretation of this word complex sees no difficulties in connecting all these disparate meanings even though the word *clear,* and accordingly the German *klar,* came to denote "castrated." The English *clear* means properly "free from guilt, innocent"; the verb indicates "to make pure mentally, to free from impurities, cleanse, to free from imputation of guilt or blame." The German *klären* simply means "to castrate."

Because these words refer to the spiritual restoration and clearing, they may also denote the proper and sound

* The best interpreter of the German vocabulary said that *heilen,* "to castrate," emphasizes not the injury inflicted on the animal but the process of healing which followed. From the noun *Heil* derived the adjective *heilig,* "holy"; thus from a basic notion "full of good vigor" developed the meaning of "good, happy." F. Kluge and A. Goetze, *Etymologisches Wörterbuch der deutschen Sprache* (Berlin: Walter de Gruyter & Co., 1948), *s.v. heilen.*

thinking. Having this implication of "clearing" in mind, one can well understand why the Latin verb *putō, -āre* unites the disparate meanings "to cut off," "to cleanse," and "to think." This is a real stumbling block for those who stick to the lexical meanings; nevertheless, various theories have been brought forth to explain how the idea "to cut off" as in *amput-ō, -āre* and the notion of "clear thinking" as in *dis-putō, -āre* can be bridged in the realm of object realities. But I think that the radical meaning referred to the castration complex.

All these various terms reveal the basic religious motivation of castration. They express the utmost rejection of man's sexuality. Castration appears as the climax of the fight man has waged against his instinctual nature since the beginning of time. It was primarily a religious ritual, like circumcision, which became its symbolic substitution. It is a significant fact that castration and circumcision were performed with stone instruments when iron knives were generally used for practical purposes; this proves that the ritual dates back to the Stone Age.

The "testes" are called in English stones, *which seems to refer to an old genuine association. This association is growing up in clinical experience, e.g., Steve, eight years, born with the left testis undescended, enacted after a successful operation a new play: "His play now consisted in building a Stevensville Museum: two marbles of special stone were on exhibit."*[48]

The Old Testament, while it introduced circumcision, this symbolic rendering of the people as a whole clean and sacral, abhorred at the same time any kind of physical castration, be it performed on animal or man. Castrated animals were by law excluded from blood sacrifice (Lev. 22:24). It is expressively said in the law about man: "He that is wounded in the stones, or hath his privy member cut off, shall not enter into the congregation of the Lord" (Deut. 23:1). Yet, despite this expressive commandment of the old law, during the age of the prophets, Isaiah promised the Kingdom of Heaven to the eunuch by using the tree symbolism: "Neither let the eunuch say, Behold, I am *a dry tree*" (Italics supplied) (Isa. 56:3). If the eunuch, Isaiah said, keeps the sabbath, the Lord will give him a place in His house "and a name better than of sons and of daughters: I will give them an everlasting name, that shall *not be cut off*" (Italics supplied.) (Isa. 56:5). This is said by the prophet in direct contradiction to the law, which is an indication that a great change had taken place in the religious evaluation of castration.

A further change in the meaning of castration was brought about by Christ's teaching. Christ taught that not only is the despised eunuch not excluded from the house of the Lord, he is also not simply tolerated there but has, in fact, the most positive promise that he will enter the Kingdom of Heaven. Christ said: "For there are some eunuchs, which were so born from their mother's womb: and there are some eunuchs, which were made eunuchs of men: and there be eunuchs, which have made themselves eunuchs for the kingdom of heaven's sake. He that is able to receive it, let him receive it" (Matt. 19:12). Whatever may be the right interpretation of these words, they are said in favor of those who castrated themselves for the sake of their salvation.

Theological experts commented on this passage through the centuries and tried to explain away its primary meaning, which is in favor of castration. They argued that the idea of "eunuch" should not be understood in this case literally but symbolically—understood as pointing out those who have renounced sexual life on religious grounds, and live in voluntary continence. If this symbolic interpretation of Christ's words is the right one (which is hard to believe) even in this case these words are the illustration of the great process of sublimation. According to this interpretation, first, all rejection of man's sexual nature appears to be the sublimation of the primary reality—which is the physical castration— and, secondly, the Kingdom of Heaven can be entered only by the good ones, those who have performed the self-sacrifice, who have made themselves sacred by having, once and for all, renounced sexual life.

Pointedly supreme, however, in the Kingdom of Heaven is the small child, for it is he who is considered in the Biblical language as the image of presexual purity (Matt. 18). Moreover, not only was he presexually pure, the child was considered also asexual, and therefore as belonging to the category of neuter objects. Thus to ensure a position in the Kingdom of Heaven, the religious man reached for castration. He would then be like a child, pure and clean.

A slight digression—finding an answer to an open

question difficult to explain otherwise—reinforces the belief that castration is religiously motivated: What is, in fact, the relationship between the German *klein,* "small," and the English *clean,* which are phonemically interrelated? The original meaning of *klein* suggests something that is "smooth" and "bright" (like the old German *kleiner Wein*), yet, at the same time, "little," "small," "brittle," with the implication of "pure" and "clean." These adjectives must have been attributed to one thing and this hardly can be anything else but the small child. If this is the case it is obvious that "cleanness" has to be understood in the spiritual sense. In the physical reality the small child is not much of a picture of cleanness.

Significantly, on the other hand, man in growing up becomes "unclean" in the religious aspect; therefore he should *cast away* that "by whom the offense cometh." This is castration in another sense, and though expressed in the following quotation (some radical thoughts by Christ) in such veiled figurative language, its true meaning should be understood by everyone (these words are said pointedly in opposition to the Old Testament law): "Ye have heard that it was said by them of old time, Thou shalt not commit adultery: But I say unto you, That whosoever looketh on a woman to lust after her hath committed adultery with her already in his heart. And if thy right eye offend thee, pluck it out, and cast it from thee: for it is profitable for thee that one of thy members should perish, and not that thy whole body should be cast into hell" (Matt. 5:27–29, also 18:7–9). The radical prevention of adultery, then, is the physical castration, and the right eye referred to is a substitute for the genitals.*

The symbolic language that Christ uses refers, by

* In the Hungarian language *szem* means "eye," *szem-ély,* "person," and *szem-érem,* "pudenda." The "eye" and the "sex organs" are in this case associated with one another: they represent the very core of the "person."

A clinical example may illustrate the specific association between blinding and castration.

A 68-year-old male patient, blind for twenty years, reported the following dream: "I saw Mrs. Jones (the director of the home) come into my room with a big scissors to cut off my *balls.* I woke up screaming. . . ." During a previous disturbed episode he had shouted: "She doesn't want me to see. When will she be satisfied—when my eyeballs are gone?"[49]

various bodily symptoms, to sexual incapacity. One such symbol is "being maimed"; the other is "limping or halting." For example, Christ said: "And if thy hand offend thee, cut it off: it is better for thee to enter into life maimed, than having two hands to go into hell, into the fire that never shall be quenched: Where their worm dieth not, and the fire is not quenched" (Mark 9:43–44). This last sentence is a recurrent one, therefore especially significant. It would be very difficult to believe that by chopping off of one arm "the worm" would die and the "fire would be quenched." This was just the underlying belief of the castration fantasies: that by the removal of the sex glands, the sex organs (the worm) would die and the sexual desire (the fire) would be quenched.

This radical teaching was valid for the apostles; so, as a result, the baptism of the chief eunuch of Ethiopia—an open protest against the Old Testament law—was the public demonstration of this new faith (Acts 8:27–39). These above-quoted Biblical instances gave to the believers the positive conviction that the utmost rejection of sexuality in the form of physical castration was an essential and integral part of Christ's teaching. Yet the radicalism of his teaching became during the subsequent centuries a great concern of the early church. Historical data illustrated the desperate fight of the church against the physical castration of the believers. The church favored the spiritual self-sacrifice by sacral continence and virginity, but abhorred the bodily mutilation. The main argument of the church was that castration does not kill "the worm" and does not "quench the fire," and that, on the contrary, it perverts the sexual desire, and thereby makes man's sinful nature even worse. The original sacral meaning implied in castration became through the polemic of church authorities turned into its opposite: the eunuch appears in the light of the church no longer as the "healed" one, "made sacer," or as the "holy" or "chaste" one, but, on the contrary, as the one upon whom all the blame and shame of moral depravity is cast.

The Greek and Roman religions are very specific in explaining the primary motive of castration. Adonis or Attis castrated himself because he fell in love with his mother Cybele; thus incest was the positive threat that he avoided by renunciating sexuality altogether. The very sin implied in the sexual desire is the sin of Oedipus, the sin most abhorred yet most deeply rooted in human nature. I want to investigate the pertinent verbal terms and ask whether the verbal forms, too, point to the incestuous desire as the very source of sin and evil.

We meet various terms for moral depravity, wickedness, and perversity, terms that carry in final analysis a sexual connotation and point to the ideas of incest and castration. Incest is a primary source of wickedness, and castration or rather the character traits of the castrated person are, in turn, a consequence of that wickedness. In other words, wickedness and depravity originate from the incestuous desire; they are not a consequence of castration, which is rather an act of cleansing, an atonement eradicating the sinful desire by extirpating the very root of its temptation. The castrated is, in this respect, cured for all his life of the temptations of sexuality, that is, cured of sin conceived from deadly mental sickness.[50] These considerations will help to understand the relationship that exists between the key words, *incest* and *castration*.

The word *in-cest* originally denoted the crime of having intercourse with the priestess of Vesta. The priestess was considered to be not simply a servant of this Mother Goddess but her image in person; she became identified with the goddess. Thus the crime in question was supposedly committed with the Mother Goddess herself. In the original sense, then, incest was not a crime committed with one's own mother but with the Mother Goddess of all. Just as Pygmalion sinned in a similar way with the image of Aphrodite (he, though, was rewarded), the vestal priestess, having committed such a crime, was to be burned according to the Greek religious law. The priestess was dedicated to sacral virginity; this quality was designated by the adjective *castus, -a,* the English *chaste* being its derivative. The crime committed against the sacral virginity of the priestess was called *in-castus,* continued in *in-cestus.* The word *castus,* denoting the sacral continence,[51] is a derivative of the old verbal form *careō, -ēre, -ui,* meaning "to not have it, to miss something." It also developed the meaning "to be cut off, to be separated from." One must infer from these terms that chastity was primarily the quality of those who did "not have" their sex organs, who were "missing them," because they had been "cut off" and "separated from" them. Secondary forms of the same verb are *castrō, -āre,* "to castrate," and *casti-gō, -āre,* properly a compound form from *castus* and *agō, -ere* and thus meaning "to drive chaste." The castrated has been "castigated," meaning "driven to be chaste." The words *in-cest* and *cast-ration* thus hang together; they developed from the same phonemic pattern; consequently there must be a common element in their meanings, too. If the lead of these verbal forms is correct, castration is conceived of as a punishment for incestuous desires. These castration fantasies reflect the anxieties and guilt feelings emerging in the child during the age of sexual maturation.

I do not dwell now upon the assumption of otherwise excellent etymological dictionaries, which suggest that the implication of "not having something," "being cut off," or "separated from" in the word *castus* must refer to the worldly life. In the more concrete aspect, however, the sacral virginity of the chaste priestess and the sacral castration of the priests are complemental to one another. The idea of chastity may well have applied primarily to the vestal priestesses of the Mother Goddess as well as to the priest who originally castigated himself in the service of the Mother Goddess by castration, and in the further course of history castigated himself symbolically as if he were "deprived of something," in the proper meaning of *castus.* The interdependence of the two words *incest* and *castration* corroborates the primary thesis that in the forgotten language of unconscious fantasies castration is apprehended as the due retaliation of incestuous desires. However, according to this interpretation castration does not mean simply a deprivation, it is in its deeper sense a delivery from sin, thus a restoration of health.

Summing up: My basic contention thus far has been that castration developed primarily not as a veterinary practice but as a religious ritual dedicating the priest to the service of the divinity. The castration of animals referred primarily to the animals selected for sacrifice; thus it represents the extension of the primary form and the symbolic replacement of man by the animal. The human aspect has been projected upon the tree, even upon stones.

If the priest as the servant of the divine needs to have

been delivered from the temptations of sexuality, one might assume that the earthly rulers also prefer eunuchs for their domestic service. By the further expansion of this thought the early farmer wanted eunuch animals as his domestic slaves and tools. The desexualization of animals prevented the animal from committing the worst of all crimes of man: incest. Considering the symbiosis of the early herdsman and his cattle, it would be inconceivable that he ever had permitted his animals to do what would be the great sin of his own life. The "good" animals couldn't possibly be the breeding type, performing again and again in their kind the most abominable type of human crimes. The great paradox of the radical rejection of sexuality in man and animal alike becomes revealed in the practice of herdsmen: on the one hand he accepted the "increase" in male children, cattle, and fruits as the blessing of all blessings, and therefore kept the procreating father animal in special reverence; on the other hand, deeply repressed guilt feelings emerging out of his own conscience forced him to reject sexuality on religious grounds, which named sexuality as a source of sin, and demanded the castration of those animals serving purposes other than procreation.

It is consistent with this view that the castrated animal and the priest were called by the same name (as in the case of the Latin *gallus* mentioned earlier). This holds true for the Greek *eunuchos,* "eunuch," which not only developed into *monachus,* "monk," but also became in Greek and Slavic languages the proper term for the castrated sheep, swine, or horse. This word denoted originally the castrated chamberlain of the harem in the Near East; his position rose sometimes to the highest ranks of confidential "cabinet" service in oriental despotic monarchies. His name has been applied to the monk; this means that the "monk" has been conceived as the "eunuch" of the Lord. It is well known that in the early Christian church the clerics were called in Latin *spadones,* "spayed men." Tertullian called even Christ by this name, which was not a blasphemy in the mouth of the patriarch;[52] on the contrary, it shows how perfectly the sublimated idea of castration had been absorbed into the ideals of "chastity" and "holiness." It is in the line of such fantasies of the early church that in Richard Wagner's *Parsifal,* Klingsor castrates himself in order to become worthy of entering the service of the Holy Grail.

That words associated with such sublime ideas were being used for denoting the castrated animals, too, demonstrates that these animals were supposed to live up to a higher purpose than did the other "lay-animals." The sacrifice to the divinity could be presented properly either by the virgin priestess or by the castrated priest. By the same token the oxen that pulled the plow used in performing the sacral nuptial of fertilizing the soil could serve their purpose properly because they (the animals) had been previously made clean and sacral by castration.

It has been observed from the biological viewpoint that the animals in the course of domestication lose the colorful pigment which protected them in the wild life. The pale and colorless pigment has been described also as a conspicuous feature of the eunuchs. By that token the white cattle, sheep, horse, goat, even the white elephant became considered as especially fit for the sacral service. The white oxen were the selected ones of the cattle to pull the plow and perform the holy wedlock with the Mother Earth.

I want to present a few of the many instances which prove that our languages have perceived "holiness" in the images of physical fitness and potency, but have reserved various derogatory terms for those men who were sexually impotent. It is a conspicuous change in opinion which casts all the blame of childlessness upon the male in contrast to the Old Testament times, when barrenness was the shame and the blame of the women. In the patristic society the sexual potency of the male is his primary distinction and impotency is the "blemish" that cannot be wiped off.

The typical example of this philosophy is the word *bad*. It derives from the Old English *baeddel*, which denotes the effeminated man, the hermaphrodite. So great was the contempt of the impotent male that he became the prototype of moral depravity. The physiological deficiency has been translated into a moral deficiency affecting the total personality. The same depravation casts a shadow upon the word *odd*. The odd fellow is not a regular one. This impaired personality is implied, though deeply repressed, by the dictionary definition describing an odd fellow as one having strange or queer behavior, not being paired with another, being without a mate. The odd one cannot be paired because he is properly a "triangle" man, according to the Scandinavian languages, in which the original meaning of *odd* is "triangle." Significantly, the triangle is the feminine symbol, incarved in caves since the early Stone Age. (The Greek letter *delta* is another denotation of the triangle.)

From Castration to Education

The preceding verbal instances suggest that Plato was not the first thinker who meditated about human eugenics and education in terms of cattle breeding. This philosophy fits the thinking of the early herdsmen. One will come in this context to a better understanding of some terms which refer to education. It can be well understood that the castrated animal became classified as the meek, good, tame, domesticated, cleaned and chaste one, obedient to the will of its master;* whereas the uncastrated animal came more or less to represent un-chastity and in-cest. An educational philosophy is implied in this.

The education of children is according to this philosophy another form of cattle breeding. We try to understand first the difficult term *e-ducation*. The Latin verb *ducō, -ere* originally meant "to pull out"; later, it came to denote "to lead." Consequently *e-ducō, -āre* means properly "to lead out." One would like to know who is leading whom out of what. According to the generally accepted explanation, "education" means the leading of the child out of the natural state to a higher "cultural" standard. Whether or not this highly moralistic and abstract interpretation really fits the facts of language is a moot point, for language refers mostly to a more elementary and primitive state of mind. Moreover, if the original meaning of *ducō, -ere,* "to pull out," is implied in the word *education,* then the supposed act is also not as gentle as it would be if the later meaning, "leading out," is implied. Let's further examine the past. Keeping in mind "cattle breeding" as the central idea of "education," one comes across the Greek term parallel to the Latin *e-ducō, -āre,* "to pull out": the Greek verb *spao,* "to extract." The relative Latin noun *spadō, -ōnis* is the common term for the "spayed man," especially for the "priest." The priests, however, were called "castrated," in distinction to the lay people—castration being

---

* The flock is led by the *bellwether,* not by the ram.

the characteristic of the life dedicated to higher spiritual purposes.

It is well possible, although it cannot be proven by specific evidences, that the "pulling out" referred primarily to castration, then to the priestly status, and became transferred, eventually, from the priesthood to education. This would be in accordance with the historical data about medieval higher education, which was essentially in the hands of the priesthood. The original saying *pulling out the fry* is still a living expression in the farmer's parlance meaning "castration" (*fry* is a derivative of the Old Norse *frijō,* "seed"). The educational process would be, if this interpretation is the right one, the sublimation of the domestication of animals. Applied to man it would refer to the abandonment of the laical state and the introduction into the higher morality of the priesthood through castration.

It could be objected that this interpretation better fits the stable than the school; however, the English *breeding* is not only the key word for cattle raising, it also denotes in a sense one's whole upbringing. Furthermore, we are strongly reminded by this word that the early herdsmen made no categorical differences between cattle, children, and women. The verb *to breed* denotes primarily the intrauterine gestation, then the process of generation in general to the hatching of the breed by incubation, and in further extension it means "education."

The German term for "education" is *Er-ziehung;* it is a strictly parallel form, perhaps a translation of the Latin *e-ducatiō,* which refers equally to children, animals, and plants. This idea is not translated as gently "leading out," however, but as forcefully "pulling out." The pertinent noun *Zucht* denotes primarily the "pulling," then "breeding" as in *Vieh-zucht,* "cattle breeding." One may ask why cattle breeding and child rearing became denoted by the concept of "pulling." The authoritative vocabulary makes this strange association intelligible by stating that this word refers to the pulling out of the calf from the cow;[53] thus it evokes the fantasy of animal parturition with human assistance. It conceives the educational process in terms of the herdsmen, much like Socrates called his profession "mental midwifery."

This German word *Zucht,* meaning "breeding" and

"education," has its strict parallel form in the Old English *teon*, "to tug, tow, pull, go, draw to, entice, allure, bind." The German noun *Zucht* and its adjective *zücht-ig* absorbed in the course of the Middle Ages all the high religious and moral qualities of chivalry, but *züchtig*, meaning "chaste, modest," carries the sexual connotation even in the modern language. This connotation becomes more apparent by its negative form: *Un-zucht* means "lewdness" and *un-züchtig*, "lewd, lascivious." The English *lewd*, which is its proper translation, derives from the Old English *laewede*, which means simply "laical" in distinction to the "clerical." This opposition of "laical" and "clerical" evokes once more the primary distinction between the unrestrained wild state and the sacral-castrated-domesticated one. The English *wanton* is derived from the Old English *wan-togen*. The first part is a negative prefix meaning "wanting, lacking," the second part is the participle *togen* of the verb *teon* "to pull out." Thus, a "wanton" person is one who has not been "pulled out," who is not castrated.

The general English term for domestication is *to tame*. This is an old genuine term with phonetic parallels almost in all Indo-European languages. The according Greek verb is *damaō* or *damadzō*, said of animals "to tame, break in, bring under the yoke," of maidens "to make subject to a husband," but in the passive "to be forced or seduced" or "to subdue or conquer." Thus in Greek the "wife" was called *damar*, properly "one that is tamed or yoked," whereas the maiden was *a-damastos*, "untamed." In German the act of seduction or rape is termed by the fantasy of "violently pulling," *Not-zucht*, which might be understood in these connections.

Summing up the whole philosophy implied in cattle raising and tilling of the soil, we arrived at the word *culture*, which denotes for our understanding the final result and product of higher education. The word is a derivative of the Latin verb *colō, colui, cultum*, which denoted primarily "to cultivate, till, tend, take care of the field"; in the same complex are *in-colō*, "to abide, dwell, inhabit," and *colonia*, "colony," a term for a settlement. The Latin *agri-cola* is the "husbandman" whose life is devoted to agriculture and cattle breeding. The Latin verb *colō, -ere* implies also "to bestow care upon, to care for"; if said of gods, it means "to frequent, cherish, care for, protect, be the guardian of." It means also "to cultivate, attend to, dress, clothe, adorn," then "to cherish, seek, practice, devote oneself to."

Almost the same meaning complex is implied in the German *pflegen: pflügen,* "attend-plow," relationship. The *colō* complex touches fairly accurately upon the emotional actions, and the values as well, implied in marriage and in the periodicity and regularity of agricultural work. This periodically repeated process is perceived as to be basically a religious ritual, and therefore is to be carried out with reverence; thus *cultus,* in the same complex, means properly "a laboring at, labor, care," then "training, education, mental discipline," next "care directed to the refinement of life, elegance, style, manner of life"; and in reference to the gods it denotes "honoring, reverence, adoration, veneration." *Agriculture* performs this religious *cultus* in relationship to the field. The regular repetition and reverence are indicative of the emotions invested in religious rituals and the well-planned activity of the husband-man.

PART THREE

THE RETURN—

CHILDHOOD LOST

REGRESSION

The wandering about of the confused and disoriented Oedipus is characterized by a salient feature: the unintentional and unconscious return to the mother. Our question is once more: How far was this blindfolded return home which touched the very core of Oedipus' existence described by the specific terms of the Greek language? Verbal fantasies may have developed long before they were elaborated on by mythology. We may trace perhaps some indications permitting a description of the underlying idea as it has been developed apart from, and long before, its dramatic representation. In fact, the Oedipus complex as the return to the mother is implicated in the prehistory of our languages, dating back as far as the early Stone Ages.

There is the Greek verb for "to return." It is *neo-mai*, from a former *nes-ōmai*. The corresponding noun of this verb is *nos-tos*, meaning "the return home"; as an adverb it means "homeward." The roaming, straying, and wandering of Oedipus implies an unconscious directive—his return home. The Odyssey is also one of the *nostoi* stories about the "homecoming" of the heroes. The Biblical story of the homecoming prodigal son is another variation on the returning-home theme. The adjectival form of this Greek verb, *as-menos,* means "well pleased, glad," properly "to be saved"; it shows the emotional significance of the prodigal son's return home that is so vividly described in the Biblical story. The separation from the mother means danger, adventure, hardship, and insecurity; while the home is the equivalent of peace, security, refuge, and safety.

Democritus, the Greek philosopher, said, "At the very first the navel (*omphalos*) grows within the womb, the place of anchor against the waves or of going loose, a rope and rampart for the becoming and growing fruit."[1] (It should be noticed for the proper understanding of the passage that "fetus" and "wave" are denoted in Greek by the same word, *kuma.*) The "place of anchor against the waves or of going

121

loose" evokes the picture of the boats leaving the harbor and going out into the open ocean. The ships leaving their place of anchor represent one aspect of life. The other aspect is represented by the boats returning to safety.

Another thread in our pattern is the word *opportunity*. It, too, refers to the returning boats. *Portūnus* was the Romans' protecting god of harbors. *Opportūnus* was "a good occasion" (e.g., the safe arrival of a ship, the saving of a ship, the blow of a needed wind)—and was derived from *ob-portūnus*, which was what the favorable wind that leads the ship homeward to harbor is called. Regression is such a favorable wind. *Portus*, "harbor, haven, port," also means, like the Latin *līmen*, "threshhold, place of refuge, asylum, retreat"; *in porto navigāre* is the standard Latin expression for "to be in safety, out of all danger." The noun *portus*, "harbor," is a derivative of *porta*, "gate, entrance, door," a term that is specifically symbolic of the female. The "return" is implied in the image of the boats brought back by divine power to their anchor place.

We may arrive at the same "anchor place" through the verbal associations. Another nominal form of the Greek verb *neomai* is *nāos*, from *nas-v-os;* the noun *nāos* reveals that the home to which man wants to return was thought of not as a physical object but as an imaginary home; therefore it can be assumed that his home perhaps means the "dwelling place" of the invisible gods, the "temple," and especially the "sanctuary," the innermost part of the temple. The verb *nāeūō*, from *nas-eūō*, denotes "to escape into the temple," an act which made even the criminal safe. There is no doubt that this imaginary sanctuary and safety is perceived in the image of the human body, specifically of the mother. This will explain, for instance, the term *nāo-phoros*, "bearing about the temple," which is used with the meaning of "behavior" as if man is himself a temple. Paul said, with this idea of the *nāo-phoros* in mind, "What? know ye not that your body is the temple of the Holy Ghost which is in you . . . ?" (I Cor. 6:19). The identification of this "home-temple-sanctuary" within the human body becomes even more transparent through the Greek verb *naiō*, which means "to dwell, abide, lie" and "to be full." The separation from the mother leaves behind in both the mother and the child the feelings of emptiness, in contrast to the "happy return," which suggests the idea "to be full." It is not by chance that the Biblical story of the prodigal son refers primarily to the alimentary canal—to whether it is empty or whether it is full. Thus we may epitomize that only a "container" can be full; this is to say, this imaginary sanctuary and place of safety may be conceived as a vessel, cavity, or hole that is empty but will be filled upon the return.

The whole meaning complex implicated in these terms appears in another form if one observes the development of the corresponding phonemic pattern in the relative languages. The Sanskrit *astam*, from *ns-tom*, means "home, dwelling place." The pertinent verb *nas-atē* describes this homecoming as a "loving approach," the drawing nearer and nearer till the happy reunification takes place; therefore it is kindly translated as "to kiss." Buddha's navel gazing is symbolic for this "eternal return" to the mother, for the navel cord, connecting generations since time immemorial, is a picture of eternity.

The Germanic languages know even more about this loving approach. They connect the same phonemic pattern with the meaning "to recover as from sickness." The Gothic *ga-nisan* and the German *ge-nesen* carry this meaning. They connect with it the idea "to keep alive, to nourish" as meant by the Gothic *nas-jan*, its German equivalent *nähren*, and the former *ner-ian*. The corresponding German noun *nara* denotes "nourishment, hail, salvation." We may observe in these words that the Germanic languages developed the fantasies about the return around the idea of the Alma Mater, the nourishing mother, for she represents the home-temple-sanctuary and safety which nourishes as well.

Thus the separation from the mother and the exposure of the helpless infant Oedipus evoke the picture of starvation, sickness, and death. The return to the mother means life, nourishment, recovery, health, and salvation. Children still like to play hide and seek—finding the real hiding place within the mother, at least under the skirt of the mother. Thus the Germanic languages elaborated the homecoming in oral terms and also in the spiritual sense of salvation.

The Greek myth interpreted the return to the mother in terms of incest. Incestuous ideas cluster not only around the verb *naiō*, "to dwell, abide," as just described, but also crystallize around the rhyming phonemic pattern *sāoō*, from *sav-oō,* meaning "to save, keep alive, heal, recover." The relative adjectival form is *sōs, saos,* from *sav-os,* meaning "safe, sound, whole"; this is preserved in such names as *Sō-kratēs* or *Sō-phoklēs.* The original meaning, as can be observed in the related languages, refers to bodily vigor and power and is translated as "to swell, grow strong, and stout." This reference to the bodily fitness implies in the concept of homecoming a sexual connotation. The idea of bodily fitness is made even more apparent by the word *sō-ma,* from *savo-ma,* "body." To this group belong such words as the Greek *sōtēr,* "savior, deliverer" from evil, "preserver" against death, in the feminine *sō-teira.* Pindar called Zeus by the name *Zeus Sōtēr.* The noun *sōtēria* means "saving, deliverance, a safe return, recovery." The noun *sōstra* is the name for "reward for saving one's life, a thanks offering for deliverance from danger, the physician's fee"; it was also used to denote "the reward for bringing back lost cattle or runaway slaves." "Thou didst make me hope when I was upon my mother's breasts," the Psalmist said (Ps. 22:9).

The return home was so heavily charged with emotions that it became the focal point of religious fantasies, just as the Oedipus complex seems to be, according to Freud, the "nucleus" of the neurotic conflicts. While the Greek myth conceived the "return" as incest, the religious language of fantasies interpreted the same "return" in the light of birth and death. The idea of *re-generation,* "to be born again," is the nucleus of Christ's teaching. "Verily, verily, I say unto thee, Except a man be born again, he cannot see the kingdom of God" (John 3:3). The question of Nicodemus is of the same order as the question with which Oedipus was confronted upon meeting the Sphinx: "How can a man be born," asked Nicodemus, "when he is old? Can he enter the second time into his mother's womb and be born?" Christ's answer to this crucial question of all regression was, "That which is born of the flesh is flesh; and that which is born of the Spirit is spirit. Marvel not that I said unto thee, Ye must be born again" (John 3:6–7).

This answer of Christ is most concise. It implies that to be born by the mother is biology and "flesh" and any return to the mother in the sense of flesh may develop into incest. Man in order to become truly human must be born a second time—"regenerated" in the Spirit of the father. The incestuous Oedipus fantasies can be overcome by the striving to be born again, but this time not by the mother. The religion of Christ, like all great religions, is an initiation religion. The initiation, properly the "going in," into the mysteries theretofore prohibited elevates the adept to the status of the father. The Christian baptism is such an initiation ritual. Christ formulated his teaching on the "return" also thus: "Except a man be born of water and of the Spirit, he cannot enter into the kingdom of God" (John 3:5). In explaining to Nicodemus this difference between "water" (the amniotic fluid of the mother) and the "Spirit" (of the fathers), Christ used a wonderful simile, which comes very near to the "harbor" of Democritus: "The wind bloweth where it listeth, and thou hearest the sound thereof, but canst not tell whence it cometh, and whither it goeth: so is every one that is born of the Spirit" (John 3:8). This is the most meaningful expression of the unconscious motivation that drives man to regenerate his own self in the Spirit of the father.

Freud explained first in neurological terms that "regression" is tension reduction and that the reduction of tension is experienced as pleasure. The organism wants to stay in a state of balance. Freud said he traces the origin of an instinct to a "need to restore an earlier state of things." Pleasurable satisfaction has as its goal the restoration of the balance that existed before the tension arose. Thus regression is an instinctual move to seeking pleasure in a state of mind which once has been experienced and is desired to be experienced again. Freud recognized sleep and dreams as such regressive states of the mind. Perhaps the decisive influence of this interpretation of regression came from his early experiences with hypnosis. The hypnotic trance is in any case the result of regression, whether a specific age regression is suggested or not.

In his later years Freud greatly expanded the meaning of the "return": The whole life process appeared to him as an excitation of the animate matter that wants to return to the inanimate state. Thus death became the great return, the final regression. The death instinct has just this goal: to undo the organic life and to restore the previously existing inanimate matter, the "dust" to which life had been given.

These metapsychological ideas of Freud's, even though they were doubted on biological ground, are consistent with and surely influenced by the Old Testament and the burial rituals. The classic Biblical expression of this understanding of death as the "return" is formulated by these words: "Naked came I out of my mother's womb, and naked shall I return thither" (Job 1:21). Thus the burial is a homecoming as denoted by the Greek verb *neomai,* and these significant words say distinctly that this is a return "thither" into the mother's womb. I do not want to analyze thoroughly in this context these repressed and repudiated *womb:tomb* fantasies. Suffice it to observe that the dead have been disposed of for ages either by fire, or by water, or by burial in the earth. The unconscious fantasies about regression may speak accordingly, therefore, in three different dialects, one in terms of burning, another of drowning, a third of being buried. These varieties of return are significant because the regressive process of falling asleep might be expressed in the picture language of dreams by one or another of the funeral techniques. Death was considered as an endless sleep, dream as the twin brother of death. Dream fantasies and burial rituals are for these reasons inseparable from one another. The "gates of dreams" of Vergil are not very different from the "gates of death" about which Job speaks.

The North Germanic people used to place the dead in a boat (Old Norse *nagel-far,* "death boat"), set fire to the pile on the boat, and let the burning vessel sail out into the open sea at night. This "departure" of the "vessel of death" into the infinite darkness is the symbolic re-enactment of the "return" and "home-going" (*Heim-gang,* as death is called in Germanic languages). The exit of the "death vessel" out onto the "bosom of the sea," out of the harbor where it once was tied down by the anchor, and the going into the ocean reiterates and reverses at the same time in symbolic language the primary exit, the separation at birth.*

* *cf.* p. 273.

BEGINNING

Whatever might be the political or religious ideology of our age, the final end of wishful thinking is always peace and happiness, the guiltless and healthy reunification of nature and civilization, or, indeed, in other words, the recovery of the lost childhood. This is the recurrent dream of mankind.

Sándor Ferenczi, surely one of the wisest followers of Freud, wrote a short summary of the ideas we want to elaborate in the following pages. He wrote: "Typical dreams recur with most people from time to time and have the same origin. They are based on the fact that there lives in all of us an undying longing for the return of the paradise of childhood; this is the 'Golden Age' that poets and Utopians project from the past into the future."[2] The significant point of this statement is the insight that perhaps all recurrent dreams are fragments of *one* universal recurrent dream, which is the "undying longing" for the return of a Golden Age.

Long before the advent of psychoanalysis or before Proust wrote *Rembrance of Things Past,* Milton wrote *Paradise Lost* with faith in the promise through Christ that "Time will run back and fetch the 'Age of Gold.' " This was also the great hope of the pre-Romantic and the German Romantic movements. German poets were fascinated by the old folk tale that once upon a time there was a beautiful city, and the people were happy, and this city lived in peace. Yet this city submerged and still exists somewhere in the depths of the ocean. Fishermen sometimes feel the lure of the depths; they know the "oceanic feeling" of Freud; they even hear—*de profundis*—the toll of the bells. Freud, with his sharp realistic criticism, stated that this oceanic feeling is nothing but the lure of the submerged infancy. The submerged world is not in the depths of the ocean, but in us, and the sound heard from deep down is the "return of the repressed." The Paradise Lost thus became the paradise of our childhood. Yet, despite this irrefutable reference to the ontogenesis of the individual, even

127

128

Freud, with a rather strange turn of thought, realized that there exists also a phylogenetic fantasy; according to it the human race once lived in a state of childlike simplicity in the Golden Age, and there remains an irremovable desire to return to it. The greater the discomfort and the feeling of guilt in our progressing civilization, the stronger grows the call for the liberation from it. The progress of civilization alienated man from his true nature. Freud, in his late years, asked the question without giving a definite answer: Is it the erotization of death which leads to the great return, the final outcome and end of all alienation? The unprecedented advances in science and technology, the reduction of physical labor through electronic devices, the prolongation of the life span, the general rise in living standards are all manifestations of a universal process that is completing the dehumanization of man, transforming him into part of a machine; he can be bought and sold on the labor market like any other item. While this process is going on, on the one hand, we can envisage the advent, on the other hand, of an expanding leisure time, of earlier retirement, the ever-increasing freedom of the individual to live in his own home according to his own desires. This may mean the dawn of a new Golden Age.

Though the new Golden Age is not the aesthetic one of beauty, of the "blue flower" Novalis was searching for and hoping to find, it is, however, the topic of the most serious diagnosticians of our age that this potentiality of our age should not result in a general "Sunday neurosis" or "existential vacuum"; neither should it result in the triumph of the death instinct, in the total dehumanization of the individual. Instead it should bring about the return of the Paradise Lost, the rediscovery of the early childhood; it should assert life against death.

We now have two fascinating and profound eschatologies of the Freudian metapsychology: One is Herbert Marcuse's *Eros and Civilization*,[3] the other is the fascinating book by Norman Brown, *Life against Death*.[4] These two thinkers did the most in restoring the true meaning of the philosophy of psychoanalysis for our own age. However different their wording may be, the common frame of reference toward which all Freudian and true post-Freudian metapsychology is moving is the return to the Golden Age of childhood, the final victory of life over death. This idea should not eventually strike one as strange as it seems to be at first. It expresses in developmental-ontogenic terms almost the same thing that Christ taught in religious-eschatological terms: the final goal of life is the "Kingdom of Heaven." Who will be the greatest in the coming "Kingdom of Heaven"? Christ gave his disciples a clear-cut answer to this question: "And Jesus called a little child unto him, and set him in the midst of them! And said, Verily I say unto you, Except ye be converted, and become as little children, ye shall not enter into the kingdom of heaven. Whosoever therefore shall humble himself as this little child, the same is greatest in the kingdom of heaven" (Matt. 18:2–4). Psychoanalysis has surely taught us to take these words of Christ not metaphorically, but literally. The "Kingdom of Heaven," the great anticipation of Christian faith, is conceived in terms of the return. When the man crucified next to Jesus said: "Lord, remember me when thou comest into thy kingdom," Jesus answered, "Verily I say unto thee, today shalt thou be with me in paradise" (Luke 23:42–43). "Blessed" are those not yet born and those not anymore alive.

We do not believe anymore as Freud did (and his American follower Stanley Hall elaborated) that the development of the child is the somewhat condensed recapitulation of the evolution of the human race, nor that the history of Western civilization mirrors the biographical categories of the Western individual development. We are concerned, however, with the fantasies about the lost happy state of childhood. Repression has wiped out the memories of infancy from our conscious awareness and relegated these memories to the realm of unconscious fantasies. These fantasies re-emerge in scattered fragments whenever the conscious awareness goes to sleep or the mind is "absent" in recurrent dreams and symptoms of neurosis and psychosis. This collective dream of earliest infancy has been dreamed by untold generations through the centuries; it has been incorporated in the early philosophies and religions and has left its imprint upon our languages.

The infantile mind raises many questions, and among all questions one is deeply buried in unconscious fantasies; it is the basic question: Who am I, from where did I come into existence, what is the origin, the beginning, of all things? These are definitely not sex questions even though some parents may understand them as such. These questions set the foundation for all further epistemology and ontology. This is the natural questioning of the wondering, infantile open mind. Miracles arouse awe and anxiety because they are strange. The greatest miracle is the source of the strongest feeling of strangeness and anxiety.

The primary anxiety still falls upon man whenever he approaches the realm of the beyond-physics (metaphysics) and becomes aware of his own possible nonexistence. Life becomes meaningful if it is held against the background of birth and death. In testing the limits of life, man experiences anxiety. His anxiety becomes objectified in the unconscious fantasies about the limitations of his existence, the beginning of his life, and of all things, as well as the eschatology of the last things to come. Cosmogony is the summary and the result of metaphysics in philosophy and theology; it is also a latent, mostly unconscious element of our everyday philosophy. The Bible begins with Genesis, and its first chapter deals with the creation. The Greek philosophy begins with the Ionian cosmogony, but Homer, Hesiod, and the disciples of the mythical singer Orpheus reveal also their fantasies about the beginning of all things.

As soon as the dual unity of mother and child becomes divided and the child emerges as a complete "one," the new duality of subject and object develops, of the I and the "something" we call the world. Man cannot simply feel, see, hear, eat, or do, but he is always doing something. There is no empty I, but this I is always filled with that which is the non-I, the "something" pertaining to the world. The Ego cannot express its specific individual feeling otherwise than by describing the kind of world it perceives. The fantasies loaded with anxiety about the beginning of its own life cannot be expressed otherwise by the child than by fantasies about the creation of the world.

This will explain our interest in the book of Genesis. *Genesis* means "birth," and *cosmogony* means the "birth of the world." The world is still perceived in terms of the I.

We do not consider the Biblical Genesis as an account of paleobiology or geology. The Bible does not deal with the physical-material reality as such; it deals with the phenomenological reality of our subjective experience as we perceive the world in the image of our own existence. Genesis is, therefore, in this understanding, a primary source book of psychology. It reveals in simple symbolic picture language the answers to the eternal human metaphysical questions. It is a book not about the world, but about the human destiny in the world.

Why are mental patients so often involved in cosmogonic fantasies? Because they are regressing to their previous state of childhood. Paranoiacs and schizophrenics are all, in some respects, cosmogonic creators. They wish to create a new world—the world of their delusions, of course. The reason for this cosmogonic element in their fantasies can be found in the fact that the world of reality has broken down in their sight, just as they experienced the "breakdown" of their own Ego structure.[5] They have lost interest in reality, which appeared to them as threatening and unbearable; it does not exist anymore for them, or it is doomed to perish. For this reason eschatological fantasies hallucinating the omens of the impending catastrophe are prominent in their perception of the world. They try, however, to rearrange their relationship with reality. Therefore, they create a new world out of hallucinations—*ex nihilo*. After the old world has been destroyed, they populate the new one with the new generation of their own creation. This might be one of the reasons why they show so great an interest in fantasies about procreation. Their cosmogonic delusions properly serve the purpose of restoration and *re-creation*.

Cosmogonic fantasies are implied in all forms of regression; they cluster around the focal points of unconscious fantasies. I insert here, as a clinical illustration of cosmogonic fantasies, a piece of free association of a highly intelligent college student, a girl, twenty, who reflects by these words upon the beginnings of her personality.

> The sky is upside down. It is in miniature. There is no end. There is only darkness and some spots of light. It goes on and on and down and down. No bottom. No top. This is my mind. And from this vastness I must find thoughts and remembrances. The difficulty lies in the first grasp. If I could just grab hold of something. All I want is one thought. From this will grow spores. Diver-

gencies which will pull more up with their own roots. Roots have an end somewhere. Then, no, for there is no end to my sky-mind. It goes and goes in flashes of light that makes the darkness blinding. So blinding that I can see nothing else. And then it passes. And in its place darkness once again. And then, another spore-thought born of the preceding light and the present darkness. But first the initial thought.

Such mythopoetic fantasies may emerge in every normal person, but they burst into consciousness with elementary force, as in the delusions, in the documents of early religions.

The First Thought of Genesis

We shall approach the textual account of the "beginning" with the same reserve as we accept the text of a dream report. We do not take the text for granted, but ask what is expressed and what repressed, what is said and what is not said yet implied, and what is behind the overt expression. With such cautious mental reservation, which is a common characteristic of any scientific inquiry, we shall consider the text of the Biblical story of creation, of the Greek and of the Germanic cosmogonies.

In order to explain our approach, I ask the reader at this point to close the book and draw a pictogram of the idea of "beginning." It should be understood that this pictogram cannot refer to any verbal expression because the "beginning" is prior to language: it is not the beginning of something, but the beginning of all later beginnings. How can this idea be expressed by a picture? This is exactly the question with which the Hebrew language community was confronted when it wanted to denote the first beginning. I shall describe how this basic concept came to be denoted in various languages. This study is not "comparative" in the same sense as this word is used in comparative linguistics. The language of the Hebrew original text of Genesis is not related to Greek, Latin, or any other Indo-European language; thus, there is nothing with which to compare it. Our comparison refers exclusively to the fantasies that became incorporated in these languages.[6] We want to hold next to one another not, as is usual, the phonemic forms, but the pictograms that project fantasies. The more unrelated the languages are, the more promising our investigation will be. We shall try to create by comparison a situation similar to that which may occur if various persons respond independently to the same question on a projective test. The naming of an idea never before met is similar to an inkblot never before seen. One answer grasps the static form, the other the dynamic motion; the one is a noun and makes a denominative verb, the other is a verb, action full of motion, and makes a deverbal noun. The responses to the same test questions are as different as are the individual language communities, yet the great continuity in the development of Western civilization brought about from totally unrelated languages some responses that look very similar. We can learn another thing from such a comparison. On the manifest surface of the languages, it does not make any difference in what language it is said that *In the beginning God created the heaven and the earth* (Gen. 1:1). Yet this seeming equality is deceptive. Every language implies something of its own in this very same proposition. As we compare the various Bible translations, despite their identical content, we will find that some of the meanings conveyed by parallel expressions will vary semantically from language to language.

The first sentence of the Bible reads in the Hebrew original: *Berēshith bārā elōhim (ēth) hasshāmayim weēth hā-āretch.*

In Greek, it is: *En archē epoiesen ho theos ton ouranon kai tēn gēn.*

In Latin: *In principio creāvit deus caelum et terram.*

In Spanish: *En el principio creó Dios los cielos y la tierra.*

In French: *Au commencement Dieu crea les cieux et la terre.*

In Italian: *Nel principio Iddio creò il cielo e la terra.*

In German: *Am Anfang schuf Gott Himmel und Erde.*

We may modify here the Latin proverb and say in comparing these sentences: If two languages say the same, it is never the same.

The "beginning" in the absolute sense is the great event of the creation *ex nihilo,* out of Nothingness. It is obvious that this pictogram can be drawn with reference, to some visual, already-existing thing. But how can language represent the picture of the Nothing that has preceded all existence and is beyond the threshold between the "to be or not to be"? How can an existing thing become expressive of the nonexistent and the beginning of existence?

THE HEAD   The first word of the Old Testament, Hebrew *be-rēshith*, "in-beginning," covers this very abstract concept; *rēshith* is derived from the word *rōsh*, meaning "to shake" and "head." It is generally assumed that the shaking of the head was the basic underlying concept. It was argued that the shaking of the head is an expression of emotions. We do not really understand why this expression of anger should be a specifically characteristic gesture for "beginning." It seems rather plausible that this "shaking" refers in general to the idea "to shake, stir, move," and intransitively "to tremble." In this case the picture evoked would be that of the Psalmist who says: "Then the earth shook and trembled; the foundations also of the hills moved and were shaken, because he was wroth" (Ps. 18:7). One could interpret that the first act of creation stirred up and shook the eternal quietness or that "trembling," the bodily manifestation of anxiety, fell upon man on the threshold of existence and nonexistence.

I do not think, however, that a verbal concept, which is abstract in itself, could properly serve this purpose. Our interpretation is based on the basic assumption, which can be illustrated by innumerable examples in all our languages, that the primary reality of man is his own body-self—the parts, the sensations, and the functioning of his own bodily existence. Why, then, is the "head" used for denoting "beginning"? We shall find the answer to this question if we observe the other meanings expressed by the Hebrew *rēshith*, "beginning." This word is used for denoting also "the first in place, time, or rank, especially a first fruit." The association of "head," "first," and "beginning" make the whole, somewhat clouded, picture clear. The head of the newborn appears first in the vertex presentation; therefore, the Hebrew pictogram of the "beginning" shows the "head" first emerging out of the Nothingness and thus starting a new existence.* We must bear

* Aristotle said, "The natural manner of birth for all animals is head first" (epi kephalēn). *Generation of Animals?* IV. 8:10, The Loeb Classical Library. (Cambridge, Mass.: Harvard University Press, 1943), p. 475.

in mind that the picture refers to the "genesis," that is, the "nativity." It is the way of primitive fantasies to understand the macrocosm of the universe in terms of the human microcosm. *Cosmogony* also properly refers to the "birth of the cosmos"; in Greek it is *kosmo-gonia*. The second part of the compound is derived from the verb *gignomai*, "to be born." In the early fantasies there is no other "coming into being" than that of being generated and being born.

It is not as obvious as is generally assumed that *rēsh-ith*, "beginning," is necessarily closely associated with the idea of being the first in social rank. The "head" of the "first fruit of the womb" to which the Hebrew term particularly applies seems to be the original point of reference in which the various meanings unite. The birth of the first son covers exactly the meaning of "genesis," "head," "first," "beginning," and also the distinguished sacred rank, which was the birthright and privilege of the firstborn son. We quote, as an illustration, the words of Paul in order to show the coherence of these meanings. Paul wrote in Greek, but his verbal fantasies are still the Hebrew ones. He says Christ is "the firstborn of every creature: For by him were all things created, that are in heaven, and that are in earth, visible and invisible, all things were created by him, and for him: And he is before all things, and by him all things consist. And he is the head of the body, the church: who is the beginning, the firstborn from the dead" (Col. 1:15–18).

Thus, "head" implied through the birthright the meaning of "chief, director," and so forth, as in our *head* and *headmaster*. The Latin *caput* also contained this meaning, and it developed in the English *chief* and the French *chef*. English words such as *ahead* and *headlong* also refer to the "head" as being "first."

The Greek language uses *en archē*, "in beginning." Though the implications are very similar, the Greek version does not say exactly the same thing as the Hebrew original. The key word *archē*, "beginning," is etymologically unexplained, so that we do not know the original object of reference; however, this noun is closely connected with the verb *archō*, "to begin" and "to lead, rule, govern, command," and *archos*, "leader, chief, commander." Thus *archē* means, on the one hand, "beginning" and, on the other hand, "the first" in time, space, or social rank and to be the first person or the first thing.[7]

As we look for the lost original object of reference, we can well observe in this special case how a mythologem—the mythology of a word—became transformed in the course of history into a philosophical, rational statement of the "first cause." Thales, the first Greek philosopher, was still deeply involved in mythological fantasies. He supposed that the "first thing" was water. Aristotle said (in his *Metaphysics*) that Thales got this idea about water "from the fact that the seeds of all things have a moist nature and water is the origin of the nature of moist things." We may interpret this by saying that Thales still thinks in the mythological-symbolic terms of *Chaos* and *Abyss*. Ovid further explains that the primary Chaos was a mixture of moist, damp, and seeds (*semina*). We have arrived again at the ideas of generation, conception, and birth implied in the Hebrew word.

THE FIRST TAKING   The first words of the Vulgate, the Latin *in principio,* show a different approach to the idea of "beginning." The key word *principium* is a compound of *prīmus,* "first," and *capiō, -ere,* "to take in hand, take hold of, seize, take by force," and so forth. Thus, the word depicts the "beginning" as an act of a grasping first. The same idea, probably through Latin influence, is present in the German *An-fang,* "beginning," properly "on-catch." While the Hebrew and Greek words convey a static nominal concept, the Latin word implies a dynamically expansive type of motion originating in an outreaching human will. The "beginning" in the Latin version supposes a prior existing will for creative action. This dynamic interpretation is far away from the "first fruit" beginning of the Hebrew original, although it still refers to the privilege of being the first in rank, the "head." As the Latin *caput* developed into *chief,* the idea of *principium,* the first taking or catching, also resulted in *princeps,* "the first, chief, the most eminent, distinguished," and thus in "ruler, sovereign, emperor." The word is continued in our word *prince.*

The notion of "taking first" should be discussed because in this "beginning" it is not perfectly clear who is "taking" whom or what "first." Generally it is assumed that "taking the first place" is implied in this word; thus, the ruler or sovereign would be the subject of this action and the place or the rank would be its object. I have some doubts concerning this primitive etiquette and must question whether the idea of the ruler as "first in rank" is the person indeed who symbolizes the "beginning" as the first grasp.

We think of the unforgettable creative hand sculptured by Rodin and called "Creation," or perhaps of Michelangelo's grandiose picture of the right hand, properly the index finger of the right hand of the Creator, awakening Adam to life—all these pictures are symbolic of the "first grasp." Even more so is the Hungarian language, for instance; it denoted "beginning" by *kezdet,* from the word *kéz,* "hand." According to the Hungarian verbal fantasies, the "beginning" starts with the hands. We would interpret that these very primitive fantasies, which are essentially dynamic, are declaring that one has to "start" by doing things, by grasping first with the hands. Grasping hands would apply to the mental patients, too, who are deeply regressed into infantile fantasies and do not understand verbal communication anymore. They understand, however, a kind gesture, a hand on their shoulder, a physical bodily contact, and they display the *"délire de toucher,"* the desire to touch or grasp. We are familiar, also, with the inscriptions that try to protect works of art in museums: "Don't touch." They suppose that in a great many people there is a desire to come in bodily contact with the things they admire. We shall show in a following section on "Creation" that the grasping hands are sexualized in the fantasies that equate the creation with shaping and forming.

We consult another Latin verb for "begin," *coepi.* Its outstanding feature is the use of the past ("began") in the present meaning; the present (*coepiō*) faded out very quickly. There must have been some reason for the suppression of the present tense, which displays the meaning implied most distinctly. We surmise that an implication distasteful to the speaker was the reason for its repression. This implication can be found by analyzing this word: it is a compound of *co-* meaning "with, together, jointly" and the verb *apō* or *apiō, -ere,* "to fasten, attach, join"; its participle *aptus* shows more of the meaning: "fitted to something" and is continued in the English *apt,* "fitted, suited." Other forms are *ad-apt* and *in-ept.* The verb *co-epi,* "began, begin," has a parallel form in the verb *copulō, -āre,* from *co-apulāre,* meaning "to couple, bind together, join, connect, unite." There can be little doubt that the meaning of "beginning" was thought of in this case as the act of generation. The verb *apō* also developed the form *apiscor,* "to reach after something in order to take, seize, or get possession of it; to pursue with effort; to take, seize upon"; this is exactly the same action which was implied in *principium.* The intention of this grasping movement is clearer in the verb *coepi,* "to begin," than in the noun *prin-cipium.*

Once more we refer to the Hebrew, which uses as a verb for "to begin," *chālāl,* "to bore, perforate, wound, dissolve, profane." This verb seems to refer to the same fantasies as the above Latin terms. The Scandinavian languages are even more explicit in this respect. The Old Norse *byrja* means "to begin" and also "to be fitting" and "to beget."

TO GO IN, TO COME   The Romance languages, which developed from Late Latin, continued the Latin notion of *principium,* but also used another Latin term: *initium,* "beginning." Thus, the Italian version begins with *nel principio* and the Spanish with *en el principio,* but the French Bible uses the other term: *au commencement.* The Latin *initium,* "beginning," properly "the going in," is derived from *in* and the verb *eō, -īre,* "to go." The verb "to go" has preserved the connotation of futurity indicating that the action will start very soon, e.g., *I am going to write* (in French *je vais écrire*); also, the English *enter upon* is used with the same meaning. All this is very obvious, and there seems to be nothing to be explained; however, one never can be sure that the reference that is obvious today was so in the early ages when the verbal fantasies took shape. The Latin *in-itium,* "going in" and "beginning," has a corresponding verbal form *in-itiō, -āre,* "to begin," but chiefly "to initiate, consecrate, admit to secret religious rites." The latter meanings suggest that this "going in" is not just an entering through an ordinary door, but an action covered with secrecy and loaded with emotional religious significance. The Romance languages generally are not satisfied with the expressiveness of "going in," and therefore add a prefix *com-,* meaning "with, together." They make the "togetherness" of the act clear, pointing out that at least two persons are involved. This *com-initiāre* is continued in the

French *commencement* and the Spanish *comenzar*. The Italian language goes even further: it adds the *in*, again, to the word, and thus derives the Italian *incominciare*, "to begin." There can be little doubt that this "going in together" is a variation of the verb "to go together," *co-eō, -īre,* which not only means also "to come together, to form a whole, to be united into a whole," but it, too, is used for "to copulate," in the same sense as *coepiō,* the faded verbal form (present tense) replaced by *coepi* (past tense): "to begin the act of generation." In Biblical language "go in" is used with the same meaning, e.g., "And he went in unto Hagar, and she conceived" (Gen. 16:4), and so forth. From all these instances it becomes more and more obvious that one cannot take even such simple expressions as this one at their face value. They refer to symbolic language. In this forgotten language of unconscious fantasies, the body is a house and the "going in" carries the meaning of generation. The Latin *in-eō,* "to go in," is the general term for the copulation of animals.

This symbolic "going in" may emerge in the delusions of mental patients. A schizophrenic patient, male, 28, said: *"I have a subconscious feeling when I see a woman that I am entering that woman. It is a mental state only."*[8]

The opposite of "to go" is "to come," which is also used to denote the "beginning." In the obsolete English *to come into being* or *it came to pass* still had a very concrete meaning; now, though, these formulas have been replaced in the revised version of the Bible by the simple "he is" or "it was." In Old English *be-cuman,* the later *be-come,* still carries the concrete meaning "to come in, arrive." The Latin *veniō, -īre* also shows the fading of the original concrete content; thus, *ad paupertatem venerit* literally means "he came to poverty"; in French *il vient à pauvreté,* hence "he came to be poor," and *il devient pauvre,* "he became poor," and finally *il est pauvre,* "he is poor."

The notion of "to go in" or "to come" with the meaning "beginning" implies the picture of an "opening." The "beginning" can be expressed by the symbolism of the door: opening signifies the beginning; closing, the end. We say in this sense, e.g., *to open fire, to open a discussion.* The German *er-öffnen* means either "to open" or "to disclose, reveal."

We shall better understand in this context that the "first fruit," "the first," as denoted by the Hebrew *rēshith*, is the "beginning," indeed, because he is the one who "opened the womb" first with his head. This was a sacred act, and part of the motivation "As it is written in the law of the Lord, Every male that openeth the womb shall be called holy to the Lord" (Luke 2:23).

Early infantile fantasies are familiar with this meaning of opening. Frankie, 5½, says: "If mommy had not opened her belly, my sister would never have come out."[9]

To "open the womb" and "to close the womb" are stereotypes of Old Testament language. It should be pointed out that these words are used in reference to the Lord, who alone can "open" the womb as in the case of Leah: "And when the Lord saw that Leah was hated, he opened her womb" (Gen. 29:31; 30:22). In the same way the Lord alone can "shut the womb," as, e.g., "the Lord had fast closed up all the wombs of the house of Abimelech" (Gen. 20:18) or "the Lord had shut up her womb" (I Sam. 1:5, 6). "Pethaiach, son of Meshezabeel" shows by his name that he is a first fruit, because the name means "opened-Jah(wē)." The Hebrew *Yiphtāch, Yephtach* properly means "he will open."

For such reason, "to be closed, locked, or shut," whether it refers to the legs, to the door, to cloth, or to the total behavior, might be symbolic for virginity, while "to be open" may appear as an invitation to seduction. I quote from a clinical report: *"Even if a guy is honorable, I tempt him so by leaving myself wide open, like a girl lying back, wide open, saying: Go ahead, go ahead and rape me!"*[10]

We may observe similar associations with eyes and windows; the "openhanded" as well as the "openhearted" behavior are symbolic for the generous personality. The associations related to the "deep" and "dark" and being empty will lead to another aspect of body fantasies.

THE LEAP AND THE SPRING   The pictogram of "beginning" as an act of a sudden leaping or springing is a concept full of motion, energy, and expansion. In dynamic perception, the "beginning" is just such a sudden, unprecedented action, a jump out of Nothingness. There is no transition between the "to be" and the "not to be." The Latin proverb *Natura non fecit saltus,* "Nature does not make a jump," implies, however, that the "beginning" is just this exceptional "jump" beyond the general rules of nature. But where there is a jump, there may be an abyss, also.

We are looking for the emotional significance of the idea of "leaping." It is a symptom of marked excitation. It can be the reaction to sudden fright; such a meaning is implied in the German *Schreck* and perhaps in the English *scare*. It can be the manifestation of exuberant joy as well: e.g., the Biblical formulas "leaping and dancing" and "leap for joy." Even the motion indicating the quickening of the fetus in the womb is called "leaping"; in Greek, too, the frequentative *skirtaō,* "to spring, leap, bound" is used in this special sense: "the babe leaped in her womb" (Luke 1:41). So is the subjective interpretation of the mother to it: "the babe leaped in my womb for joy" (Luke 1:44). These subjective sensations of the mother were thought to be the very "beginning" of a new life. Perhaps the meanings "to shake, move, stir" implied in the Hebrew *rōsh,* "beginning," should be explained in this context as a sign of "quickening."

This dynamic idea is spectacularly expressed by the German *Ur-sprung,* "origin," literally "primordial jump." A closely related term is *Ab-sprung:* the first part of this compound, *ab* (meaning "off" or "from"), indicates that the leap is made away from something; therefore, this word is used also for "springboard." The English equivalent is the Old English *of-spring,* now *off-spring.* The child is perceived in this sense in the dynamic aspect of a "jump from" the mother into existence. In German the "primary thing" of Thales, the "cause," became denoted by the static concept of *Ur-sache,* "cause," literally "primordial thing," but the process of origin was perceived as action. "Jump" and "beginning" are denoted by identical words in other languages, too (e.g., in Lithuanian).

The English *start* carries similar implications. This word has acquired the vigor of a popular expression, and it is already outmoding the more respectable *beginning.* We must suppose that this higher intensity of the word originates from the repression of a dynamic concept. The verb *to start* has the primary meaning "to move suddenly with a leap"; it also means "to issue suddenly and violently, to fly, to protrude, to seem to protrude." As a noun, the Old English *steort* primarily means "tail, cauda," just as does the relative German *Sterz,* "tail." The association between "to jump up," "to soar," "to protrude," "tail" can be found in other languages, too. The original meaning of "tail" might be the reason for repression and the subsequent career of the word in colloquial language. Yet, even the present surface meaning, too, may be deceptive. We may recall the words of the prophet about the glory that "shall fly away like a bird, from the birth, and from the womb, and from the conception" (Hos. 9:11), or the similar fantasies of Sophocles in *King Oedipus:* "See how lives like birds take wings like sparks that fly when a fire soars to the god of evening" (5. 168-74). Such verses will make us wary of any naturalistic interpretation of verbal fantasies. Behind the vigorous verb *to start,* a large cluster of fantasies seem to loom; they seem to connect the ideas of "tail," "soaring," "bird," "egg," "conception," "flying." These fantasies emerge in the various flying and bird dreams or in such verbal expressions as the German *Schwanz,* "tail"; *schwanger,* "pregnant"; *Schwinge,* "wing, swing"; and so forth. Even though the primary references to the human body and body processes are obvious, it is not the anatomical reality but the fantasy, the imaginary picture language, to which the verbal expressions refer.

The second sentence of Genesis says: "And the earth was
without form, and void; and darkness was upon the face of the
deep. And the Spirit of God moved upon the face of the
waters." The Hebrew term for this primary "deep" and
"dark," which is also "without form" (*thōhū*) and "void" (*wā-
bhōhū*), is the word *techōm*. The text shows that it also means
"waters." Today we use the terms of the Greek cosmogony to
denote the same concepts. "The very first Chaos came into
being," Hesiod says in his theogony. The Greek word *chaos* is
closely connected with the verb *chainō*, "to yawn, gape"; a
derivative is *chasma*, "yawning hollow, chasm, gulf" and also
"the open mouth." The corresponding verb *chasmaō* means
"to yawn, gape wide." One may again ask whether the
yawning mouth or the chasm of the earth was the primary
reference; however, if by all signs the anthropomorphic associations prevailed, the chasm in the earth has been perceived
in the picture of the human body.

The same fantasies are found in the Germanic myth.
The primordial Deep is called in the Old Norse *Ginnunga-
gap,* "yawning opening or abyss." Our English distinguishes
between *gap,* "opening, cleft," and *to gape,* "yawn," but the
verb *to gape* covers both meanings.

As we consider more closely the qualities of the
Chaos, we find that it is not a reality concept, but mythology;
it is deep and dark, filled with moisture, vapor or water; Ovid
mentions specifically that it was also a mixture of "seeds"
(*semina*), of germinal material. The Hebrew word used in
"the face of the waters" is significantly a plural, *mayim;* it
also means "juice, urine, semen." Thales' idea that water
moisture was the primordial thing, the beginning, sounds very
much the same as the Biblical account. The Greek *Okeanos*
personifies this primeval water. He is the son of Heaven and
Earth, of Uranus and Gaia; Homer calls him the generator of
gods and all things (*Iliad* xiv. 246, 302).

Thales thought of the earth as a flat disc floating and partly covering this primary water. The borderland was an abyss (as in *Abyssinia*) or an outer darkness (as in *Scotia* or Scotland, from the Greek *skotia,* "darkness," and *skotos,* "dark"). The concept of the world in the Old Testament is very similar. The Hebrew *techōm,* used without determination as a personal name, denoted a very concrete reality. It was the mystery of the creation to lay "the foundation of the world" upon this primordial water. It was the revelation of the creative power of God for the Psalmist when he obviously submerged in this primary abyss so that "the channels of waters were seen, and the foundations of the world were discovered"; but after that the Lord drew him "out of many waters" (Ps. 18:15, 16). God can shake these "foundations of the earth and the heaven." (The Irish language has kept this idea by using one word for both "world" and "deep.")

This ancient world concept has changed, and since Copernicus the "primary thing," *Chaos,* and great *Techōm* have lost their strongly felt reality. However, while we think in Copernican terms, we sometimes speak according to the fantasies of a much older mythology; yet Shakespeare says: "Creeping murmur and the poring dark fills the wide vessel of the universe." We, too, still refer to the "bottomless pit" of the Revelation; this is the *abyss* (from the Greek *a-byssos,* a compound of the privative *a* and *byssos,* "bottom").

This is especially true for the language of psychology. Freud liked to compare consciousness to the small part of an iceberg which looms above the surface—while the rest of the iceberg floats submerged in the deep waters. Therefore, the deep waters represent the primordial element, not only the separate individual unconscious, but the all-embracing trans-individual one of the whole race.* This picture of the mind recalls the cosmic picture of the world as Hesiod, Thales, or

* Pierre Janet once called the gradual transition toward the "threshold" of the unconscious "the lowering of the conscious mind" (*abaissement du niveau mental*), thus suggesting that there might be something like upper and lower parts of the human mind. The unconscious state appears in this symbolism as if it were covered with a primordial darkness; the conscious mind accordingly cannot be more than a small flickering light moving around in the great abyss.

the Old Testament have conceived it. We must ask whether our concept of psychic reality is still a residue of ancient cosmogonies, or is the cosmogonic idea of an earth-disc floating upon the bottomless darkness still the projection of untold psychological experiences upon physical reality? My answer is: Cosmogony is a symbolic picture language dealing with inside experiences. The prophet who was seeking the "foundations of the world" and discovered them in the channels of the deep waters was expressing the striving of all "deep" psychology to discover the foundation of the conscious mind somewhere in the bottomless pit of the unconscious. Thus, the Psalmist praises the Lord because he drew him "out of many waters." All those who are familiar with mental disturbance will grasp the psychological truth of the saying that the Lord can shake the foundations of earth and heaven, or even pull someone out of the deep waters.

We speak of psychological concepts in terms of spatial relations. We cannot do otherwise, but we have to bear in mind that everything we say about the nonmaterial mind is figurative anyway. Though we can speak of the mind only in symbols, this does not mean that psychological facts are not real. The unconscious is generally denoted in our language as if it were an abyss or a deep well mirroring in its bottom "the face of the deep," the dim reflection of the unconscious Ego. Why do we call a sleep "deep," and why do we "fall" asleep, as if one were submerging in a bottomless gulf? "Darkness like a dream," or "darkness of death," Shakespeare says. The first day of creation, the separation of light from the primordial darkness, reflects the great human experience of the birth of a new consciousness out of the deep and dark unconscious state. The cosmogony of the world depicts another process: the psychogony of the mind. The Biblical cosmogonic fantasies are still interwoven with primary body fantasies. For instance, Job says: "Who shut up the sea with doors, when it brake forth, as if it had issued out of the womb?" (Job 38:8) and "Out of whose womb came the ice?" (Job 38:29). The same fusion of body symbolism and cosmogonic mythology can be found in the language of the New Testament: for instance, when it is said by Christ, "out of his belly shall flow rivers of living water" (John 7:38). Such symbolic expressions were possible in an age when the identity of the Ego and the world was still a living reality, and the cosmogonic pictures were still understood as illustration of the human mind. The fusion of the creation of the inside and outside world is complete when it is said that the Lord created the world in "the heart" of man: "He hath set the world in their heart, so that no man can find out the work that God maketh from the beginning to the end" (Eccles. 3:11). Such a saying should warn those who want to make an unscientific textbook of geology out of the Biblical cosmogony. The great *Techōm*, the Deep and Dark, is in us; it is the symbolic expression of unconscious experiences.

The verbal fantasies implicit in Deep and Dark reveal other significant characteristics. Our languages show that this Dark is at the same time a very substantial "moist, wet" darkness. This can be seen in the relationship of the German *dunkel*, "dark," and the corresponding English word *dank*. The original concept must have united both qualities: it must have been very concrete and substantial. An indication of this is the fact that the word is used often in the plural, as the Latin *tenebrae*, properly "darknesses." Moreover, this "darkness" is "hiding" something. Perhaps it is just the "light" that lies dormant or hidden in the primary darkness. We come to such a conclusion by observing that the Latin *ob-scūrus*, "dark," originally meant "covered, sheltered"; the corresponding German form, *Scheuer*, means "shelter" (Old High German *scūr*). The English *dark* corresponds to the Old High German verb *tarchan-jan*, "to conceal, hide." This dark abyss is indeed not empty: it hides something unknown to us.

We may understand on these suppositions the word *beginning* and the old verb *begin, began, begun*. The origin of this word is marked "dubious" in our best vocabularies, but if we keep in mind the whole context in which the ideas of genesis, conception, and birth appear in describing the "beginning," the English word will appear less enigmatic. The word surely belongs to an old Germanic stock, as indicated by the vowel change of the verb. The Old English noun *ginn* means "gap, abyss, opening"; as an adjective it means "lying open, spacious." It appears in the verbs *on-ginnan, a-ginnan, ginnan*, all meaning "to begin"; the primary meaning, however, must have been "to open up," as does the corresponding Old High German *in-ginnan*, "to cut open, open up, begin." There exists also a parallel Old English verb *gi-nan, gy-nian,* whose meaning "to gape" is continued in *to yawn;* also corresponding are the German verb *gäh-nen,* which means "to yawn," and the noun *Gähn-ung,* "yawning," "abyss." These Germanic words are in some way related to the corresponding Latin *hi-āre,* "to gape, yawn, open." Thus, one may say that the underlying associations are very old. In fact, the word also seems to be deeply rooted in the Germanic mythological fantasies; we shall trace its role, therefore, in the Old Icelandic language, which is the best representative of the Old Norse language and the chief source of Germanic mythology.

The Old Icelandic *ginn-* is a so-called "mythological prefix," an intensifier of other meanings to which it is prefixed. We can observe in many instances that such intensifiers for the most part expressed the meaning that was the source of anxiety, and in consequence of repression they were used frequently.[11] An illustrative example may be the frequent use of the word *awful* or *terrific.* The word *awe* is derived from an Old Germanic form that denotes just this characteristic "mixed feeling of reverence, fear, and wonder, caused by something majestic, sublime." This is the description of the awe observed when man is confronted with the *mysterium tremendum.* The Old Icelandic *ginn-* also means "numinous" (great and holy), just that quality which leaves man filled with awe, wonder, reverence, and anxiety. The Old Icelandic *ginn heilög godh* means the "most holy gods," in distinction to the deities of the lower order; *ginn-regin* or even *ginnungar* are the *magna numina,* the chief gods; and Odin, the chief of all Germanic divinities, is called simply *Ginnar.* His abode is called *Ginnunga-vē;* the heavenly vault covering it is the *Ginnunga-hinin;* and the primary abyss, which was preexistent to the creation and which contained damp, moist vapor and the creative power in germinal material, is the *Ginnunga-gap.* After repression took place, this word *ginn,* so heavily charged with meaning, became a common, everyday intensive, used most frequently without the slightest anxiety implied in its original meaning, just as *awful* or *terrific* is used in colloquial English. So the Old Icelandic *ginn-viti* means "great fire" and *ginn-fasti* means "very fast." The same "mythological prefix" appears also in Old English; for instance, *faest* means "fast," *gin-faest* "very fast."

We understand now the whole realm of associations out of which our verb *begin* emerged. The prefix *be-* is of newer provenience; it is added to *gin* as in the relationship of *get* and *beget, hold* and *behold, have* and *behave, love* and *belove, come* and *become, long* and *belong.* This prefix *be-* functions as an intensifier.

Therefore, when the Germanic ancestors had to find a cosmogonic picture for the beginning of all things, their fantasies could not help but be similar to the Hebrew and Greco-Roman fantasies: this is the picture of the maternal organ projected into mythological proportion. These fantasies were loaded with anxiety.

There is an abyss between existence and nonexistence, between something and nothing, between reality and unreality. The act of creation implies just this abyss by bringing things into existence out of the nonexistence, making things to exist where they did not exist before. Creation connotes in this primary meaning "generation." The Biblical account does not say that Elohim created heaven and earth out of nothing, yet this idea became deeply implanted into the theological literature through the centuries, and the reference to the idea, to the "no-thing," confirms our interpretation of the unconscious fantasies implied in the "beginning."

The deep and dark "bottomless pit," the symbol of all beginning, has its fascination. Where there is an abyss there is also the ambivalent fear and desire "to fall" and "to be swallowed" by this primary darkness. Vertigo as a neurotic symptom is the call of the abyss. It represents the self-perception of regression. Róheim has demonstrated by a wealth of clinical evidences that the "falling" dream is the "basic dream," the self-perception of *falling asleep.* So, the hypnotic experience of "going under" implies this feeling of "falling" into the abyss. The abyss is a temptation for the infantile mind. Reality situations are always tempting us to do something, such as a match tempts us to make fire. One can understand, then, that the abyss is tempting us to jump: it is the "call of the depth."

The unconscious fantasy to go down the "bottomless pit" might be reinforced by the small child's various falling experiences, for instance, by falling from the chair. A female patient in induced hypnotic age regression screams: "I am falling. . . . I am falling. . . . Oh, please catch me. . . . Oh, doctor, please catch me. . . .[12]

In religious fantasies the "call of the depth," vertigo, might be interpreted as the temptation of the devil. The devil tempted Jesus: "and set him on a pinnacle of the temple, and said unto him, 'If thou be the Son of God, cast thyself down from hence.' Jesus answered: 'It is said, Thou shalt not tempt the Lord thy God' " (Luke 4:9, 12).

The idea of "falling down" may mobilize some rather passive oral fantasies; therefore the abyss is described frequently in oral terms as "yawning" or "swallowing."[13] *Also, the idea of "falling" in the symbolism of oral fantasies can be expressive for the "falling" on a genital level, which, in turn, implies "defloration" or "castration." Therefore some "falling dreams" might be rooted in these types of anxieties, and the visual representation of these anxieties is the "abyss," or the "bottomless pit."*

Heaven and earth are, for Greek mythological thinking, much like the Biblical record of creation, the "first" things in existence. They precede all others. The Greek *Ouranos* and *Gaia* are the generators of the gods—*ouranos* meaning "heaven" and *gaia,* later *gē,* meaning "earth." Heaven is represented by a male divinity, the earth by a female. This distinction is maintained by our languages in so far as they express gender; thus we have in German *der Himmel,* "heaven," and *die Erde,* "earth," and in French *le ciel,* "heaven," and *la terre,* "earth." It would be unwise in cases like this one to consider the genders as mere formal grammatical categories without meaning and to deny that unconscious fantasies have impressed upon our languages in some cases the masculine, in other cases the feminine gender—a relationship that cannot be reversed, at least in our patristic culture. However, it is because the unconscious fantasies are, indeed, so irrational and elusive that generally the linguistic thinker hesitates to consider them. Nevertheless, the various concepts of heaven and earth will be examined here still more closely.

The Greek *ouranos,* "heaven," is masculine, and the reason for the adherence to the masculine gender becomes obvious when we observe that the Greek word denoting "heaven" has close parallel forms in the Greek *oureō,* "to urinate," in the Greek *ouron* and the Latin *urina,* "urine," and in the phonemically closely related Sanskrit *varsati,* "it is raining." We still say "it is raining, it is thundering." But, we may properly ask, who or what is in fact meant by "it"? The Greek language is more expressive and says exactly what we repress; it says *Zeus huei,* "Zeus is raining." All these words referring to "rain" and "urine" imply also the idea to "emit semen," because infantile fantasies identify "semen" and "urine." These words also have relative forms with corresponding meanings in the other related languages, so we may

150

readily infer that they represent an old genuine Indo-European idea of the raining sky fertilizing the Mother Earth. The masculine gender of "heaven" seems to be rooted in this repressed layer of fantasies. (*cf.* p. 265.) *

One will meet these age-old cosmogonic fantasies associating "rain" and "urine" in a clinical setting. I refer to an asthmatic boy, 8, playing. He stands on a chair and says that he is big. He has a paint brush and twirls it and splatters paint all around. He says: "Rain all around. . . . Like penis water all around."[14] *We may add the linguistic interpretation that the "paint brush," the German* Pinsel, *from the Latin* penicillum, *"little penis," came to this identification perhaps through the mediation of "tail" as a "brush." Gulliver's fantasies or Rabelais' Gargantua reveal similar identification of "rain" and "urine" as expressed by the Greek language.*

The wife of *Ouranos* is the Mother Earth; she is sometimes even considered to be his mother. The Greek *Dēmētēr*, from the former *Gē-mētēr*, is the personification of this mother-goddess. In Latin *Terra Māter*, "Mother Earth," is her most general name. Her cult is a living element in the folklore of many people. The marriage between the Father Sky and the Mother Earth is called in Greek *hieros gamos,* "holy wedding." This is perhaps the most general sublimated projection of sex upon the universe. This may be the reason why the "earth" cannot be conceived otherwise than in the aspect of the feminine gender. The Latin *hūmus, -i,* "earth," and *tellūs, -ūris,* "earth," are also feminine, even though the grammatical endings would suggest the masculine gender. Plato says: "For in her pregnancy and childbirth it is the woman who imitates the earth, and not the other way around" (*Menexenus* 238a). On finding such old associations we can conclude that the feminine gender of the nouns denoting "earth" is not simply a grammatical formality.

The Greek *ouranos,* "heaven," is conceived of as a concave hemisphere resting on the verge of the earth and held up by the pillars of Atlas and wrapped in clouds. This hemisphere was supposed to revolve together with the stars

---

* In Egypt, however, the "sky" (*nut*) was feminine, the earth masculine (*to*). This is in accordance with the matristic religion and social order.

fixed on it. Above this great dome was the abode of the gods.

Our languages do not share this elaborate fantasy of the Greeks about the heaven in every respect. It seems that there exists an even older and more primitive picture of it. The dark night sky is the sky of the primitive herdsmen. Their outdoor life had its most exciting moments at night. The Old Testament people were of this kind. The starry sky appeared to them as the very meaningful sky. The shepherds lived in tents, not in houses. Thus, the sky was thought of as an immense heavenly tent, made not out of solid material but of garment. We can understand this better if we remember that the "dark" is thought of as having such substantial nature: it is a thick garment which actually "covers." "Darkness shall cover the earth, and gross darkness the people," the prophet says (Isa. 60:2). This is the "dark" of the "heavenly tent." "Heavens like a curtain," the Psalmist says (Ps. 104:2). The darkness of the great *Techōm* or of the *Abyssos* is complemented by the "deep" darkness of the sky. The Lord, the Psalmist says, covered the foundation of the world with darkness. "Thou coveredst it with the deep as with a garment: the waters stood above the mountains" (Ps. 104:6). In the classical Greek the night is characterized by its "black cloak" and is called *melampeplos nux,* "black-robed night." Shakespeare evokes the same fantasies when he says: "The day begins to break, and the night is fled whose pitchy mantle overveil'd the earth." The same ideas are implicit in Old Testament language when it speaks of the "thick darkness" or "gross darkness." Darkness as such is neither thick nor gross, but the garment of the heavenly tent is so. The black garment is the "darkness which may be felt" (Exod. 10:21). The Lord appears to these people, who are more familiar with the night sky than with the day sky, with the sky not in shining brightness, but covered with darkness. The Lord "made darkness pavilions round about him, dark waters, and thick clouds of the skies" (II Sam. 22:12).

Because the night sky displayed to these people (who lived otherwise under the most intense sunshine) the very meaning of heaven, the clouds assumed a meaning similar to the night. The clouds to them also meant "darkness" and "covering." "Clouds and darkness" is a Biblical formula of synonyms, a connection of two aspects of the same thing. We would say, according to our more abstract logic, instead of "clouds and darkness," simply "dark clouds." The mountain of Horeb burned "with darkness, clouds, and thick darkness" (Deut. 4:11). "Clouds and darkness are round about him," the Psalmist says (Ps. 97:2). "A day of darkness and of gloominess, a day of clouds and of thick darkness, as the morning spread upon the mountains" (Joel 2:2) is another expression of this fantasy.

The English *sky* originally meant "cloud" in Germanic languages, proving that the dark, "covered" sky, the night sky, was, in Germanic perception, the true sky itself. This word is etymologically connected with the Latin *ob-scū-rus* and other words meaning "to cover." The Old German *scūr* meant "shelter"; the form is the same as in the Latin *scūt-um,* "shield." In the other Indo-European languages the meanings of "sky," "cloud," "cover," and "dark" are interchangeable in many respects. The Old English *wolcen* (plural *wolcnu*) means "cloud" and "sky," whereas the German *Wolke* denotes only the "cloud." The related English *welkin,* "sky," became obsolete, but remained in such formulas as "make the welkin ring."

One can observe in connection with all these words that the perception of an outside object is always partly the projection of an inside experience. In the Norse languages, e.g., "cloud" and "thick darkness" are identified; thus, the Swedish *moln* means "cloud," while the Danish *mulm* means "darkness," but the latter means also "mist," "dim sight" or even the "confused state of mind." Significantly, the French *brouillard,* "mist," is connected with the verb *brouiller,* "to mix up," and the identical Italian form *im-broglio* means "confusion." For such reasons the English words *dim, dumb,* and *damp* are interrelated forms occurring with various meanings in Germanic languages. The Greek *nephos* and *nephelē* mean "cloud," while the corresponding Latin *nebul-a* and German *Nebel* denote the "mist." The Old Norse *Nifl-heimr* is the mythological name of the outer darkness of the realm beyond the world, the realm of death. It seems obvious that this conception of the great Beyond is the projection of people who felt their blindness and confusion in the face of death. The horror of darkness is the main topic of the Babylonian

Gilgamesh epic. Gilgamesh, the legendary king, traveled through the realms of gods and men in order to find a remedy against the eternal darkness of death. He prayed to the god of light that he may give some light to the dead souls, for light would dissipate the anxiety of dying.

The shepherds living in tents projected upon the clouds their anxieties. This is indicated by the identification of "sheep" and "cloud." One can find in almost all our languages such denotations as *fleecy clouds* (in German *Schaf-wolken* and *Lämmer-wolken,* literally "sheep-clouds"; in French *nuage moutonné*). "As a shepherd seeketh out his flock in the day that he is among his sheep that are scattered; so will I seek out my sheep, and will deliver them out of all places where they have been scattered in the cloudy and dark day" (Ezek. 34:12). The nomad Arabs thought of the clouds as wandering camels; they called the thunderclouds "the bellowing ones" (*alhanāna*) because such clouds were in their perception camels bellowing in their longing to reach home. The rain cloud was called by the same token "a camel with a heavy burden."

Such Arabic concepts of clouds perhaps reached Shakespeare in some way, because he performs almost a perfect projective "cloud test"* in the dialogue of Hamlet with Polonius. Hamlet asks: "Do you see yonder cloud that's almost in shape of a camel?" Polonius answers: "By the mass, and 'tis like a camel, indeed." Hamlet: "Methinks it is like a weasel." Polonius: "It is backed like a weasel." Hamlet: "Or like a whale?" Polonius: "Very like a whale." Shakespeare described another cloud test by these words: "Sometime we see a cloud that's dragonish/ A vapor sometime like a bear or lion/ A tower'd citadel, a pendant rock/ A forked mountain, or blue promontory/ With trees upon't, that nod unto the world/ And mock our eyes with air."

Many poets before and after Shakespeare have depicted the subjective interpretation of the cloudy sky. The clouds were considered in mythology as giants, as in the Germanic myth where the face of the first living beings,

* The German psychologist William Stern used the interpretation of cloud pictures as one of the first projective tests. William Stern, "Cloud Pictures: A New Method of Testing Imagination," in *Character and Personality,* 1937, pp. 132–46.

preceding man, were just such giants born of damp and vapor, fire and water. The Old English *wolcen-wyrcend* expresses the Latin *de nube genitus,* "one engendered of a cloud," i.e., of a centaur. The Greek *Kentauros,* "Centaur," a savage race—half-horse, half-man—are sons of *Nephelē,* meaning "cloud"; thus, Virgil calls them *nubigenae,* "cloudborn" (*The Aeneid* 7. 640).

In Old English *clūd* means "rock, stone, hill." Its derivatives are the English *clod* and *cloud.* How can the concept of "cloud" be derived from "rock, stone"? We shall find the answer to this question in the following observations about the stone sky. Such an answer is suggested by the words of Job: "Who can number the clouds in wisdom? or who can stay the bottles of heaven, When the dust groweth into hardness, and the clods cleave fast together?" (Job 38:37–38).

The sky conceived of as a stone building represents a higher stage of cultural development than that represented by the huge black canopy of the herdsman. This difference between the city dwellers in stone buildings and the shepherds living in tents is brought out distinctly in the two different types of fantasies about the rising sun. In Eastern languages (also in Hungarian) the sun is "rending" the sky (in Hungarian *hajnal hasadás*).[15] In the Late Greek the plural *charamata* means "dawn" and the singular *charagmos* means "incision, cut." This obviously refers to a garment that can be rent and cut. This also shows that the "thick" darkness "can be cut." In distinction to these tent fantasies, we say *day-break*. This word suggests the violent bursting of the vault, the breaking through of the solid material by the rising sun, not just the cutting apart of a thick garment.

The English *heaven* and the German *Himmel* are closely connected forms. The origin of these words is not very clear, but whatever may be their affiliation, one will always arrive at the meaning of "vault" (as the phonemically related Greek *kamara*) or "stone" (as the Persian *asman,* which means both "stone" and "sky").[16]

The Latin *firmamentum* is also founded upon such fantasies. The word is a derivative of *firmus,* "firm, fast, constant, immovable." The translations seem to fit a general description of a huge vault built of stones; certainly the description applies neither to "canopy" nor to the airy character of the sky. Moreover, this stone building fantasy does not exactly correspond to the Hebrew word that it translates (*rāgīya*). Nevertheless, the Hebrew term is, though, a derivative of the primary root *rāqa*, which means "to pound" in the sense of hitting hard so that it may become larger and expand. Therein is a connection between "stone" and "sky"; of course another one is found in the concept of the "firmament of heaven," which is frequently used in Old Testament language. Shakespeare was quite near to the original Hebrew concept of "expansion" when he said: "This brave o'erhanging firmament, this majestical roof fretted with golden fire." And let's not forget that the stars were considered to be precious stones on this stone vault, which the Greeks called *ouranos*.

It is consistent with the fantasy of stone builders that the heaven is thought of as a three-storied building. The words referring to it are used, therefore, mostly in the plural. There are "heavens" and "heaven of heavens" (Deut. 10:14) and a "third heaven" (II Cor. 12:2). The clouds and the air seem to fill the lowest part, the sun and the moon belong to the second story, and the highest heaven is the abode of God and the angels. This whole construction rests, according to the Old Testament, on pillars. The Lord has the power to make "the pillars of heaven tremble" (Job 26:11). The "gates of heaven" are also the projection of stone builders. Jacob wandered in his important dream in this highest of heavens and it is described thus: "And Jacob awaked out of his sleep, and he said, Surely the Lord is in this place; and I knew it not. And he was afraid, and said, How dreadful is this place! this is none other but the house of God, and this is the gate of heaven" (Gen. 28:16–17). This fantasy refers to a stone building.

Children are sometimes disturbed by such fantasies which refer to the experience of strangeness. They are at home in the familiar setting, but are frightened if they venture beyond the boundaries of the familiar home. The word *danger*, therefore, deriving from the Latin *dominium*, refers to the boundaries of familiarity. The unknown is dangerous. The primitive antithesis of "familiar" and "unknown, danger" became overruled later on by the polarity of "right" and "wrong." The dog, like the small child, does not know the difference between "right" and "wrong," but he knows the difference between the familiar home and the strange setting.

Similarly, we should understand why Jacob said in his dream: "How dreadful is this place!" He was not at home in heaven.

The stone sky, although it is a huge vault, is not necessarily bright. On the contrary, one will find that the stone vault is primarily a "cover" filled with darkness. The bright sky is not an Indo-European concept either. Shakespeare speaks of the "vaulty prison" which "stows away the day." The sky, as the counterpart of the ocean, is as high and dark as the ocean is deep and dark. The Hebrew term for "heaven" is derived from the root meaning "to fold back"; this is a reference to the curved shape of the vault. Likewise, the Greek *koilia* refers to the "innermost" cavity of the body. This can mean "stomach, belly," but it mostly means "womb": e.g., in the New Testament Greek, *ek koilias mētros* is a recurrent formula meaning "from the mother's womb" (Matt. 19:12), the very symbol of "beginning." This Greek word translates as "the innermost parts of the belly" (Prov. 18:8) or the "inward parts of the belly" (Prov. 20:30).

The interpretations which try to derive the "sky" from the idea of "bright, brightness" do not fit the old picture of the dark sky. Another illustration of the "dark sky" can be shown with the old Latin variant meaning "sky," *coelum, coelestis,* which is phonemically related to the Greek *koilia,* "cavity," and *koil-os,* "hollow." As a consequence of the relationship between the Latin *coelum* and the Greek *koilia* and *koilos,* we may assume an association between these words and a later Latin word for "sky": *caelum.**

A Greek formula such as *aitheros kolpos,* "the bosom of the sky," approaches the idea of "vault" and "cavity" through bodily fantasies. The same idea found expression also in the Old English *heofen hwealf,* "heavenly vault" or "heavenly bosom." The corresponding Latin stereotypes are *cāva caeli,* "the cave of heaven," and *magnas caeli cavernas,* "the great caverns of the sky." The sky appears as "deep" as the ocean in an old Latin expression: *caelus profundus.* The original masculine gender of the word speaks for the genuineness of this association.

The English *ceiling* is a derivative of the Latin *caelum,* "sky." In Old English the "ceiling" is called *hūs-heofan,*

* The Latin *caelum* is generally considered to be of unknown origin; however, it is difficult to suppose that it developed completely independent of *cēlāre,* "to hide."

"house-heaven," or *heofon-rōf,* "heaven-roof." These examples prove that the "sky" was named first and that the ceiling of the house received its name from the imaginary cavity of the sky. The belief that the imaginary sky vault is prior to the reality of the house runs against the common-sense interpretation of our best dictionaries, which, therefore, resort to assorted explanations; for instance, one is that the "ceiling" was called "sky" because the vaulted ceilings of churches were often painted blue and decorated with stars. Plausible as such historical interpretation seems to be, the basic question remains unanswered: Why was the ceiling decorated in the image of the sky if such an association was not already present in the mind of the decorator? The decoration proves the very fact which is implied in the verbal expression itself—that the ceiling of the house was perceived in the image of the sky (the blue sky and the stars in combination also indicate its imaginary character).

The rising of the sun is the great event of the cosmic order, just as the rise of the consciousness is the great event of human life; thus, one is reflected in the mirror of the other. For untold ages both have evoked the very problem of existence: the origin and beginning of all things and all life.

The dawn, also called *daybreak* (cf. the German *Tagesanbruch*), suggests the dramatic opening of the "Golden Gate." It is conceived in the ancient myth not as a mere transitory state between night and day, but generally as the personification of a young maiden, the daughter of Night and Day, displaying a double nature and enjoying but a short twilight life. This is characteristic of the Sanskrit *Ushas,* the Greek *Eos,* and the Latin *Aurora.* The English *dawn* received its name from *day;* the Old English *dagung,* "dawn," and *dagian,* "to dawn," literally mean "to become day." The twilight character of "dawn" can be traced in our languages by the various color associations connected with it: the dawn is associated with "white" as in the Latin, where *alba,* "dawn," is the feminine of *albus,* "white"; thus, the Italian has *alba,* the French *aube,* and the Spanish *alba.* "Dawn" is associated with "gray" in the Swedish *gryning,* for this term for dawn is literally "to become gray" (from *gry,* "gray"), and also in the German, where *Morgen-grauen,* "morning-graying," is the term for "dawn." "Rosy" is the persistent epithet in the Homeric language; the Greek *rhodo-daktulos Eos* means "rosy-fingered dawn." The dawn is "reddish" in Sanskrit (*arusa-*) and positively "red" in the German *Morgen-rot,* "morning red." It may be associated with "darkness," for the German *Morgen-dämmerung,* "morning-twilight," contains the old noun *demar,* "darkness." The Slavic languages also associate the dawn with the darkness of the waning night. In contrast, though, the Latin *prima lux,* "first light," and the Greek *augē,* "light," conceive of the dawn as an aspect of the beginning of daylight.

There is scarcely any other word—in all its disguises— charged so heavily with symbolism that is at the same time so transparent in phonemic structure and meaning as the name of the deity identified with the brightly shining day sky. This name regularly appears connected with the idea of the father. This is, of course, a very complicated symbol blending such disparate concepts as those of the sky and the father. Of course, just the fact that this symbol appears as a most persistent element in our languages dating back to the Indo- European prehistory proves once more that not the words denoting reality objects but the words denoting vague uncon- scious fantasies represent the primary element in our lan- guages.

The Sanskrit *Dyaush, dyū, div* means "sky" and "day" and is frequently called *pitar,* "father"—so much so that *Dyaushpitar* becomes one word in the Vedic literature. The corresponding name in Greek is *Zeus,* or *Zeu-patēr.* Homer defines the meaning by saying "the father, the most glorious, the greatest who rules over all mortals and immortals" (*Iliad* 1.545). The Latin vocative *Ju-piter, Jovis,* with the restored nominative *Dies-piter,* corresponds phonemically to the Greek and Sanskrit names; the Latin *diēs,* "day," and *deus,* "god," are related forms. In the Old Norse Edda *Tyr, Tys, Tu* is the phonemic equivalent of the name. In Old English the name does not occur independently, but is preserved in *Tiwes-daeg,* our *Tues-day. Tiwes-daeg* and *Tuesday* stand for the Latin *dies Martis,* but they translate literally the Latin *dies Jovis,* "Jupiter's day."

The day, the sun, and the day sky are conceived in most of our languages as of masculine character, while the moon and the night are thought of as feminine. It is rather a strange exception that the German language, while implying the masculine gender in *der Tag,* "the day," and in *der*

Himmel, "the sky," looks upon the "sun" as feminine (*die Sonne*). On the other hand, the "moon" is considered to be masculine (*der Mond*) in opposition to the feminine "night" (*die Nacht*). There is no proper explanation of this phenomenon, which must have arisen out of some strong psychological motivation. Perhaps this is a symptom indicating that the night sky and not the day sky was for the Indo-European languages, as well as for the Hebrew-Arabic world, the primary fantasy.[17]

The "earth" is called the "dry one" in the Hebrew *yabbasēth.* The same holds true for the Latin *terra* (a much disputed word), for it comes, we suppose, from *ter-sa,* which could be related to the Greek *tersomai,* "to become dry, to dry up," and the Latin *torreō, -ēre,* "to dry a thing by heat" as well as "to roast, parch, bake." We also speak about the "dry land" as clearly distinguished from the water. Thus, we suppose that the "earth" emerged from the pre-existent water. In one way or another, though, these words once more suppose that the great watery abyss, the *Techōm,* was the primordial element and that the earth was born, like Venus, out of the water. This should not be taken as a primitive geophysical theory about the origin of the earth. Such a problem did not exist for the primitive mind. In primitive thought the world always was and is the same and will remain so. The cosmogony of the earth is the projection of primitive theories about the origin of life; it reflects the process of the emerging of the fetus out of the amniotic fluid.

The conscious mind is called into existence according to this belief, like the light by the primary *fiat* of the Creator. Consciousness and thinking are thus perceived in the aspect of "light" and the universe accordingly as the work of a superior conscious mind. Order, harmony, consistency, and unity—these qualities of sound thinking—are also revealed in the universe. The Latin word *uni-versum* (from *ūnus,* "one," and *vertō, -ere, versum* "to turn") literally means "to be turned into a unity"; obviously chaos has been turned into a consistent wholeness. This consistency, order, and wholeness, the knowledge of the beginning and the end are the basic qualities of conscious thinking, as has been demonstrated most impressively by Hegelian phenomenology.

The Greek mind, otherwise static, perceived the universe from the viewpoint of Zeus, i.e., as a dynamic process. (The idea of "fast motion" is implied in our word *to run* as we use it in reference to a car, to water, or to an affair; significantly, the idea of the primordial liquid is still implied.) Zeus still "runs" the world. This is the meaning of the shaking of the aegis that frightens gods as well as men; therefore Zeus is called *aigi-ochos,* "aegis-shaker," and also *gaiē-ochos,* "earth-mover."[18] The word *ochos,* "vehicle," may refer to anything that carries, as in *ochetus,* "a waterpipe, channel, aqueduct," which enables water to "run"; the primary reference is implied in the following words: *ocheusis,* "sexual intercourse"; *ocheuō,* "to copulate" (used both of male and female), also "to uphold, sustain, carry, continue, keep doing," and even "to ride, to sail," and of a ship, "to ride at anchor." Obviously, the idea of "running" is deeply embedded in unconscious fantasies and may account for the sexual symbolism of the various running vehicles in dreams. Furthermore, the primary "running vehicle" for infantile fantasies is the mother or the father; for fantasies regarding the cultural respect the vehicle is the horse, the Latin *equo vehi;* eventually, "riding" became expanded to all kinds of vehicles—cars, trains. For such reason a streetcar could be named "Desire," or "to ride together" could, in the dream language, replace "to walk together," which is the Latin *co-īre,* of the complex implying generation.

The Greek concept of the universe supposes the work of a clear conscious mind, and, therefore, the idea of "order" is brought out in its very name. The Greek *kosmos* means "order" primarily, and then "good behavior, decency." It also means "ornament, decoration, embellishment," especially of women; *kosmetikē* is the art of dress adornment. The idea of beauty and harmony is implied in this Greek concept of the universe, just as implied in the Biblical language by "the morning stars sang together" (Job 36:7).* The Latin *mundus* translates the Greek *kosmos* and also refers to "order, ornament, decoration"; the Latin adjective *mundus* means "clean"

* On the auditory perception of harmony, con-sonance and sym-phony see the classic study of Leo Spitzer: *Classical and Christian Ideas of World Harmony. Prolegomena to an Interpretation of the Word Stimmung.* Edited by Anita Granville Hatcher. Preface by René Wellek. (Baltimore: The Johns Hopkins Press, 1963.)

and its derivatives in Italian and Spanish (*mondo*) mean "neat, pure."

Not very different from this Greek concept of the orderly universe is the equation of the universe with light. In Slavic languages "light" (*svetu*) and "world" are equated as they are, e.g., in Hungarian (*világ*); thus, we may suppose that creation is the transition from darkness to light. "The worlds were framed by the word of God, so that things which are seen were not made of things which do appear" (Heb. 11:3). The world of light is the Apollonian world, where *kosmos* means "order" and "good behavior," where the morning stars sing together in harmony; this is the daylight world of reason and enlightenment. It is not difficult to discover that this daylight world is born out of the night, never the other way around, for the Night is never the child of the Day. This means, in other terms, that the Apollonian conscious Ego is imposed upon the unconscious abyss; that is, it is somehow sustained and fixed upon the bottomless pit, just as the "foundation of the world" is based upon the depth that no man could explore. Nevertheless, another world is reflected upon the abyss of darkness: the Dionysian world, which means not the "order" and "good behavior" but the freedom in the outburst of instinctual demands.

The Germanic concept of the universe is not as clearly restricted to the visible world. It denotes the world as the "middle yard" (cf. the Gothic *middjungards* and the Old English *middan-geart,* or *middan-eard*). The visible world is thought to be situated in the "middle," between the "mist-home" (*Nifl-heimr*) of death and darkness, which is below, and the abode of the gods, which is above. The Ego is such a "middle yard" in psychology.

The English *world* implies the idea of "lifetime, age." The strange equation of the short-lived human lifetime with the timeless universe can be explained, as we will find, on the ground of the Golden Age, where the lifetime means eternity, where there is no death, only eternal youth. The Old English *wer-old* is apparently a compound form: the first part *wer* means "man," as in Old English *wer-fulf,* "man-wolf"; the second part is the Old English *yldo, yld,* "age." Thus, *wer-old* literally means "man-age." The concept of time thus implied is still strongly felt when, for instance, the Biblical "for ever and ever" (Ps. 9:5), translated in Latin as *in saeculum semper saecula,* appears in Old English as *on woruld a woruld,* properly "from man age to man age," from world to world.

The Gothic language developed still another original concept of the "world": *mana-sēth,* which literally means "the seed of man." The idea of generation and human lifetime is once more implied.

CREATION

"So God created man in his own image, in the image of God created he him; male and female created he them" (Gen. 1:27). We understand by these simple words that the essential moment of creation has its meaning not in the material of creation, but in the form into which this material was shaped; therefore, it is said, "And the Lord God formed man of the dust of the ground" (Gen. 2:7).

The Latin *hōmo*, "human being, man," the equivalent of the Hebrew *adam*, is, as is generally supposed, related to *humānus*, "human," and *hūmus, -i*, "earth." This word is found also in the Germanic languages: the Gothic *guma*, "man," and the German *Bräuti-gam* (the English bridegroom, from the Old English *bryd-guma*, literally "brideman") have preserved remnants of this old term.[19] This reference to the "earth" is generally explained as alluding to the terrestrial existence of man as opposed to the celestial existence of the gods. In Greek, too, man is called "earth-born" (*gē-genēs*), and there was the belief that some people, such as the Athenians, never migrated, but are *auto-chthōnos* (*chthōn* meaning "earth"), properly, born out of the earth. The Mother Earth being the mother of all living beings, man is consequently the "terrestrial" being.

The Biblical account of creation differs in one essential point from this terrestrial perception of man which is implied in the Indo-European prehistory of our languages. In the Biblical concept only the material is the dust of the ground; the form is the celestial "image of God." What was formed is not as important as how this material was formed. "Art thou a man? thy *form* cries out, thou art," Shakespeare said.

There is an abyss between existence and nonexistence, of something and nothing, of "to be" and "not to be." Our languages express this difference. The Latin verb *creō, -āre*, "to bring forth, create, beget," points to the activity that makes the difference between being and nonbeing; this verb is the transitive form of the intransitive *cre-sc-ō, -ere,* which corresponds to the English *grow* and refers to an organic process.

Creation is generally understood in terms of generation. The *mater-ial* represents the maternal element, whereas the form is derived from the will of the father. The shaping of the material by the work of the hands is, in the symbolic language of fantasies, the same process as begetting a new life. Such fantasies were in Plato's mind when he wrote: "The Earth as the mother brought forth men, but God was the shaper" (*ho theos platton, Politics* 414). Similar fantasies are present in the Old Testament language, which uses "to shape," "to form," and "to beget" interchangeably. Jeremiah said: "Then the word of the Lord came unto me, saying, Before I formed thee in the belly I knew thee; and before thou camest forth out of the womb I sanctified thee" (Jer. 1:4–5). Similar associations are present in the words of Isaiah: "Woe unto him that striveth with his Maker! . . . Shall the clay say to him that fashioneth it, What makest thou? or thy work, He hath no hands? Woe unto him that saith unto his father, What begettest thou? or to the woman, What hast thou brought forth?" (Isa. 45:9–10). These primitive sex theories suppose that conception is brought about by the solidification of body fluids, notably of the blood. The complete fusion of the idea "beget" and the work of the potter forming the clay is present in these words: "But now, O Lord, thou art our father; we are the clay, and thou our potter; and we all the work of thy hand" (Isa. 64:8). This association of "to generate" and "to shape" is most clearly expressed by the Hebrew language in *yētsēr,* meaning "form" and "conception"; *yātsār,* "to form" and "to determine"; and *yotsēr,* "the potter" and, literally, "the former." An equation between "man" and "vessel" is thus implied by the identification.

The word *potter* could never express adequately in our languages the sublime concept of the Creator and Shaper.[20] The reason for this inadequacy can be found in the fact that the Father, who is called in Hebrew the "Shaper" or "Former," is characterized in our language by the product of his work, the *pot,* a word which does not imply the generation of man. The word *Maker* renders the original Hebrew more correctly by its unconscious implications, because the Old

English *macian*, "to make," developed from the primary meaning, "to form, fashion," and is probably related to the Greek *massō, emagen*, "to handle" and "to knead the dough."* This concept of the "potter" as shaper prevails in the Celtic and Slavic languages; it is also reflected in the Latin *figulus*, "potter," literally "shaper," from the verb *fingō, -ere*, "to shape, mold." However, it is significant that this Latin "maker of forms" makes only "figures" (from the Latin *figura*); thus, the verb *fingō, -ere* developed in English as *to feign*. (The Latin *figulus* does not create but simply imitates the true images of the created things.)

The potter's work implies some paradox for infantile fantasies. The potter works with the wet, soft, sticky material, but he puts this material finally in the oven, where it becomes dry, hard, clean, and brittle. So his work appeals to the fantasies of the child in a transitory stage of development.[21] The child has given up the smell of the dirty material to play with, but enjoys its soft, wet, and sticky qualities, which make the molding easy. He will soon, however, learn to play with clean, dry, and more solid substances. The original smell perception may still emerge in fantasies as, e.g., expressed in such children's rhymes as: "Mud is very nice to feel—all squish-squash between the toes—I'd rather wade in wiggly mud *than smell a yellow rose.*" The word cluster with such "rhyme ideas" as *squash-smash-mash-dash* may also refer to this primary play material. We call this "dust of the earth," as said in the Bible, *plaster of Paris*. This is the common name of that soft, oily, and limy composition which the sculptor uses for molding figures. The full emotional significance of this plaster of Paris can be observed in Greek, from which the word ultimately originated: the Greek *plassō*, "to mold, form" (rhyming with *massō*, "to knead, form, mold"). Its derivatives are *plasma*, "anything formed, molded," "image, figure," "the body fashioned by the Creator"; *plastēs*, "molder, shaper"; *koro-plathos*, "modeler of small figures," thus the maker of the *korē*, "child-doll." The unshaped material out of which the *koro-plathos* makes the forms is equated, in our languages, with earth, dust, mud, mire, and primarily with

* The Hebrew word for "trough" means also "cradle." It is otherwise significant that even in our forefathers' days the "trough" and the "cradle" were identical in their form.

"faeces." The German *Kot* covers both meanings: "excrement" and "mire"; the Old English equivalent *cwead* means "dung." The oily and sticky quality of the material is perceived in our term *clay,* which is related to *glue* and *cleave;* the same relationship exists between the German *Lehm,* "clay," and *Leim,* meaning "glue," and a derivative of the Latin *līmus.* The English term for this earthly material is *dirt* (as in *dirt road*), which developed from the Old English verb *dritan,* "to excrete"; the original meaning of "excrements" is still implied in "dirty." The German *Schmutz* ("dirt"), related to the English *smut,* also referred to a wet and greasy substance originally. These original qualities of the shaped material have been gradually given up, and instead a dry material, still liquid or in the form of a powder, is perceived, not by smell, but by its gray color. This is implied in the Greek *pēlos,* "clay, earth." Man is sometimes so called—since made of *pēlos* by Prometheus. *Pēlos* also means "mud, mire"; it is related to the Latin *palleō, -ēre,* "to be pale," as is the English *pale, pallid.* The Hebrew term for the "dust of the ground" is *aphar;* the primary meaning is either "to be gray" or "to pulverize." These concepts represent an advanced stage in the development of infantile fantasies.*

Most of our languages have lost the true meaning of the primary forming and shaping of the raw material as the expression of spiritual creation; thus they perceive the "shaper" of forms by the practical and useful results of his work as a "potter." Prometheus, when he tried to shape men out of clay, was not a potter, but a shaper or maker. One can find the English *pot:potter* relationship in the German *Topf: Töpfer,* the Gothic *kas:kasja,* the Old German *hafa:*German *Hafner,* the Latin *olla:ollārius* (and hence the Spanish *ollero*), the Slavic *grunici, grinicari:*Russian *gonchar.* All these words conceive the idea of "potter" in the static way, visualizing the end result of action, the "pot," whereas the more dynamic aspect of action is implied in the Greek *angeio-*

---

* These infantile fantasies may influence the adults' language. Calvin says: "I will in the first place state what in my judgment Moses intended. We have already heard that before God had perfected the world, it was an *indigested mass.* . . ." John Calvin, *Commentaries on the First Book of Moses ·Called Genesis,* translated by John King (Grand Rapids, Mich.: Wm. B. Eerdman), 1:73.

plastēs, from *angeion*, "vessel," and *plastēs* ("molder"), from *plassō*, "to mold, form"; in the Old English *croc-wyrhta*, a compound from *crocca*, "pot, crock" (cf. the German *Krug*, "jug"), and the noun *wyrhta*, "artisan." The Dutch *potten-bakker*, "pot-baker," sees the final act, the baking of the pottery, as the essential moment of its making. In many cases the potter gets his name from the material with which he works. Such is the case with the Greek *kerameus*, "potter," from *keramos*, "clay." The same is true of the Old English *lam-wyrhta*, literally "clay-artisan."

These various terms referring to pottery illustrate the process of the gradual fading out of the primary symbolic meaning that was alive in Biblical ages when the shaping of raw material was symbolic of generation and of creation. The material meant almost nothing, the sovereign will of the shaper everything. This infinite distance between the insignificant motherly material and the all-powerful fatherly will of the potter is pointed out in such sentences as: "O house of Israel, cannot I do with you as this potter? saith the Lord. Behold, as the clay is in the potter's hand, so are ye in mine hand" (Jer. 18:6). Such thoughts (as in Isa. 29:16) reverberate in Paul when he says: "Shall the thing formed say to him that formed it, Why hast thou made me thus? Hath not the potter power over the clay, of the same lump to make one vessel unto honour, and another unto dishonour?" (Rom. 9:20–21).

The earthenware, the work of the potter, became the symbol of human nature. Man is "frail, fragile, brittle"; the "weaker vessel" especially is said to be so. "I am like a broken vessel," the Psalmist says (Ps. 31:12). "Women, being the weaker vessels, are ever thrust to the wall," Shakespeare says. The crack on earthenware, called "craze" (minute cracks in glaze or enamel), became expressive of man in the word *crazy*, which literally means "full of cracks." The relationship between "clay" and "potter" came to be used as an illustration of the complete dependence of the creature upon the will of its creator. He who generates the life of the individual also has the right to destroy it, according to this primitive philosophy of creation. The free will of creation is complete in the freedom to destroy one's own creation. "Thou shalt break them with a rod of iron; thou shalt dash them in pieces like a potter's vessel," the Psalmist says (Ps. 2:9). Also it is said: "And he shall break it as the breaking of the potter's vessel that is broken in pieces; he shall not spare (Isa. 30:14). If creation is perceived as the shaping of the raw material, then the actual spiritual destruction consists in the destruction of the form and the return from the formed existence back into the unformed material. By depriving a thing of its meaning, which is manifested by its form, "all form is formless, order orderless," Shakespeare says. Since the primary shaping of life takes place in the womb, the separation from individual form reduces existence again to the *mater-ial*. Thus, the same Shaper of forms who set the beginning of life by these words: "Let us make man in our image, after our likeness" (Gen. 1:26) also set the "end of all flesh" by these words: "Return unto the ground; for out of it wast thou taken: for dust thou art, and unto dust shalt thou return" (Gen. 3:19). This is the meaning of the return to the mother. The idea of creation is complete only in the idea of destruction. Every beginning is an ending, and every ending a beginning. Perfection means both. "I am Alpha and Omega, the beginning and the end, the first and the last" (Rev. 22:13). Freud also postulated the eternal antagonism of the creative life instinct and the destructive death instinct. This teaching elaborated in biological terms the Old Testament philosophy about life and death.

The English *like* originally meant the same as the Old English *līc*, "body." The Old English *līcian*, "liken," and *ge-līc*, "equal" and "similar," refer positively to the body as the reason for being *like* or *alike*. The corresponding German *gleich* originally meant both "equal" and "similar"; now it means only "equal." "Similar" has been expressed by *ähn-lich*, formerly *ein-lich*, "one-body." These words present the problem of "embodiment"—especially if one also takes into consideration the English verb *to like*. Why do we like someone or something? It would be difficult to maintain that "we like it" because it has the same body we have. The emotional attraction denoted by this verb is generally explained as the result of a gradual shift in the meaning: from "to be of the same form," then "to be like," then "to be suited to," next "to be pleasing to," and finally "to like it." This tightrope walking from one meaning to another is not the way in which meanings usually change. In this special case, for instance, the related Gothic *leikan* is used in Ulphilas Bible translation for both the Greek *areskō*, "to please, be pleased," and *eudokeō*, "to be well pleased." The Old High German *līchan*, also, means "to be pleased, to like it." The examples of the related languages thus prove that the meaning "to like it" did not result or come about by a gradual shift from one concept to another, but was *a priori* implied in this verb. Extremely indicative of this is the fact that the Gothic language uses this verb with the addition of the word *faura:* thus, we have *faura-ga-leikan*, which could be translated as an "advanced liking, pre-ference or pre-dilection." How can we like someone or something before we are actually confronted with this particular person or object? It seems misleading to read into this word a modern-day interpretation of "body" and to assume in the idea "to like someone" primarily a bodily suitability. Bodily attraction or repulsion cannot be denied as one important facet of personal relationships; however, there is no proof to attest such subtle motives of sympathy to social conditions much more primitive than ours. The "liking" of one another which is supposed to appear in those who have a bodily "likeness" leads to the supposition that they are in one way or another "brothers and sisters" or blood relatives, that the psychological attraction is based upon a common ancestry. People may *long* for one another because they *be-long* together as members of one extended family.

This primitive feeling of belonging together and being attracted to one another by some inherent bodily similarity is better reflected in Greek thinking than in the philosophy of modern man. Aristotle explained that the *morphē*, "form," is but the visible appearance of an intrinsic idea that is the very essence of things: this is the first principle of existence and also its completion (called *entelecheia*). These intrinsic ideas represent the timeless primordial *para-deigma*, paradigms and archetypes of all factual physical and temporal existence. The coming and going and the turmoil and strife of the ever-changing actual world does not reach to the eternal quietness of the timeless ideas. These Aristotelian ideas are not conceived as abstractions; on the contrary, they really exist, and all the forms of things we perceive are but a dim reflection of the eternal perfection of the ideas. The forms we perceive *liken* the ideas, but they remain their imperfect *likeness*. The

Platonic philosophy explained the "longing" of the imperfect "likeness" to the original perfection as *anamnēsis,* "recollection" of the oneness that existed once before in the ideal essence. The German *ähnlich,* literally "one body," explains in this way the phenomenon of "similar": i.e., similar things originate from prior existing unity.

The Biblical concept of the "image of God" as a generative creative act expands the idea of the father and of the family to man in general. All men are *a-like* because they are all created in the same image of the father; they are brothers and sisters of one universal family.

The English language is still sensitive to the differentiation of *liking* and *loving.* This difference is apparent in the following fragment of a student's report on her feelings:

> I know that he loves me and wants to take care of me. We know we want a family together. Our love wasn't a sudden thing. It has taken three years. We learned *to like* each other, then something bigger happened: we were in love. I believe this is the meaning of love. I believe that you have *to like* someone before you can love him.

The English word *shape* is based upon slightly different fantasies of creation. The Old English *sceap* and *ge-sceap* denote the "generative organs" and also "shape, form, creation" and "creature," and are derivatives of the Old English verb *scypan, scop, gesceapan,* "to form, create, make" with the idea of "to draw" (as water). It is again intriguing to find some connecting link between "to create, make" and "to draw out of something." (Generally the answer is sought in some reality object, rather than in cosmogonic fantasies.) The original German verb *schöpfen, schuf, geschaffen* split into two different verbs: one is *schöpfen, schöpfte, geschöpft,* "to draw"; the other is *schaffen, schuf, geschaffen,* "to create." In the potter's workshop these two actions are not different as are the relevant verbal expressions. To be drawn out of the deep is a symbolic dramatization of the birth process. Botticelli's "Birth of Venus" (out of the waves of the ocean) is a well-known representation of this idea. According to gypsy folklore, a newborn babe still has "to be drawn" out of a deep well. "He sent from above, he took me, he drew me out of many waters" (Ps. 18:16). Christ said: "Except a man be born of water and of the Spirit, he cannot enter into the kingdom of God" (John 3:5). To draw out of water and to be born in spirit are, in this case, synonymous expressions for two interrelated events, just as they are in the case of the German *schaffen*, "to create," and *schöpfen*, "to draw." This applies to baptism also, which is the ritualistic expression of rebirth.

The identification of man, as well as of the woman, with the idea of "vessel" is supposed by these Biblical words: "giving honour unto the wife, as unto the weaker vessel" (I Pet. 3:7). Both are the creations of the Shaper of forms. The idea of the "ship" is closely associated with "vessel." This connection is very common in our languages, proving that this association must have some common psychological basis. As a typical example, we may note the Latin *vas*, "vessel, dish"; the English equivalent *vase;* the Latin diminutive *vasculum*, "a small vessel," "a small beehive," "the seed capsule of certain plants," "membrum virile"; and also *vascellum*, "small vase or urn." "Ship" is continued in the Italian *vascello*, the French *vaisseau*, and the English *vessel*. It may readily be asked why a "small vase" is used to denote a ship, which is a rather "large vase." This question is in order especially in French, inasmuch as *vaisseau* denotes only a very large ship, while a smaller boat is called *bâteau*. In this case, the diminutive appears again, however, but as an indicator of the imaginary quality of the "ship," not as an indicator of physical smallness. The English *ship* originally referred to a "pot"; the same holds true for the German *Schiff*. Our lexicons see no connection between the Old English *scyppan*, "to create, form"; *ge-sceap*, "creation, forming, shaping," and "genitals"; *ge-sceaft*, "creation, origin, world"; *ge-sceapenis*, "creation, a created thing"; and *ge-sceapu*, "form, beauty," on the one hand; and *scyp, scip*, "ship"; *scipian*, "navigate"; and *sciper*, "sailor," on the other. The separation of these two groups of words can hardly be maintained on formal phonemic grounds; the separation is due only to the divergence of the meanings. However, the unconscious fantasies suppose, in this case, as in the former ones, the identity of "vessel," "ship," "creation," "generation," which is also implied in the Old English *ge-sceap*, "creation, creature," and the English *shape.* If unconscious fantasies about the female body had not entered the idea of "ship," one hardly could explain the grammatical peculiarity that one refers to a "ship" by a female pronoun. The ship may be called "George Washington," but one says "she arrived." In Latin even *nauta,* from *nāvita,* "a sailor, seaman, mariner," is a feminine noun— because it is derived from *nāvis,* "ship." There must have been a very forceful psychological motive implied in the fantasies about this "ship" in order for it to succeed in breaking through an equally powerful general rule and establishing a rare exception. Only a few other obvious mother-symbols, such as "furnace" and "city," succeeded in the same way. The word *ship* shares another characteristic of some taboo words referring to the body: after its meaning became repressed, it became a formative element of the grammar and was used as a grammatical form repetitiously. In a similar manner, the word *like,* "body," became transferred from the vocabulary to the grammar, and we speak of "lady-like" or "child-like" behavior; in further development it became the ending *-ly*—as in the adverbial forms: *clearly, nicely,* or *fatherly*—and became used most frequently. In the same way, the noun *ship* became transferred to the grammar. We say "friend-ship," "lord-ship," "kin-ship," and use the word without meaning, repetitiously. We would not use it so frequently if there were no tabooed and repressed meanings behind it.

It can be observed that some children receive the pet name *Skipper.* The name implies some jocose derogatory meaning, much like the word *naughty.* We suppose that this implication, as well as the frequency of the repetitious use, derives from a repressed fantasy. We do not find this unconscious fantasy either in the meaning of "captain of a small vessel" or in the "skipping insect." The repressed object of reference is neither the insect nor the small vessel but the "pot." Not a coincidence is the fact that in German the verb *schiffen,* meaning "to navigate," also refers to urination. The difficulties of toilet training are recalled by this word.

PARADISE AND GOLDEN AGE

Cosmogonic fantasies imply the creation of man, but they also suppose that man, once created, must start on the long road of human history. Thus, the Biblical Creation would not be complete without an account of the Paradise and the Fall of man, however disjointed this narrative may appear otherwise (the Lord of Creation is denoted by the Hebrew plural *Elohim;* the Lord of Paradise is called *Jahve*). The Greek cosmogonic fantasies as described by Hesiod are also completed by the description of the "Golden Age." There is no historical or genetic coherence between the Paradise of the Bible and the Golden Age of Hesiod. These accounts of the primary state of man do not even refer to any prehistoric reality evidenced by archaeological or anthropological facts. Their intrinsic truth cannot be substantiated by history: it is a truth founded not upon history, but upon psychological realities. These stories recorded in the Bible and by Hesiod are real not "once upon a time," not at any moment of history, but in a perennial sense, for all ages and all men. Their truth, timeless in character, is therefore, as is all religious truth, valid forever. These stories do not record historical events, but reveal human motives and situations which may occur anywhere at anytime because they are founded on human nature. They project unconscious fantasies upon the prehistory of a race (much as utopian fantasies project upon its posthistory). They depict the metaphysics of wishful thinking.

We consider these products of religious fantasies primarily as the result of projection. They project in a negative way: they show just what we are not, what we lack and fear in our present situation. The Golden Age is the dream of the people who live in the Iron Age. One may readily suppose that these fantasies about the primordial existence of man have some similarities with dream fantasies. Freud once wrote about the "never-forgotten dream of the Golden Age," but he

174

was inclined to believe in the historical foundation of this dream. Our analysis will proceed along linguistic lines and select by way of phenomenological description a few verbal expressions which make these fantasies meaningful. We shall rely upon the pertinent verbal expressions because the tradition that is embodied in language is much older than any text or any myth recorded in this language.

Unreality

Fantasies are detached from reality. The essential unreality of these fantasies is expressed by their distance from the here and now of the present moment. Fairy tales indicate this unreality by referring to the remote past, as in the English "once upon a time," in the German *es war einmal,* or in the Oriental languages that say, "it happened once when it did not happen." A small boy said to his pal: "when I was a big man. . . ."[22] Some languages indicate the unreality of wishful thinking by using the past perfect tense or subjunctive mood. In English, for example, "I think *I have* never met him" means something true, but "I wish *I had* never met him" means something which is not true as a matter of fact.[23]

The unreality of this imaginary world may also be indicated by infinite spatial distance. In the Greek myth the "Blissful Island" is somewhere far away in the west, at the end of the earth and the ocean. American Indians seek the "Palace of Heaven" on the top of the Rocky Mountains, on a "high place," so high that no man can see it. The examples of all races and cultures are numerous.

The infinite distance in time becomes in these cases expressed by infinite distance in space. The visual perspective of this distanciation might be expressed in dreams by miniature figures, as Freud plastically expressed it, as if one would see the world from the wrong end of a telescope. As the past perfect refers to the distant time, we shall find that the diminutive might be the spatial expression of unreality. I propose to call such diminutive "imaginary diminutive." Here is a clinical example:

One can observe this use of the diminutive in the language of Schreber:

It is evident that he is endeavoring to distinguish the "soul
Flechsig" from the living man of the same name, the real
Flechsig, from the Flechsig of his delusions. . . . Flechsig,
whom he called a "soul-murderer"; and he used to call out
over and over again: *"Little* Flechsig!" putting sharp stress
upon the first word.[24]

This imaginary diminutive may be used primarily to
denote with some personification the split of the infantile part
of the Ego, a part which has not been assimilated by the
conscious mind. It might be just a fragment of the oral
complex.[25]

The unreality of these Lilliputian fantasies is also
indicated by their quality of inaccessibility. Their realm might
be encircled by a high wall. The meaning of the "high wall"
is, in this case, the same as of the use of the past perfect in
English. When Moses exhorting his people depicts the Promised Land, he speaks about the cities there "great and walled
up to heaven" (Deut. 1:28; 9:1). In the Zend-Avesta Yma's
Garden is just such an ideal place enclosed by insurmountable
walls.[26] The idea of "enclosure" is also implied in the word
Paradise through the Latin *paradisus,* a derivative of the
Greek *para-deisos,* which in turn is a loan word from the
Zend-Avesta *pairi-daēza* (literally "walled around") meaning
"enclosure"; it later developed the meaning of "garden."
Thus, there exists a linguistic relationship between Zoroaster's
teaching about Yma's garden and the Biblical teaching of
Paradise as "Jahve's Garden."

All these pictograms of the inaccessible places, especially the "high walls," are the symbolic expression of the
defenses that man tends to build up against the pressure of
reality while protecting his infantile complexes. The neurotic
is always escaping behind the "high wall" into his imaginary
Golden Age.[27]

The high walls depict not only the separateness of this
divine territory from any historical reality, but they indicate
also in spatial language the characteristics of the Golden Age,
an age of safety and peace. Within the walls of this garden
there is "joy" and "pleasure." The Hebrew name of this
garden, *Eden,* means "pleasure, delight." "The Lord shall comfort Zion . . . , he will make her wilderness like Eden, and

her desert like the garden of the Lord; joy and gladness shall be found therein, thanksgiving, and the voice of melody" (Isa. 51:3). The infantile world is a world of pleasure.

Upon closer inspection one will discover the inside bodily fantasies implicit in the notion of "garden."[28] The sphere of associations proves again that the idea of "garden" refers primarily not to some reality object, but to an imaginary "garden" of fantasies. The English *garden*, as well as *orchard* (from the Old English *ort-geart*), originally meant "enclosure"; the same holds true for the related Latin word *hortus*, which also refers to a place fenced around and enclosed. This is the original implication of the English *town;* the corresponding German *Zaun* means "fence," recalling the idea of cities "fenced to heaven." The Old English equivalent *tun* continued to express the primary idea of "enclosure, garden."

The inside bodily character of the whole fantasy complex becomes apparent in the pertinent Greek and Latin terms: both the Greek *kēpos* and the Latin *hortus* mean "garden" and also "womb" and *pudenda muliebra*. This primary idea of "garden" is generally associated with "joy" and "pleasure" as in the English *pleasure garden* and the German *Lust-garten* (and also *Lust-haus*, "pavillion within the garden"). The *Kinder-garten* has the same implications. The Old English *feltum* means "enclosed place, garden," and also "privy, dunghill." This ideal garden is not necessarily an orchard; it may be a *vineyard* (from the Old English *wingeard*); it may just as easily be a "pasture" or "meadow" such as the Greek *keinon* and *pedion*, "cultivated fields" and *pudenda muliebra*. The corresponding German *Weide*, "pasture," reveals once more that this ideal pasture is within the body: the German *Ein-ge-weide*, literally "inward-pasture," denotes the "intestines." Realistic-minded interpreters were startled by this absurd identity of "pasture" and "intestines"; therefore, they considered it to be either a chance homophony or sought a hidden connecting link in some agricultural realities. However, such reality explanations break down when one considers that the Latin *pastura* also developed the meaning of "intestines" in the Romance dialects. A derivative of the verb *pascō, -ere,* "pasture," also means "to feast, to gratify." The German *Weide* is interchangeable with the synonymous *Wonne*, "joy, pleasure," which also means "pasture"; for instance, *Augen-weide* and *Augen-wonne* both mean "delight to the eyes," and both *Wonne-monat* and *Weide-monat* are obsolete names for the month of May, as the month of pleasure.

The connecting link between "pasture," "intestines," "joy," and "happiness" can hardly be found on the level of agricultural realities because all these words are rooted in the reality of inside fantasies about the "pleasure garden." Another instance of this association can be observed in the Latin verb *laetō, -āre,* which, on the one hand, means "to make joyful, delight, cheer, gladden," and, on the other hand, "to fertilize, manure." Accordingly, the noun *laeta-men* means "dung, manure" and *laetitia,* also the feminine name *Laetitia,* means "joy, especially unrestrained joyfulness, gladness, pleasure, delight." Even though these words were applied to the soil, their primary reference was beyond doubt the human body. The Latin *Stercutius,* from *stercus,* "dung excrements, ordure," is an attribute of Saturnus, ruler of the Golden Age. We recall, in this context, the often-quoted words of Francis Bacon: "Money is like manure, very little use except it be spread." Reference to the deification of manure and excrements is found also in the Old Testament. It is said about Egypt: "And ye have seen their abominations, and their idols . . ." (Deut. 29:17). The Hebrew text properly says instead of "idols": "dung-gods."

Gold and Iron

How do these fantasies about the inside "pleasure garden" correspond to the names of the metals—gold, silver, iron—that Hesiod used to denote the ages? Hesiod designated as "golden" the age that was supposed to be farthest from present reality. We are condemned, he says, to live in the Iron Age. "I would that I *were* not living in the fifth age of men, but that I *had* either died before them or *been* born later"[29] [italics supplied], says the text of the translator. The formula "golden age" thus denotes time by space, as verbal expressions *always* do; it also denotes the most remote past by the name of the metal that is supposed to be found in the deepest parts of Mother Earth. This indicates once more and in a concrete way that these mythical ages are just as inaccessible to human experience as is the inside of the earth or the garden or city "fenced up to heaven."

These metals are extracted from the "entrails of the earth." Their patently Plutonian character may serve as a connecting link with the previous terms of the pleasure garden, which also refers to the intestines. Infantile fantasies about the internals of the body became projected upon the inside of the earth.

The meaning of "gold" has been thoroughly investigated by clinical research. Gold is considered to be the most precious of metals. The small child considers in the struggle of toilet training his excrements as the most precious gift to his mother; thus, an equation of "gold" and "excrement" is meaningful to his mind. In Old English *gold-hord-hūs*, properly "gold-hoard-house," is the proper term for the toilet. Many associations connected with "business," "job," "currency"— the unconscious fantasies about capitalism—still center around this basic equation of gold and excrements.*

The whole realm of associations which developed in connection with mining is replete with fantasies about the human body, especially about the inside of the Mother Earth. The "secret of the miraculous birth of iron" is the great topic of the Finnish national epic Kalevala.[30] The matrix of the mineral deposit is called *Mutter-gestein*, "mother stone," in German and *roche mère*, "mother stone," in French; the entrance of the mine is called *Mannes-fahrt*, "man's way," in German. The melting *furnace* derives its name from the Latin *fornax, fornacis*, from *fornum, furnus*, "oven"; the primary meaning, however, seems to refer to the "vaulted" quality of the dark, hot inside of the oven. The word also developed the meaning of *fornix*, "vault," and of *fornication*. Realistic-minded interpreters have the explanation at hand, that fornication was practiced in the vaulted subterranean brothels of Rome; yet the imaginary identification of the "furnace" with the female genitals is such a widespread and age-old association of latent meanings that one need not resort to an incidental historical motivation. The English *cupola* is the proper term for a "furnace used for melting metals." In German the same word is associated again with the idea of

* *cf.* p. 89.

"brothel." The melting furnace is referred to in the language of the miners, just as the vessel in the language of the sailors, by the feminine *she*. And the gold is separated according to this language from the *dirt*, "the gravel from which gold is separated." One still speaks about a "cast-iron stomach."

The crude casting of the metal running directly from the smelting furnace is called the "pig" or the "pig-iron." In the Greek *delphax*, "pig, piggy," actually means the "uterine" animal (from *delphus*, "womb"). The cast iron that has cells is called a *honeycomb*, a significant association to be explored later on. These instances can be multiplied, but they would not alter our preliminary result indicating that metals and mining evoke infantile fantasies about the inside of the body.

It seems rather difficult to answer the question as to why gold is a "good" metal and iron is a "bad" one, since both are extracted from the earth.* The question is the more in order because both "gold" and "iron" became identified in the language of fantasies with "excrements." The answer to this question is that though both refer to the same thing, they reflect two stages in the development of the child. The small child presents his excrements first as a gift representing the "good" child, thus as "gold"—and in a later stage, under the influence of toilet training, he learns the disgust and the "bad" connotations, the implication of "iron."

In this sense, said Plato in *Kratylos* (p. 398), "gold" implies "good" and "iron," "bad." In interpreting Hesiod he made the following rather sarcastic statement: "I think he did mean by the 'golden race of man' that they were good and noble. I can prove it because he called us the iron generation." In Greek "iron" is in fact sometimes termed *kakos phuton*, "bad plant."

These fantasies have left their traces in our languages. In English *scoria* means "slag or dross from melting metals out of ores," also "slaggy lava." The word *scoria* is derived from the Greek *skor*, "dung, ordure"; *skoria*, "the dross of metals, slag"; in Latin called *stercus ferri*. The same ideas expressed by a catatonic schizophrenic will clarify the delusional absurdities of Hesiod's metal ages. The patient unwit-

* In Greek, silver is *leukos chrusos*, "white gold," it is the same in Sanskrit, *ragatam heranyan*. But Sanskrit attributes to gold the "good color," *sa-varna*, while silver is of "bad color," *dur-varna*.

tingly explains the Greek idea of "iron" as *kakos phuton,* "bad plant."

A thirty-two-year-old woman with an episode of catatonic schizophrenia said to her therapist:

> It's the duty of people to grow things in the earth, to plant and to sow and to reap. People should give up the evils of metal and of work in the city [here she preaches with dogmatic emphasis]. They should stop digging [now shouting petulantly in rage] down inside the earth to draw metals out of it. That's digging down into Mother Earth and taking things that shouldn't be taken. They should leave them there. . . . All these machines and cars are wrong. All those materials should be left in the earth and we should grow things on the surface of the earth the way we were meant to—on the soil.[31]

The Biblical language is, in this respect, as expressive as the Greek. "Iron" is almost synonymous with "bad." When the afflictions of man are described, the Lord says: "I will punish you seven times more for your sins. And I will break the pride of your power; and I will make your heaven as iron, and your earth as brass" (Lev. 26:18–19). It is one of the great curses: "And thy heaven that is over thy head shall be brass, and the earth that is under thee shall be iron" (Deut. 28:23). Moses, referring to the utmost misery, says: "But the Lord hath taken you, and brought you forth out of the iron furnace, even out of Egypt" (Deut. 4:20). This expression is repeated several times: "out of Egypt, from the midst of the furnace of iron" (I Kings 8:51); "out of the land of Egypt, from the iron furnace" (Jer. 11:4). There can be no doubt that the iron furnace means something very bad.

The moral interpretation of body chemistry holds that the food taken in is "good" and the excrements are "bad." Gold and silver, being "good," represent the food taken in; iron is the "output." It is consistent with this primitive philosophy that our languages denote taste and smell by the moral attributes "good" and "bad" and attach moral qualities to the biochemistry of the alimentary canal. The Biblical stereotype *sweet-smelling,* Old English *sweet-stinking,* refers primarily, by the infantile synaesthesis of taste and smell, to the peculiar smell of their food, particularly milk and honey, which tasted sweet. The Greek words show that the intake of food and the accompanying "good taste" are synonymous in the latent meaning with "pleasure" and "lust"; thus, the Greek *hēdus,* "sweet, agreeable," refers to taste; the derivative *hēdonē* refers to "lust" and *hēdumos* to "pleasure." By such associations "gold" assumed as well the meaning of "sperm, semen." The best-known illustration of this meaning of "gold" is found in the story of Danaë, mother of Perseus. Zeus fertilized her in her prison tower in the form of a golden rain.

On the other hand, the Greek *kakos,* "bad, evil," refers to *kakkē,* "excrements," and *kakkaō,* "void." Consequently, "gold" took on the meanings of "sweet, pleasure, lust," while iron became associated with the various attributes of excrement. The smell is "cast" like iron. The words *smell, smelt,* and *melt* show a conspicuous structure despite their independence of one another in phonemics as well as in their meaning. Thus, we may suppose some hidden coherence in the implied unconscious fantasies. In summing up all these observations, it may be stated that the age called "golden" refers to an age of mankind which corresponds to the earliest stage of infancy.

Nature

The division of man and nature does not exist in the Golden Age. The "natural state" of man before the Fall also leads the fantasies beyond the dichotomy of conscious and unconscious existence. It supposes an age when man simply lived like the animals and plants and did not reflect upon his own existence. He lived according to the vegetative pattern of nature, existed in complete unity and harmony with nature. He was under no necessity of choosing or deciding about his own way of life; we would say that he could follow his natural instincts without repression. He did not know the pangs of conscience which result from the conflicts with his instinctual desires. The Biblical account refers in a pictorial way to the nakedness of man as descriptive of his primary natural state. Animals are naked in this sense—they are not ashamed of their instincts. The great turning point in human history came about, according to the Biblical account, when man first acquired knowledge. With knowledge there came into existence consciousness about one's own self, feelings of guilt and shame, and the awareness of death. Man experienced, from then on, the pressing feeling of internal fear and anxiety. He also started on the human way, the way of hard labor in shaping his own destiny. The natural state of man as reflected by these characteristics refers again to the unity of mother and child. The fetus within the mother represents the perfect oneness of man and nature, the Golden Age of the human lifetime.

It is consistent with these fantasies that *nature* (from the Latin *nātūra,* a derivative of the verb *gignō, -ere, gnātus,* "to beget") primarily denoted the "natural parts, organs of generation." The estrangement of man from nature begins with the separation of the child from the mother. The maturation of man into a self-reliant person appears in the light of these words as the fulfillment of being born into a separate being. The process of growing up is in this sense always an act of disobedience. Freedom is a revolt, not only against the will of the parents, but against the limitations of nature. Man experiences his freedom through this disobedience, by not accepting the imperative of nature, by imposing his will upon it. If we consider the process of growing up not simply as an individual process, but as a general development of history, we shall find that man tries to break down the barriers restricting his existence, tries to subjugate those forces that he feels were imposed upon his will. He realizes his freedom as the fruit of the Tree of Knowledge. Myth and religion, however, with a deep understanding of man's predicament, conceived the experience of human freedom as a revolt against a will higher than man's own.

Hesiod, not an analyst, is very conscious of the fact that the Golden Age of life is but the reflection of prolonged childhood. He says concerning the second age, the Age of Silver, which is never as perfect as the previous Age of Gold:

> . . . but for a hundred years indeed a boy was reared
> and grew up beside his wise mother, in her house being
> quite childish—but when one happened to age and

184

reached the stature of manhood, for but a brief space
used they to live suffering griefs through their impru-
dence. . . .

One may readily suppose that in the Golden Age man never
grew up, was never separated from his mother, was never
alienated from his natural instincts. He was one with nature.

Ever since the prehistoric age of our languages, there
has existed an over-all fantasy about generation and growth as
a natural process, as the sprouting, swelling, rising, growing,
and springing up from the germinal state into full existence:
Dionysus is the Greek personification of this abounding
sprouting. His surname is *Phlō-ios,* the Greek equivalent of
the Latin *flō-s, -ris,* the Italian *fiori,* the French *fleur,* the
English *flower,* and many other related words. The season of
spring obviously has something in common with growth,
youth, and love in this Dionysiac aspect of life. The swelling
and sprouting of the spring foliage is depicted in the Greek
word *phullon,* akin to *phallos* and meaning "leaf," and in the
Latin *fōl-ium* and all its derivatives. The English *blade* and
the German *Blatt,* however, originally meant "leaf, shoot, that
which springs forth," in the same sense as is implied in the
Bible by "when the blade was sprung up, and brought forth
fruit" (Matt. 13:26). The Old English *blō-ma,* from the same
sound pattern, does not mean "bloom, flower," but is the
proper name for "the iron flowing out of the glowing furnace," an expressive symbol showing once more that the
production of the metals has been correctly understood in the
fantasies about the reproduction of human life. The glowing
ore running directly out of the furnace also is called *Blume,*
"bloom," in German; it is symbolic of the creative process of
nature. Shakespeare's language, rich in symbolism, reveals a
deep understanding of the unconscious fantasies implied in
flower symbolism: he speaks of "spring-time flowers" and
"summer-swelling flowers" and expresses the implication of
"de-floration" by such simple flower language as "before milk-
white, now purple with love's wound," or the "pale and
maiden blossom became bleeding." The universal process of
organic conception, growth, decay, and death is the law of
nature followed by animals and plants, but man alone has the
privilege of being also aware of it.

Security and Innocence

The primary state of man, conceived of as a state of innocence, was projected out of feelings of guilt and anxiety. The very reason for fear, the unconscious motivation of anxiety and guilt, becomes apparent through the picture of the opposite pole, of the primary ideal state of man. There is no fear without an object. One can observe a remarkable change in the objects feared most. The various descriptions of the bliss of the Golden Age display the gradual change in the objects of fear and ultimate concerns of man. I give in the following a few examples:

In the third millennium B.C. a Sumerian stone inscription reads as follows [in Kramer's translation]: "In those days there was no snake, there was no hyena, there was no lion, there was no wild dog, no wolf. There was no fear, no terror. Man had no rival."[32]

According to the Zend-Avesta, Yma's garden is the place of the Golden Age: "In the reign of the valiant Yma there was neither cold wind nor hot wind, neither old age nor death, nor envy made by the Daevas (evil spirits)."[33]

While the objects of fear in the Sumerian text are aggressive animals and men, dangers threatening from outside, the objects of fear according to Zoroaster's interpretation are the internal enemies of man:

> There shall be no humpbacked, non-bulged forward there; no impotent, no lunatic, no poverty, no lying, no meanness, no jealousy, no decayed tooth, no leprous to be confined, nor any of the brands wherewith the Evil Spirit stamps the bodies of mortals.

Hesiod, in his *Works and Days,* is more specific about the objects of fear in the negative aspect; he points out in particular "hard work," "sickness," "wretched old age," and "death." These are the worst of evils which have fallen upon man. "Once, indeed, the races of men . . . used to live on earth apart and free from ills, and without hard labor and painful diseases which have brought death upon mortals."[34]

In the Iron Age in which we live, Hesiod says, man is never free from evils and people "corrupt as they are, gods will give them severe cares, yet nevertheless even in these shall good be mingled with evil." The "golden race of speech-gifted men" was free from these afflictions. No death, no frail old age, no sickness mean in a positive aspect eternal youth and immortality. These are the privileges of the gods, but these divine attributes were also enjoyed by the inhabitants of Elysium. They lived in an eternal present, knowing no past, no future, no history; their existence had no relationship to the flux of time.

The Latin *se-cūrus* originally meant "free from fear, without anxiety" (*sine cūra*), "free from the black fury, the messenger of death" (*atra cūra*). *Secūrus* denoted literally the life "free from care, untroubled, tranquil, serene, cheerful, bright," which man enjoyed in the Golden Age, and which the deceased heroes also enjoyed under the rule of Kronos on the "Blissful Isle." We may observe—in the change of meaning from *sine cūra* to "secure"—the transition from the subjective "free from fear" to the objective "free from danger, safe, secure"; thus, we may suppose that through some unconscious fantasies both meanings were originally one. The German derivative of *secūrus* is *sicher,* "safe, secure"; it originally meant "without guilt, innocent," thus suggesting that there existed a correlation between innocence and security. Man remained innocent, "without guilt," as long as he lived in safety, but when he was driven out of the enclosure of safety into the world of dangers, he became guilty. The Latin *innocent* literally means "not harmful," from the verb *noceō, -ēre,* "to do harm." It implies the fantasy of harmful aggressiveness. This means, in other words, that things which are harmful in our world were not so in this imaginary world; that those who are guilty today were not so in the ideal state; that the dangers feared most were not dangers in this golden age of life. Ovid (*Metamorphoses* 4. 96–105) depicts this supposed unity of "secure," "free from fear," "free from guilt," and "not harmful" as the natural state by saying:

> But that pristine age which we have named the golden age
> was blessed with the fruit of the trees and the herbs which
> the ground sends forth. . . . nor did men defile their lips
> with blood. Then birds plied their wings in safety through
> the heaven and the hare loitered all unafraid in the tilled

fields, nor did its own guilelessness hang the fish upon the hook. All things were free from treacherous snares, fearing no guile and full of peace.

The lion is one of the "harmful" animals enumerated as nonexisting in the Golden Age by the Sumerian inscription. Yet a lion and a leopard peacefully pull the chariot that brings Dionysus and Ariadne to the great wedding festival at Naxos. This tame lion and meek leopard of Ariadne represent *in-nocence* in the sense of "not being harmful." The meaning "not guilty" applies only to man. Perhaps the lion of Dionysus and the leopard of Ariadne are also symbolic of the "innocence" of the animal in man if his animal instincts are free from guilt. The nakedness of man is the symbol of the innocence of his animal nature.

One can well observe in clinical situations that such fantasies of the Golden Age are brought about by the defense mechanism of denial. I quote the following passage from the analysis of a child in order to illustrate that fantasies may serve like dreams as a "safety valve," as Freud termed it, to alleviate his anxieties.

In the case of a seven-year-old boy, all essential character traits were largely determined by this mechanism of denial. Fear permeated his entire life pattern. . . . He developed a fear of death and a tic which bore the imprint of his particular mechanism of denial. . . . He showed great fear of wild animals. Within a few hours, however, he appeared to have mastered it. . . . He played with toy animals, talking to the lion and tiger, of whom he had been so frightened in the morning, in a friendly, loving tone. . . . He explained very quietly that he was no longer afraid of them. ("The animals are my friends, and we are on such good terms that they won't do anything to me.") He did admit that they might be dangerous, but only to strangers—not to him, their good friend; they would in fact protect him against all enemies.[35]

The tame lion and the meek leopard do not disturb our sleep; thus, their "in-nocent" character might be the result of the sleep-protecting dream work.[36]

When he leaves the "fenced around" garden of safety and innocence, man is exposed to "danger." This word is a

188

derivative of the Latin *dominium*, which refers to the "right of ownership, domain." Shakespeare says: "You stay in my danger." One's own *dominium* is "homely" (cf. the German *heimlich*); this means "homely, snug, cozy" and also "secret." Beyond this familiar sphere begins the realm of "danger," the *dominium* of fear and anxiety. Our subjective "fear" corresponds with the object of fear in German *Ge-fahr*, which means "danger." The German *un-heimlich* means "not homely" and also "uncanny." The interrelationship of these various negative expressions (*se-cūrus*, "free from fear," *innocentia*, "not harmful," the German *un-schuldig* and *sicher*, "free from guilt") becomes meaningful through their positive aspect if they are related to the primary situation of mother and child. The lap of the mother is homely, cozy, snug, and a place to hide in secrecy. Apart from it, there are dangers and other frightening, uncanny things.

Timelessness

Somehow implied in bliss and happiness is timelessness. Happiness wants eternity. This is the characteristic feeling of elation. Freud pointed out that collective elation in festivals and carnivals is characterized by a subjective confusion between day and night times. Elation and ecstasy may produce the sensation of time standing still.[37] The person who is completely absorbed by an object of pleasure or love, may forget about the passage of time and may even "forget about himself." In the Greek conception *ekstasis* implies a state of mind in which man is "beside himself" and thus "alienated" from his own self because his mind has left his self and has become united with the deity. On the other hand, *enthousiasmos*, from *en-theos*, "having the god within," means that the deity has entered the mind and, by absorbing it from within, makes man and the god identical; man is then "full of god." This feeling of timelessness may thus be brought about by the identification of the mortal man with the immortal god; it may also derive from the identification with another person through love. The identification is, however, in the last analysis, the repetition of the primary unity and its first repetition, the reunification of mother and child in the nursing situation.[38]

The relevant words of this reunification refer either to the breast of the mother (like *fē-lix*, "happy") or to the sweet taste (as the Greek *hēdus*, "sweet," and *hēdomai*, "to be happy") or to something which is "smooth" (as *please, pleasure*, the French *plaisir*). The Latin *laetus*, "happy," refers to the verb *laetō, -āre*, "to fertilize, manure." It is a common characteristic of these words denoting "joy" and "pleasure" on the oral or anal level that they have absorbed the meaning of sexual gratification also. The Greek *hēdomai*, "to be pleased," and *hēdumos*, "agreeable," developed also into *hēdonē*, "lust." The Latin *volup*, "pleasant, agreeable," developed into *volup-tas*, "satisfaction, enjoyment, pleasure, delight." The German *lust-ig* means simply "gay," but the noun *Lust* is equivalent with our "lust." Such implications are present also in the English *joy* and *enjoyment, pleasure* due to wantonness.

In the German language *selig* means, on the one hand, "blessed," as the dead ones on the Island of the Blest, and "sensually happy" on the other hand. These two disparate meanings must have once coincided: the Island of the Blest must have also been an island of libidinous satisfaction. We can receive a more comprehensive picture of these meanings by looking into the Old English background of this key word: The Old English *sael* primarily referred to "time," then it referred particularly to the "good time," i.e., a time of "prosperity"; the noun *saeld* meant accordingly "happiness, felicity, enjoyment, prosperity, wealth." Significantly, all these are characteristics of the Golden Age. The word is continued in the adjective *silly*, which originally denoted in Middle English "good, blessed, innocent." After the original fantasies recessed, however, the new meaning emerged, first as "helpless, weak," then as "foolish, stupid." Thus, this word reflects the decomposition of the original religious fantasies.

The Greek word *orgasmos* reveals the same background. It is derived from the verb *orgaō*, "to swell with lust, to wax wanton"; applied to the soil, it denotes a land "well watered and ready to bear a crop." Another derivative of this verb is the plural *orgia*, "orgies, secret rites, secret worship"— but most commonly of the rites of Bacchus, with their dedications and purifications which were indeed partly shown to the uninitiated, but left unexplained.

The shadow of a bad conscience is conspicuous in the word *delight,* from the Latin *de-lectō, -āre* (which is, in turn, from *de-lacerō, -āre*), which means, on the one hand, "to delight, please, charm, amuse" and, on the other, "to allure from the right path, entice away, seduce." In the Biblical account we see the close association of *Eden,* meaning "delight," and the act of enticement: claiming to be seduced or enchanted relieves the Self from a bad conscience and responsibility by projecting one's own guilt upon the source of the delightful gratification. In contradiction to this negative attitude to "pleasure" stands the affirmative praise of "bliss" and "fecundity." Both are timeless; they overcome the futility of time.

Metals are also symbolic of timeless persistence—*aere perennius,* "more persistent than metal," being the Latin formula for eternal existence. The ages named as metals indicate that each of them has been considered as exempt from corruption in time. Each represents in its own way timeless eternity. The relevant verbal expressions reveal that there must have existed some fantasy out of which the singular meaning of "eternity," "human life-time," and "generation" has developed. This imaginary. timeless state of man supposes that once the "duration of human life" and "eternity" meant the same and both were inseparable from "generation." This idea became elaborated in the fantasies of the Golden Age in which the human lifetime was eternal, unceasing youth, and generation.

I quote a clinical instance of the schizophrenic symbolization of "eternity": "On that day, she recognized herself as Mother Eve, and the place as the Garden of Eden, the First Paradise; thus everyone should be going around naked as primitives, for this was the beginning of time and of the world. She felt her watch was of solid gold, *which meant that it could not move and* thus time stood still." *One cannot interpret these fantasies without reference to the Golden Age.*[39]

Various languages struggled with the problem of how to express, by a visual picture, the abstract idea of time, especially of "eternity." How could the invisible and inconceivable be made visible? "Gold" was used for symbolizing eternity; e.g., the golden ground behind the Byzantine mosaic figures expressed just this unreal, irrational, and visionary moment in the lives of saints. But there was also need for an adverbial form for the "everlasting." Our *always* translates time into space through the picture of *all ways* (Old English *allne waeg*); the same form was used in obsolete German (Luther used *allewege*). The origin of this expression seems to be rooted in the Biblical language, in such formulas as "The Lord shall preserve thy going out and thy coming in from this time forth, and even for evermore" (Ps. 121:8).

The Hebrew language sought another solution of this problem. The Hebrew adverb for "always" is *olam, olawn;* it means, as a noun, "eternity," and as an adverb "ever," but the primary meaning implied is "covered, concealed, secret," just as the German *heimlich* means "snug, cozy, secret." These references to the warm and secret home evoke the picture of the lap of the mother. One may interpret: Eternity is inside the mother and not visible to the outside world. Eternity, that is, timeless existence, is sought in life before birth. The babe enjoys the bliss of timeless eternity.

The Greeks and Romans approached the picture of eternity by the idea of generation. The power of procreation represented to their mind the continuity beyond the individual life. The transcendent generative power of man and woman alike was located, according to their primitive biological fantasies, in the marrow of the bones, especially in the spinal fluid and the brain. It was called in Greek *aiōn* (from *aiwon*), which denoted primarily the "spinal marrow," but also "eternity," "age," and "human lifetime." The relative adverbial expression was *aiei,* "ever, always." Eternity was something divine, the privilege of the immortal gods. Man participated in it either by *enthousiasmos* or *ekstasis*. In the climax of sexual union the I and the Thou, the subject and the object, time and eternity, become fused in unity. The Greek *aiōn* wonderfully expresses this unity of "human lifetime" and "eternity," and also the sexual potency as the true representative of the Self. In Latin the corresponding form developed as *aevum* and *aetas* (from *aev-itas*), uniting the three meanings "age," "eternity," and "human lifetime."

It seems to be a specific Germanic development which implied in this associative complex the meanings of "law" and "marriage." One readily may ask, What has "eternity" to do with "law" and "marriage"? They seem to be disparate ideas. So they do, but they appear genuinely connected with one another in the mythological fantasies of the Golden Age. An analysis of our languages can substantiate this belief. First, however, we must recognize that eternal peace is a requisite for eternal bliss. Then we can accept the idea that the eternal bliss of the Golden Age was also a state of "eternal peace" in which the "golden rule"—the ideal law of mutual respect— prevailed. (This ideal law is represented by the "righteous" ruler of this peaceful community.)

If we examine now the idea of "law" in our languages, we should find much evidence of how the deeply rooted fantasies* of an "eternal peace" supported the synonymity of "marriage" and "law" and their position in the complex of "eternity."

The Germanic equivalents of the Greek *aiōn* (from *aiw-ōn*) are the Old English *aew, awa, ae* (preserved in the adverb *ev-er*). These Old English words as nouns mean "eternity" and "law," and as adverbs, "ever." The law, of course, is the divine law, which is often called in the Biblical language "ordinance forever." Similarly, the Old German *ewa* means "eternity" (as preserved in the German *Ew-igkeit,* "eternity," and *ew-ig,* "eternal") and *aiw* or *eo* means "ever." This old form, *ewa,* for "eternity" remained preserved in the German *je* (from *eo*), "ever." *Eo-mer,* properly "ever," is preserved in *immer,* meaning "always." *Ewa* is also present in the German *echt* (from *ē-haft,* "lawful"), meaning "true, real." The implication developed obviously supposes that the "true" or "real" things are also in accordance with the divine law and eternity.

The Dutch *echt* means "marriage"; the German word for "marriage," *Ehe,* is derived from *eo* and therefore contains the same reference to "eternity." Thus it could be interpreted that "marriage," in referring to "eternity," is perhaps also "lawful" in accordance with the divine ordinance. However, we shall reason in the following that in the original state of innocence, marriage is never unlawful. Why? For nature does

---

* Immanuel Kant, writing on the topic of "eternal peace," readily referred to the "empty longing" (*leere Sehnsucht*) of wishful thinking fostered by "the shadow of the Golden Age much praised by the poets."

not discriminate between the "lawful" and the "unlawful" marriage. So in the Golden Age every "marriage" is "lawful"; thus, as a result of this relationship, "marriage" and "law" became synonymous. This legalization of the union of man and woman, symbolically depicted in the wedding of Dionysus and Ariadne, is one of the characteristics of the Golden Age.

Milk and Honey

The infantile fantasies of returning to the primary nursing situation are symbolically represented by "milk" and "honey" in the concept of "abundance" as found in the eternal and blissful garden of the Golden Age.

Before examining the whole complex piecemeal, we should gain some insight by first reading some associated literature: A Sumerian stone inscription describing the blissful state of man, says that Shubur (East) was "the place of plenty"[40] and that Uri (North) was "the land having that what was needful."

The Zend-Avesta described more explicitly Yma's enclosure:

> Thither thou shalt bring the seeds of every kind of tree, of the greatest, best, and finest kinds of this earth; thither thou shalt bring the seeds of every kind of fruit, the fullest of food and sweetest of odor. All those seeds shalt thou bring, two of every kind, to be kept inexhaustible there so long as those men shall stay in the Vara. . . . In Yma's "reign" both aliments (food and drink) were never failing for feeding creatures, flocks; men were undying, waters and plants were undrying. . . .[41]

Hesiod's description of the Greek Golden Age refers to the same abundance and freedom from want. He says:

> As gods they (men) were used to live, with a life void of care, apart from and without labors and troubles. . . . All blessings were theirs, of its own will the fruitful field would bear them fruit much and ample: and they gladly used to reap the labors of their hands in quietness: along with many good things, being rich in flocks, dear to the

blessed gods. . . . [At the Isles of the Blest where Kronos was the righteous King] thrice in a year doth the fertile soil bear blooming fruits as sweet as honey.[42]

The Latin *sat-is* or *sat-urus* means "satiated" and *sat-ietas,* "satiation"; the "platter filled with the first fruits offered to the gods" was called *lanx satura,* it was a symbol of abundance. The ideal law was called *lex satura.* We shall understand this strange association of "law" and "satiated abundance" by the above-mentioned implication of the "eternal law." It hardly can be accounted for as mere chance that the ruler of the Golden Age, Kronos, has found his Latin equivalent in *Sāt-urnus.* His festivals, which evoked the timeless elation, revelry, and license, were the *Sāt-urnalia.* The personification of the natural instincts and Dionysiac drives in man was the *Sāt-uro,* the satyr. We will call the Sabbath day *Saturday,* in remembrance of *Sāt-urnus.*

The distinctive feature of abundance is often denoted in the Biblical language as well as in the classic antiquity by the formula "milk and honey." Seneca in describing the wedding feast of Dionysus and Ariadne said, "The dew became honey and the springs gave milk." Socrates said, according to Plato, that the Bacchae, the women participating in the Dionysiac festival, took milk and honey out of the rivers if they were in the maniac state, but could not do so when their minds returned to normalcy. Seeking for a psychological interpretation of this statement, one will think of the illusions that can be brought about by the hypnotic suggestion.

The reference to the milk makes it once more very obvious that the whole complex reflects the primary nursing situation. Only the mother is abundant with milk. Separated from the idea of mother, "the rivers of milk and honey" would be a schizophrenic delusion. The opposite of the generously giving attitude is expressed in our language by the reference to the symbolic gesture of "tight-fistedness." In the Hungarian the same attitude is characterized by the expression "of a narrow breast" (*szükmellü*).

How the cosmogonic creation fantasies may flow together with early feeding memories might be illustrated by the verbalizations of a male patient. He said:

The dream was just haze. Like looking at a cloud. I see it now. It's white. Now I see a pug nose on it. A lit

red light bulb. A baby's head? A darning egg, to hold in
the hand? Now it has become a rain cloud. It's angry and
raining, now. The nose has gone. Lightning and rain
come out of it. I see the tree. My tree. It's not a successful
feeding. An angry one. A bad old deal. The storm might
kill the tree. Then it would be dead, decayed wood. Worms
would eat it like they ate my mother. Now the storm is
leaving and the sun's coming through. God. If I were well,
I'd have nothing to work on. I'd have no aggressive need.
I'd be so satiated. (Bryce Boyer, "A Hypothesis Regarding
Time of Appearance of the Dream Screen," *International
Journal of Psycho-Analysis* [1960], 41:114–22.)

The reference to honey is not as transparent as that to
milk.[43] "Gold" and "milk" were according to the infantile
fantasies inside products, one deriving from the inside of the
earth, the other from the inside of the mother. By the same
token "honey" was also considered as a mysterious inside
product; it came from the inside of the beehive. The Greek
sumblos denotes the "beehive," but also any kind of store,
hoard or treasure house. It has long since been symbolic for
"the deposit," which is—especially when collected by indus-
trious work—the armor of the savings banks. As we say "a
sack of money," the Greeks said in the same way "a beehive
(*sumblos*) of gold." Honey has been associated with gold; by
its sweetness it seemed to be symbolic of the food taken in, by
its color it appeared as "fluid gold." *Meli-chrusos* ("gold-
honey-colored") is the Greek term. The internal bodily character of the honey will become more apparent if one takes into
account the ancient methods of honey production: for instance, the Egyptian practice was to kill a calf and expose it;
and in nine days, it was said, bees would swarm within the
carcass. Herodotus also told a story of how a human head
was suspended over a gate and soon became filled with
honeycomb.

Continuing in the "honey-gold" complex is the name
of the bee, a recurrent personal name of women: in Hebrew
Debōrāh, the name of Rachel's nurse; in Greek *Melissa* or
Melitta, the name given to the priestesses of Delphi, of
Demeter, and of Artemis. In the language of Neo-Platonic
philosophy "bee" is the name of any pure soul coming to
birth. Moreover, the idea of the bee being the fetus in the
womb is further implied in both *meli-pais-symblos*, "the hive

with its honey-children," and *simbl-euō,* "to shelter as in a hive." The infantile fantasies about the beginning of life during the Golden Age are present in all these words. The "queen wasp" is called in Greek *mētra,* "womb." In Hungarian the "womb" is called *méh* or *anya-méh,* "bee" or "mother bee." These repressed fantasies are also present in such formulas as the Latin *lūna mellis,* i.e., "honeymoon." On the reality level such words may be ridiculed as sheer nonsense, yet they are meaningful in terms of the unconscious fantasies implied.

It is an old folkway to prepare the honey *cake* (from the Old Norse *kaka*) in the mold of a babe, evoking the idea of the fetus. Such "cake" was called in Greek *plakous,* hence the Latin *placenta.* According to these fantasies the fetus in the uterus was fed on honey. It has been also observed that some mother animals (cattle) are eager to consume the ejected placenta after birth.

When milk and honey were flowing, no hard work was forced upon man. "Hard work" is according to these fantasies the opposite of the pristine abundance. Man lived at the beginning of history like the primitive food gatherers do, just collecting the seeds and fruits nature produced with inexhaustible abundance. Man in this Golden Age perhaps wanted an apple from a prohibited tree, but if this was indeed his great crime, he was surely not the rapacious dangerous cannibal as he appeared everywhere during the prehistoric ages. The life of the carnivorous hunter implied fight, effort, danger, whereas the food gatherer chose the easy way of life.*

Work and Pain

It is a conspicuous general feature of our languages that the words for "work" are synonymous with "pain," "suffering," "hardship," or "distress." They often also imply the idea of "plowing, tilling," which is a clear indication that the agricultural "work" marked the end of the primary blissful state thought of as life without work. The Greek *ponos* means "toil" and "pain," the Latin *labor* means "toil" and "suffering," and the German *Arbeit,* though it now means "work,"

* This easy way of life is pungently denoted by the English and French word *nonchalance,* which is a derivative of the Latin *non calet,* "that which does not make hot."

meant in the old language "distress, suffering." The implied misfortune of "work" holds true in many other pertinent words in Old English and in the Scandinavian languages, as well as in the work of Herodotus, who says about the Thracians (5:6): "To be idle is accounted the most honorable thing, and to be tiller of the soil the most dishonorable. To live by war and plunder is of all things the most glorious."

The French *travail*, "work," and the Spanish *trabajo*, "work," are derivatives of the Latin *tripālium*, which is an instrument of torture. The Greek gods on Olympus surely did not work: their life was *leisure*. This word derives from the Latin verb *liceō, -ēre*, "to be permitted," "to be free." The idea of work was felt to be the opposite of being free, thus it became associated with "slavery." The Greek *doulos*, "slave," is continued in the New Testament Greek *douleia*, "work"; Slavic *robota, rabota*, "work," derives from *rabu*, "slave." Obviously, the association between "pain" and "work" and "slave" seems transparent enough without any reference to unconscious fantasies.

In contrast, however, there are many examples (e.g., the English *labor* and *travail*) in other languages in which the "pain" of "labor" is a specific kind of pain, like the Dionysiac pain, which is lust as well—a pain that is not a "pain unto *death*" but a pain unto *life*. For, while to the Golden race of man parturition was free from pain and fear, to Biblical man it was said, "In sorrow thou shalt bring forth children" (Gen. 3:16)—this divine pronouncement marking the end of the primary state of man. Birth and death, the entrance and the exit of life, became the two sources of anxiety, but they were not so dreadful for the early man. "They died as if overcome by sleep," Hesiod says. The desire for sleep follows immediately the infant's desire for "milk and honey." If the instinctual needs become satisfied the infant will fall asleep. And sleep is not only the recovery and counterbalance of "hard work" but also the sign of the great peace of mind and the freedom from want.

The Forbidden Fruit

The "tree of the knowledge of good and evil" is the only prohibited tree of Paradise. This tree was "in the midst of the garden" and the commandment said: "Thou shalt not eat of it: for in the day that thou eatest thereof thou shalt surely die." Endless theological, philosophical, and psychological disputes have tried to unravel the meaning of these words. We shall try to approach this age-old controversy from the angle of the verbal expressions.

The traditional commentators on theology and those on psychology who stressed independence and individualism (Otto Rank, Erich Fromm), in discussing this passage, pointed out the motive of disobedience. According to this interpretation the decisive point of the narrative is that the fruit was *prohibited*.

It should be pointed out that the verb *pro-hibit* derives from the Latin *pro-hibeō,* from *pro-habeō,* which properly meant "to have before, in front of." This means in more explicit terms that someone has something before one is permitted to have it, or that someone has something even in front of someone else who is objecting to it. If the fruit is prohibited it may mean, according to infantile fantasies, that it is something prematurely eaten in anticipation of later days. The knowledge of the prohibited fruit is the driving power behind the gradual growth into maturity starting from infantile dependency and ending up at self-responsible independence. Rebellion and disobedience are the symptoms of growing up. It is the human predicament that man must become free through knowledge and become the master of his destiny. In traditional religious terms this means: the root of evil is disobedience and rebellion against the divine commandment.

It could be said in support of this understanding that the "voice of conscience" (the Superego) is primarily auditory in character. This is wonderfully illustrated in the Biblical narrative by having Adam hear the voice calling his name—"Adam, where art thou?"—just at the moment when he wanted nothing more than to hide. *Con-science* properly means "joint knowledge," thus "knowing together." The verbal command is a voice heard from within, and the surrender to this voice is obedience. *Ob-edience* is a derivative of the Latin *ob-audīre,* properly "upon hearing."

The traditional reference to disobedience explains the rebellious behavior of Adam but does not account for the symbolic act of eating the fruit nor the role of the woman in it. Immediately after the prohibition has been declared, the Lord says: "It is not good that the man should be alone; I will make him an help meet for him" (Gen. 2:18). So the creation of the woman is told a second time in the same narrative. The first time it is said that Elohim created man in his own image: "Male and female created he them. And God blessed them, and God said unto them, Be fruitful, and multiply" (Gen. 1:27–28). The second version says that Jahve took out the rib of Adam while he slept and from the rib "made he a woman, and brought her unto the man" (Gen. 2:22).

These two versions of the creation of Eve are generally referred to as revealing the inconsistencies in combining the Elohim and the Jahve oral traditions in the story of the Creation; from a psychological viewpoint, however, these two aspects are not inconsistent at all but illustrate the two characteristic stages in the development of infantile fantasies.

In the earliest stages the child perceives male and female as one undifferentiated unity, thus "male and female created he them." For this reason primordial beings are thought of as bisexual all over the world from the *androgynos* or *hermaphroditos* to the Germanic progenitor *Tuisco*, whose name refers to the numeral "two" or "twisted," or to the Hebrew *Leviathan*, from *liwyāthān*, which properly means "twisted." In Hungarian, for instance, the word for "man" or "mankind," *ember*, is an old compound of *em-ber* meaning properly "woman-man." So is our word *wo-man* a compound form meaning also "wife-man." It is not so unreasonable to suppose that according to earliest infantile fantasies there existed but one sex, the "male-female," which became dissected later on in order that man and woman should multiply. Thus not man was born out of the woman but the woman was taken out of man, the male became effeminated and made into a *woman*, i.e., *wife-man*. Plato, in the famous passage of his *Symposium*, explains the eternal longing of the male for the female by saying that both once were one: "Zeus in pity invented a new plan: he turned the part of generation round the front, for this had not always been their position, and they sowed the seed no longer, like grasshoppers in the ground but in one another." There are the sexually deviated who do not experience this basic split and turn around of the sex organs, but remain fixated on the infantile androgynous level and thus confuse the front and the back aspects of anatomy.

The taking out of the rib represents another version of splitting the primordial "male and female" unity. The rib is the curved bone taken out of the man. It seems to be significant how often it is silently implied in theological literature that the rib had been taken out of the *left* side of Adam, even though the Bible does not say it. The unconscious fantasies suggest this elaboration of the Biblical account.[44] Whatever might be the role of Eve, her creation is *a priori* conceived of as eliciting the evil out of man: "left," "crooked," "wrong," from *to wring,* portends evil.

The fruit of the Tree of Knowledge has been interpreted in many different ways. It has been pointed out that if disobedience is not conceived of as the "original sin," the eating of a prohibited fruit would be too insignificant a transgression for bringing about the condemnation of the whole human race.* This relatively minor transgression would project upon the Lord the revengefulness of paranoiac proportion. Therefore another interpretation of the prohibited fruit must be sought.

We start from the generally known equation of "woman" and "tree." The Biblical expression "fruit of the womb" definitely identifies the woman with the tree. In the Latin language *mater-iō, -āre* means to "build of wood"—the mother being equated with the timber. The feeling of natural kinship of the woman and the tree has been greatly emphasized by castration fantasies, seeing in the scar of a cut-off branch the simile of the female organ. This primary experience of primitive thinking pervaded the Roman mind when, for example, Vitruvius wrote about the *mater-ial,* which is the timber that should be felled between the early fall and the spring: "For in spring all trees become pregnant. This is also the case with women who have conceived. Their bodies are not considered perfectly healthy until the child is born: hence pregnant slaves, when offered for sale, are not warranted

* Theodore Reik, *Myth and Guilt: The Crime and Punishment of Mankind* (New York: George Braziller, 1957). He supposes that the eating of the prohibited fruit is symbolic for the cannibalistic crime of killing and eating one's own father.

sound."[45] We surely have lost this primordial feeling of blood relationship with all organic life, an elementary experience that cannot be recovered any longer in our age.

With these implications in mind we approach the interpretation of the concept of the "Tree of Knowledge" as a symbol of the female principle, just as found previously in the curved rib. The "pro-hibited" fruit is termed in the Hebrew original *periy*, derivative of the verb *pārāh*, "to bear fruit." Perhaps it is more than a chance homophony that this word also means "cow, heifer, kine," which also bear "fruit" in the image of themselves. Our term *fruit* is a derivative of the Latin verb *fruor, frui, fructus*, "to enjoy"; thus it refers to the primary pleasure principle. The Biblical text does not say that this "fruit" of the Tree of Knowledge was an apple; nevertheless, once more the gravitation of unconscious fantasies made this interpretation almost obvious. The "tomato" became called *love apple*—in German *Paradeis*, "Paradise."

It is a question of theoretical significance whether or not the *apple* is symbolic of the breast of the mother; for, if so, the eating of the apple is suggestive of sucking. Freud asserted that "fruit stands for the breasts, not for the child."[46] We propose, on the other hand, that in the absolute "dependent" situation the breast and the child were perceived as a perfect unity, and thus that the apple is symbolic of just this dependency: as the apple fruit hangs from the tree and is still a part of it, so the child hangs from the breast of the mother. Such expressions as "fruit of the womb" or "fruitful" are too general to exclude the equation of "fruit" and "child." The Greek *karpos*, "fruit," properly means the "plucked one," as something cut off from the tree. *Omphalo-karpos* means "bearing fruit like a navel." The Latin *pōmum, -i*, "apple," from a former *po-ēmum*, carries the same implication. Thus these words may be interpreted on the oral level as referring to the separation of the child from the breast; they may be interpreted on the genital level as "enjoyment." The Hebrew language uses also another term for "fruit": *zimrāh;* it denotes the choice fruit but this noun may also mean a "musical piece," "the playing of an instrument"; the pertinent verb *zāmar* means, on the one hand, "to trim, prune," and, on the other hand, "to touch with the fingers the strings of the musical instrument, to play." We suppose that in this case genital fantasies became reinterpreted in regressive oral terms. The Garden of Eden's delight was "full of melody."

We quote first a clinical example in order to illustrate the primary nursing situation.

Marguerite Sechehaye, who introduced the symbolic relations in psychotherapy, described the case of her patient Renée, a schizophrenic girl, nineteen, who suffered oral frustrations in her early childhood.

> On my observation that she need only eat the beautiful apples I gave her, she stopped me abruptly and pointing to my bosom, said, "Renée doesn't want the apples of grown-ups, she want real apples, mama's apples." For me this was a shaft of light. I perceived the deep symbolism of the apples and the course I must adopt to relieve the patient. I at once gave her a piece of apple (no more apples in quantity) saying "It's time to drink the good milk from mama's apples; mama is going to give it herself to her little Renée." And Renée, her head resting on my shoulder, ate her piece of apple with all the concentration and contentment of a nursing baby.[47]

The prohibited fruit being the fruit of the Tree of Knowledge necessarily implies that the eating of this fruit represents "oral knowledge," the primordial way of acquisition by internalizing the object. We follow in our interpretation the same line which we have previously drawn from the verbal expressions concerning "knowledge." The verbal instances prove that knowledge was primarily genital knowledge. It is one of the ineradicable misunderstandings, though one with an honorable history, which maintains that the Biblical words "Adam knew Eve his wife; and she conceived" (Gen. 4:1) should be understood as a euphemism.* The Hebrew *yādha,* "to know," is *not* a euphemism but says exactly that which is meant. The epistemological act of

* William Graham Cole: *Sex in Christianity and Psychoanalysis* (New York: Oxford University Press, 1955). "It is a popular distortion to interpret the original sin of Adam and Eve in the Garden of Eden as the sexual act, but this represents a complete misunderstanding of the myth" (p. 11). See also his *Sex and Love in the Bible* (New York: Association Press, 1959).

knowing is inseparable from the biological act in early thinking. The Vulgate translates the Hebrew intensive as "Adam
vero cognovit uxorem suam Hevam," which means "Adam
knew very much or thoroughly his wife Eve." To interpret
"knowledge" otherwise runs against the testimony of the
Hebrew and all Indo-European languages. The fruit which
brought sin, evil, and disobedience to man was prohibited; it
was the satisfaction of sexual desire. The reference to the
breast of the mother is the result of regression from the
genital knowledge to the infantile oral internalization by
sucking. There is much evidence available proving that *eating*
may stand on the regressive oral level for the active sadistic
component; *to be eaten,* for the passive, masochistic position
in genital knowledge.

*I quote as illustration of this regression from the
genital level to the oral level a Biblical instance from the Song
of Solomon. He describes the union of the bride and the
bridegroom (Song of Sol. 8). The lying position is suggested
by "His left hand should be under my head, and his right
hand should embrace me" (Song of Sol. 8:3). The bride is
occupied with incestuous fantasies:*

*"O that thou wert as my brother, that sucked the
breasts of my mother! . . . Who is this that cometh up from
the wilderness, leaning upon her beloved? I raised thee up
under the apple tree: there thy mother brought thee forth:
there she brought thee forth that bare thee" (Song of Sol. 8:1,
5). This "under the apple tree" stands for the oral knowledge
as "under the fig tree" stands for genital knowledge. Christ
answered the question of Nathanael "Whence knowest thou
me?" by saying: "Before that Philip called thee, when thou
wast under the fig tree, I saw thee" (John 1: 48).*

In this context we might consider the "Adam's apple,"
pōmum Adami, the general term for the protruding thyroid
cartilage. Why has this male characteristic been called so?
The original Hebrew *tappūach ha ādām* reveals more about
this expression. The Hebrew *tappūach,* "apple," is a derivative
of the primordial root *nāphach,* which means "to blow" and
may refer to all kinds of protrusions. One may surmise that the
protruding thyroid cartilage was considered as an anatomical
indication of a strong masculine voice, and this voice as an
index of potency. The regression from the genital male

position to the pregenital oral one may explain this anatomical term.[48]

Shame and Sin

In the beginning of time man did not know the pangs of guilt and shame, so says the Biblical analysis of eternal human nature. This seems to be, once more, the negative projection of the positive truth that guilt and shame were experienced beside death and work as the great afflictions of human destiny. Because they were considered as being so painful, they were supposed not to exist in the ideal state of life.

The Biblical account of the phenomenon of shame is given by these words: "And the eyes of them both were opened, and they knew that they were naked; and they sewed fig leaves together, and made themselves aprons" (Gen. 3:7). Shame is specifically referred to as the exposure of the genital organs. The Biblical Hebrew term *ervāh* means both "shame" and "nakedness." "Shameless" and "nude" are also covered by the same word, *gālāh*, which also referred to both "captive" and "stripped"—because captives were stripped of any clothing. The Greek *aidos* means "the sense of shame," "modesty," "respect," "reverence for others," "scandal," on the one hand, and "dignity" and "majesty," on the other. The word *aidoion* and its plural *aidoia* denote "privy parts, both of men and women." The Latin *pudor*, "shame," is by the same token related to the word *pudenda*. The same relationship exists between the Old English *sceamu*, "shame" and "nakedness," and the German *Scham*, also covering both meanings. These linguistic instances permit little doubt as to the original situation implied in "shame."

Blushing might be a bodily manifestation of "shame," for both are often mentioned together, as in "I am ashamed and blush . . ." (Ezra 9:6). Because blushing is an involuntary reaction one must suppose that shame overcomes the individual independently of his will. Because the autonomous nervous system is responsive to fantasies, blushing and shame may result not from a real situation but from an imaginary one. Blushing occurs (especially during the stage of puberty) if one feels observed in fantasies or in the factual situation just in the moment one wanted to remain unnoticed, or if someone is hurt just on his "Achilles Heel," the hidden weak spot of his personality. Shame has an object, and this object is the shortcoming, the failure of one's own self. One wishes nothing more than to hide, to cover up this "shame" in the objective sense; yet blushing, the concomitant bodily symptom, betrays publicly that one is conscious of it. The deeply repressed unconscious fantasies implied in shame work through the symptom of blushing in favor of public exposure. Because shame exposes a part of the personality structure we want to hide, repress, and forget, it makes one very conscious about a motive in the whole personality which is not noticed under normal conditions. The English language also uses as a synonym for "shame": *self-consciousness,* thus pointing out that in the state of embarrassment one will reach a higher level of consciousness about one's Self than normally.⁴⁹ Nakedness might be the natural nakedness of innocence. The small child and the primitive man are not ashamed of their body-selves. There is no ground for shame either in the primary state of love and intimacy between man and woman, if they are "one flesh," between the I and Thou. Shame enters this situation by social implication. It supposes an estrangement between man and nature, between mother and child, or between the lover and the beloved. The Biblical account connects "shame" with the estrangement of man and the Lord; therefore shame is associated with the concepts of "sin" and the "Tree of Knowledge." The Lord said to Adam: "Who told thee that thou wast naked? Hast thou eaten of the tree, whereof I commanded thee that thou shouldest not eat?" (Gen. 3:11).* The presence of shame is in this case indicative of the estrangement, of the opposite of love, and therefore reveals at once the transgression of the divine commandment.

The idea of "sin" is just as that of "shame"†: the fruit of the Tree of Knowledge. However, the idea of "sin" refers to the *conscious* transgression of a known commandment. Granted, of course, there might also exist an innocence of

---

* The Hebrew *Adam* derives in the final analysis from the verb *adam,* "to show blood in the face, i.e., to flush or turn rosy"; thus *Adam* properly means "ruddy."

† The word *sin,* the German *Sünde,* developed from the same phonemic pattern as *shame;* this indicates that the meanings of both words are related to one another.

transgression without sin, for we read "they know not what they do." Yet, in the original natural state man cannot act otherwise than in harmony with nature, therefore he is without sin. Nevertheless, as we observed previously, the idea of sin was conceived by our languages primarily as an error or blunder; it was expressed by stumbling, by going astray, or by the fall of man. Thus it was a particular act that could have been avoided. In other words, in having sinned man has transgressed a divine commandment, and, according to Biblical interpretation, he transgressed this commandment willfully; therefore he is held responsible for his transgression. Specifically, sin supposes the choice between right and wrong, and also the freedom of man to choose and to decide by himself the course of life. In this case man is not guided any longer by his natural instincts but he is the master of his own fate, he is free to shape his own life, either to honor or to dishonor his Maker.

"Shame," on the other hand, refers primarily to the uncovering of sex or of the most vulnerable spot of the unchangeable personality before our fellow men. In the state of shame one painfully perceives one's helplessness and defeat in front of the ideal Ego one has formed about oneself or from what others expect from one. In the moment man tasted of the fruit of knowledge and self-consciousness, he progressed on the way to maturation; he abandoned his primary natural state; he was driven out from the paradise of earliest infancy; he was to experience shame. "And they shall be afraid," the prophet says, "pangs and sorrows shall take hold of them; they shall be in pain as a woman that travaileth: they shall be amazed one at another; their faces shall be as flames" (Isa. 13:8).

Thus, because there is no guilt implied in shame, there is no forgiveness of shame: because there is guilt in sin, there is forgiveness of sin; so to be *shame-less* is a fault, and *sin-less* a virtue.

Fertility

The opposite of hard work and slavery is the personal freedom, the implement of all the pleasures, which the Golden Age bestowed upon man. Mention has been made previously of the Latin *fē-lix* ("happy"), which refers to "sucking" and is thus indicative of the primary nursing situation that makes both mother and child happy. The suckling child, however, seems to be rather a picture of helplessness and dependency than one of personal freedom. The question arises, how did the idea of freedom enter this context, inasmuch as the suckling or the fetus suggests rather a parasite relying completely upon the mother?

The freedom of the Golden Age is not the same as the freedom of free choice between right and wrong. This latter freedom of decision implies that man by this very act of self-decision has taken his fate in his own hands. Through the fruits of knowledge man ceased to remain simply the creature of his Maker, he himself wanted to become the maker of his own destiny. He is not any longer a product of nature, he does not follow as animals do the course of life prescribed by nature, he does not enter the world like a guided missile, the course of which is predetermined by those who made it. When man assumed the responsibility for his own choice, his own existence, he, once and for all, left the Golden Age of childhood. He reached the state of maturity. The predicament of this freedom is the consciousness of the own-self, anxiety, shame, guilt, hard work, the knowledge that life will come to an end—all these mean the end of the Golden Age.

The freedom of the primary state of man is different in kind. It is the freedom *of* dependency. It means freedom from the evils of the true personal freedom and all the frustrations of the responsible life. It is the freedom of the suckling and of all creatures which are one with nature. All their desires are met by nature; satisfaction is given with the need itself and not frustrated by shame, not loaded with fear, anxiety, and guilt, not burdened by social demands.

The timeless bliss of this coincidence of personal desires and nature became expressed in the various terms about the "blessings" of fruitfulness and the abounding plenty by which every instinctual need freely can be satisfied. The German term for "pleasure," *Ver-gnügen,* is a derivative of *genug,* "enough"; it supposes this abundance. The underlying implication of this freedom can be shown best by these two aspects: one refers to "suckling" as *fē-cundity,* the other points back beyond the nursing situation to the *pre-gnancy,* from *prae-gnātus,* to the pre-natal unity of mother and child, as *fer-tility,* from the verb *ferrō, ferre,* "to bear." The English *birth,* the German *Ge-burt,* and all the words that refer to the "carrying" of the fetus evoke the picture of the fulfillment of fruitfulness and blessing. In both aspects, as fecundity and as fertility, the blessing of abundance supposes the bliss of procreation.* The fantasy of the abounding prolificness appears in the dynamic aspect necessarily as the highest intensity of the instinctual drive for procreation. It is the age of "eternal youth," there are none impotent; thus the Zend-Avesta characterizes the life in Yma's garden.

In contrast to the negative attitude to pleasure stands the affirmative praise of prolificness and the religious sanctification of procreation. In this positive aspect the abundance of the Golden Age is conceived as fertility and permeated with the unconscious fantasies about the primal scene. Dionysus, the "golden-haired" god, *chruso-komēs,* in whose way honey drips from the trees and milk springs from the fountains, the god of abundance, is also the mythological personification of the libido.[50] The fantasies about the Golden Age received through him, and through all the other mythical personifications of the generative process, their first reinterpretation. This interpretation is mythical, too, but compared with the gold-silver-brass-iron myth it appears as the first biological view of life; it reflects the eternal human reinterpretation of the child-mother relationship during the sexual maturation of the child.

The Dionysiac reinterpretation of "hard work" and "pain" has made it evident that these objects of fear did not exist in Hesiod's Golden Age, yet became a part of the bliss and the blessing of fertility by the universal expansion of the generative process: "labor" and "travail" are not only the feared messengers of slavery but also the wished-for signs of the new life. Similar associations merge in connection with the Gothic term for "birth." The underlying idea is again "to bear," which developed the following meanings: *ga-baurth,* "birth"; *ga-baur,* "tax, gain, profit"; *ga-baurjabē,* "agreeable";

* Sophocles, also, says: "fruit of the earth, fruit of the womb." (*Oedipus King,* line 266.)

and *ga-baurjōthus,* "libido, lust." In this case, "birth" is associated not with any idea of "labor," "travail," or "pain," but with the ecstatic elation of the bacchanalian carousals and with libidinous pleasure.

The implication of "tax, gain, profit" in this complex derives from the identification of "gold" with the interior of man. We refer here as to an illustrative example to the English noun *job,* from which there is a monetary gain. The frequency of the use of this word is high; this alone points to the obsessive repetition of a repressed meaning. The origin of this very common noun is said to be uncertain; however, Middle English *jobbe* meant "lump" and "lump" means "indefinitely shaped mass." The word is still in general use in the nursery language denoting the child's excrements. Other languages use the same idea of the "small" and "big job." In German the noun *Geschäft* covers the same meaning complex; it derives from the verb *schaffen,* "to create"; thus the "job" in German refers primarily to creative activity.

The head has been considered to be the location of the generative power: this notion of the head, the Latin *caput,* became transferred to the prolificness of the *capital.* The same fantasy is present in the Greek *phor-os,* "tax," once more referring to the fertility of "bearing," which is inherent in the gold of the capital. The belief in the righteous "fertility of the capital" is one of the living residues of the over-all fecundity of the Golden Age.[51] A similar complex idea can be observed by analyzing the implications of the English verb *to win,* the German verb *ge-winnen* and the noun *Ge-winn,* "gain," which may be either the result of hard work or the symbolic fruit of the capital. These terms derive from an age-old cluster of words which reaches back to the prehistory of our language. This word complex was prolific and its bringing forth various meanings is a telling indication that it was charged and covered up a repressed intensive desire. This meaning, still repressed, is the libidinous desire, the Dionysiac drive for fertilization and exultation in the sexual union.

Freedom and Liberty

It was out of the unconscious libidinous fantasies that the idea of Golden Age freedom came—freedom from shame, guilt, anxiety, and frustrations of maturation—the freedom to which the subconscious of man wants to return.

The infantile fantasies—desires for the excessive, bacchanalian way of life and love—though rejected and thus repressed in the adult mind are a psychic reality that can still be found preserved in our languages. The original core of these fantasies is present in the Latin *ven-us,* which originally meant "sex appeal," all the qualities which excite love. The derivative *venereus* means things "belonging to sexual love, venereous, venereal, wanton, lascivious," or all the qualities personified in the goddess who stands for the Greek Aphrodite. The akin Sanskrit *van-as* denotes "desire" with the implication of love. The Germanic languages repressed this original meaning but developed instead the following ones: "desire" (the German *Wunsch*), with little doubt as to what kind of desire this originally was; "libido" (Old English *wyn-lust*), implying the original meaning through a compound form; "to live, to dwell" (the German *wohnen*), much like the Latin *habitō, -āre,* only with the added implication of *co-habitāre,* which is obviously difficult to avoid; "usual, common" (the German *ge-wöhn-lich*), this connection being about the same as between the German verb *pflegen,* "to use to," and *pflügen,* "to plow"; "delusion" and "elation" (the German *Wahn*), with the implication that this ecstatic state of mind derives from the libidinous desire; "ecstasis, exultation" (the Old English *wyn-dream*); "joy" (the Old English *wyn, wyn-sumnes*); "gain" and "to win" (the German *Ge-winn* and *gi-winnen*); "to labor, toil with grief and pain" (the Old English *winnan*); "pleasant" (the Old English *win-sum*); "lust, voluptas" (the German *Wonne*); "the month of May as spring month" (the Old German *Wonne-monat*); "land of joy" (the Old English *wyn-land*), much like *Eldorado,* the gilded land; "pasture" (the Gothic *win-ja*); and so on. It seems of little value to find out some transitory meaning for one of these words or another because all these words so apparently hang together. They derive from one deeply repressed complex in which *libido, voluptas, ecstasis, delusion, pain,* and *gain* cheerfully exist together. The name *Wyn-land* is the geographical term for this Dionysiac Golden Age for which the month of May is symbolic: "love whose month was ever May," Shakespeare said. The over-all subjective feeling of this kind is best represented in the world by the fertility of the pasture. The German *Wonne-monat,* a month for lust, joy, is interchangeable with *Weide-monat,* "pasture month"— joy and pasture being used as synonyms. America was called *Wyn-land* by the first Germanic discoverers.

Venus-Aphrodite appears within this cluster of meanings as the feminine complement of the god Dionysus. It seems significant that in the Dionysus myth this god, the personification of libido, had been brought up as a girl. After having been reborn from the bosom of his father, from "the thighs of Zeus," he became entrusted to Hermes; consequently he inherited some elements of the Hermes mythologies. Hermes and Aphrodite are thought to be in an inseparable unity in the hermaphrodites, each of whom is sexually both man and woman. In early childhood, also, before the age of sex recognition, both the masculine and the feminine characteristics are seen in an undifferentiated state that implies a permanent heterosexual unity (*con-iugium,* "a joint together"), as in the yoke of marriage. The permanent wedding festival as ceaseless honeymooning is an essential component of the fantasies of the Golden Age.

The attribute of Dionysus is *eleutherios,* referring to the place Eleutherai on the border of Boeotia, just as Athens is to Athena. He may have inherited this attribute from his father, who was called also *Zeus Eleutherios.*[52] There is, however, more implied in this name than a simple geographical reference. The feminine complement and counterpart of Dionysus is called *Eleuthera.* Her name is a derivative of the verb *eleusomai,* a future with the meaning "I shall come." This attribute shows that Dionysus is the god of fertility and of futurity that is implied in the seeds, that he is the eternal "coming one," *ad-venturus,* that he is coming, traveling, to the wedding festival with Ariadne, that he is the mythical personification of the universal process of *be-coming.* However, although the attribute *eleutheros* belongs to the god of fertility and growth, it is found in Greek also with the common meaning of "free," used especially in the sociopolitical sense as the opposite of "slave." The coherence of these two meanings—"the future coming one" and "free"—hardly can be found on the reality level, but certainly the fantasies that created in Dionysus a living symbol do explain this verbal identity of the god of fertility and the idea of freedom.*

Restricting our observation to sociopolitical realms, we can observe that it was a custom of the Greek and Latin festivals in honor of Kronos-Saturnus, ruler of the Golden Age, that the slaves were set free for December 15–17, the days of the Saturnalia. These were the feasts of freedom; they were also called *feriae servorum*, "holidays of the slaves"; real *sacrae feriae*, "holy days." The schools remained closed on these days; one could go out in the most informal dress; people invited one another for common carousals; it was not a shame to be found drunken during these days, but the special performance during this general relaxing and rejoicing was the custom of the master eating with the slaves, who on that occasion were also served first, or even served by the master. Of course, there was a saying *non semper Sāturnalia erunt,* "there are not always Saturnalia." The liberating of the slaves for two days in honor of the Golden Age was a significant ritual of these festivals. It was also customary that people gave one another gifts in the form of clay puppets and of *cerei;* these are candles made of wax, of the product of the honeycomb. Both presents are characteristic of the inside fantasies involved. The orgiastic Bacchanalia, festivals of Dionysus-Bacchus, were perhaps of Thracian origin, but being once introduced and accepted by the Greek people, they reinterpreted the old festivals of Kronos and the Golden Age. They introduced the orgiastic libidinous element of the old fantasies about the "freedom from fear and want."

In the Latin tradition Dionysus-Bacchus has been equated with an Italic deity called *Liber,* who was also the god of generation and growth, of wine and ecstasies, of puppets and masks. He was the Latin alter ego of the Thracian-Greek Dionysus. As Dionysus Eleutherios became complete through Eleuthera, so, in the same way, was Liber inseparable from *Libera,* goddess of birth and fertility. Linguistically, *lib-er, -era, -erum* (from the Old Latin *loeb-er*) is

---

* The same holds true for another name deriving from *eleusomai,* "I shall come": Eleusis, the name of the old city of Attica and sacred to Demeter and Kore-Persephone. As a noun, *eleusis* is used in the sense of "a coming, arrival"—as in the New Testament Greek for the coming of Christ in the Advent.

the proper Latin phonemic correspondent form of the Greek
(*e*)-*leuth-er*(-*os*). The Latin word, just as the Greek, carries
besides the names of the deities also the meaning "free"; the
orgiastic Bacchanalia were called on Latin soil *liberalia,* thus
leaving little doubt about the original implications of *liber-tas*
(Old Latin *loeber-tas*), "liberty."* *Lib-er, -era, -erum* developed also the meaning of "birth" and of "child," *liberi,* used
only in the plural, in the grammatical category of prolificness.
These two lexical meanings, "free" and "child," have been
overbridged in linguistic literature by sociopolitical considerations; however, the whole sphere of their associations, their
relationship with the futurity of the "coming" god, with the
puppets and masks displayed in the vineyards at the Liberalia
point to a deeper coherence. The notions of "free" and "child"
have grown together in the veneration of the deities of
procreation and fertility. This complex idea of *lib-er* (the Old
Latin *lub-er, loeber*) has been acted out through the liberalian
festivals. This word became fused in the meaning—even if an
old kinship did not exist—with the words *lib-et est,* formerly
lub-et est, "it is permitted," from the verb *lib-eō, -ēre,* "to
have lust, desire"; its derivative is the word *lib-idō,* from *lub-
idō.* The change of meanings from "I desire" (*lib-eō*) to "it is
permitted" (*lib-et est*) supposes again an imaginary situation
in which the libidinous forces were set free and permitted.
"Freedom" in this original sense meant the freedom from
frustrations and social prohibitions.

The original libidinous meaning of this old complex
became strongly repressed in the Germanic languages, and
consequently it developed instead a luxuriant variety of substitute meanings. All these new words have seemingly nothing in
common with one another except their phonemic relationship.
And their common phonemic form points to a common

* On the Liberalia see Georg Wissowa, "Religion und Kultus
der Römer," in Iwan Müller, *Handbuch der Klass: Altertumswissenschaft* (München: Beck, 1912), 5:138 ff. He comes close to our position in stating: "Die Göttin Libertas vertritt nicht . . . *Libertas
publica populi Romani,* sondern die persönliche Freiheit des einzelnen
Bürgers." ("The goddess Libertas represents not the *Libertas publica
populi Romani,* but the personal liberty of the private citizen," p. 138).
See also W. Warde Fowler, *The Roman Festivals of the Period of the
Republic* (London: The Macmillan & Co., Ltd, 1899).

214

meaning. This meaning, however, has been repressed and many related forms mushroomed in its place. The following meanings were expressed by words belonging to this cluster: "love, beloved" (the Gothic *liuf, -s,* the German *Liebe,* the English *love*); "permission" (the English *leave,* the German *Ur-laub,* the English *fur-lough*); "to praise" (the German *loben, Lob*); "to vow" (the German *Ge-lüb-de, ver-lob-en,* "engage"); "to believe" (the English *be-lief,* the German *Glauben,* from *ga-laub-an*). All these lexical meanings are found together in the mysteries of Dionysus, in the Bacchanalia and the Liberalia.

It may be doubted by rational considerations that the fantasies of "love" and "freedom" hang together as suggested by the pertinent Greek and Latin terms. Yet we shall demonstrate in the following that the same coherence of "love" and "freedom" once existed in the Germanic languages, too. The Germanic deity *Yng,* or *Yngvi,* is just another mythical personification of the libido, a Germanic variant of Dionysus. This deity was first called *Yngvi-Frey,* "Yng-Lord"; then by omitting the numinous name, he was simply called *Frey,* "Lord." His sister was *Freya,* the goddess of love and fertility. These deities were venerated by the Germanic people in the form of symbols and rituals which were very much like those displayed at the Liberalia and Bacchanalia, by phallophoric processions or ecstatic obscenities (*aischologia*), excesses described for the Greeks by Euripides in the *Bacchae* (about 407–406 B.C.). Frey is the child of Nerthus, the Mother Earth, and of her brother Njordr, who is thus a kind of uncle-father, provider of all good things, just an "uncle" as illegitimate children of promiscuous mothers sometimes call their father. An Icelandic idiom says: "as rich as Njordr." Nerthus and Njordr were supreme in the Germanic Golden Age fantasies, just as was Kronos-Saturnus in the classic traditions. Their procession across the land elicited joy and exuberant happiness as it has been already described by Tacitus in *Germania.* Frey, being the child of this brother-sister marriage, inherited the fantasies about the Golden Age, just as Dionysus inherited those of Apollo and Hermes in the Greek tradition. Frey, however, lives also with his mother in a permanent honeymoon, keeping her fertile—just as Dionysus did with his.

Euripides commented, "Hath he mirth in the joy of the Earth, and he loveth constantly her, who brings increase, the Feeder of children, Peace . . . only on them that spurn joy may his anger burn."[53] Frey "bestowed peace and joy upon man," as Adam of Bremen said, just as did Dionysus. During this "Peace of Frey," the Icelandic source says, "No man injured another, even if that were his brother's or father's slayer. No thief, no robber was known and a gold ring lay long untouched on Jalang's sheath."[54]

A much feared animal seems to be *in-nocent,* "harmless," in the fantasies about the Germanic Golden Age: it is the boar. It is the "golden boar" which pulls the chariot on which Frey "is coming" (*ad-venturus*); it is the "Battle-Boar" —shining with bristles of gold—on which Frey is even riding.

Frey is fair and beautiful, as is his sister-wife Freya. Saxo Grammaticus said that the cult of Frey was utterly repellent for the "effeminate gestures," "the play of mimes," and the "ringing of bells," especially for the "unseemly songs" that were "sung during the human blood sacrifices." All this recalls the "girl-faced stranger" in the play of Euripides, the golden-haired god, "a fair shape for a woman's eye," "long curls," "and a white skin," "with white red of cheeks that never face the light!" Frey lives with his sister Freya in incest, as his father did with his mother. We are informed of at least the Germanic father-god that reprimanded Freya reproachfully because the giants had found her in the bed of her brother. The discarding of sex taboos has been pointed out by many stories in the Germanic tradition as characteristic of these most popular deities who "bestowed peace and joy upon man." The father-god reprimands Freya (in the *Edda*) by saying: "Keep silent, Freya, I know you well, you are not free of faults. You have made happy all the Aesir (giants) in turn." That a goddess is prone to being the object of much gossip was obvious when the father-god continued, "In the night like a she-goat you leap after the goats." The goddess of love seems to be promiscuous. She appears also as a newcomer among the Germanic Olympians. She crowded out and replaced the older goddess of fertility, Frija, who was originally equated with the Latin Venus. It is now merely an academic question to try discerning Frija from Freya. In the living myth they are but one. Freya appears as the new

216

Germanic Venus, even as "Venus vulgivaga." *Veneris diem* and the French *vendredi* became interpreted in the Germanic languages as *Fri-day,* the German *Frei-tag,* the original term being *Aphroditēs hēmera* in Greek.

Just as from the Grecian Eleutherios and the Roman Liber myths came the idea and word *libertas,* "liberty," from the Germanic mythifications of the libido came the idea of *free-dom,* the German *Frei-heit.* The interrelationship of *Friday* and *free-dom* is conspicuous. The whole sphere of associations with which the idea of "freedom" was originally connected is indicated by the following phonemically related words: "to love" (the Gothic *frī-jon;* the English *friend;* the German *Freund,* from *frī-jonds,* "loving"); "love" (Old English *frigu*); "beloved, dear" (Old English *freo-bear,* "dearchild"); "lord" (German *Fron-leichnam,* "Corpus Christi"); "woman" (German *Frau*); "to marry" (the German *frei-en,* later "to engage"); "joy" (the German *Freude*); "peace" (the German *Friede*); "joyful, merry" (the German *froh* and *fröhlich*). Other meanings found in connection with this verbal form are most distinct in Sanskrit, as "to spring up," "to move to and fro," "to hover." These meanings make the original implication of the whole word cluster even more concrete.

These associations corroborate the former observations made in connection with the parallel Greek and Latin words. The idea of freedom has not developed primarily as a sociopolitical concept, but emerged out of unconscious libidinous fantasies. "Freedom" has the same psychological etiology as "liberty," meaning freedom from shame, guilt, anxiety, and frustrations originating from the prohibitive Superego.

Latent unconscious fantasies shaped verbal forms in prehistoric times but sometimes became personified in the living myth of historical events. The French Revolution created the popular personification of "Marianne" as the national ideal of liberty, the living political myth, indeed. This image of a national heroine was not an individual arbitrary creation but the product of common fantasies. It absorbed many traits of older existing national figures such as Jeanne d'Arc—especially some characteristics of *douce France,* "fair France," the nourishing-mother image. The popular figure of Marianne reinterpreted these older ideas and transformed them according to the desires of the French Revolution, just as the new Freya transformed the older Frija image, or as the Bacchanalia revived with a new meaning the old Saturnalia. "Marianne" as the symbol of the republican French government carries a "slightly lewd connotation."[55] Her name was often given to women of easy virtue; she demonstrated just that revolutionary spirit in opposition to the father-state authority. She bestowed joy and happiness generously upon all her lovers.

The national figures "Liberty" and "Uncle Sam" are the creations of historical times; yet they, like brother and sister, are inseparable from one another, both being descendants of an imaginary Golden Age. Uncle Sam is the mythicizing of the two letters of the abbreviation U.S.—the result of a very expressive fantasy projected upon these two letters. He is surely not a variant of the father figure of John Bull representing the English sentiment. He is not really a father, but an "uncle"[56] who is said to be personified as a tall spare man with chin whiskers; dressed in a red, white, and blue costume of swallowtail coat, striped trousers, and tall hat. His outstanding qualities are that he is rich, very rich indeed, and good to his children. Soldiers liked to sing at Bataan: "We are the bastards of Uncle Sam." Liberty and Uncle Sam appear as the modern variants of the age-old mythical personifications and fantasies represented in the Greek culture by Dionysus Eleutherios and Kore-Eleuthera and acted out in the Bacchanalia; in the Latin culture by Liber and Libera-Proserpina and acted out in the Liberalia; in the Germanic realm by Frey and Freya and ritualized in the excesses of their festivals. These unchanging infantile fantasies became rejected and repressed by the adult mind in the course of history; language, however, kept the imprints of their psychic reality, of unconscious fantasies as rich and elusive as the images of dreams, yet so factual, old, and meaningful that they can be deciphered just as the Sumerian stone inscriptions of the third millennium before Christ.

Finally I present a clinical illustration of the unconscious fantasies referring to the Golden Age. I quote extensively from the excellent study, "The Curative Function of Symbols in a Case of Traumatic Neurosis with Psychotic Reactions," by Marguerite A. Sechehaye. The paper, and thus the patient's verbal productions, were originally in French.[57]

The Case: *Demeter, sixty years, is a highly intelligent woman. She read even the outstanding work of her analyst on "Symbolic Representations." Thus she knows a lot about symbolism but does not understand her own symbolic representations. She fell sick twenty years ago. She described the subjective experience of her sickness saying this: "When I am sick, I am unable to do anything, any work whatever, to make any appointment and least of all to speak to people. I avoid everybody. I lose all contact with both people and things. Inside and mentally I know that I live, but I feel that I do not live, that I am like dead, similar to the feeling just before losing consciousness when being anesthetized. I suffer the entire time for not feeling alive. I must stay in bed tortured by this impotency but not really tired. And I am hostile."*

During the twenty years of her sickness she consulted a number of psychiatrists and psychoanalysts but psychotherapy did not work. She spontaneously discovered the cure of her depressive sickness:

> I began to feel I was dying inside when I had just re-
> covered from pneumonia. But I believe I did not realize
> this feeling of being dead, or half alive, until it was over,
> thanks to the library. The public library is the only thing
> which for a period of time has cured me. . . . This ex-
> perience has been repeated eight times in a period of nine
> years. Now I am absolutely sure it is only the library which
> cures me. Before the war, I consulted a number of doctors
> who treated me—psychiatrists included—but nothing suc-
> ceeded in improving my condition in the least. No one
> ever showed the slightest interest in the library and yet,
> I repeat, this was the one and only thing that helped.

The patient thus realized that the "Library" is her curative symbol. She says: "I also have a symbol, but no one wants to understand it." So she turned to Marguerite A. Sechehaye, the excellent Swiss analyst and author of the book Symbolic Representations.

Diagnosis: *The analyst diagnosed this borderline case as a "psychotic reaction to a traumatic neurosis." The onset of the sickness followed, indeed, a traumatic experience. In the wording of the patient, the trauma struck her twenty years ago: "I fell sick at the age of forty, consequent to the abduction of my daughter, an event that was fully approved by my country's Court of Justice, which is entirely under the influence of the Church."*

Treatment: *The analyst first of all verified the fact that this traumatic event had taken place and the patient did not even exaggerate the shock she suffered thereby. She was able to show to the patient and work through with her that her depressive feelings were rooted in the image of a prohibitive, vindictive and castrative Superego, i.e., her mother. Her mother was indeed perceived in the image of a bad, revengeful mother. Demeter perceived her daughter as an inseparable part of her own-self; the legal abduction of her daughter was perceived by unconscious fantasies as a factual castration. Being deeply hurt by and disappointed in the "bad mother," she found in the search for the "good mother" the symbol of the Library. The Library became her home. In the process of analysis it succeeded to shift the image of the good mother from the Library to the female analyst; through this transference the morbid fixation to the Library was resolved and the patient became again able to work and to establish normal human relationships. This is just the outline of the treatment in a very condensed and necessarily oversimplified description. The treatment consisted of 144 interviews.*

Interpretation: *The intelligent patient had a grasp of the fact that the "Library" affected her illness in a symbolic way. She realized that the "Library" was somehow related to her complexes but she never went beyond this cognizance. Her analyst says: "She never realized their exact nature and contented herself with re-experiencing them intensely in the manner of a presymbolic magical participation. This sufficed to cure her." We would say that this magic effect represents the first degree of symbolic understanding of the "Library."*

The successful cure by the analyst's interpretation of the "Library" symbol goes far beyond the original understanding of the patient.

The patient's understanding remained strictly on a presymbolic magical level. Not for one moment did the patient realize "the meaning of the castration represented by the symbolic figures in the surrender of the document. . . ."

Through "transference the patient learned to substitute the mother-analyst for the library-hospital." In place of the magic treatment of the library, the treatment by analysis made the pathologic emotions conscious and effected the lasting cure. We would call this elucidation of the symbol "Library" a second degree of understanding.

The linguistic interpretation, we suppose, opens up the way for a third degree of understanding. The report of the analyst is material we shall examine.

Liberty: This seems to be the focal symbol of the patient's fantasies. This symbol appears to her in the original meaning of Libera, the good mother who bestowed fertility and freedom upon man. She grasped this living symbol in her revolt against her tyrannical mother, who took away her freedom. "Everything was prohibited with her. . . . It was prohibited to go out of the park. . . . I was not allowed to study. . . . It was also forbidden to swim or to ride. . . . She isolated us from everybody and everything. . . . I hated her and had but one wish: to run away from her." So she did but in a most significant way. At twenty-four she broke away from her family.

Contrary to all her family stood for . . . she became an ardent member of the liberation party. She married an outstanding liberation-fighter. Her mother was horrified, she considered this marriage a disgrace to the whole family. Her husband was a man of strong conviction. He was placed in a high post by the revolutionary government. He was imprisoned by the government of the opposing party which again had come into power. To protest he went on a hunger strike and died after seventy-five days, a martyr to his political conviction.

He surely died for the idea. The patient identified herself with her husband; both, thereby, represent Liber and Libera in a modern setting.

There seemed to have emerged but one point of difference: religion. The father wanted their only child (their daughter, who was four at the father's death) to be brought up in the tradition and Church of his own religion. The patient was opposed to it. She identified the Church with her mother. *The Church, so she felt, was the enemy of liberty.* "*My mother made a mystery of everything and particularly of sexual matters. The anguish I felt toward her and toward the Church was the same; she forbade me both all action, all knowledge—leaving me in anguish and darkness.*"

In revenge against her mother she harbored the great desire: to bring up her only daughter in the worship of liberty, and instill in her her own deepest conviction. After the death of her hero-husband she undertook another revolutionary step: she conceived from an indifferent man an illegitimate child. "*I purposely wanted the child to be illegitimate,*" *so she told her analyst,* "*in order to protest against the middle-class and religious conventions opposed to love and life.*" *Her liberty, just as the Roman Liberalia, was aimed at the liberty of instincts, the glorification of love and life. Her Golden Age was the Age of Liberty, of free love and marriage.*

Light and Darkness: *The contrast between liberty and the tyrannical mother appears in another form in the polarity of "Light" and "Darkness." The Age of Liberty was also the Age of Enlightenment defeating the "dark ages" of the past.* "*To give light to them that sit in darkness*" (*Luke 1:79*) *is a primary religious experience, and the patient found in it the true meaning of life. The mother and the Church, and later the Court of Justice threatened her as powers of Darkness, while knowledge, liberty, became equated with Light.* "*My mother,*" *said the patient,* "*spread around her the fear of the unknown, she was always mysterious, always silent and icy.*" *In the fight for liberty against Darkness, Demeter lost her daughter.* "*The child was my power, and the document, by depriving me of my child, deprived me of all my power . . . and this is why I could no longer work.*"

It is significant for this intelligent patient versed in symbolism that she wanted to be called Demeter (*this from* Gē-mētēr), "*Earth Mother,*" *the image of the fertile, nourishing mother. Her daughter is in Greek* Persephonē, *in Latin* Proserpina, *which is another name for* Libera. *Persephone-Proserpina has been abducted by Pluto and the dark powers of the nether world. She originally belonged, just as her brother Liber-Bacchus did, to the world of Light. In Greek the names* Eleutherios *and* Eleuthera *properly denoted the divinities who "are coming" from the bright sky to the Earth*

Mother. The patient felt in the same way. *"Ignorance is the unknown and it is the unknown that has destroyed my daughter. Had I had more extensive knowledge, they would not have been able to take my daughter away for I would have defended myself."*

Library: *Why did the library become her healing symbol?* She considered the library in opposition of the Church (also in opposition to her mother, who read very little) as a place of liberty and enlightenment. The library is a place of knowledge, and represents in her fantasies the Tree of Knowledge. It seems to be significant that she attributed the curative influence only to the public library. *"But if a library is to be of any use to me, it must necessarily be a large, clean, well-ordered, and easily accessible room. If I have to make an effort to reach it, it is not the same thing and does not operate."* The public library represents the light shining in darkness. The "public library" is the image of the good mother, Libera, open to all, full of light: *"There you find long, undivided tables with a number to each place: it's equality and justice to all people, no differences are made between the readers. . . . And then the library is light and clean. The Church, which prevents instruction, is dark. And the Court of Justice must necessarily be dark too. My mother never taught us the truth."*

The patient found her Golden Age realized in the public library. This library which is open to all is at the same time separated from the reality just as Yma's garden or the Island of the Blest. *"The library, like a hospital, can cure people. It has the same vast dimension and silence; one feels protected there from the external, hostile world, where one receives mortal shocks."* This seclusion from the dangers of reality is a particular characteristic of the Golden Age.

The analysis reached a deeper level when the patient came to the association between "library" and "child"—the book as a substitute for her lost daughter. The Dionysiac fantasies grew out distinctly when she said: *"The library is full of life, whereas my mother's house was full of deadly silence. My mother was opposed to life, to children, to love, as is also the Church."* The identification of the idea of "library" with life, love, and children definitely belongs to Libera and is quite incongruent with the general concepts of libraries.

The fact that "library" became the substitutive symbol of the "good mother" is not very explanatory in itself without the grasp of the interconnecting link: the library is, so to say, the temple of liberty, and liberty is the healing-mother symbol. The patient herself came to this point by saying: "The cupola on the public library in my town always reminds me of a breast; it has the same shape, this breast which nourishes the child and gives strength to it." As we mentioned previously the names Liber *and* Libera, *from* lib-er, -era, -erum, *are therefore inseparable from the plural* liberi, *which means "children." So the library itself appears here in the picture of the Alma Mater, "Nourishing Mother," of milk and honey, and the children are in her protection. Thus the library, the books in the library, return to her some of the feelings she had for her daughter. "Books! (the French* livres) *How my daughter loved them! Later on, it's she who would have instructed me.* It's my daughter who is in the library; there I rediscover my spiritual child *whom no one can steal away from me."*

We come to the nodal point of her fantasies and must ask: Why did the library become as a mother symbol the representation of liberty? In Latin there is not only an apparent coincidence, as observed previously, between the pertinent words Liber *and* Libera, *the names of the deities;* liber, -a, -um, *meaning "free"; and* liberi, *meaning "children"; but also between them and the word* libr-um, -i, *the word which means "book" and from which the word* library *derives. The origin of the word* librum *is not very clear and the coherence of the idea of "book" with the idea of "child" is not simply a problem of the Latin language. The interdependence of the meaning of* liberi, *"children," and* libri, *"books," is difficult to disregard, e.g., in view of the fact that the early printings were* in-cunabula, *a compound form of* in *and* cunabula, *"cradle." It originally denoted the "swaddling cloth" in the cradle. This refers rather to the "child" than to the "book." It makes no difference whether the patient in question spoke French (*bibliothèque, *"library") or another language, because the whole field of literacy is permeated with genital fantasies. The Dionysiac freedom in the gratification of instincts has been implied in many manifestations of writing and reading, which were in the view of the small child* *a privilege of the adults just as making fire was the prerogative of Father Zeus. Libidinous fantasies have made writing and reading indeed symbolic for lust, love, and life, for fertility, procreation, and children.*

The books were formerly scrolls, volums, *from the verb* volvō, -ere, *"to roll," but the scrolls were sometimes called* penis. *Their knob was called in Greek* omphalos, *in Latin* umbilicus; *the book was in Greek* sōma *or* somatikon, *in Latin* corpus, *both meaning "the human body." Later the manuscripts were called* caudex *or* cōdex, *sometimes* codicillum, *of which all are terms referring to* cauda, *"tail, penis." The homiletics, preachers and writers of theological sermons, used the nominal form of the verb* homileō, *which is the classic term for having "sexual intercourse." The fertility magic of plowing and procreating is still implied in many of our present fantasies concerning writing and reading; their most transparent representation is the noun* pencil, *from* penicillum, *meaning "little penis."*[58] *The English verb* to read *has its equivalent in the German verb* raten, *"to guess, to decipher" the magic signs.* Spelling *still recalls the magic* spell. *Reading meant for the patient Demeter this deciphering of the dark symbols of her unconscious fantasies.*

When she recovered through the therapy with her able analyst, she returned to her work. "Happily," says the analyst, "Demeter is more active than she was before becoming sick and also more interested in her apostleship, i.e., her work for freedom and the rescue of oppressed children and adults." Thus she returned from the library *to the service of* liberty, *and the* libri, *the books, were once more replaced by the* liberi, *the children.*

CONCLUSION

I started this investigation with the statement that we are not prepared to interpret our languages as we interpret our dreams. We seem to stand blindfolded in front of the abundance of material that is laid before us in the volumes of vocabularies and dictionaries. The difference between language and dream is obvious: the "language of the dream" seems to speak a more individual idiom, and its archaic underground, the "recurrent" elements, are rather seldom perceptible. The opposite holds true for language. The individual accent appears as a rather superficial element that does not affect language's fundamental structure. Recurrent fantasies and their verbal expression are the rule; individual variants, the exception.

One may compare the development of language with the flow of a river. We know well, as described in vocabularies, the surface of this stream. We see the usage and the debris of everyday life floating on this surface. No doubt there is also a lot of sand and refuse carried along, but this undesired material soon submerges—no eye will see it and after a while it will be sedimented. We take it for granted that language flows like a stream from distant sources of the early Stone Age, connecting our mind with the mind of our ancestors. Yet, it is a strange fact that people mostly proud of their ancestry are rather ashamed of the language community of their heritage. We do everything possible to forget the messages that come to us from the past. True, our forefathers surely expressed themselves in a way other than our way; they spoke perhaps as food gatherers, cave dwellers, cannibals, or basketmakers are supposed to speak. Nevertheless, I wanted to study not those things floating on the surface of our language, but rather the sedimentation of past centuries. Perhaps one could call this kind of study linguistic paleontology because it deals with the messages of the past as they become ossified and preserved in our present-day verbal material, but I preferred the term *psychoanalytical interpretation.*

What is the use of such a study? We are always confronted with the here and now of a unique actual situation. How can we profit from studying messages of a long-forgotten past? Perhaps one will not see any connection between the general practice in using languages and our study of verbal expressions. In answer to these questions I may say this: All symptoms are fragments and debris; they become meaningful if we perceive their relationship to the whole that has been lost. *The peculiarity of the singular event stands out only if one holds it against the background of the general.* The unconscious fantasies incorporated in verbal forms always display a unique individual accent while they speak a common language. We are remiss if we attribute to individual speech that which belongs to the forgotten common language or that which is generally human.

Ever since man lived on earth there was cooperation and hostility, love and hatred, struggle for life and fear of destruction; there was anxiety and guilt, also longing for peace and security, seeking pleasure and avoiding pain. The eternal desire for a life that is truly human—one that will set free the creative capacities of man—is reflected in recurrent dreams and in the verbal expressions that became the rock bottom upon which the stream of our language flows. In the reality of historical time, no verbal utterance can be said twice in exactly the same way, in exactly the same situation, just as one cannot step twice in the same river, as Heraclitus said. One can never grasp the same speech a second time either. Yet rivers flow since time immemorial and despite all individual changes languages remain ever the same.

ADDENDA

DICTIONARY OF SOME
PERTINENT CONCEPTS

This book was intended to be an exploratory pilot study, therefore many questions remain unanswered. But even so, the reader will reserve his judgment on many statements for good reasons until he has gained a general orientation in the field. This appendix should facilitate independent judgment and stimulate personal insight into everyday problems that have no easy answer. It presents in alphabetical order a few basic concepts that served as guideposts and directed the course of my thinking through the labyrinth of unconscious fantasies as they are reflected in verbal expressions.

Ancestor

The position of the father was defined in the family by his function as priest. The family was a community of worship and sacrifice, a community held together by the "familiar spirit," the spirit of the ancestors. Laius and Oedipus are Labdacids, descendants of the ancestor Labdacus. The family name still unites the family by the name of the ancestor.

We are looking primarily into the linguistic manifestations because the testimony of our languages is older than their written records. In Latin, the ascendant line is called *pater*, "father"; *āvus*, "grandfather"; *proāvus*, "great-grandfather"; *abāvus*, "great-great-grandfather"; and his father, *atāvus*, from which our word *atavism* derives. Only *pater*, *āvus*, and *proāvus* are considered to belong to the restricted personal family unity; the *abāvus* and *atāvus*, not known personally as a rule, are fused in the idea of ancestors. The farther remote the past, the more depersonalized the ancestors become. The word *ancestor* derives from *ante-cessor*, which properly means "he who goes before, the forerunner," and which is also used significantly in Late Latin in the sense of the "Holy Ghost."[1]

This over-all concept of the ancestors becomes more complicated if one considers the pertinent German words.

The grandfather and the forefathers are called *Ahn*. This word developed a diminutive form: the German *Enkel*, which properly meant "little grandfather," but actually denotes the "grandchild." Our words *grandfather, grandmother* are patently inspired by the French language, but the attribute of "great" is used also in other languages, for instance in Sanskrit. In Latin *maiores*, properly "the greater ones," usually denoted the "forefathers, ancestors." We can well understand that the old head of the household was called by the attribute "grand," but it is more difficult to explain why the youngest generation also received this attribute in "grandchild." These are indications proving that there existed a positive relationship between grandfather and grandchild.[2] Naturalistic interpreters will say that often a similarity is observed that is inherited from the grandfather by the grandchild; this must be the special reason for denoting the grandchild as "little grandfather." Sometimes the grandfather may even claim some right upon the grandchild. Odysseus (meaning properly "one who is angry") received his name from his maternal grandfather (*Odyssey* 24:115–19; 19:399–466). But linguistic expressions grew out of much deeper unconscious fantasies. They suppose that the "grandchild" is, in fact, identical with the "grandfather." The grandfather, or forefather, passed away, but he returned in the person of a little child.

In the light of this fantasy, which identifies the child not with the father, but with the grandfather as returning into life, one may understand the idea of spiritual generation in a more positive way. For the primitive mind, the living soul does not spring up from nothing.[3] It can originate only from another living soul. Someone has to die first in order that a new life can be born. The child has thus a double paternity: it is begotten by the earthly father, but generated in spirit by the grandfather, if he passed away, or by one of the ancestors. The reincarnation of the generative spirit in the son closes tight the family circle. The father in his central position unites both the living memory of the grandfather and the personal presence of the son as the repetition of the grandfather. The attribute "little," which is expressed by the diminutive, does not primarily refer to physical smallness, but indicates the model which is symbolic and imaginary. Generation is thus understood to be always an incarnation of the ancestral spirit, a regeneration, a return from the detached, merely nonpersonal existence into the earthly life through the womb of the mother. It shall be remembered in this connection that the spirit of the departed is represented as a miniature of a child in Eastern and Western paintings and sculptures.

The whole construction of this spiritual regeneration appears in our cultural development as a pronounced patristic conception. There is technically no room for the woman, except as the medium of birth. The woman is not considered to be a full-fledged human being in this patristic philosophy; she serves simply as the *material*. The mother's family, even its male members, were generally excluded from the community of family worship formed by father, son, and spirit.

Considering the idea of regeneration from the psychological angle, it appears to be an effective weapon against the reality of death. The elaborate funeral ceremonials, also, are an acting out of the emotions connected with the disappearance of an important person. By its whole performance, the ritual spoke perhaps in an early age when man was not able to express himself in language on such abstract ideas; thus, the language of the ritual said that death is not really the final end of life. The person who has died has simply changed his status and will return soon in a renewed form to the earthly existence. The dead one who was present in person in the family a short time ago has not disappeared for good; he is still present and active within the family, though in an exchanged status, but even this absence is only a temporary one.

This denial or mitigating of the reality of death had, in its reverse side, grave consequences as far as the protection of human life was concerned.

The stereotype of funeral sermons, "Thy spirit will remain with us," carried an actual concrete meaning for the primitive mind. It implied the duties of the living toward the dead ones. These duties had to be carefully observed, especially if they served also as a relief for a disturbed conscience toward the dead person. Grief and guilt are often inseparable. The dead one expected that the living would attend him and observe faithfully his duties toward him "beyond the grave." The Greek tragedy of *Antigone* is based upon this idea. She

232

says: "I shall rest, a loved one with him whom I have loved, sinless in my crime; for I owe a longer allegiance to the dead than to the living; in that world I shall abide forever."

The building of the tomb as a house or the erection of subterranean palaces for dead rulers is based upon such fantasies. The regular offering of food and drink to the spirit of the dead is another duty of the head of the household. But there are many other services, e.g., to give the spirit an opportunity to take a bath periodically, providing the dead person with practical necessities and personal belongings, even with wives, slaves, and servants, with favorite horses, dogs, also with weapons and utilities; such funeral customs serving the departed souls are attested all over the world for all people.

Generally, a difference is made between those spirits which are introduced in a solemn ritual way into the community of the venerated ancestors, on the one hand, and those spirits of the dead ones who were buried around the house, but who were not attended regularly in a religious way, on the other. These spirits, roaming homelessly around, were considered mischievous troublemakers, interfering in daily life and haunting men in their dreams. The verbal expressions also discriminate between the attended spirits and the unattended ones. The attended spirit is called in Greek *hēros;* this word seems to imply the idea of worship, "hero worship." The heroes represent to the Greek mind a generation of supermen, semigods; they are called also *theoi patrooi,* "divine parents." The Romans called them *di parentes,* "divine parents"; *dii manes,* "the good ones"; or *penates,* "the internal ones, dwelling inside the house." A son, collecting the funeral ashes of his father, says: "He is now a god."[4] The Greek *daimōn,* "demon," and the Latin *gēnius* are also venerated ancestral spirits.

Ancestor worship is well known as a characteristic feature of the Greek and Latin polytheism, but it can be demonstrated that beneath the Mosaic religion of the Old Testament there was still flourishing a popular layer of ancestor worship which never could be fully eradicated. The deification of the father was idolatry, indeed, but this idolatry had despite all condemnations a deep influence upon religious development. The deification of the father has paved the way for the paternalization of the Lord. We would perhaps not call our Lord "Our Father which art in heaven" without an almost universal prehistoric belief that the father after death became in fact a deity. *Zeus-patēr* and *Jup-piter* have absorbed the attributes of the deified father. Such minor gods, semideities, are supposed by these words of the Psalmists: "God standeth in the congregation of the mighty; he judgeth among the gods [*elōhim*]. . . . I have said, Ye are gods; and all of you are children of the most High" (Ps. 82:1, 6). Also in the Old Testament are some outstanding personalities who died not simply as men but were raised above the human status: they became "translated" to heaven. They were semigods like the Greek heroes. Such was Enoch, who "walked with God: and he was not; for God took him" (Gen. 5:24); such was Elijah the great prophet who went up to heaven by a whirlwind carrying a "chariot of fire, and horses of fire" (II Kings 2:11); even Moses was raised immediately to the Lord without going first through "Sheol," the underworld through which all human departed souls must go according to the Hebrew religion. The Lord himself buried him: "And he buried him . . . but no man knoweth of his sepulchre unto this day" (Deut. 34:6).

The generally known literary example of the reappearing ancestral spirit is Hamlet's nightly encounter with the spirit of his father on the terrace of the castle of Elsinore.

The Old Testament offers an example of similar vigor, though it is not the father, but the father figure of the prophet Samuel who appears in spirit to King Saul. In both cases the spirit of the dead says to the living heir of power just that which the guilty conscience knows but does not dare to confess. It is the voice of the heir's own conscience which speaks. It is the voice of an internalized father picture which tells the repressed truth through the hallucination. Saul has just eradicated those who believe in the idolatry of "familiar spirits." Yet, when he was in great distress, he himself went to a "woman that hath a familiar spirit at En-dor." He said to the woman: "I pray thee, divine unto me by the familiar spirit, and bring me him up, whom I shall name unto thee. . . . Bring me up Samuel." The woman significantly saw "gods ascending out of the earth." The spirits of the dead do not come from heaven, they ascend from the grave. Snakes were considered as carriers of ancestral spirits. "An old man cometh up; and he is covered with a mantle" and says to Saul: "Why hast thou disquieted me, to bring me up?" Saul answers by the

234

confession of his sins (I Sam. 28:7–20). We may conclude from this example that a guilty conscience which is heavily loaded with anxiety and fear, as it may explode in nightmares, may lead on the religious plane to the belief of the spiritual reappearance of the dead.

The ancestral spirits are "ascending out of the earth" like the spirit of Samuel. It is a prophetic utterance: "Thou shalt speak out of the ground, and thy speech shall be low out of the dust, and thy voice shall be, as of one that hath a familiar spirit, out of the ground, and thy speech shall whisper out of the dust" (Isa. 29:4). The ancestral spirit imposed fear, awe, and reverence upon the family.

The ancestral spirits were also venerated in figurative representations. The tutelary spirit was considered a household god to whom special offerings had to be made. The "molten gods" (Lev. 19:4) and the "graven images" (Deut. 27:15) definitely show that the wealthier families especially kept the vestiges of the primitive ancestor worship.

The first commandment therefore places the strong prohibition on this popular religion: "Thou shalt not make unto thee any graven image, or any likeness of anything that is in heaven above, or that is in the earth beneath, or that is in the water under the earth" (Exod. 20:4). These figures must sometimes have been human representations, otherwise Michal, David's wife, could not personate David by an image when Saul wanted to kill him. She took an image, laid it in David's sickbed and put a pillow of goat's hair for his bolster and covered it with a cloth (I Sam. 19:13). Such images (teraphim) represented a high religious value for the whole family. Rachel, when she left the house of her father Laban, carried away surreptitiously the teraphim of the house. We hear the desperate search and outcry of Laban: "Wherefore hast thou stolen my gods?" (Gen. 31:30). One may surmise that these "molten gods" were the altar, the central part of the worship unity of the house. "A man also or woman that hath a familiar spirit, or that is a wizard, shall surely be put to death: they shall stone them with stones: their blood shall be upon them" (Lev. 20:27). One can well observe the gradual transition of the ancestral representation into an "image of God," the strictly forbidden material representation of the Lord himself. So Micah's mother "took two hundred shekels of silver, and gave them to the founder, who made thereof a graven image and a molten image: and they were in the house of Micah" (Judg. 17:4). The ancestral spirit worship had been assimilated in this way into the course of religious development.

The head of the house served as priest and the whole family was present in person on the special occasions when the dead ancestors were worshiped. The ancestral spirits were remembered by the head of the house at every meal. In Greek and Roman antiquity the dead were customarily called three times by their names and thus invited to participate in the daily family meal. Such daily feeding of the dead ones must also have been a general custom of the Jewish people, otherwise we can hardly explain why every single giver of the tithes, when he delivered his taxes to the Levites, had to make an oath with the subsequent statement: "I have not transgressed thy commandments, neither have I forgotten them: I have not eaten thereof . . . nor given ought thereof for the dead" (Deut. 26:13–14). Such religious oaths obviously counteracted a strong tendency of the people to give one part of the victuals not to the priest but to their own dead ones. In Latin the sacrifice for the dead parents or forefathers is called *parentalia;* the verb *parentō, -āre* means "to offer a solemn sacrifice in honor of the deceased parents," as well as "to revenge the death of a parent by that of another, to make therewith an offering to his name."[5] This proves that the service to the *di parentes,* the deified parents, consisted not only in continuous sacrifices but implied also the obligation of blood-feud.

The occasion of the funeral was generally the first of such family gatherings. The funeral was followed generally by an elaborate banquet, feasting and drinking; the funeral obsequies consisted of just this *parentatio* at the fresh grave. This family sacrifice was usually repeated several times during the year. The Latin *feralis,* "of or belonging to the dead or to corpses, funeral, offerings to the dead," refers to the *feralia,* "the general festival of the dead" kept on the seventeenth or twenty-first of February. This Latin feast of the ancestors has been adapted by the Church as the feast of All Saints' Day, November 1, and of All Souls' Day, November 2. Our *Hallowe'en,* from the former *all hallow even,* celebrated now with fun making and masquerading, kept the vestiges of the ancient festivals that took place at the grave in connection with the funeral. The acting out of sorrow and mourning, on the one hand, and of joyous and frivolous exuberance, on the other, can be interpreted in different ways. It may reveal the deeply repressed ambivalent and antagonistic emotions toward the dead person. It can be equally possible that the masquerading is an outlet of anxiety. If man cannot deal otherwise with the necessity of death, he makes fun of it. In the German language the Latin *feralia* developed into the meaning of *Ferien,* "vacation." The attendance of the familiar sacrifices was imperative for the members of the family—these were the males, for the women were regularly not admitted, and if so, only as servants of the feasts. At funerals the lamentations were their duties.

One can observe in the Old Testament one case when David asked Jonathan for leave "that he might run to Bethlehem his city: for there is a yearly sacrifice there for all the family." He said: "Let me go, I pray thee, for our family hath a sacrifice in the city, and my brother, he hath commanded me to be there: and now, if I have found favour in thine eyes, let me get away, I pray thee, and see my brethren" (I Sam. 20: 6, 29).

When such Feralia were over not only the guests but the ancestral spirits were also dismissed sometimes in a very disrespectful way: *Edistis, bibistis, animae, ite fores, ite fores!* "You have eaten and drunken, spirits get out! Get out!"

Summing up all these observations, we may say: the position of the father in the family appears in the light of ancestor worship to be that of a priest. He is the mediator between the spiritual community of the ancestors and the actual family. His authority, the *patria potestas,* is derived from this suprahuman power attributed to the ancestral spirits. He acts in the trust of the ancestors. He has the right to fertilize, to call into existence a new life; he has also the right to kill, to set an end to the life of his children.

See: CANNIBALISM, INITIATION, SENICIDE.

Anxiety

The verbal expressions describe the primary bodily sensations of anxiety. They refer to the language of the body. Two bodily manifestations can be distinguished, though not always clearly separated: one describes a sensation in the throat as being throttled; the other refers to the paralyzing effect as being tied down, especially on the feet; thus one feels the inhibition either in respiration or in locomotion.

The word *anxiety* belongs to the Latin verb *angō, anxum,* which means, on the one hand, "to bind, draw, or press together; to throttle; to strangle." On the other hand, it refers to the emotional experience "to cause pain; to distress, torment, torture, vex, trouble; to suffer." A pertinent noun is *angor,* which denotes the sensations of "strangling" and of "anguish, torment," as a sudden spell, while *anxietas* describes the same sensations as a permanent condition. The equivalent terms in Greek are *angchō* and *sphingō*—the first meaning "to press tight, to strangle," the second, "to bind fast and tight." Thus, *Sphinx* and *anx-iety* are twin words with parallel meanings. The German *Angst,* the English *anguish,* the French *angoisse,* all refer to somewhat similar subjective experiences, which are described objectively as a state of being uneasy, or of being worried about what may happen. The state of painful suspense is its characteristic. This holds true also for the English *worry,* which derives from the Old English *wyrgan,* meaning, as does the German *würgen,* "to throttle, strangle." The German *bange,* "worried," and the noun *Bangigkeit,* "anxiety," derive from *be-ange,* the second part of which means "narrow," referring to the inhibition either in breathing or in motion. The same bodily symptoms are described in the Slavic terms for anxiety. Thus, is felt an inside pressure that seems as if it would constrict the throat or the chest, or paralyze the whole body as if it were tied down and immobilized in a situation when one wants to fight or to escape.

The Latin *angor,* denoting the choking, strangulating anxiety, and the noun *anguis,* "serpent," seem to be two different words from linguistic viewpoint but the Greek myth made some connection between the ideas of "anxiety" and "serpent." Laocoön, the priest of Troy, is the personification of anticipatory anxiety. He warned his people against the Greek wooden horse. Two huge serpents came up from the depth of the sea, one may interpret, from the depth of his unconscious. The serpents suffocated him together with his two sons.

Respiratory and circulatory sensations are involved in such English terms as *breathless, breath-taking*. Patients in describing an anxiety attack say, "it was a sort of tightening of the throat," "it seemed as if my breath stopped," "the feeling of fear gripped my heart." Anxiety is indicated by the increased rate and depth of respiration, frequent sighing, hyperventilation.[6]

Sensations in the alimentary system are verbalized by patients stating that "the bowels are tied into knots" or that they have "the sinking feeling" or "butterflies" in the pit of the stomach.

Skin reactions are described by Greek and Latin terms. The Greek verb *phrissō* means "to be rough or uneven on the surface, to bristle," like the bristling surface of the water; it also means "to shiver or shudder" of fear and anxiety. The anxiety reaction upon the skin is the same as of cold; therefore, the Greek verb refers also to the feeling of chill when one's skin contracts and forms what we commonly call *goose-flesh,* or when the hair stands up on end, as in the Latin *horrent comae, steterunt comae*. It denotes, particularly, "to feel a holy shudder or awe as at the approach of a divinity." This is the metaphysicum beyond sense perception to which man reacts with *phrikē,* "anguish, shiver, chill," "shivering fear," "shuddering especially from religious awe," also "frost, cold." The same skin reaction is described by the Latin verb *horreō,* which means "to stand on end, stand erect," then "to move in an unsteady, shaky manner," "to shake, shiver, tremble, shudder, quake with fright." The verb *horrescō, -ui* means "to rise on end, stand erect, bristle up, grow rough," "to begin to shake, shudder." The English "the hair stands up on end" corresponds exactly to the Greek and Latin perception of horror.

Another characteristic bodily reaction is trembling. The trembling man, *homo tremens,* became symbolic for fear and anxiety. "Fear and trembling" are almost synonyms in the Biblical language. "Fear came upon me, and trembling," Job says (4:14). This trembling is felt not only in the extremities, but all over the body. Thus, the "trembling heart" (Deut. 28:65) is as true an experience as that felt when it is said: "When I heard, my belly trembled" (Hab. 3:16). The "cup of trembling" is the symbol of a life ridden by fear and anxiety in the picture language of the Bible. The Greek *tromos,* the Latin *terror* and *pavor,* and many Slavic terms also refer to this trembling and describe the painful experience of fear and anxiety by it.

Our languages discriminate between "anxiety, worry, care," on the one hand, and "fear, fright, being scared, being afraid," on the other. Similar distinction is made in German between *Angst, Bangigkeit, Sorge* against *Furcht* and *Schrecken,* or in French *angoisse* as against *peur, crainte, effroi.* The borderlines separating the two concepts are not always the same. The bodily reactions seem to be identical in both; however, the essential difference in the verbal expressions is, *to fear* has an object (one fears "something"), while *to be anxious* doesn't (one is anxious "about"). This means that fear refers to a reality, while anxiety refers to no reality. Anxiety is anticipatory, it does not face any specific real or imaginary danger situation, it is free-floating and ever-changing, clearly distinguished from the attention fixed upon one object which is feared. The cause of fear is known, conscious, it is present as the danger inherent in a situation or thing, whereas the cause of anxiety is hidden, unknown, buried in the unconscious, it is *no-thing.* "Eternal troubles haunt thy anxious mind, whose cause and cure thou never hop'st to find." For this reason, anxiety has no mobilizing effect as fear has, but a paralyzing influence. If man is confronted with an overwhelming danger, with the superior power that makes flight or fight impossible, the result is the "frozen" immobility, the skin reaction to cold, and trembling. Anxiety is "binding fast." The paralyzing effect of anxiety was depicted in the Greek myth of Niobe, whose feet "took roots" while she was fleeing with her children. Anxiety *petrifies,* which says properly, "it makes man to be a rock or stone." Anxiety dreams produce such paralyzing sensations.

In pavor nocturnus *children may dream that they want to run away from a danger, but their feet remain stuck in a "gluey substance," they cannot move.*[7] *Freud also described such an anxiety dream: A child is pursued by a man with a hatchet, the child tries to run away, but he cannot, he is paralyzed and "cannot move from the spot."*[8] *A female college student, in free association, said: "As a child, I was so over-ridden with fears that I felt as though there were extra weights tied to my feet."* *The* foot-fetter *association emerged spontaneously.* Because anxiety is so often experienced in the feet, inhibiting walking, one may readily suppose that the swollen feet of Oedipus may be interpreted as the bodily symptoms of anxiety.

A specific kind of anxiety is concerned with the loss of a loved person or object. The English adjective *anxious* absorbed some of these qualities. It means "worried over a possible failure or impending sickness, to be concerned about something future and unknown." On the conscious level this "impending" evil and "future and unknown" is death. There are many terms that identify "anxiety" with "sorrow, grief," even with "mourning, lamenting." The persistence of this tension is pointed out by the words which identify "anxiety" with "care." Our word *care,* Old English *cearu,* originally meant "sorrow," and this meaning remained preserved in the German *Kar-freitag,* "Good Friday." Out of the original concept of "grief, sorrow" developed the concept of "anxiety." The idea of death was implied. This is also the case with the Greek and Latin terms. The Greek words *phrōntis* and *merimna* both mean "care" and "anxiety," especially the anxious care which is a fixated, permanent condition. The Latin *cūra* denotes primarily the careful attention and concern, on the one hand, while, on the other hand, it means "anxiety, disgust, grief, sorrow"; the connotation of mourning is again implied. The common point of reference in these terms is the concentration of attention, in one case, upon a person or situation one is afraid of losing, and, in the other case, upon somebody or something not existing anymore, leaving behind the pain of separation, loss, and helplessness.

Anxiety is a central topic of analytical and existential psychology. The interpretation of its origin and meaning is manifold.[9] It was a haunting problem for Freud, and it stayed with him since his early writings, through the various stages of his thinking. The formulations of Freud's anxiety concepts sometimes sound confusing in the English translations because the German *Angst* has different connotations than the English *anxiety,* thus it is sometimes translated as *fear* or *to be afraid.*[10] Freud changed his interpretation several times. According to his last formulation (1932), anxiety is a signal of danger; separation, deprivation connected with pain is the primary anxiety-arousing experience of the helpless child, which becomes repeated in later life. It may be the separation from the mother, castration fear as a painful separation from a part of the body, or it may be repeated in the pain of mourning the loss of a beloved one.[11] Freud paid little attention to the pertinent verbal expressions, although he may have found strong support for his viewpoint, for instance, in the verbal identification of anxiety and mourning, or in the English *to be anxious about,* which is not implied in German.

According to the existentialist interpretation of Kierkegaard and Heidegger, anxiety is the response to nonexistence. I tried to demonstrate that however different the wording and the frame of reference might be, the existentialist "No-thingness" is, in essence, not very different from the visual representation of negation, castration, abyss which are implied in Freud's interpretation. (*cf.* pp. 70–71.)

See: FEAR.

Birth

The noun *birth* is a derivative of the verb *to bear,* Old English *beran,* "to carry," and thus refers to the result of carrying in the body. It is related to *burden.* The Middle English *burdon of nature* means "excrements." The German equivalent words are *Ge-burt,* "birth," and *Bürde,* "burden." The act of birth is thus perceived not as "delivery" from a burden, but in the sense of "gestation"; the word *gestation,* also meaning properly "the carrying," is a derivative of the Latin verb *gestāre,* "to carry," the intensive form of *gerō, -ere,* "to carry." As in the word *child,* properly "uterine," no distinction is made between the prenatal and postnatal state.

The mother "bearing" the fetus was obviously a primordial experience; therefore, it was charged with anxiety, magic, rituals, and taboo avoidances. The term *birth* seems to be a cover word replacing an ancient term which was in Old English, *cenning* ("birth"), from *cennan,* the equivalent of such related terms as the Greek *gen-nauō,* "to beget," the Latin *gignō, -ere,* "to beget," said of the father, and the Latin *nascō, -ere,* from former *gnascō,* "to bear." The awe implied in the beginning of life resorted to cover words—just as for the end of life, instead of *died,* we say "departed, passed away." Other familiar circumlocutions for "to bear" are *to bring forth, bring to the world*—like the French *mettre au monde*—and *to be delivered*. The hospital is called the *lying-in*, like the French *accoucher*. The Old English used the term *aweccan*, "to awake," for the concept of "birth"; thus it does not consider the biological act, but the psychological awakening of consciousness, the separation of light and darkness as the beginning of life. Other Old English terms are *strynan*, "to obtain," in a sense somewhat similar to "beget"; also the verb *tēman*, "to teem" in the sense, now rare, meaning "to be full or ready to bring forth, generate." A remarkable feature of the old generic verbs is that in the transitive active form they refer to the father, in the passive form to the mother, in the medium to the child.

The sublimation of the primary biological meaning resulted in such abstractions as "to turn out," like in the vertex presentation, "to bring forth, produce, result, be born out, appear, obtain, gain, get." According to infantile fantasies, the mother did not *be-get* the babe, but simply *got* it. The choice of a euphemism is, in some respects, as much a problem as the choice of a neurosis. It seems to be probable, in some cases provable, that a specific euphemism was chosen for cover because it derived itself from the same crude meaning which it was to replace. Many euphemisms illustrate "the return of the repressed." However clean, white, or sublimated the euphemism seems to be, by covering up a "hot" meaning, it can become "hot" again and subjected to newer repression. We call this phenomenon "secondary" repression. If the verb *to bear* covered up the primary cruder concept of *cennan*, it became charged in the secondary way with all the repressive anxiety invested in *cennan;* thus it developed a luxuriant variety of abstracted and sublimated notions such as "to support," "to endure, tolerate, suffer," as the pregnant woman does, "to render or give," as *to bear testimony, to bear in mind,* to conduct oneself in a given manner as *to bear oneself* with dignity. Thus the basic idea of all these abstractions is still *to bear,* as the pregnant woman is bearing, "to endure with patience" as the woman must endure until the delivery. The old verb *cennan* developed such desexualized meanings as implied by the related words *kind, kindness, kin, kinship,* or the German *Kind,* "child."

The underground communication between the old repudiated meaning and the new cover word can be demonstrated also in the case of *be-get* and *get,* "obtain," but this secret unity is also clearly exposed by the Latin verb *pariō, -ere,* "to beget," in the abstract dimension "to bring forth, produce, create, accomplish, invent, procure, acquire," and the parallel *parō, -āre,* which means not only "to get ready, pre-pare, provide, order," but also in the transferred sense "to procure, acquire, get, obtain," just as the original *pariō. Separation* thus properly means "to be born asunder."

The birth process was surrounded with magic and ritual in the early ages.[12] The lying position at birth seems to be a rather late Western accommodation. The "lying down" was perceived as the distinguishing feature in the obsolete German *eines Kindes liegen,* properly "to lie down for a child," so also in the French *accoucher.* An earlier position at birth was the "kneeling parturition." The Egyptian hieroglyph for "birth" depicts the kneeling woman. In the ancient Greek tradition, as revealed by Homer, the kneeling parturition was the normal one, therefore, the goddesses of marriage and childbirth were frequently presented in the kneeling position.[13] However, we do not think that the genitalization of the "knee," as expressed in many languages, is the consequence of the kneeling birth.

In the Old Testament ages the "stool" was used for birth as indicated by the saying of Pharaoh to the Hebrew midwives: "When ye do the office of a midwife to the Hebrew women, and see them upon the stools . . ." (Exod. 1:16). The interference of the midwife marks another step in the over-all cultural development.

Infantile birth theories are inseparable from the infantile fantasies about conception. First, the child knows nothing about birth. At this level of ignorance or complete repression in later age, the newborn is simply "obtained," "received," "acquired," or it simply "appears," is "brought to light." On this level the Old English term for "birth," *ge-strynan,* "gain, obtain," with the pertinent noun *strēon,* "gain, treasure," accepts the newborn as a precious "gift" and the mother, though passive, as the receiver of this gift. Jonathan, from the Hebrew *Yehonathan,* properly means "the Lord has given." The same is true for *Theodore,* from the Greek *theos,* "god," and *doron,* "gift." The point in these words is that it is not the act of "birth" that is questioned, but only the location, from where the newborn was brought home and by whom it was brought into the house. The babe must have lived somewhere else before. This infantile attitude toward birth might be one reason for the innumerable foundling stories in legends and myths.[14] For instance, the Roman Romulus and Remus were found and nursed by the deified *Luperca,* "she-wolf"; however, the once glorified name developed a derogatory meaning in Latin, as it did in English (the female of the wolf or dog being called *bitch*). Like the other females of uncastrated animals living around the house, it became symbolic of promiscuity; so the Latin *lupa-nar,* a house of ill-repute, means properly "the house of she-wolves." The parents did not generate the child, according to these fantasies, they simply adopted it; thus adoption doubts may grow up in the small child. Oedipus was also such an adopted foundling.

The two most-common variants of such fantasies within our culture are the child "brought" by the stork and the child "found" on the cabbage leaf.[15] In the Orient the lotus flower has the symbolic function of child bearing. However veiled these infantile birth theories seem to be, they tend either to the patristic or to the matristic conception. To "plant a cabbage," in French *planter des choux,* the same in all Slavic languages, means to generate a child. So, according to French folklore, newly wedded pairs ought to eat cabbage—obviously an old fertility rite. The Greek *kaulos,* also its Latin derivatives *caulis* and *colis,* means the "stalk of a plant" (especially the "cabbage stalk," the *cauli-flower*), "the bony part of an ox's tail," and the "membrum virile." The word is, then, in the final analysis, a derivative of the Greek verb *kueō,* "to bear in the womb, to have conceived, to be pregnant."

Whereas the cabbage refers to the male, the stork story implies the female. This story was originally popular in the eastern part of Europe in the homeland of this migratory bird. It comes in late spring to the northern countries and returns during the fall to its hibernating home in North Africa, specifically to the swamps of the Nile Delta. This implies the covered meaning. The *delta* appears, since prehistoric ages, as the symbol of the female. In English, the delta is called the "mouth" of the Nile, but it must be noticed that this "mouth" is an outflowing into the sea. "Yea, the stork in the heaven knoweth *her* appointed time," the Bible says (Jer. 8:7). Moses was found in the mouth of the Nile in an "ark of bulrushes" daubed "with slime and pitch" (Exod. 2:3). No doubt the foundling child had some affinity with the papyrus, reed, and weed which covered the outflowing of the Nile. These plants were not planted; they grew wild like illegitimate children. In Greek *spartos,* properly "sown, grown from seed" (from *speirō,* "to sow"), means the "shrub" that was used for making cords and brooms, but *spartos*—and *speirō*—also refers to the planless, scattered seeds and not just to the "inserted" ones. The *Spartoi* are the men who claimed to descend from the dragon's teeth "scattered" by Cadmus.

On an advanced level, as compared with the fantasies about the pre-existent child, are those children who have some vague ideas that the babe was formerly within the mother, that it came out of the mother somehow, but the father still remained excluded from these fantasies. How did the mother "turn out" or "bring forth" the babe? The most common of this stage of infantile fantasies is the "anal birth." It identifies the "belly, stomach" with "womb " and thus the "child" with "excrements," or birth with defecation. The "excrements" are called by the English generic term, Old English *sceadan,* which properly means "separation." For such reason, the derogatory pet name "my excrements" came to mean "my baby," as in French *ma crotte;* the French *merdeux,* "little child," comes from the Latin *merda,* "excrements."

The anal birth supposes the conception through eating, as, for instance, eating the "mandrakes" in the Old Testament. Rachel says to Leah: "He shall lie with thee to night for thy son's mandrakes" (Gen. 30:15). In this instance the mandrakes were more important to Rachel, who desired a child, than her husband.

The anal-birth theory was reinforced in the infantile mind by observing the laying of eggs as implied in terms of *ovaries* and associations connecting "wings" and "birds" with pregnancy. For example, the mother of a schizophrenic girl said about her pregnancy: "I had the impression of carrying a canary."[16]

See: CONCEPTION.

Blessing

The word *blessing,* from former *blod-sung,* is a derivative of the Old English *blodi-sō-jan,* from *blood, bleed, bled,* and properly means "to make bloody." Interpreters were struck by this meaning. Why should *blessing* mean "to make bloody"? The plain commonsense answer will seek for a logical "missing link" between "blood" and "blessing." Thus our vocabularies construct a transitory meaning that is not attested but only supposed to have existed: "The etymological meaning was thus to mark or to affect in some way, with blood or sacrifice, to consecrate" (NED, *s.v. blessing*). The line of development was according to this explanation: "blood: blood consecration: blessing." Nothing is more misleading than such logical rationalization of unconscious fantasies. Moreover the transition from "blood consecration" to "blessing" still remained quite a jump. It implies that man is "blessing" God, not God blessing man; otherwise it could not be maintained that "to mark with blood" should be the core of the meaning of blessedness. So rationalistic interpreters insist that "blessing" denotes primarily an act of man: "to consecrate a thing by religious rite, the utterance of a formula of charm, in later time by prayer" (NED, *s.v. blessing*).

One will agree that the verbal ritual of praising the Lord for receiving and subsequent thanksgiving, also the imploration for receiving, can be fused with the original notion which means to confer blessing, not to receive it. In fact, the Greek *éulogia* and the equivalent Latin *benedictio* suggest human action. The only Biblical passage that can be quoted in support of this interpretation—"The cup of blessing which we bless, is it not the communion of the blood of Christ?" (I Cor. 10:16)—is obviously a secondary application of this notion.

According to primitive fantasies the conception of new life in the female occurs as the coagulation of the blood, which otherwise appears as menstrual discharge. They suppose that the cessation of regular periodicity is caused by the clotting of the blood. Inside the mother this blood is the carrier of a new life, the incorporation of a new soul; the clotting of the blood is an act of the supernatural Spirit, it is the "fruit of the womb." When discharged, it is "flower" translated as "uncleanness"; it is filthy, dirty, loathsome, an object of fear, disgust, and taboo. But inside the body, it implies "life," "child," "progeny," "fruit of the womb." Shakespeare so used this word in "O thou the earthy author of my blood" and "a gentleman of blood." Physiologically, the blood is the most changeable body fluid; symbolically it is the most constant one, for otherwise such a term as "blood relatives" would not make sense. It refers to the imaginary coagulated blood, to the "fruit of the womb," which is a "gift" given by the grace of the Lord. This primary meaning of "blessing" can be found in the instances in which this word is used still in our language: "God bless you!" Shakespeare says, "Heaven bless you!" "Jesus bless you!" but he never uses the word with the meaning of "Praise the Lord!" In the meaning of receiving is the word used in the stereotyped formulas of the Bible. It suffices to quote only a few from the first Book of Genesis: "And God blessed them, saying, Be fruitful, and multiply" (1:22, 28); "I will bless her, and she shall be a mother of nations" (17:16); "I have blessed him, and will make him fruitful, and will multiply him exceedingly" (17:20); "That in blessing I will bless thee, and in multiply-ing I will multiply thy seed" (22:17; 26:24); "blessings of the breasts, and of the womb" (49:25). The fruits of the field are bestowed upon man as the blessing of the Lord: "The smell of a field which the Lord hath blessed: Therefore God give thee of the dew of heaven, and the fatness of the earth, and plenty of corn and wine" (27:27–28). The fruit which grows on the tree is also called "blessing": "There shall be showers of bless-ing. And the tree of the field shall yield her fruit" (Ezek. 34:26–27). The very meaning of blessing is phenomenologi-cally described when Moses said: the Lord "will love thee, and bless thee, and multiply thee: he will also bless the fruit of thy womb, and the fruit of thy land, thy corn, and thy wine . . ." (Deut. 7:13). The final formulation is attained in Elisabeth's saying: "Blessed art thou among women, and blessed is the fruit of thy womb" (Luke 1:42).

The Greek fantasy of the "Islands of the Blessed," as the place where the departed souls gather, illustrates the repres-sion, the great return implied in death.

See: CONCEPTION, DEATH.

Cannibalism

Among various prohibitions two areas stand out still in our culture. One is the prohibition of cannibalism; the other is the prohibition of incest. Both are equally met in our culture with horror, yet one must suppose that once, in prehistoric ages, both represented a temptation to man. In the course of his cultural development, however, man has found out that both the unclean food and the defiling of the marital relationship are loaded with explosive dangers which will automatically do harm to the transgressor. These two areas of taboo are strongly protected by law even in our culture.

It is difficult to explain how these two chief prohibitions hang together. They are obviously interrelated with one another because the primary object of reference is in both cases the human person. Cannibalism once was general and, except for some remote parts of the world, has been completely eradicated within the realm of our civilization. One may suppose that its suppression was a great event of human history. There can be no doubt that such cultural change could be brought about only through drastic punitive measures which implied the certainty of retaliation and inflicted fear. The negative abhorrence and loathing of human meat developed when on the positive side man became aware of the sanctity of human life and personality. The prohibition of consuming human flesh and blood must have been the first of all taboo prohibitions. It set the pattern of all following food prohibitions. Anthropophagy was long forgotten in Greek antiquity, but a few other food taboos developed instead. The Pythagorean sect, for instance, abstained from eating beans as unholy food. Plutarch said that Pythagoras had his followers "abstain from beans as from human flesh." Such saying shows that human flesh was still to his mind the primary food taboo.*

The consumption of food does not serve only the biological need of nourishment but is at the same time a spiritual act expressing the primitive desire of participating in the spiritual being of the consumed one. It is a solemn act of incorporation, identification, and spiritual regeneration. It appeals to the most primitive satisfaction of man's desire of immortality. To be consumed by his own children means to perpetuate in them, to be absorbed in their life, to continue to

* The Pythagorean maxim was: It is equal crime to eat beans and the heads of one's parents. Pliny says about beans: "The souls of the dead (*animae mortuorum*) are in them" (*Natural History,* 18:118). Alfred C. Andrews, "The Bean and Indo-European Totemism," *American Anthropologist* (1949), 51:274–92.

live within them. Even in later historical time when anthropophagy was long abhorred, the idea remained that eating means the communion with the ancestral spirit. The great emphasis on the food aspect in sacrifices and various religious rituals becomes much more plausible by this prehistoric custom. The ancestral spirit became incorporated by the family through the sacral eating of the dead one.

The consumption of human flesh, a universal custom during the prehistoric ages, is well attested over all the world through the prehistoric relics, historical data, and anthropological evidences.[17] "Cannibalism prevailed until recently over a great part of West and Central Africa, New Guinea, Melanesia (especially Fiji), Australia, New Zealand, the Polynesian Islands, Sumatra, other Indian Islands in South America, and in the earlier days of North America."* The Mohawk, a tribe of the Iroquoian Indians, lived in the Mohawk Valley in New York; it received its name as *mohowauuck,* meaning "they eat animate things," which might then include the meaning "man-eaters." The term *cannibal,* from the Spanish *caníbal* or *caribe,* referred originally to the Carib islands. In Ethiopia human flesh formerly was exposed for sale in baskets on the market.[18] The Indo-European people were in no way exempt from this over-all characteristic of prehistoric man.

These facts are difficult to reconcile with those characteristics of primitive culture which exclude by their very nature cannibalism. Some tribes are found and described still living on the Stone Age level of simple food gathering and they definitely show man as frugivorous, much like the anthropoid apes are. They abstain from hunting or eating animals, just as man was supposed to do in the Golden Age of innocence. The primitive man is often called *savage,* French *sauvage,* Italian *selvaggio;* these words are derivatives of the Latin *silvaticus* (from *silva,* "wood, forest"), "belonging to the wood," "wild," thus "a wood-dweller." This word properly does not necessarily imply that man was a predatory animal: The pygmies are such peaceful sylvan people; they do not hunt, they do not kill. The great anthropoid apes living in the

* *Encyclopedia Britannica* 4:745, *s.v. cannibalism.* The word *Eskimo* is said to derive from the Labrador-Algonquian *eskimantik,* "eater of raw meat." What kind of raw meat was eaten cannot be decided.

virgin forest were called by the aborigines of Borneo *orang-utan,* which means in the Malayan language "wild man," from *oran,* "man," and *utan,* "wild," but this anthropoid ape does not consume meat either.

Somewhere in the human prehistory occurred the great change from the type of the frugivorous man into the carnivorous rapacious type that is present everywhere at the beginning of history. Some anthropologists do not hesitate to call this great turn in human destiny the Fall of Man. Man is, indeed, when he appears in the light of history, as William James said, "the most formidable of all beasts of prey and indeed the only one that preys systematically on its own species."[19] This is the distinctive feature between man and ape. This should be kept in mind when the origin of the human family is sought along evolutionist lines in the social grouping of anthropoid apes. These apes are strict vegetarians while man appears as a predatory, carnivorous being.

What may be the reason that man differs so conspicuously from his nearest animal relatives? The difference consists just in this: man is endowed with fantasies. Man does not simply feed like the apes do, but his eating is besides feeding a spiritual act. By eating, man will acquire spiritual power and strength. Not the flesh but the spirit in the flesh is the final goal of nourishment.

The desire for incorporation may represent esteem, sympathy, or love, through which the eater wants to identify himself with the eaten one.

By sharing his food and eating together, man seeks spiritual communion with his fellow men. *Com-panion* means this sharing the bread. But this sharing of the bread appears in the light of prehistory to be a secondary derivation. The original implication of this sharing was the participation in the flesh and blood of the dead person, whose spiritual powers man wanted to acquire. Head-hunters do not kill for food but for the other's brain, which they consider to be the stuff of vitality. Man became a cannibal when he became aware of his spiritual nature. He differs in this respect from all predatory animals. Cannibalism is a human characteristic. Through cannibalism, man became the consumer of animal meat. People of the Hindu religion feel the same abhorrence for our slaughtering animals and eating their flesh as we feel loathsome toward the consumption of human meat. Empedocles and the Pythagoreans, who believed in the kinship of all life, maintained that once upon a time an age of love preceded the ages of strife. When Aphrodite was supreme, men did not shed blood and did not eat flesh. The animals had no reason to fear man. Beasts and birds were tame. The fantasies went so far as to say that even the trees kept their leaves and their fruits the whole year. "But no altar was wet with the shameful slaughter of bulls. Nay it was held the foulest defilement to tear out life and devour the goodly limbs."[20]

One may conclude from these observations that simple food cannibalism as an addiction for the taste and smell of human flesh and blood relatively seldom occurred. It must be a late degeneration of the original cannibalism. The ancient historical records, for instance, Herodotus and Strabo describe only the original, sacral form of anthropophagy.

Herodotus says about the Issedone people:

> But the Issedones are said to have these customs. Whensoever a man's father dieth, all his kinsmen bring flocks, and having slain them and cut the meat up, they also cut up the dead father of their host, and mingle all the pieces together and make a feast thereof. But the head of the dead man when they have plucked off the hair and cleansed the inside, they gild over and have it ever afterwards for a precious ornament performing great sacrifices to it every year.[21]

This is an exact description of this primordial kind of ancestor worship.

Herodotus says about the Massagetae, another neighboring people of the Greeks (1:216):

> Each marrieth a wife but they use them in common. For that which the Greeks say that the Scythians do, it is not the Scythians but the Massagetae which do it. For whatsoever woman one of the Massagetae desireth, he hangeth up his quiver before her wagon and useth her without fear. And they have no appointed limit of life but this that whensoever a man grew exceeding old, all his kinsmen come together and slay him. And much cattle also. And then they seethe the flesh and devour it. This is held by them to be the most blessed lot; But the man that

perisheth of sickness they consume not but bury in the earth. And they deem it a calamity that he liveth not to be slain.[22]

This picture reminds one, in fact, of the fighting anthropoids as described by Darwin, but in this case again there is not the slightest indication of a "jealous sire" and the competitive fight of the males for the possession of the females.

As an example which applies to the Indo-European people of the Celts, Strabo (6:5, 4) reported about the people of Ireland:

> Concerning this island I have nothing certain to tell except that its inhabitants are more savage than the Britons, since they are man-eaters as well as heavy eaters, and since further they count it an honorable thing when their fathers die, to devour them, and openly to have intercourse not only with the other women, but also with their mothers and sisters.[23]

The taking possession of the women of the disposed father seems to be in this case the climax of the funeral ceremonial and the public demonstration of the shift of power from the father to the son. This description illustrates, indeed, the Oedipus situation in anthropological projection.

Many more examples could be given but these few may suffice to show a family situation that differs so widely from the concept we are used to connect with the idea of family. The consumption of parts of the flesh of the murdered man as a magic incorporation of and identification with his spirit had its legal consequences. The act also served as an appeasement. It abated the blood revenge. No retaliation was expected when the murderer consumed parts of the body of the murdered one, because by this act they became one in spirit. That this question of blood revenge still bothered the guilty conscience of the sons can be seen in the example of the Germanic Heruli people, who preferred that the deadly blow should be applied by an agnate of the family because the cognates, obliged to blood revenge, would not like to be involved.*

* _cf._ p. 354.

The drinking of human blood demonstrates even more distinctly than does the consumption of flesh that no actual hunger or thirst had to be stilled by this act, but the "life," the spirit, had to be incorporated. The liver, the brain, and the marrow of the bones were for such reasons the preferred food. But the eating of another man's flesh and the drinking of his blood did not mean simply the acquisition of his vital powers, but, paradoxical as it may seem, it had at the same time the effect of reconciliation. It was an act of covenant. By this consuming of the vital power of another man one became identified, reunified, in spirit with him; one surely became safe against any retaliation. If murder, however sacral, was the source of guilt feelings, the sacral consumption of the murdered was considered to be a palliative against the blood revenge.

There exists a close association between the drinking cup and the skull. Historical data prove that the skulls of the killed enemies have been used as drinking cups.* In the Germanic tradition of myth and legend many instances could be shown that the skull was used as a vessel for drinking. Besides the historical data and mythical evidences actual archaeological material has been found: in this case, drinking cups with elaborate gold framing and decoration made out of a human skull. This use of the skull was so ingrained in primitive fantasies that the drinking utensils were often decorated with the features of the human head. "Pitchers have ears." The drinking from a human skull made the act of drinking into a spiritual appropriation even if wine was used instead of blood. The verbal expressions illustrate the same identification of "skull" and "cup." It has been said, this identification resulted from a given "similarity" of the two objects. Farfetched as this supposed similarity may be, the evidences of history and archaeology prove beyond doubt that this age-old connection between the meaning "skull" and "cup" is a residue of cannibalism.[24]

The Latin *cupa*, "a tub, cask, tin for holding liquids, especially wine," developed into the Late Latin *cuppa*, the English *cup*, and the German *Kopf*, "head." The Latin *testa* means "tile, brick, earthen pot, pitcher, jug, urn"; this mean-

* Urns are often made in the similarity of the head: this suggests even more the spiritualization of the vessel.

ing is continued by the French *tête*, "head." The Old Norse *hverna*, "cooking vessel," and the according Gothic *hwairnei* and Old High German *hwer* mean "head." The same connection is found in the Slavic languages and in Sanskrit (*kapāla*, "cup, bowl," and "skull").

In view of this association so old and so widespread it is rather strange that some of our vocabularies try to separate words that are so closely linked together as *skull* and *shell*, the German *Schale*, "shell, cup," and *Schädel*, "skull." This separation becomes impossible in the Scandinavian languages, in which, e.g., Swedish *skal* means "bowl, cup, shell" and *skalle*, "skull." The concepts of "skull," "cup," and "shell" are in the same way connected in the other Scandinavian languages. In the Gothic language there is also the word *skalja*, meaning "brick," but it means also the material of the brick, the clay, as does the Latin *testa*. The corresponding Old English term is *scel*, or *scell*, "shell, cavity, testa." There has also been found in a Latin inscription on a Roman gravestone of Pannonia a very old Germanic instance of the meaning "head." A Roman with the name of Cassus Musa buried his wife, who was a Germanic woman. Her name was *Strubilō-scalleō;* this means properly "tousle-head" (in German *Struwelkopf*). The meanings of "shell," "cup," "head," "skull" were thus connected in the Old Germanic language.

As one cannot draw a strict borderline between the cup or chalice used in the sacral ritual and the drinking vessel used every day, similarly, no strict separation is possible between the ritualistic religious consumption of human flesh and blood and the vulgar food cannibalism. A case of the simple food cannibalism was described by Amerigo Vespucci. He visited the shores of Brazil in 1501 and met there the Tupi tribe of the Indians. He reported to Lorenzo Medici:

> If they are the victors, they chop the defeated people to pieces, consume them and assert that this is an excellent meal. They nourish themselves on human flesh, too: the father consumes his son or the son consumes his father, as the case or the chances of the fight may be. I have seen a horrible man who bragged of having eaten more than three hundred men. I have also seen a place where I lived for twenty-seven days. There pieces of salted human flesh were hanging on the posts of houses, just as by us

at home salted or smoked pork or sausages are hanging. They were very surprised that we do not eat the flesh of our enemies like they do; they told us that nothing could be juicier or more delicate.[25]

Such vulgar food cannibalism was present in all those instances where prisoners were kept, like slaughter cattle, over a period of time in order to be fatted before they were killed for consumption. Such instances are attested for the American Indians. Such food cannibalism seems to go hand in hand with the sacrificial slaughtering of humans.

It was surely one of the great steps in human development when the eating of human flesh was abandoned. We know little of why and how this change came about in the prehistoric period of mankind, because in the light of history the custom is already, if not extinguished, in recess.

The custom of eating human flesh and drinking human blood may have been repressed and abolished by some unknown moral resource in man, yet the disappearance from the actual practice does not mean that cannibalism has disappeared also from the world of fantasies. Myth and tales are fraught with its motives as if they would compensate for the banishment in actual reality. Like after sunset the clouds on the horizon are still colored red, so the products of fantasies seem to be colored long after cannibal man has disappeared below the horizon.

Some examples from the language of the Bible will illustrate the case. They prove that the fantasies may still preserve residues of a long-forgotten past: The Psalmist speaks about the evil men, their works and says that they are "corrupt," they have done abominable works," "they are all gone aside, they are all together become filthy"; "who eat up my people as they eat bread, and call not upon the Lord" (Ps. 14:1–4). Jeremiah the prophet, in foretelling the catastrophes of his people, says, "for they are come, and have devoured the land, and all that is in it; the city, and those that dwell therein" (Jer. 8:16). In another passage he says, "for they have eaten up Jacob, and devoured him, and consumed him, and have made his habitation desolate" (Jer. 10:25).

It may be objected that these figurative expressions have no direct reference any longer with actual cannibalism, but I think the scripture exactly says what it meant to say.

256

The direct reference is obvious in these words of the prophet Micah:

> Who hate the good, and love the evil; who pluck off their skin from off them, and their flesh from off their bones; Who also eat the flesh of my people, and flay their skin from off them; and they break their bones and chop them in pieces, as for the pot, and as flesh within the caldron. Then shall they cry unto the Lord, but he will not hear them: he will even hide his face from them at that time, as they have behaved themselves ill in their doings (Mic. 3:2–4).

This is figurative speech, yet the liveliness of description speaks for itself. It is the language of an age in which cannibalism was not completely forgotten.

One may hold against this historical background the generally known fact that cannibalistic fantasies emerge with great intensity in cases of oral-sadistic regression in dreams and nightmares, in psychoses, especially in the hallucinations of alcoholics.[26] However rejected and repressed this heritage of human ancestry might be, it is still looming on the borderlines of the Ego, and time and again it succeeds in becoming an open expression. These fantasies, which are so general, cannot be understood on a limited individualistic plane.

I select among the many clinical examples the following ones:

To a patient, a stammerer, a "very narcissistic character," following active therapy directed toward abstinence from smoking, another cannibalistic dream emerged. "In it a man seemed to be attempting an assault on a young woman and the patient pounded the man's head on the floor and killed him. Then he ate the man and the human flesh seemed to taste like chicken. In another dream, the patient seemed to be eating his father's testicles. How the castration took place was not indicated in this dream, but it seemed quite natural to eat the testicles without any sense of guilt."[27]

A woman, sixty-two years of age, with many symptoms, complained: "I had a strange, frightening dream: I invited all my student tenants for a big evening meal. I served chopped meat, a kind of goulash, and I do not know how this happened, the goulash was made out of my three darling grandchildren. I can't understand it. . . . Could you explain?" (File.)

Henry, 4½ years old, said to his analyst: "I have to smash and destroy things. I can't help it. Something inside me always wants it. . . . Do you know what I do with people I like? First I kill them, cut them up in little pieces, roast them and then eat them up." By the "people I like" this boy may have his parents in mind.[28]

Cannibalistic fantasies are fused with castration fantasies in these cases.

The important role of eating and drinking in religious observances would be difficult to understand without considering the underlying idea of spiritual incorporation. This holds true particularly in respect to funeral ceremonials. The "funeral meal" (Greek *peri-deipnon,* Latin *silicernium*) originally was held upon or around the grave or around the funeral pile. The spirit of the dead was thought to be present, or to be even the host of the whole feast. The same presence of the spirit was also supposed at the sacrifice. The meal that followed, mostly debauching, excessive eating, drinking, exuberant feasting, seems to indicate the very essence of the ritual. Orgies were not exceptional. Seeking the reason for this drunken banqueting and merrymaking upon the just-covered grave, one hardly can avoid the conclusion that the dead person himself was the original victim of this sacrificial meal. The consumption of his flesh and blood implied a particular meaning. People felt relieved because the meal was thought to be the expiation of the guilt feelings toward the dead. Those who gathered around the grave felt some reason to reconcile the spirit of the dead by eating from his body and drinking from his blood, thereby absorbing his life in their own flesh and blood.

The sacrifice of human beings has been often described in detail by eyewitnesses all over the world during the early ages of history. If the interpretation is correct in asserting that the sacrifice is primarily the communion by eating the food offered to the spirit, we must concede that man offered the best of his food. Offering human life to the gods supposes that these gods liked this human food—an idea which betrays that people were still cannibals in their fantasies. The idea of man-eating gods is the outgrowth of cannibalistic fantasies.

In the course of cultural development the human body became an unholy food. The horror and disgust which became associated with the idea of its consumption show how powerful was the repression of cannibalism. The Ten Commandments say nothing among the "thou shalt nots" about anthropophagy. This must have been in the age of the commandment an abomination abhorred so thoroughly that no formal prohibition was any longer necessary.

When anthropophagy was wiped out as a source of food, it developed various substitute forms. One such substitute is the social anthropophagy as a privilege of the highest, most exclusive social caste. This was the case with the Indians who lived around Vancouver. Their highest social class was the *Hamet,* meaning the "man-eaters." It took four years of strenuous preparation to become admitted to the most respected aristocracy of these Indians.

The sacrificing of human beings and eating of their flesh as a solemn religious ritual was perhaps the most persistent form of cannibalism. When human flesh was rejected as daily food, it was still eaten in religious ceremonials. Men were slaughtered with sacral purpose in the Greek and Roman antiquity even though their flesh was not eaten any longer, but simply offered as food for the gods. The Germanic people made much use of human sacrifices in all their religious performances. Their wholesale slaughtering of people on the altars differs from the mass sacrifices, e.g., of the Aztecs in Mexico, only in that the Germanic people did not eat the slaughtered any longer. Man was the first and foremost object of sacrifice before the dawn of historical consciousness. Spirit has to be fed with spirit, thus the offering of human life, the human flesh and blood, was the most valuable gift. "The gods are thirsty," but their thirst wanted human blood according to these primitive fantasies. All blood sacrifices imply the killing of an animated being and sharing this food between the worshiper and the worshiped. This killing and communal eating received its full meaning when its center was the human spirit. For this reason it follows that the sacrifice of man was the archetype of all following blood sacrifices of animals. The primary object of the sacrificial meal was man himself; the meal itself was sacral anthropophagy. "The most beautiful among the victim animals is man," Procopius said.[*]

The interrelationship of cannibalism, human sacrifice, and ancestor worship is best illustrated by those instances showing that the chosen victims for sacrifice were venerated before their slaying. Such was the case of the Mexican yearly sacrifices. The chosen victim was first venerated as a prince, worshiped as divine, attributed with all luxuries and benefits of life, but all this for one year only until the day of sacrifice came. Then he was slain and eaten by the people. Similar to this custom, approaching the idea of theophagy, was the Aztec worship of their god Huitzilopochtli. They made from dough mixed with the blood of children a statue of the god of seeds. Then by a symbolic gesture they "killed" the idol and ate it. They called the feast "the eating of god."

See: ANCESTOR.

Christian Influence

The conjugal monogamous family developed in the Western World under the influence of the Christian religion. The teaching of Christ is radically opposed to the family system that prevailed in the Old Testament within the Judeo-Arabic culture at this time and that, one may add, was conducive to the Oedipus situation.

This opposition in principles went even so far that Christ himself, the prototype of love, displayed no signs of emotional attachment to his mother. It is difficult to understand otherwise such harsh words as those spoken in rebuke of motherly tender thoughtfulness: "Woman, what have I to do with thee? mine hour is not yet come" (John 2:4). The first part of this saying seems to deny radically any closeness to the mother, just as the following Greek saying does: "I do not care for Hecuba." Even in the last scene, the last word to the mother, the archetype of the *Mater Dolorosa,* reaffirming the sonship, is void of any expression of personal filial love

---

[*] Procopius, *The Gothic War* II:15. With an English translation by H. B. Dewing. Vol. III. The Loeb Classical Library. (London: William Heinemann, and New York: G. P. Putnam's Sons, 1919), p. 19. See also, O. Schrader, *Reallexikon der Indogermanischen Altertumskunde,* 2nd ed. (Berlin and Leipzig: Walter de Gruyer, 1929), 2:59, *s.v. Menschenopfer.*

and of the tenderness which Christ extended even to his executioners. He said: "Woman, behold thy son!" Then saith he to the disciple, "Behold thy mother!" (John 19:26–27).

Christ's teaching, simply by implication, positively precludes the practice of polygamy. However, his family ideal is patristic; it is the patristic conjugal family, the absolute unity of father and son which leaves no room for the mother. This is just the reversal of the Oedipus situation. Attachment to the father and remoteness from the mother is characteristic of Christ's family concept.

This new philosophy of life is based on the re-evaluation of sex. While sex was venerated as the magic creativeness in the male and condemned as an inherent evil in the female; Christ's teaching recast this whole doctrine. He repudiated sex altogether, no matter whether male or female. The child, considered as sexless, was declared to be nearest to the Kingdom of Heaven. At this age of general polygamy the male, we may suppose, displayed the large size of his harem with proud arrogance as a demonstration of wealth and sexual power. He surely looked down on his servant, the eunuch, who was deprived of power. What a revolution of thinking must have been proclaimed when Christ extolled the lowest, the eunuch (who was not even permitted to enter the temple), and preached that the eunuch, especially if he castrated himself and renounced sexuality by his own will, was entitled to enter first the Kingdom of Heaven. It made no difference to Christ whether the male or the female was concerned; sex was declared to be the source of evil, the seed of Satan.

Virginity and continence appeared in a new light as seen by this religious philosophy. Christ surely did not accept the prevailing system which approved the union of a virgin bride with a sexually experienced male. Virginity applies in Christ's teaching to the male as well as to the female. It is not just the quality of the chosen woman to be "without blemish" because it is supposed to raise her sales value, promising more thrill to the male. Virginity is a religious and moral quality, inseparable from holiness. It became the attribute of the holy life for man and woman alike.

Even more radically re-evaluated was the concept of adultery. "Thou shalt not commit adultery" was rather a loose concept in the Old Testament; it may have referred to incest, sodomy, fornication, and to the stealing of the wife of the neighbor as far as the male is concerned, but it meant a capital crime for the female. Christ pointedly turned the concept of adultery against the male. The turn was made in such outspoken terms that it must have shocked the men who felt secure in their sexual liberty. Adultery is by the definition of Christ an intentional act. "Ye have heard that it was said by them of old time, Thou shalt not commit adultery: But I say unto you, That whosoever looketh on a woman to lust after her hath committed adultery with her already in his heart" (Matt. 5:27–28). This is decidedly the adultery of the male; it is committed in fantasies. "If any man take a wife, and go in unto her, and hate her" (Deut. 22:13) and is indulging meanwhile in sex fantasies about another woman, he is guilty of the worst adultery.

While Christ's teaching is hard in brandishing the male's sexual transgressions, it is—again in opposition to the rigor of the Old Testament—rather lenient and understanding in respect to the female. When the woman, "taken in adultery, in the very act," was brought before him, Jesus seemingly did not even listen to these accusations, but, writing in the sand, indicated that the misdeed of the woman should be forgotten and forgiven just as the wind will blow away the writing on the sand. Then Jesus turned against the men and said, "He that is without sin among you, let him first cast a stone at her." He said to the woman, "Neither do I condemn thee: go, and sin no more" (John 8:1–11). It is also surely a remarkable fact of the Biblical tradition that Christ, when foretelling the great secret that he would rise from death, was not believed by his disciples; thus the risen Christ appeared first just to Mary Magdalene. "Now when Jesus was risen early the first day of the week, he appeared first to Mary Magdalene, out of whom he had cast seven devils" (Mark 16:9). The identification of the "seven devils" of the woman is open to interpretation, yet we surmise she would have been stoned under the Old Testament law.

The Christian marriage offers according to this philosophy not as perfect a form of life as does virginity and continence. Marriage is simply a tolerated evil. Paul, the first and most powerful interpreter of Christ's teaching, developed most distinctly the principle of Christian marriage (I Cor. 7). "It is good for a man not to touch a woman. Nevertheless, to avoid fornication, let every man have his own wife, and let every woman have her own husband. . . . But if they cannot contain, let them marry: for it is better to marry than to burn."

The new aspect of marriage is the proclaimed equality and reciprocity of husband and wife. This principle wrecked the polygamous family structure in its foundation.* True love could develop under polygamous conditions only in relation to the mother and at best become transferred from the mother to another woman. The Oedipus complex developed out of this supposition that the only genuine source of love is the attachment to the mother. In contradiction to this mother-centered love Paul said that the heterosexual love will develop from the narcissistic self-love as in fact it may replace auto-erotic fixation. "So ought men to love their wives as their own bodies. He that loveth his wife loveth himself" (Eph. 5:28). The Oedipus complex, the radical evil of the polygamous family, is cast out like the seven devils by these very words: "For this cause shall a man leave his father and mother, and shall be joined unto his wife, and they two shall be one flesh. This is a great mystery: but I speak concerning Christ and the church" (Eph. 5:31–32). That Paul symbolizes the unity of Christ and the church by the union of husband and wife expresses the utmost spiritualization of marriage as a sacred institution.

Divorce also became radically re-evaluated. In full contrast to the general practice that permitted the man to dismiss his wife but did not allow the wife to separate herself from the husband, the new question raised was rather this: How is divorce possible at all if man and woman are one flesh? How can man separate what has grown together into an inseparable unity? Christ's answer restricts divorce to a situation in which this unity of man and woman does not exist

---

* For the sake of contrast, I quote what Procopius said about the widows of the Germanic Heruli people: "And when a man of the Heruli died, it was necessary for his wife, if she laid claim to virtue and wished a fair name behind her, to lie not long afterward beside the tomb of her husband by hanging herself with a rope. And if she did not do this, the result was that she was in ill repute thereafter and an offense to the relatives of her husband." *The Gothic War* VI, 14: 3–11. With an English translation by H. B. Dewing, Vol. III:405.

spiritually, i.e., in cases of adultery which, as pointed out before, might be committed in fantasies. Christ's psychology searches deep in the human mind and realizes that the polygamous family life may disappear from the surface of the social order; it may even be condemned and prosecuted as bigamy; but deep in their hearts, in the fantasies of their wishful thinking, men will remain polygamous. The intentional ethics of Christ removed the mask and hypocrisy of physical monogamy which is conjugal. He claimed faithfulness in the sexual fantasies from his believers. Of course sexual fantasies appear and disappear in the mind as if they were written in the dust of the ground. While the woman was looked upon formerly as a possession, the new gospel led her out of servitude and opened the way toward her acceptance as a human being equal with her master in rights and dignity. She finally deserved to be addressed as *potnia, domina, Frau,* or *lady.* This was the first step on the long road of emancipation. However, Christ's concept of the Christian family is decidedly patristic. It was pronounced again and again by Paul that the woman is still on a lower level of human existence than the man. It was perhaps necessary for Paul to emphasize this for the time being because Christ's equalizing man and woman was too radical a reform on the way to emancipation. Paul said: "But I would have you know, that the head of every man is Christ; and the head of the woman is the man; and the head of Christ is God" (I Cor. 11:3). He explained by this that the head of man should be uncovered but the head of woman must be covered in worship services. "For if the woman be not covered, let her also be shorn: but if it be a shame for a woman to be shorn or shaven, let her be covered. For a man indeed ought not to cover his head, forasmuch as he is the image and glory of God: but the woman is the glory of the man" (I Cor. 11:6–7). Paul even recapitulated the age-old prejudice that the woman is made out of man. "For the man is not of the woman; but the woman of the man. Neither was the man created for the woman; but the woman for the man" (I Cor. 11:8–9). This sounds like a justification of polygamy, yet this was not Paul's intention. His last word is still the praise of love and reciprocity of man and woman in Christian marriage. "Nevertheless neither is the man without the woman, neither the woman without the man, in the Lord. For as the woman is of the man, even so is the man also by the woman; but all things of God" (I Cor. 11:11–12). In this way the Christian teaching fomented a new emotional climate in family life, a climate in which the child may grow up with the feeling of security, of being loved and wanted, without hatred of one parent and incestuous attachment to the other. The conjugal monogamous unity of husband and wife became the foundation of Western civilization; it represents the final solution of the Oedipus complex.

Conception

The original meaning of the verb *to conceive*, from the Latin *con-cipiō, -ere*, unites in a paradoxical way "togetherness, closeness," and "aggression." The prefix *con-* denotes "close connection." The verb *capiō, -ere*, "to take, lay hold, seize, grasp," refers to aggression. This verb, like *perceive, apprehend, grasp*, reveals another characteristic feature: it can apply to physiology as well as to philosophy. The classic example is the Biblical sentence: "Adam knew Eve his wife; and she conceived" (Gen. 4:1). The "concept" is a term of philosophy, it refers to genital knowledge.

The emotional relationship between parents and children is to a great extent dependent upon the early sex theories. Different types of families developed their characteristic sex theories. If the child is perceived to have grown in the mother the matristic type of family can be expected. For example, in the Biblical language, the patristic type is represented in such formulas as "seed of Abraham" and the matristic fantasies are implied in the expression "fruit of the womb."

The total ignorance about the elementary facts of procreation, which is characteristic of the small child, has been found and described by anthropologists as a condition of the primitive level of culture.[29] Sexual ignorance has been used, in fact, as a criterion of primitivity. This means that people procreate almost as animals do but the people, too, have no insight into the biological process; they remain ignorant particularly about the role of the father in the conception of the child. The father's relationship to his children is almost that of a stepfather to his stepchildren. He considers his children not as his own but as the children of his wife. He remains a marginal figure and all his children are more or less like adopted children.

The childish ignorance is on the same level. The child in the stage of growing can well accept as a matter of fact that it has grown as an embryo in the mother, but the idea of previous sex relation between the parents is still unbearable for his infantile fantasies. Thus it supposes that the fertilization of the mother was brought about by artificial means. Repression has blocked out the father as the begetter of his child. This might be one of the reasons why the concept of "parents" is unknown in the early Greek language as well as in the Old Testament Hebrew.

Three types of conception theories have developed under such premises. One, the most repressive theory, admits neither the father nor the mother in generating the child. Another admits the mother but not the father; and a third, rather uncommon variant, considers the child born from the father without a mother. Strange as these primitive sex theories may appear to our minds, they are all well attested in various cultural settings.[30]

The image of the father, once removed, has to be replaced by natural processes such as rain, wind, lightning; the ocean, too, is often considered as the fertilizing agency. Venus emerged out of the waves of Okeanos. The "wave" is called in Greek *kuma*, "anything swollen as if pregnant," "a wave billow," "the fetus in the womb." The ocean is the "mother-water" also in the Chinese picture writing. The "dolphin," the Greek *delphinos,* means properly the "uterine" animal; it is also symbolic of the fetus. The people of the Trobriand Islands in Melanesia, described as being ignorant of the physical part of the father, believe that unmarried girls should not expose themselves by bathing at high tide because they may become pregnant.[31] The ocean as the primary abyss was considered in the oldest Greek and Latin cosmogonies to be filled with germinal materials.

The rain is also interpreted as a father substitute in myth and folklore. We say "it is raining" and fantasies may question: "Who is behind this *it?*" The Greeks said exactly *Zeus huei,* "Zeus, the father god, is raining." Rabelais' Gargantua and Swift's Gulliver re-enact such fantasies. Zeus fertilized Danaë in her prison tower, by a "shower of gold."

The wind, another celestial agency, is often considered as the true father of the child. Hera conceived Hephaestus by inhaling the wind. In Longfellow's *Hiawatha* (1855) the west wind is claimed to be the father of the Mohawk Indian chief. It sounds rather strange that this infantile substitution of the father is carried over into the field of realistic agriculture and animal husbandry. Vergil, in all seriousness, attributes the fertilizing of the mares to the Zephyr wind (*Georgica* 1:273). The Greek *Zephyros,* and the corresponding Latin *Favōnius,* the warm, wet spring wind from the west was considered as a fertilizing agency. The word *favōnius* is again used with the sense of *spurius,* "illegitimate child." Repressing the father image always makes the conception of the child spurious. *Pater semper incertus,* "the father is always uncertain," is a classic Roman axiom. The Latin *favor* carries a connotation that can be recovered only by knowing its background. The Latin noun *favor,* "good will, inclination," is a derivative of the verb *faveō, -ēre,* "to be favorable, well disposed"; this, however, if not a direct derivative of *foveō, -ere,* "to be warm, keep warm," also "to cherish, caress, love, favor, support, assist," surely became contaminated with it. The warm fertilizing *Favonius* wind of the spring is charged with associations of "warm" and "wet," which makes its fertilizing effect understandable. It is a formula of the English Bible saying of the woman in respect to her husband: "to find favor in his sight."

The English *wind* is "blowing," in German *wehen,* which again became confused with the plural of the noun *Weh, Wehen,* properly the *woes,* which denotes the labor in birth. It seems to be that the idea of "blowing up" referred to both the pregnant woman and the wind. So the German *Winds-braut,* "whirlwind," properly meant the "winds-bride." Similar expressions are found in Greek and Roman traditions. These are examples of the "everyday mythology" that found expression only in language, not in Germanic mythological representations. However, Ovid described how Flora was ravished by Zephyr (*Fasti* 5:195–202).

Adding a clinical illustration, one can sometimes observe that some seeds are, indeed, floating in the air and may suggest fertilization through the wind. Some insects, too, flying around may become suspicious in infantile fantasies as germ carriers.

A five-year-old girl with such insect phobia was very outspoken and explained that the male semen was emitted in order to fly around and enter the female, but she added doubtfully that she did not really believe it because the semen has no wings like flies and butterflies.[32]

One may add to the clinical report as background illustration that in Greek vase paintings one can in fact see how the winged Cupido-Amor ejaculates seed, which develops into butterflies and flies away. Similar fantasies are attested for deeply regressed schizophrenic patients. A female patient expressed her loneliness by stating that people can be turned into bugs, and bugs can turn into persons, in this way she would have something "to call her own."[33]

The position of the father appears to be somewhat marginal in the light of these fantasies. He is not really the father of the child because his part in procreation is substituted by a natural or superhuman agency. The father is not begetting the child but adopting it. He accepts the child by the birth ritual of lifting it up from the Mother Earth and placing it on his lap. It is well known through dream interpretations that the father appears frequently in dreams as an intruder, a stranger who is interfering with the child and mother relationship.[34] The Trobriand Islanders call the father *komakava,* "stranger," or, even more correctly, "outsider."[35]

Despite such repression people were multiplying, fathers begot children; consequently the primitive mind introduced a fine distinction within the concept of procreation. The father may "beget" the child, but "generating" a new life appeared as the prerogative of a spiritual, superhuman power. In this consists the wisdom of the often ridiculed primitive sex theories. The physical act of the father does not explain the origin of a new life. The primitive man seems to confess his ignorance and believes that the conception of a new life is a miracle beyond any rational human understanding. So they think the father may create the conditions for the true fertilizing act; some primitives go even so far as to say: Man must first "open the womb" so that the creative spirit may enter, but the agency of the spirit is an act of grace, independent from human will.

The Biblical conception theory goes along these lines of thinking: The Lord "opens the womb," the Lord "shuts the womb" like a door or mouth. Man has nothing to do with it. We hear Rachel's desperate outcry addressed to her husband Jacob: "Give me children, or else I die." Whereupon Jacob retorts angrily: "Am I in God's stead, who hath withheld from thee the fruit of the womb?" (Gen. 30:1–2). The Hebrew *Joab* properly means "The Lord [is] his father." To address the Lord as "Our Father" is not simply figurative speech but is understood literally. The Creator, Maker, is in fact the father. "As thou knowest not what is the way of the spirit, nor how the bones do grow in the womb of her that is with child: even so thou knowest not the works of God who maketh all" (Eccles. 11:5). The personal relationship of man to God is strengthened by the conception theory that tends to replace the earthly father by God as the true spiritual father of man. In the light of this thought we shall better understand the strange statement of Christ: " . . . and call no man your father upon the earth: for one is your Father, which is in heaven" (Matt. 23:9). The wording of Paul sounds even stronger: "And because ye are sons, God hath sent forth the Spirit of his Son into your hearts, crying, Abba, Father" (Gal. 4:6).

It might be stated that the negation of human paternity has cast an air of irresponsibility upon the male even in cultures that emphasize the virginity of the female. The male could achieve sexual gratification without the moral obligations inherent in it. Paternity is not instinctive, has no biological foundations. It has to be ingrained, learned by culture. The denial of physical paternity in some cases may be the expression of the primitive nature of the male: sex without the heavy burden of paternity which religion, morals, and knowledge have imposed upon it.

The great interest of the child in procreation has a lasting effect upon the fantasies of the adult. The curiosity of the child concerning the conception of its life is a legitimate desire for knowledge; it is still one of the greatest and deepest problems of metaphysics. And it is still a miracle. The relationship of man to his parents in respect to conception remained, beyond all emotional ties, a metaphysical problem. There is a Latin saying mostly misunderstood as referring to history: "Not to know what came to pass before you were born means to remain always a child." (*Nescire quid antea quam natus acciderit, id semper est esse puerum.*) This saying expresses the much more vital psychological truth concerning the conception of a new life.

See: BLESSING, BIRTH, DEATH.

Death

We are primarily interested in early verbal expressions that reveal some characteristics of man's conception of death. No one really knows what death is like; one can only guess what the idea of death meant to various language communities; one can define it in the negative as the end of life or describe it objectively as the dying of someone else, but one can speak and think of one's own death in no other terms than in terms of life. It has been said often that there would be no religion, no philosophy, no great works of art without the fear of death and the according desire for immortality. By the same token, one may state that by studying the terms about "death" and "dying," the whole theory of verbal expression and repression can be explored.

There once was one common term for "death." This old genuine term is reflected in many of our languages, as in the Latin verb *morior,* "to die," and the noun *mors,* "death"; and to this group of words the English *murder* and the German *Mord,* "murder," belong. These words indicate the nature of "death." What we consider as "natural" death did not exist for early thinking. According to this thinking, man does not simply "die," but is always "killed" by some agency; the killer might be some disease, old age, or even a god, but man is always "put to death" against his will. This belief implied that death "strikes" as a fatal blow, as an accident which could have been avoided. Death happens by chance, not as necessity. Wishful thinking always appealed to chance when necessity became unbearable. The accidental death—by a strange twist of our culture—became increasingly accepted, once again, as normal.

The necessity of death emerged as a rather late and painful insight. No animal has it, even though it may fight for the preservation of its life. Because this insight is painful, man avoided calling it by name. He resorted to cover words and substitute expressions. Circumlocutions for the unspeakable and unknowable idea reflect, as do projective tests, the return of the repressed fantasies that man developed in defense of his Ego. One can well distinguish two categories of these cover words: one type is represented by the so-called transitive verbs, which perceive "death" as "killing," as the action of an outside agency; the other type of cover words suggests that dying is an "intransitive" process, the dying person "departed" or "passed away" by his own volition.

The first type, "to be killed," might have been the meaning of the genuine prehistoric term, the remnants of which remained preserved in the Latin *mors* and the English *murder*. The original meaning seems to coincide with the concept "to crush," which implies a superior power that destroys its helpless victim. This is also the implication of the Old English *cwelan*, "to die"; the according noun *cwalu* denotes "violent death, slaughter, a quelling with weapons." The most general concept supposes that death "strikes," thus that dying is the consequence of "a stroke," sometimes specified as "a stroke on the head." A deadly blow appears in verbal fantasies as the reason of death. The Latin *nex* denoted such "violent death" when the noun *mors* assumed the meaning of natural death. This noun, *nex,* is a derivative of the verb *necāre,* "to kill." The English *slay* originally meant "to strike to death"; the according German verb *schlagen* also means "to strike." Even the verb *to kill* originally also meant "to strike, beat, knock," particularly on the head.

Man is not always the passive victim in this attack against his life; this is indicated by the Latin verbs with the prefix *inter-,* "between," as *inter-ficiō, -ere,* "to kill," from *facere,* "to do, make"; this is implied still in the verb *to interfere,* from the Latin *inter-,* "between," and *feriō, -īre,* "to strike, smite, beat, knock, cut, thrust, hit," but it means also "to kill by striking, to give a death blow, to slay." It is the "violent" accidental death which seems to be generally accepted by the verbal expressions of early ages. The French verb *tuer,* "to kill," derives from the Latin *tutāre, tutāri,* "to make safe (*tūtus*), safeguard, protect oneself against." It is supposed, for the most part, that this "killing" for safety refers to the "extinguishing of fire," which could be a secondary symbolic expression, but it was, in any case, the protection of one's life which resulted in "killing."

A change from the conception of death or of being dead as a condition caused by an outside agency to the conception that it might also be a condition caused by a natural happening may be seen by examining the English words *death, dead,* and *to die. Death* and *dead* are respectively represented in German by *Tod* and *tot.* From them developed the corresponding verbal derivative *töten,* "to kill," as did the Old English *ādiēdan* and the Gothic *dauthjan,* both also meaning "to kill." Obviously the words *death* and *dead* attribute death to an outside agency. On the other hand, the verb *to die* was adopted by English from Scandinavian. Why? Most likely as both a replacement for some outmoded idea and an expression for a new one. We say: "He *has* died." In other words, he *has* something, he is in possession of something. The word *is* (not *has*) is used with the old-concept word *dead:* e.g., he *is* dead. In German, too, the expressions for the idea of the violent death, killing, slaying, had to be augmented by a new one for the new concept of death, the natural death. The replacement is the altogether different verbal form *sterben,* "to die," as a necessity of all life. This word is related to *starve.* The necessary death was a source of even greater anxiety than to be killed by an outside agency. "They that be slain with the sword are better than they slain with hunger, for those pine away, stricken through for want of the fruits of the field" (Lam. 4:9). The "natural death" was called "the death of death," "the own death," in Latin *morte suimet mortuus est,* "he died the death of his own self." This "own death of death" is recorded on the old Persian stone inscription on the rock of Behistūn in which King Darius paid his last tribute to Cambyses.*

The intransitive cover words such as *departed* or *passed away* describe death as someone's own doing, mostly in terms of travel or change of domicile, that is, in terms of life because one must be alive in order to do something. So the Latin says *ex-eō, -īre,* "to go out or away," which can refer to someone going "from one's house," "to move out"; it is also another way of saying "to decease, die"—instead of the usual *ex-cedere* or *de-cedere de vita,* "to depart from life." The Old English also used such cover words as *forth-faran,*

---

* The oldest Hungarian text, the "Funeral Sermon," also says of Adam: "Thou shalt die the death of death" (*halalnac halalaval halsz*). See the classic paper of Wilhelm Schulze: *Der Tod des Kambyses.* Sitzungsberichte der königl. Preussischen Akademie der Wissenschaften. (Berlin, 1912), p. 32–34, and 685–703.

"to go forth, depart, die," and *forth-fore* for calling the "death"; and since *fore* means "went," it is said and thought that the deceased "went forth."

Infantile fantasies perceive the beginning of life as if the newborn had lived somewhere else and simply was brought home from another location; by the same token the end of life is perceived as if the dead one has left the home and continues to live somewhere else. The funeral ceremonials are, in this case, expressive of death fantasies of early ages, much as is the verbal heritage. The funeral ceremonials appear in our understanding as if they were made in preparation for a long journey. They provide the departing life with all the personal belongings, weapons, and food which the traveler may need; he is also provided with his favorite animals—which are killed for the journey—and even with his wives, who are supposed to accompany the deceased to the land beyond. Herodotus tells us about the burial of the Scythians: "In the open space around the body of the king they bury one of his concubines, first killing her by strangling, and also his cup-bearer, his cook, his groom, his lackey, his messenger, some of his horses, firstlings of all his other possessions and some golden cups" (4:71). The travel was often depicted as the crossing of a river or a big water; therefore, the boat or ship, in the function of the coffin, was widely used in the language of fantasies.[36] The Greek ritual did not forget to provide the dead with one obol, the established tariff fee of the ferryman, Charon; he was waiting in his boat to transfer the psyche of the dead. Medieval Christianity often ascribed to saints the symbol of a "little ship" or boat. This does not mean that the saint is necessarily the protector of seagoing vessels; the small boat may indicate that the saint is the protector of the souls when they "depart." For instance, Saint Melanesius is depicted as lying dead in a ship sailing against the stream; Saint Werenfrid's attribute is a "little ship" which he holds in his hand, but this ship has a coffin on her deck! Dante, the great fountainhead of medieval symbolism, speaks also about himself as if his soul would travel on a little *navicella* across the ocean of the eternal Beyond, from which no man ever returned (*Paradiso* 2:1 ff. and 23:67 ff.).

As a clinical illustration, a dream of Lincoln may serve. In this dream Lincoln feels that he is in a singular indescribable vessel. It is always the same throughout his life,

and the whole substance of the dream picture is moving with
great rapidity toward a dark, indefinite shore. The biographer
connects this dream with Lincoln's strong attachment to his
mother and also with the obvious regressive tendencies.[37]

The departure becomes meaningful if death is accepted as the fulfillment of life, as the return to the beginning.
The journey into the unknown has in such cases an inner
direction, it is the "going home," the German *Heimgang,*
"going home to the mother." Death is understood, in the light
of unconscious fantasies, not simply as separation from life,
but also as the reunification with the mother. Pictures of the
infantile past in this way become blended with the expecta-
tions of the unfathomable future. The "Islands of the Blessed"
is the picture of the Golden Age of infancy. Oedipus reached
his goal at Colonus; he arrived home at the grove of the
chthonian Mother Goddesses. In the same way Goethe's Faust
also arrived at the end of his long journey to the "Mothers."
Many people have died with this idea in mind: the last word
uttered by the dying lips was "mother." Erasmus of Rotter-
dam, the great humanist who spoke and wrote only Latin and
Greek and was alienated from his mother tongue, uttered his
last words in Dutch: *lieve moeder,* "dear mother." Toulouse-
Lautrec, also alienated from his aristocratic family, died with
these words (in French), "dear mother, soon I shall be with
you." Pope John XXIII, who by his holy coronation became
elevated above his humble origin, died with these words:
Mamma mia, mamma mia! Instances can be multiplied; they
illustrate the regressive fantasies in death which have no
bearing on a matristic social order. The regression to the
mother is also expressed by the symbolism of the various
funeral rituals. Whether the dead body is enwrapped in
swaddling clothes like the babe or buried in the fetal crouch-
ing position, ideas of the beginning of life are implied. The
coffin and the *casket,* as well as the funerary urns, are
symbolic for the return to the Mother Earth; the death boats
of seagoing people depict the return to the Mother Water, as
the ocean is called, for instance, in Chinese.

Some expressions define "death" in the nihilistic way
simply as the undoing of life. Such terms are, in Old English,
ealdor-gedāl, "death," saying properly "separation (*gedāl*)
from life or age (*ealdor*)." Another one is *for-weordhan,* the

opposite of becoming, "to become nothing, be undone, perish, die."

Old English uses two other verbs descriptive of "dying": *sweltan* and *steorfan*. The according noun *swylt*, "death," reveals a characteristic feature of this negative philosophy of death. It is a general over-all observation that life supposes some humid, warm, pliable material, while "death" is equivalent with dehydration, cooling off, and thus suggests the ideas of cold, stiff, numb, and, especially, dry. We still have preserved the verb *to swelter* in the original meaning, "to be oppressed with heat, to sweat profusely"; it refers to the same process that was denoted in Old English *sweltan,* in Gothic *swiltan*. In Scandinavian languages *to swelter* means primarily "to starve." This also explains the Old English verb *steorfan,* meaning both "to die" and "to starve." The according German verb *sterben,* however, implies just the general idea "to die"; on the other hand, the English *starve* still means specifically "to die of hunger"—but in the English dialects it also means "to perish of exposure to cold, to freeze to death."

We shall understand these verbs if we consider that primitive people, living in close contact with nature, sometimes in equatorial heat and burning sunshine, consider the liquid substances of the body as the ingredients of life: blood and semen are such substances; and even fat, which can melt, and especially the spinal liquid, the brain, and the marrow of the bones were considered the seat of vitality and sexual capacity.

Job says: "One dieth in his full strength, being wholly at ease and quiet. His breasts are full of milk, and his bones are moistened with marrow" (21:23–24). Because the sexual vitality was supposed in the marrow, Job can say: "His bones are full of the sin of his youth" (20:11). The moisture is the condition of growth in nature, the Psalmist says: "Thou hast the dew of thy youth" (110:3). The liquid is the very life substance, the symbol of vitality, and this should be in mind when Christ speaks to the woman of Samaria about the "living water" (John 4:10). "To be born of water" (John 3:5) should not be interpreted as referring simply to the amniotic fluid, nor to the ocean as a mother symbol in general, rather to the concept that life is implied in the liquid secretion and excretion, as in nature humidity is the precondition of vegetation.

The opposite of life means the loss of liquid, the gradual drying up of the organism. The sweat covering the dying face, the fever burning up from inside this vital substance are steps in this process that ends life. For an illustration may serve the word *skeleton,* from the Greek *skeleton sōma,* "dried body, mummy," and, in turn, from the verb *skellō,* "to dry up, parch." While the bones of youth are teeming with moisture, the "dry bone" skeleton becomes symbolic of death. One is reminded of Ezekiel's vision of the valley of dry bones, the valley where the bones "were very dry" (37:2). The heat consumes the vital liquid. The Psalmist says: "For my days are consumed like smoke, and my bones are burned as an hearth" (102:3). So says Job also: "My skin is black upon me, and my bones are burned with heat" (30:30). The dying man withers like the plant in the dry land. He is thirsty, he desires the "living water."

According to the Greek Orphic tradition, when the soul arrives at Hades, it cries out: "I am dry with thirst and perish."[38] With this in mind one will recognize the meaning of the seldom understood last words of the dying Christ: "I thirst" (John 19:28). This outcry might also be motivated by the great "return." While he avoided any reference to his mother in his parables, dying Christ said: "Woman, behold thy son!" (John 19:26). He returned to his infancy when he was truly the son of the mother and received the "living water" from the mother.

The idea of starving and thirst implied in death may explain that, in regressive fantasies, the Golden Age of the dead ones appears as an age of abundance and plenty. Funeral ceremonials provide the deceased with food, drink, and shelter. The custom of *libation,* from the Latin *libō, -āre,* "to pour out as an offering," means "a pouring of a liquid, as wine, either on the ground or on a victim in sacrifice, in honor of a deity." This custom may hold the explanation of the German verb *schenken,* "to give." Its original meaning is still transparent in the verb *ein-schenken,* "to pour," properly "to tilt."

Perhaps the drying up of nature in winter and the reawakening in the moist of spring was perceived as the general background of these images of death and of the returning life. The technical fumigation and dehydration of corpses at such funeral rituals as are attested to for the pre-Greek Mycenaean and for the Germanic graves preceded the complete incineration, which radically transsubstantiated the corpse into dry ashes. These ashes, once again, can be poured into the urn, like any liquid. The Psalmist says: "I am poured out like water, and all my bones are out of joint: my heart is like wax; it is melted in the midst of my bowels. My strength is dried up like a potsherd; and my tongue cleaveth to my jaws; and thou hast brought me into the dust of death" (Ps. 22:14–15).

This proverb seems to be the best explanation of the term *to liquidate,* in the meaning "to wipe out by killing or murder." The Old English *sweltan,* "to die," is the twin word of *meltan,* "to melt," which denotes the transformation of the solid body into the shapeless liquid. How old and interrelated these fantasies are can be observed in the Greek verb *cheō,* "to pour, melt, smelt." The corresponding *chutra* denotes the "earthen vessel," and *enchutos* means "poured in, infused, a cake cast into shape"; consequently one may elaborate according to folklore that the cake often became cast into the shape of a swaddled babe. The Greek verb *en-churidzō* means "to expose children in earthenware vessels"; *en-chustristria* accordingly denotes either "the mother who has exposed her child in an earthen pot" or "the woman who gathered the bones from the funeral pile in the urn." These two meanings of the same word indicate that both acts, however different, were perceived as collateral and essentially the same. The English slang term *to go to pot,* meaning "to come to an end," is also used in classic Greek. The return to the *chutra,* "pot, urn," means the final end of life. This process of liquidation reversed the imaginary prenatal process of incubation, melting, molding, and solidifying of the body fluids, notably of the blood, which was the *blessing* of the mother.

The formal difference between the noun *death* as accidental "killing" and the verb *to die* supposes a still deeper change in the concept of human life. It is not by chance that the prehistoric forms of houses, as used by Germanic people, are known as "house-urns," urns shaped in the form of little houses. They are the strict parallels of the Old English *bān-*

hūs, properly "bone-house," an old term for the human body. "Body," "house," "urn" are closely associated with one another. The: are figurative expressions suggesting that the body is just a shelter for the indwelling spirit. The spirit enters the body at conception and leaves the body with the last exhalation. "Primitive paternity" rejects the full responsibility for a new life for the good reason that this would also imply the idea of complete annihilation in death. Total death became replaced by the concept of "partial *dying,"* which means while the mortal body is "drying up," the immortal soul is leaving the body and returning to its origin. The dead one, the corpse, is considered, accordingly, as a "cover," as in the German *Leich-nam,* from the former *līh-hamo,* properly "body cover." The question may be asked : What is the body covering? The corresponding Old English terms for the "body" suggest the answer: they call the "body" *flaesc-homa,* properly "flesh-cover"; *ban-cofa,* "bone-cave"; *ban-faet,* "bone-vessel"; or *ban-hūs,* "bone-house." The "house," the "cave," the "vessel" made of flesh and bones are all "cover" for the invisible agency that has chosen the house, cave, vessel for its dwelling place. All these terms reveal a basic dualistic concept of man.

While the monistic concept of man implies the idea of total death, the dualistic aspect accepts death only as partial, as the separation of the mortal "cover," "vessel," "house," from the immortal essence. This dualistic concept of man alleviates, in some respects, the fear of death. The Greeks held the belief that *Thanatōs,* "death," is the twin brother of *Hypnos,* "sleep"; death is just like falling asleep and awakening again. Despite such obvious consolatory fantasies, it would surely result in complete misunderstanding if one would consider the effect of consolation to be the cause and origin of this most general belief which is shared by the greater part of all humanity. This belief in immortality of the soul is rooted in the very foundation of all life; this is the polarity of the inside and the outside, the subjective and objective pole of perception. As stated before, death belongs exclusively to the objective perception, and is never experienced subjectively; thus the idea of death refers to the objective reality of the body and does not interfere with the subjective conviction that rejects the assumption of total annihilation.

The Old Testament concept of man, as well as Homeric anthropology, went even further and substituted the dualistic aspect by a tripartite division. They distinguish the mortal body, the life soul, which perishes with the body, and the immortal soul, which transcends the individual life.

The classic Greek thinking supposes that the "body," *sōma,* is charged with "something vaporous," *thumos,* related to the Latin *fumus,* "smoke." It is located in the blood and other body fluids, in the whole cardiovascular system; especially the *phrēn,* "midriff," and the lungs are charged with it. The respiratory and circulatory systems are perceived in their interdependence as the seat of the *thumos;* it keeps the body alive and wastes away in death. These Greek concepts defy translation; *thumos* cannot be properly replaced by the English "mind" because the meanings are different. The Old English *sawol,* "soul," however, comes very near to the ancient belief of a conscious mind located in the warm body fluids, particularly in the blood. The equivalent Latin term is *animus;* it also denotes the agency that keeps the body alive. The Old Testament Hebrew uses the term *nephesh* in the same restricted sense. It says explicitly: "For the life of the flesh is in the blood" (Lev. 17:11). When it is said, "The voice of thy brother's blood crieth unto me from the ground" (Gen. 4:10), not the blood as such, but the *nephesh* in the spilled blood is still crying out to the heavens.

In distinction to the Greek *thumos,* Latin *animus,* Hebrew *nephesh,* another concept developed. This is denoted by the Greek *psychē,* Latin *anima,* and the Hebrew *ruach.* These terms refer to the immortal essence of man. They never identify this transcendental principle with the blood; they refer generally to respiration. They perceive respiration as the continuous exchange of the inside and outside world, as the invisible communication between the subjective and the objective reality; thus respiration became the carrier of the immortal and divine share of man. Yet this belief, which is deeply ingrained in almost all our languages, did not remove the doubt and the conflict between the objective reality of death and the subjective belief in immortality. As Job said: "For there is hope of a tree, if it be cut down, that it will sprout again. . . . But man dieth, and wasteth away: yea, man giveth up the ghost and where is he? . . . So man lieth down, and riseth not: till the heavens be no more, they shall not awake, nor be raised out of their sleep. . . . If a man die, shall he live again? all the days of my appointed time will I wait, till my change come" (Job 14:7–14).

Family

The word *family* is derived from the Latin *familia,* which originally meant not the conjugal unity of parents and children, but "the slaves in a household, a household establishment" and, with the idea of the house predominating, "a house with all belongings, a family estate, property." The word is a derivative of *famulus,* "servant, slave," as belonging to the house. The *pater familias* has kept this original meaning, which was also implied in the Greek *des-pōtes,* the Sanskrit *dampati,* "lord of the house."[39]

The family was polygamous at the beginning of history, at least among all people from the Indo-European stock who have built up our Western civilization. Only two exceptions are noteworthy: they are the Greek and the Roman; these people were in principle monogamous. The Persian men—as Herodotus reported—each of them has many women, "and a still larger number of concubines" (1:135). He said concerning the Thracian people, too, that "each man has many wives" (5:5). Similar documentary evidences are furnished concerning all the other people of Indo-European descent; the German people are no exception in this respect. The people of the Old Testament, who, although belonging to the Semitic-Hamitic stock of languages, contributed abundantly to our Western heritage, were equally polygamous. Even the Greek and the Roman families, though monogamous in principle, were still far from the ideal of conjugal monogamy as we understand it today. Their monogamy was rather a legal fiction. The important role of slave women and concubines (Greek *pallakides*) within the household, and the consequent great number of illegitimate children (*nothoi*) suggests that the actual condition of family life still preserved many remnants of an earlier polygamy.

The transitional state between monogamy and polygamy was marked by the ever-growing distinction of the first, favorite wife from the other wives, who became gradually declassified as concubines and servants. The total family appears not as a closely knit unity, but as an extended compound of subfamilies. Such a joint family was the rule with the Old Testament people; the same family structure must be supposed for Indo-European prehistory, too. The subfamily may be grouped around the wives or the sons who were also married; it may be formed by various conjugal families.

One will realize that within this rather loose structure of the joint family unit the emotional relationship between its members was quite different from all those characteristics found in the close unity of the monogamous conjugal family. The ruling head of this unit, spoken of as the "Himself," was its provider and master.

The conflicting emotions of the growing child lead to the complex phenomenon summarized by the term "family romance."[40] This Oedipus complex developed as a plastic psychological reality under the conditions of patristic polygamy. Within our modern conjugal monogamy only the vestiges can be detected of this emotional conflict which was in full force during the early ages of patristic polygamy. The same archaic heritage is present in the Oedipus complex as in castration fantasies, guilt feelings, and food predilections; it is the world of our early ancestors which we try to forget, and which is therefore submerged in the oblivion of unconscious fantasies. The etymology of words leads us to the etymology of emotions that are still operative in our present-day society. It is obvious without much scientific demonstration that the "husband" of the polygamous family is emotionally not the same as the husband of conjugal monogamy; by the same token the father of fifty or more boys and uncounted girls is emotionally not the same kind of father as is the "daddy" whose children internalize his image in the closely knit conjugal monogamy. The Bible says about Solomon: "And he had seven hundred wives, princesses, and three hundred concubines: and his wives turned away his heart" (I Kings 11:3). This multitude of wives and concubines cannot be considered even as an extended biological affiliation. Even though it is said, "his wives turned away his heart," the atmosphere of emotional intimacy of the conjugal family is *a priori* excluded. The husband of the many wives is not loved but feared; he is reflected in our languages as the *despot,* the ruler and lord of the house who is distinguished primarily by his absolute "power" to use sexually all his female subjects. He bought his wives as he bought slaves or cattle; no wonder it makes little difference to him whether the woman is his wife or his slave, maidservant, or concubine. Each is his private possession whose price has been paid. The sadistic fantasies of the male are sometimes best satisfied by the woman who is his purchased possession, even if only for an hour. It is a distinction for the wife, one of the many, if she is selected.

The worst evil of polygamous social order is the competition of the wives for the favor of the one master. This competition may have an advantage for the male, but it surely undermines the security of the females. The Old Testament is replete with this female rivalry and reveals quite clearly its real motive. It was not really the love of the man but the claim for inheritance of the sons and for the exalted position of the mother when the son followed his father as ruler. The Old Testament law found it necessary to legislate in such cases: "If a man have two wives, one beloved and another hated, and they have born him children, both the beloved and the hated . . ." (Deut. 21:15–17). The man should not disinherit his firstborn son even if he is the son of the hated wife. Children identifying themselves with their mother grow up in an atmosphere of suspicion and envy. They share not only the negative feelings of their mother, but they will come to hate one another because they have to compete with one another for the favor of their master, just as do the wives. From Cain and Abel, the Old Testament exposes in a long sequence of pictures an irreconcilable antagonism which separates the brothers in the polygamous family. There are favorite sons as there are favorite wives. Israel, too, is a chosen people, the favorite people of the Lord. The birthright of the firstborn son does not eliminate the evil that is inherent in the discrimination of children; bitterness is the share of those who do not participate in the privileges of the one. Shakespeare, the great psychologist, has fully expounded the ambivalent feelings of the favorite son in the picture of Brutus, who loved Caesar but stabbed him: "I slew my best lover for the good of Rome." Caesar's famous last words: *Et tu me fili Brute?* ("And thou, too, my son Brutus?") is the classic formulation of the pain of the father struck down by the favorite son.

There grows up in the male child an admiration of the father, especially in the firstborn son, who hopes to replace the father one day. He may side with the father and accept in early age the philosophy that women are contemptible, including his own mother. For the other members of this family, however, the whole situation breeds fear and hatred turned against the father. The estrangement between the one privileged ruler and the many subjects, may they be wives, servants, concubines, slaves, or children, prevents the upsurge of tender emotions toward the one whose will can mean life or death. The father image will loom on the horizon of the small child as a permanent threat. The desire to eliminate this source of despotic power is natural. The unconscious hatred that Oedipus harbors against his father is somewhat out of place in our modern society, and we would not stress as much as Freud did the motif of jealousy in this hatred, the jealousy for possessing the mother. Of course the possession of the mother as very true ownership was real for the early ages but is not true in the same way for our day. However, the antagonism of the son against the despotic father had a much deeper and wider foundation in the polygamous system than in our days.

The more frightful and distant the father image becomes, the more will the child invest all his desire for love and security in the mother. (Freud in describing the case of Leonardo da Vinci pointed out that Leonardo, being an illegitimate child, knowing no father, was exposed to the "tender seduction" of his mother, for he was her only consolation.[41]) If no father responds to the emotional needs of the growing boy, the attachment to the mother will grow more intimate. This is mostly the case when a mother has to bring up her child alone. The emotional climate that the growing child needs was centered in the mother and the small subfamily around her, which was the familiar segment of the large structure of the polygamous family. In Old Testament times each woman had her own tent. This tent was, in fact, the "house" symbolized by the mother. It is obvious that within the realm of this closer circle the mother was supreme and the organization of such a subfamily may look like matriarchy.

The family unit of the grandfather spirit, father, and

son appears from the religious angle as a communion of worship and sacrifice. The same family represents from the legal aspect the communion of inheritance and blood feud. One is a privilege, the other a sacred duty; both are inseparable from one another, both are strictly affairs of men. In the legal sense the family is considered as a private property owned by the head of the household. If the ruling father died, his successor, the son, inherited all properties, widows and children included. The son became the master and lord of his mother. His own mother is thus not exempt from this general law. After the death of the father she becomes inherited by the son, as do the other women. If the family was polygamous, and this was generally the case, the son inherited the whole harem of the father. The turnover of authority became ostensibly expressed by the son taking possession of the father's women.

The Old Testament describes for instance the revolt of Absalom against his father David. It is said: "So they spread Absalom a tent upon the top of the house, and Absalom went in unto his father's concubines in the sight of all Israel" (II Sam. 16:22). This was the most positive demonstration of the shift of power from the father to the son.

Father

The various Indo-European languages agree in emphasizing that the husband-father was the absolute master, center, and foundation of the whole family. The Indo-European family was as patristic as was that of the people of the Old Testament. One can also observe that all these people display a strong leaning toward polygamy: the recognition of the right of a man to keep many women as wives. Such family structure supposes that the position of the one husband was exalted high above the plurality of wives.

This high position of the father-husband is clearly expressed by the old genuine root *poti-*, which denoted the "husband" as "lord" or "master." The husband was called "my lord" by his wife. So Sarah called her husband Abraham: "After I am waxed old shall I have pleasure, my lord, being old also?" (Gen. 18:12). Shakespeare's Juliet says of Romeo: "How does my lord?" The term denoting the "lord of the

284

house" remained preserved in the Greek *posis*, "husband," from a former *poti-s*. This Greek word is contained in the second part of the compound *des-potēs*, which properly meant "the lord of the house," from a former *dem-s-potis* (the according Sanskrit word is *dam-pati*, "lord of the house"), but the "house" meant the "family." The first part of the compound is identical with the Greek *domos*, the Latin *domus*, "house"; the Latin *dominus* also denoted properly the "master of the house," then, "master, possessor, ruler, lord" in general. The slaves addressed their master in Greek with *despotēs*, in Latin with *dominus*. The Greek word was generally applied to Oriental rulers, whose subjects were slaves. So also ruled the "lord of the house" upon the family. This word can be found in the Slavic languages (*gospodi*), in the Germanic languages by the Gothic *faths*, "lord," as in *brūth-faths*, "bride-groom," properly "lord of the bride." In the Latin the same word is present in *pot-estas*, "ability, power," also in *potis sum*, properly "I am the master," which developed into *possum*, "I am able, I may, I can"; the English noun *power* is a derivative of this verb.

This power of the individual referred primarily to his *potency*, and when projected upon objects it suggested their *potentiality*. The most significant Latin word in this connection is the adverb *ut-pote*, "namely, inasmuch as, as"; it refers to the true "own-self." The Lithuanian *pats* means "self" and "husband," while *pati* means "self" and "wife." Even in the ancient Hittite *-pat* means "self." In the Russian popular parlance the lord of the house is called *samo*, "himself"; he is also called so in Scandinavian. The Latin *ipse*, "self," is also used in this sense. By way of eminence, *ipse* is used to indicate the "chief person, host, master"; it expresses distinction. Even in obsolete English, *himself* is used as a noun, perhaps influenced by the Irish language, especially when referring to the head of the household. It was an expression of reverence that people did not take the ineffable name of the lord of the family in vain, but used the emphatic personal pronoun instead and said "Himself." This pronoun, however, referred primarily to the sexual power, to the semen as representing the true himself. The seed was ever the symbol of the potential existence. In Hungarian the "Himself" is called "his seed" (*magam*). If the father and head of the house was perceived primarily by his power of procreation, one may assume that the corresponding birth fantasies considered the child primarily as the product of the father. The Biblical equation of "child" with "seed," as in "the seed of Abraham," is the expression of a patristic society that considered the sperm of the male as the carrier of life, the very substance of immortality.

Many other expressions for "husband" are of newer origin and refer to the procreative power of the male in a more veiled or symbolic disguise. Such a term is the English *husband*, which properly denotes man in his relation to the soil as yeoman and not to his wife. Plowing and sowing were conceived in almost all Indo-European languages as symbolic for the male, while the "furrow" was associated with the female. The whole idea, once again, is basically unfair to the woman. It implies that the child grows out of the sperm cell as the plant develops from the seed sown into the furrow, which is, of course, a complete misrepresentation of the fertilization of the ovum.

Other languages also use symbolic expressions for describing the head of the household in his relationship to the women. The Slavic languages call the "Himself" the "owner of the fireplace": *ogni* means "fire"; *ogniste*, "hearth"; and *ogniscaninu*, properly "owner of the fireplace," is the generic term for "man." The English *lord*, "master, ruler," is beyond doubt a compound form. The Old English *hlāf-ord* seems to derive from a former *hlāf-weard*, "loafward," meaning properly the "guardian of the loaf." This Old English compound has a parallel word in *hord-weard*, "treasure-keeper, guardian." The meaning implied in this case is a question open for discussion. Such a question is the more justified since the corresponding *lady* derives from the Old English *hlaef-dige*. The first part of this compound is again *hlāf*, "loaf"; the second part possibly hangs together with *daegee*, "kneader." The realistic interpretation which states that the lord is the provider of bread fits the concept of the master, but the kneading of the dough does not fit the lady. What kind of marital relationship might be associated with the preparation of the bread, making the man act as guardian, the woman as kneader? I surmise, in contradiction to all our best vocabulary sources, that this whole picture language is of the same order as the plowing "husband" and the "owner of the fireplace." It is another veiled reference to the marital relationship.

See: FAMILY, MOTHER.

Fear

The English language distinguishes *fear, fright, to be afraid,* or *to be scared* from *anxiety, worry, to be anxious,* even though the bodily changes characteristic of these internal experiences are often blended with one another. One fears "something," which means that fear has an object, it is the "emergency reaction" of the conscious Ego to a perceived or anticipated danger. The reactions in fear mobilize the resources of the body in order that one shall be able to face the critical moment of stress, thus they are useful in the expected resistance—fight or flight. Sometimes anxiety may interfere— with its paralyzing effect as trembling. The symptoms of fear may, in their expression, also coincide with the expressions of anger.

The terms for "fear" are descriptive of the reaction to the perceived "danger." The Greek noun *phobos* is the most common term for "fear"; it belongs to the verbs *phobeō* and *phebomai,* which specify the reaction as "to put to flight, to flee." A special kind of fear is *panic,* from the Greek *pānikos,* properly belonging to the demigod Pan. It denotes the "groundless" fear, which means that from a grove or grotto the sudden loud shouts that made the hair bristle were attributed to Pan. He was believed to frighten people who disturbed his sleep. The English *fear* originally denoted the "sudden attack" in Old English; the same word in Old High German, *fara,* specifies this "sudden attack" as coming from "ambush," "deceit." The German parallel of *fear, Ge-fahr,* means "danger." These words demonstrate that the subjective experience "fear" refers to an objective "danger."

The English *scare* is said to be of Old Norse origin. It might be so, but even in this case it referred primarily to the sudden reaction to the perceived danger. The German noun *Schreck,* "fright," derives from the verb *schrecken,* which originally meant "to leap, jump up"; the meaning remained preserved in *Heu-schrecke,* "grass-hopper." The Old English term for the "grasshopper" is *secge-scere,* a word misinterpreted in vocabularies as "sedge-shearer." I think *scare* became identified with "jumping up" in this case. This is an old perception as shown by the saying of Job: "Canst thou make him afraid as a grasshopper?" (39:20).

Fear implies the perception of the imminent or anticipated "danger." This apprehension of danger is the objective content of the subjective experience of fear. It belongs to the psychological wisdom of the English language that *apprehension,* from the Latin *ad-prehendere,* "to take hold of," originally meant "to arrest, to take into custody." This meaning was used, on the one hand, to depict the paralyzing effect of anxiety and, on the other, it denoted the quick mental grasp of danger; thus it means "to anticipate with fear." "The sense of death is most in apprehension," Shakespeare said. Thus *apprehensive* means both "quick to understand, grasp" and "worried by fear, anxious." *To apprehend* also carries this double reference: the original concrete meaning "to seize, to arrest" developed into "to grasp, to understand the meaning of" and, at the same time, "to anticipate with dread or fear." It supposes the grasp of the meaning of danger. By the same token, the word *afraid,* like *affray,* and the French *effroi,* "fright," is a derivative of the blended Latin-Germanic *ex-fridāre,* meaning properly "to be out of the state of peace" and thus exposed to danger. There is no fear without the apprehension of danger.

The case of Oedipus is revealing in this respect. Having realized his tragic mistake, he put the blame primarily upon his eyes, which, he thinks, have failed in apprehension. He says, while blinding his eyes: "You looked enough upon those you ought never to have looked upon, you failed long enough to know those whom you ought to have known, therefore you shall be dark." His eyes did not perceive the danger. Simple sensation without perception does not signal the danger; it is like the light which "shineth in darkness; and the darkness comprehended it not" (John 1:5). By blinding himself, Oedipus delivered himself to a permanent danger situation, to the mistakes and errors which the blind will make—which are also known as the recurrent motives of anxiety dreams and neuroses. He may, like any blindfolded man, stumble, trip, fall into an abyss; he may go astray; he

288

will experience the fear of darkness as many children do. He will avoid open spaces where he will be exposed and be seen when he himself cannot see; he might tremble when crossing a bridge or when losing orientation, being caught in blind alleys and unable to find the way out of a maze. "Miserable that I am! Where am I going? Where am I cast away? Who hears my words?"

Blindness implies darkness, invisibility as the objective qualities of "danger." Darkness is like a general ambush for powers that remain unknown and unknowable and strike invisibly. Security implies the realm of Apollo, light and visibility, enlightenment and "foresight"; while darkness is the realm of insecurity, implying fear. The Latin word *tūtus*, "safe," seems to belong to the verb *tueor, tuitus,* meaning primarily "to see, look, gaze upon, watch"; thus one may interpret that safety is primarily a matter of clear vision, but insecurity and danger, the consequence of darkness or blindness. Fantasies about danger situations are, for this reason, projected into either the depths of the earth, the ocean, inside the human body, or beyond the limits of human vision. Instructive in this respect is the term *dragon.* The word, deriving from the Latin *dracō, -ōnis* and the Greek *drakōn*, is a derivative of the Greek verb *derkomai,* "to see." The dragon has many eyes, is superior to man, and can see when man cannot. The limitations of human visual perception are projected into their opposite, into the many-eyed monster. This is the typical paranoiac fear—to be watched and not to see, to always be observed by an all-seeing eye, which remains invisible, seeing everything, knowing everything, leaving nothing to hide.

See: ANXIETY.

Guilt

A manifestation of belonging to the family was the obligation of blood revenge. This was a duty inherited within the family; it served the unity of the family by mutually protecting each member's life. It was a sacred religious obligation, a sacrifice presented to the spirit of the dead ancestor, the father or brother who had been killed.

One can well observe at the beginning of the historical

ages that the principle of retaliation was still a living obligation of the male family members.[42] The law commanded: "And thine eye shall not pity; but life shall go for life, eye for eye, tooth for tooth, hand for hand, foot for foot" (Deut. 19:20). Yet the law remained so only in principle. In practice it could be "redeemed" by the payment of valuables. Protesting against this general mitigation of the original blood revenge, the Old Testament law rigidly demanded that "the revenger of blood himself shall slay the murderer: when he meeteth him, he shall slay him" (Num. 35:19). The law expressly prohibited the acceptance of ransom payment instead of the factual killing: "And ye shall take no satisfaction for him . . . So ye shall not pollute the land wherein ye are: for blood it defileth the land: and the land cannot be cleansed of the blood that is shed therein, but by the blood of him that shed it" (Num. 35:32–33). However, even the Old Testament law did introduce and accept the idea of "redemption money" (Num. 3:49) but only in respect to the Levites, who represent another form of spiritual sacrifice to the Lord. The law otherwise protested vigorously against the acceptance of this "redemption" instead of blood vengeance because the tendency to accept it had been growing ever stronger—until finally it became generally accepted in the community. If someone is found slain by unknown hands, the Old Testament law requires that a heifer should be beheaded and all the elders of that city which is next to the slain man shall wash their hands over the heifer and shall say, "Our hands have not shed this blood, neither have our eyes seen it" (Deut. 21:1–9).

One must keep in mind this shift from the actual blood revenge to the fiscal dealing for proper redemption (as described in detail in Lev. 27) if one wants to come to a proper understanding of the psychological implications of *guilt*. There can be no doubt that the feeling of guilt, and its various manifestations, is the great problem of metaphysics and metapsychology. It seems to be ingrained in man, it is implied in all anxiety, it has grown with the cultural progress, thus religion has conceived the idea of the "original sin" of man. The origin of the universal guilt with which human conscience is charged is a psychological problem of primary importance. The psychoanalytic "scientific myth" of the killing of the forefather became interpreted in this sense as the primary crime, which, "since it occurred, has not allowed mankind a moment's rest" (Freud).* Plausible as this assumption was, it remained a reconstruction without objective evidences. Moreover, it may be objected that senicide was such a self-perpetuating custom sanctified by religion and justified by law: Why should it be then the origin and explanation of the universal guilt spread upon all men? Instead of mere construction, however explanatory such hypothesis might be, I prefer the testimony of language, because in the verbal expressions I hope to find the relics of the oldest and most universal associations with the idea of "guilt."

I do not doubt that "Thou shalt not kill," properly "not murder," is the supreme commandment in human relations and its transgression is the primary source of guilt. This negative commandment has been turned into its positive fulfillment: Not sex lies at the root of guilt feelings but the unconscious desire for the death of those who stand in our way. But killing was inseparable from blood vengeance, or, during the progressing civilization, from the payment of a redemption. The various verbal instances speak for this connection of the idea of "crime, sin, guilt" with the due payment for it. One must realize that murder was still a private family affair and the case had to be settled by the male members of the family. We shall understand in the light of this family obligation the strange association between *debt* and *debtor* with "sin" and "guilt." The prehistoric man was not so highly commercialized as we are in our capitalistic society; thus the failure to pay one's debts hardly could be pointed out as the archetype of all crime. This is the implication also of the German singular noun *Schuld*, "guilt" which means in the plural *Schulden*, "financial debt." The corresponding Old English noun is *scyld*, "sin, crime, guilt," and also "debt." This association between "crime" and "debt" is age old and can be demonstrated also by Greek, Latin, Sanskrit and Slavic data. This means, in other words, that the original "debt" was the ransom one had to pay for having committed a crime. In Latin *redimō, -ere*, "to buy back, repurchase," also "to pay

* Freud once said it was his intention "to represent the sense of guilt as the most important problem in the evolution of culture." *Civilization and Its Discontents*, 1929, *Standard Edition*, 21:123–43.

for, make amends, atone, compensate for," is a derivative of
re- and emō-, ere, "to buy." This implies the original meaning
of "redemption": to regain the possession by the payment of a
due amount. We may interpret: by the act of killing the
murderer has lost his right to live but by the payment of a
redemption he may repurchase it. In a religious sense "redemption" means the deliverance from the consequences of
sin and guilt just as in the original meaning. The English *debt*,
referring to "sin, guilt," derives from the Latin verb *dēbeō*,
-ēre, "to owe, have on loan," which, in turn, is from *de-
habeō*, *-ēre*, meaning "to have in possession from him, or in
respect of him." Derivatives of this Latin verb through French
are the English *due* and *duty*. There is a moral imperative
implied in the word *duty;* and *due* refers to the idea of
fairness and justice. Both concepts derive their moral implications (together with the relative *debt* as "sin" and "guilt")
from the primary "duty," by which each member of the
family was bound to the others. In the same way the German
Schuld and the Old English *scyld*, "crime, guilt," developed
with the parallel verbal forms *shall, should,* Old English
sceolan, German *sollen*—all expressing the imperative obligation of blood vengeance or of payment.

The English word *guilt* is said by the authoritative
sources to be "unexplained, of unknown origin." In the light
of the above synonymous words we shall not hesitate to
consider the connection of "guilt" with the payment of a
ransom. The Old English nouns *gylt*, "crime, sin, fault, debt,"
and *gyltend*, "a debtor, offender," and the verb *gyldan* (*he
gylt*), meaning "to pay, restore, requite, render" and "to make
an offering," are in the same relationship with one another as
we found previously in connection with the other words for
"crime." The English derivative of this verb is *yield*, which
originally also meant "to repay, restore, recompense," but it
implies significantly the idea of "to surrender under force, to
submit." The obligation of blood vengeance or its redemption
was an absolute pressure, indeed. The related German verb
gelten originally implied the meaning of "to pay back." This is
the meaning of all retaliation. The German *Geld* assumed
during historical development the meaning of "money"—the
original reference of the word being "payment" as well as
"sacrifice." The Old English *geld* carried this meaning, too.[43]

With the progress of Christianity this old Germanic

292

concept of *guilt* became replaced by the word *sin*. The word does not refer any longer to the ransom to be paid as retaliation but seems to point to the notion of "shame," which is the internalization of a criminal act into its psychological consequences.

Summing up these observations made on the empirical material of our languages, one must accept that the idea of "guilt" is associated with the "obligation to pay back," to repurchase something lost. I think that this forfeited right of man who committed murder was the right to live. He must, according to the old tradition, either flee to a place of safety or redeem his deed by the payment of a ransom. No crime committed can remain unavenged. Murder is still frequently considered as a private family feud, not as an act of public offense. The sense of guilt so deeply ingrained in modern civilization is often retraced to the early sex experiences of the child. Sex and guilt feelings are, indeed, closely associated, but the above observations suggest that their association developed in a secondary way. The primary content of guilt feeling is the idea that one has to pay for everything. Sex means lust, but according to the fantasies implied in language it is not guilt or sin. Nevertheless, one has to pay for it. One has to make a sacrifice because, so says the Greek mind, the gods are envious. They are offended by human happiness and must be satisfied. "Thou shalt not kill" is the supreme commandment of the ancient law; if man transgressed this law, it was obligatory to pay the ransom of his deed. The neurotic guilt feeling, as has been well observed, always involves the tendency to pay for a factual or imaginary crime, to restore something taken away, to establish peace with the spirit who has been offended. The desire to suffer, to humiliate oneself, to confess, to accept the due punishment, or to sacrifice oneself as redemption are the well-known and often described symptoms of the neurotic guilt feeling.[44]

Incest

The Oedipus story in the Greek interpretation is the "family romance," the story of an incest. In our culture incest is as revolting in character as cannibalism. The Greek legend of Oedipus proves that incest with the mother was abhorred from the earliest ages of Greek antiquity. It became as much a primary taboo as the eating of human flesh and blood, which also has grown into a horrifying abomination. The motivation of this horror was sought by various social philosophers in biological, sociological, or economic considerations; yet all these rational interpretations proceed on the modern utilitarian plane. They do not fit primitive thinking. They do not consider other primary taboo restrictions such as the repression of cannibalism.[45]

There exists a difference between animal mating and human intercourse. No animal shows any sign of the repugnance we feel with respect to the mating between mother and son or father and daughter. In fact, inbreeding is a frequent procedure in animal husbandry. Thus it follows that the horror of incest is neither innate nor instinctual with man, nor is it simply a sociocultural pattern that has been set up by some arbitrary ruling. The horror of incest came about by the simple acknowledgment of the fact that the mother belongs to the father and not to the son. Intimacy necessarily develops within the close family circle; it may be conducive to sex relations. Sex supposes such closeness. Hesiod advised man "to marry in particular those who dwell closest with you." The Latin term *affinis* or *affinitas*, "relationship by marriage," properly refers to those who are "on the border" (*finis* means "end, border"), who live in the neighborhood. The "dwelling together" may result in *cohabitation* or sleeping together; however, this is just the point in question: human intercourse is not simply the outlet of a natural instinct like the mating of animals. It is also a breaking away from the dependency upon nature, from the dependency upon the mother; it is an act by which man wants to select his mate, to make a choice, to reach a decision and thus experience his will. In early times the marriages of the children were contracted by the parents, and thus were carried out in obedience to a paternal will, but this was not the satisfaction of a natural instinct. Incest with the mother would prove that man has never grown up, never could free himself from the dependency of early childhood; it would prolong the mother-child relationship *ad infinitum*. Man would, in such a case, never venture to explore the unknown, never "uncover" the secrecy of another person, never could perceive life as an adventure or a challenge to power. If man remained attached to the mother, he would continue, so to say, his parasitic existence in the womb. He would remain sheltered in his sexual life—and surely would grow into a neurotic. The taboo of incest averts an evil. The evil avoided in this case is perennial infancy.

The return of Oedipus to his "unknown" mother might be understood, not, however, as the unconscious desire of lingering in infantile dependency, but, on the contrary, in terms of the struggle for independence and identity. In order to grow up, the child must break the ties of dependency and defeat his parents. The developing boy, especially, has to overcome his fear of the female. It was the age-old symbol of conquest to kill the males and rape the females, then abduct them into servitude. The victory of the male implied this aggression of killing and raping. Oedipus, the rejected child, killed the father and took possession of the mother; she was given to him as a reward. No love was implied. Even though he was not conscious of so doing, he in fact dared to beget his own self with his mother. The desire to be "born again" was made real by entering the maternal womb the second time and to be born the second time in his true identity through the children who are truly his own blood. Legends and myths of progenitors describe the racial purity of the descents in terms of endogamous, incestuous marriages.[46]

Among all incest prohibitions the mating of mother and son appears as the primary taboo; we suppose just because the dependency of the son upon the mother is also the most elementary.

The daughter is not in the same sense biologically dependent upon the father as the son is upon the mother. For this reason the incestuous relationship between daughter and father, the so-called Electra complex, is felt less repugnant than the Oedipus situation.[47]

The incest between brother and sister also tries to prolong the infancy of both parties—as if their whole life would remain on the infantile level of "playing house." The taboo prohibition set against it is less rigorous and, we shall see, in special cases such marriage is recommended.

Various historical sources throw some light upon the prehistory of marriage within our Western civilization and positively speak in favor of Freud's assumption that an inborn instinct is not the *horror* of incest but, on the contrary, the *desire* for it. The Old Testament law would not specifically prohibit the sex relation of the son with his mother or of the father with his daughter if the propensity toward it had not been recognized.

In support of Freud's thesis I refer to what could be called "the tendency toward marginal cases." The abhorrence of incest on the negative side is proportionate on the positive side with the frequency of cases that show but a slight variation from the prohibited one. It could be demonstrated almost with statistical exactness that the frequency of the marginal cases indicates how powerful was the repressed tendency. Incest with the mother was a "peril of the soul," as Sir Frazer aptly characterized the taboo in general. The boy who is prohibited to mate with his mother will finally succeed in marrying his stepmother. Or he will try to replace the mother by his sister, or in case his sister is unapproachable, he will finally end up in marrying his cousin.

The first substitute of the mother was at hand within the polygamous family in the person of "the other woman," who was equally the wife of the father. The Old Testament for instance says that Reuben, Jacob's son, started a prohibited love affair with his father's wife Bilhah. Jacob heard about it (Gen. 35:22) and never could forgive Reuben. "Unstable as water, thou shalt not excel; because thou wentest up to thy father's bed; then defiledest thou it: he went up to my couch" (Gen. 49:4). Such a relationship was positively forbidden by the law. It said: "The nakedness of thy father's wife shalt thou not uncover: it is thy father's nakedness" (Lev. 18:8), or "Cursed be he that lieth with his father's wife; because he uncovereth his father's skirt" (Deut. 27:20). Yet the psychological forces were stronger than the words of the law. It might be objected to on the grounds that the stepmother is not a relative in the genetic sense and, therefore, that no incest is involved; but this objection does not explain why just she became the object of preferential mating. The marrying of the stepmother has grown into a sacral duty of the son, in case the father died, among some Indo-European people. Procopius, for instance, writing about the Gothic people, mentioned this as an ancestral custom: "Radiger, my son, shall marry his stepmother for the rest of his life, according to the custom of our fathers." This custom is attested to for the Anglo-Saxon people as well as for other members of the Indo-European family.

Somewhat different is the case of incest between father and daughter. The Biblical account of Lot and his two daughters (Gen. 19:30–38) is told as a rather exceptional case of emergency implying many excuses, but showing no signs of moral indignation. The incest served in this case the purpose of racial purity of Lot's children and descendants, the people of the Moabites and of the Ammonites. By the same token the Zend-Avesta holds that Ahura Mazda begot with his daughter Spenta Armaiti a mighty people; thus inbreeding was the beginning of their history. Mythological fantasies explain in this way that the progenitors of people were so high above any human status that they could multiply only by mating with their own kind. The daughter or sister is in such cases a substitute of the mother. Another substitute may be found in the aunt, a sister of the father or the mother.

The Old Testament law prohibited such intercourse (Lev. 18:12–13), but such prohibition proves, we shall show, that there was a trend to do it. Diomedes of the *Odyssey* (7:66) married his mother's sister. Such a hero, a descendant of a nephew-aunt marriage, was Moses. "And Amram took him Jochebed his father's sister to wife; and she bare him Aaron and Moses (Exod. 6:20). Because Amram was the grandchild of Levi and his father's sister was the daughter of Levi, it follows that Moses descended from pure Levitical blood.

The frequency of marginal cases once more exhibits the tendency toward this kind of incest, more than any mythological account.[48] If the father cannot marry his daughter, he will feel attracted by the daughter of his brother or sister. Such uncle-niece marriages were prohibited by the Roman law but were admitted by the Old Testament, and one may surmise that people made use of this freedom. This practice has left some traces upon our present society. Another substitute for the daughter was the daughter-in-law. It has been proven by plenty of evidence that the father held some marital rights upon the wife of his son in the early period of our culture. This follows from the absolute power, the *patria potestas*, with which the father ruled over each member of the family. In India the daughter-in-law, bought by the father for his son and introduced as a newcomer into the family, was advised to behave with particular modesty and discretion in respect to her father-in-law.

The Old English term for the father-in-law is *sveor;* its kindred equivalents are the German *Schwäher,* the Greek *hekuros,* the Latin *socer,* all derivatives of a former *sve-kuros.* This compound form contains in its first part the same *sve*-element we meet in the original form of *sister,* from *sve-sor.* If this analysis is right, the word would originally mean "the own lord," i.e., the proper lord of the house. In the large group-family, the real lord and master was not the married son but his father. The right of this over-all lord of a family compound extended also upon the grandchildren. The father-in-law was the father of the son in relationship to his daughter-in-law. It did not refer to the father of the wife in relationship to the "son-in-law." Because every woman in the family was more or less the personal property of the father, the Old Testament law found it necessary to point out: "Thou shalt not uncover the nakedness of thy daughter in law: she is thy son's wife; thou shalt not uncover her nakedness" (Lev. 18:15). "And if a man lie with his daughter in law, both of them shall surely be put to death: they have wrought confusion; their blood shall be upon them" (Lev. 20:12). There are evidences showing that when the father-in-law visited his daughter-in-law at night, he wore the frightening mask of an ancestral spirit. His act was a kind of initiation much like Zeus's various visits in human disguise.

The gods must have felt lonely in Olympic seclusion and desired human embrace. This was perhaps once the case with the illicit adventures of the Olympic fathers in the setting of a large family. It is characteristic of the patristic family setting that the Indo-European languages have developed an old genuine terminology for the relationship which exists between the wife and her husband's family, but no such terms are found denoting the relationship between the husband and the family of his wife. This means, in other words, that the wife became a member of the husband's family but that the husband had no proper relationship with the family of his wife.

For the grandfather and granddaughter relationship the Old Testament law set the warning with this specific motivation: "The nakedness of thy son's daughter, or of thy daughter's daughter, even their nakedness thou shalt not uncover: for theirs is thine own nakedness" (Lev. 18:10).

The relationship between son-in-law and mother-in-law is safeguarded by the most rigorous taboo prohibitions in many parts of the world. The English "in-law" speaks rather in legal formalistic terms, avoiding any emotional implication. The French *beau-père* and *belle-mère* with the according *beau-fils* and *belle-fille* seem to be complimentary for both parties. It was customary in the Old French to address family members respectfully by the French adjective meaning "beautiful," e.g., *beau sire, bel ami*. Even husband and wife addressed one another endearingly as *beau-frère, belle-soeur*. Yet the addressing of the "in-laws" by the word meaning "beautiful" seems to be a secondary euphemism which replaced a repressed connotation. It is a cover word, which hides the true emotions. On the other hand, the people of the Pentateuch had to be warned: "Cursed be he that lieth with his mother in law. And all the people shall say, Amen" (Deut. 27:23).

The frequent form of incest is the brother-sister marriage. It was prohibited as incestuous, yet it was often recommended; it was for the son a substitute for the union with the mother. It represents in myth the authenticity of racial purity and genuineness of the descendants. This was the implication of such marriages in ruling dynasties, famous examples of which are the Ptolemies in Egypt or the Incas in Peru. These rulers, too, were separated by their divine nature to mate with humans; thus, similarly, they were destined by their unique position to mate with one another. Similar motives have brought about that in myth the progenitors often blend the brother-sister consanguinity with the husband-wife relationship. The primitive fantasies suppose that the primary beings were always brothers and sisters and thus could mate only with their own kind. Zeus was brother and husband to Hera. Isis and Osiris were twins and husband and wife. The Rig-Veda, the oldest monument of the Old Indian literature, expounded the whole dialectic implied in such union. The Indian Yama, the brother, speaks against incest; Yami, the sister, insists on it and succeeds. These two names suggest that they were twins. Various people require the marriage of brother-sister twins; they are led by considerations according to which the twins were married since the womb, they were united by nature, thus should not be separated by man.

Perhaps such undifferentiated unity of husband-wife as brother-sister is in the background of the word *sister,* the German *Schwester,* the Latin *soror,* from former *svestor.* These words are related with one another through an old Indo-European compound form that seems to mean "own-wife." This can refer, of course, only to the mythological fantasy of the primordial sister, not to the reality. Such mythical marriage of brother and sister is characteristic of the fantasies that belong to the prehistoric ages, but that do not necessarily reflect upon existing social situations. These fantasies, however, grew out of the natural desire that is characteristic of early childhood and that becomes properly repressed during maturation. The frequency of marginal cases in the most various cultural settings speaks eloquently for them, indicating that the repressed desire was strong and broke out vehemently on the borderlines of the prohibition. (Bronislaw Malinowski says that the Trobriand natives used three kinds of incestuous curses: the mildest is "cohabit with thy mother," much more offensive is "cohabit with thy sister," but the worst imprecation and insult is the "cohabit with thy wife."[49])

The sister being a denied taboo, the repressed desire asks: Who is next and not prohibited? The nearest substitute for the sister is the stepsister. She may be the stepsister either through the common father or through the common mother. The concept of "brother" or "sister" is, however, different in various cultures. In the early age of our culture, "brother" and "sister" were defined as such either by the common father or by the common mother. We would call such a relationship "half-brother" or "half-sister" because our concept of "brother" or "sister" supposes that *both* parents are identical. Such distinction was significant, especially if a man had many wives, for the number of children having a common father was regularly greater than the children having the same mother. Such children are called in most of our languages by a term using the mother as the reference point, terms such as the Greek *a-delphos,* "brother," properly "uterine" brother, and *a-delphē,* "sister," properly "uterine" sister, both from *delphus,* "womb." The Latin *frāter* and the Greek *phrātēr* derive from an old genuine Indo-European word, the meaning of which seems to have been restricted to the descendants of one common father—who include in the age of polygamy a great number of "half-brothers." The word in Greek denoted properly the membership in a "brotherhood," *phratria,* which included all adult male members of a kinship. They were all considered to be "brothers" even if they were not the sons of the same father. It seems to be also significant that our languages did not develop an old genuine collective term for the concept "brother(s) and sister(s)." The term *sibling,* used in this sense, just as is the German *Geschwister,* is of newer origin. Brother and sister were felt as belonging to two such different categories that no common name comprising both could be developed.

The Old Testament law properly prohibited any sexual connection between brothers and sisters, half-brothers and half-sisters. It said expressively: "The nakedness of thy sister, the daughter of thy father, or daughter of thy mother, whether she be born at home, or born abroad, even their nakedness thou shalt not uncover" (Lev. 18:9; 20:17). This prohibition of the law, however, was never fully effective in the culture of a people whose progenitors are Abraham and Sarah. Abraham took advantage of this situation and introduced Sarah either as his wife or as his sister; it depended on the given situation: "And yet indeed," Abraham says, "she is my sister; she is the daughter of my father, but not the daughter of my mother; and she became my wife" (Gen. 20:12). Ezekiel the prophet, enumerating the sins of Israel, says: "And one hath committed abomination with his neighbor's wife; and another hath lewdly defiled his daughter in law; and another in thee hath humbled his sister, his father's daughter" (Ezek. 22:11). Not the "adelphoi" relationship, the sameness of the mother, but the identity of the father is pointed out in this instance as sinful.

The classic Biblical illustration of the incestuous relationship between half-brother and half-sister is found in the story of Amnon and Tamar (II Sam. 13), both children of David. Because, however, their mothers were different, Amnon did not thus consider Tamar to be truly his sister, so he called her "my brother's sister." When he "took hold of her, and said unto her, Come lie with me, my sister," Tamar resisted. She said, "No such thing ought to be done in Israel: do not thou this folly"; but it seems to be significant that she suggested that Amnon ask the permission for this incestuous marriage from their father King David: "I pray thee, speak unto the king; for he will not withhold me from thee," she said. The half-brother was not an absolute taboo to her feeling; she was rather convinced that the royal father could waive the obstacle to their union.

Still similar to the brother-sister unity, yet somewhat more distant, is the kinship with the first cousin, with the son or daughter of one's uncle or aunt. It is clearly a marginal case; some state laws prohibit it, others do not. There are communities which strongly prohibit the marriage of parallel cousins (children of the mother's sister or of the father's brother) but make almost obligatory the marriage with a cross-cousin (child of the mother's brother or of the father's sister). Some languages differentiate strongly between the paternal cousins and the maternal cousins, e.g., the Latin *frater patruelis* denotes the child of the *patruus,* the paternal uncle. For the child of the mother's sister they used an altogether different term; this is the *con-sobrinus,* contracted from *sororinus* (from *soror,* "sister"); our word *cousin* is its derivative. These words show that the blood relationship through the father represented to the Latin mind something categorically different from the consanguinity through the mother. The notion of "brother" and "sister" is implied in these terms; the cousins were classified so when these words were shaped.

Cousin marriage is, if not prohibited by law, frequent in present days. It is almost the rule in some Near Eastern countries. In the Arabic the cross-cousins call one another "husband" and "wife" even if they are not married. On the other hand, they are called "brother" and "sister"; their marriage is patently on the borderline between incest and nonincest. The typical example of this kind of union is in the Old Testament in the case of Jacob's marriage with the sisters Rachel and Leah. The sisters were the daughters of Laban, who was the brother of Jacob's mother, Rebekah; thus they were to him maternal cross-cousins. According to the Biblical text, Laban said to Jacob: "Surely thou art my bone and my flesh"; this is the old formula for true consanguinity. When Jacob asked for Rachel, Laban answered by these words: "It is better that I give her to thee, than that I should give her to another man: abide with me" (Gen. 29:12–19). This means in other words that marriage within the kinship or consanguinity (endogamy) is preferred to marriage with an outsider (exogamy).

This case involving Jacob represents a marginal case of incest also in another respect. He married two sisters, and had both as wives at the same time. Polygamy made such arrangements possible. However, positive prohibition was set against this custom, too, in the law: "Neither shalt thou take a wife to her sister, to vex her, to uncover her nakedness, beside the other in her life time" (Lev. 18:18). In England such marriage was forbidden even after the death of one sister—till recent times. It was also incestuous according to the Old Testament law to marry and to keep as wives at the same time the mother and her daughter, the grandmother and her granddaughters, "for they are her near kinswomen: it is wickedness" (Lev. 18:17).

See: MATRIARCHY, UNCLE.

Infanticide

The slaughtering of children at the altar, the preparation of their flesh as meat for consumption, was the most general form of human sacrifice and cannibalism.[50] Its traces are recorded in the Old Testament as well as by the historians of antiquity. Children were considered like cattle, as property of the father; therefore they were as exposed to sacral killing as were cattle and old people. Homer tells us that Achilles put on the pyre of the dead Patroclus "four proud horses," then "the dead hero had nine house dogs: two of them did Achilles slay and throw upon the pyre; he also put twelve brave sons of noble Trojans to the sword and laid them with the rest . . . then he committed all to the resistless and devouring might of the fire" (*Iliad* xxiii. 174). So children were sacrificed together with horses and dogs by the Greeks as a burnt offering.

One may observe in the case of animal sacrifices that the young ones were chosen because they were thought to be preferred by the gods, we surmise for their tender meat. "And Samuel took a sucking lamb, and offered it for a burnt offering wholly unto the Lord" (I Sam. 7:9). The small children appealed to the repressed cannibalistic fantasies. The belief in reincarnation also suggested that the ancestors had a special claim upon the children, by which they returned to life. In the naming of the children there is often expressed the idea that they are just a "gift." *Joab* properly means "the Lord (is) his father." Phoenician names with the ending of -*bal*, such as *Hanni-bal, Hadru-bal,* indicate that the child is a gift of *Baal,* god of fertility and seeds, who was particularly eager to receive children.

Keeping this historical-anthropological background in mind, one will better understand the observations of some keen analysts (L. Szekely) that the "basic fear" in some children is that of being eaten, possibly by their own parents.[51] The *sarko-phagos,* properly the "flesh-eating," devouring mother, remained preserved in *sarcophage.* Some parents express their love in terms of oral sadism, acting as if they want to devour their baby. The Old Testament curse refers to such propensity: "And thou shalt eat the fruit of thine own body, the flesh of thy sons and of thy daughters" (Deut. 28:53). A clinical instance of a father who frightened his daughter, Renée, by saying that he would eat up the mother has been described.[52]

The carnivorous mother is a haunting idea in the fantasies of infantile anxiety. Let us not close our eyes in front of the facts that often emerge in clinical practice: the abortive parents' behavior toward the unwanted child. The parents who want good riddance of their child on the moral pretext of sacrifice are not exceptional in our culture. Clinical practitioners know more about it. They can observe in analysis that "the ill-treating parents do not belong to the dim prehistoric past." Such parents are rather "still very much alive," says one observer of parental sentiments.[53] The facts as revealed by child analysis show that many a child knows that he was born unwanted and that the parents tried abortion, to kill him, but did not succeed.

The child sacrifice comes to the fullness of meaning and all its emotional implications if the father sacrifices his only son. The Biblical story of Abraham and Isaac (Gen. 22) supposes an atmosphere in which the sacrifice of children was still a living memory; otherwise the Lord never would have tempted his faithful servant by such a demand. The Biblical account exposes with classic simplicity the emotional complication that must have arisen between father and son when they went to the land of Moriah. "And they went both of them together" is the returning refrain of the fateful journey.[54] An actual sacrifice is reported about the king of Moab, who, when pressed hard by the enemy, resorted to the sacrifice of his son: "Then he took his eldest son that should have reigned in his stead, and offered him for a burnt offering upon the wall" (II Kings 3:27).

In the Old Testament two gods, Moloch and Baal, are specifically mentioned as venerated by the sacrifice of children. They were divinities of the neighboring peoples; yet, we must suppose that their veneration was deep-rooted in the Hebrew people, too. When Jehu started to extirpate the worship of Baal, "the house of Baal was full from one end to another" (II Kings 10:21). Moloch (properly *melek,* meaning "king" as in names like Nathan-melek, Abi-melek) was the popular divinity of the Phoenicians. He was worshiped by the Phoenician colonies as he was at Carthage. When this city was besieged two hundred sons of the aristocracy were made burnt offering in one day. The god Moloch received the children in his arms in a particular way. His statue was not only a molten image, but practically a furnace that could be heated from the inside. The children were placed into the glowing arms of this furnace-idol. The Old Testament laws had to prohibit again and again the burnt offering of children, to impose the death penalty for it, which is an obvious symptom that the propensity to do such sacrifice was an old actual custom that could not be stamped out easily.

He "that giveth any of his seed unto Moloch; he shall surely be put to death" (Lev. 20:2). Such negative prohibitions indicate the presence of a positive tendency to be repressed. Moses had to warn the people not to imitate the other nations: "every abomination to the Lord, which he hateth, have they done unto their gods" (Deut. 12:31). These warnings were in vain. King Solomon erected a molten image for Moloch on one of the summits of the Mount Olive (I Kings 16:3). The child sacrifice was again officially introduced by King Ahaz, who himself "made his son to pass through the fire" (II Kings 16:3). The custom was particularly made popular also by King Manasseh, who sacrificed his own son (II Kings 21:16) and even more of his children to Moloch (II Chron. 33:6). The prophets fought with all their power against these remnants of cannibalism among the Hebrew people. Ezekiel said about Jerusalem: "Moreover thou hast taken thy sons and thy daughters, whom thou has borne unto me, and these hast thou sacrificed unto them to be devoured. Is this of thy whoredoms a small matter, That thou hast slain my children, and delivered them to cause them to pass through the fire for them?" (Ezek. 16:20–21).

The Phoenician sacrifices to Moloch suggest the *holocaust* form of sacrifice; this means "burnt as a whole," from the Greek *holos,* "whole," and *kaustos,* "burnt." The people did not any longer eat from this sacred food which was dedicated in the whole to the god. The above words by Ezekiel, however, mention the devouring. The Hebrew custom did not follow this burning alive, nor did the Mohammedan Arab tribes who used to bury alive their daughters, but the old Hebrew ritual set the pattern of first slaughtering the child and then burning it. The above words of Ezekiel clearly distinguish these two acts. It is also said that the people "caused to pass through the fire all that openeth the womb" (Ezek. 20:26): this means the "first-fruit" child. By this we still recognize the original implication of the law of the first-fruits as Moses gave it to the people: "Sanctify unto me all the first-born whatsoever openeth the womb among the children of Israel both of man and of beast, it is mine; and every firstling among thy cattle, whether ox or sheep, that is male. But the firstling of an ass thou shalt redeem with a lamb: and if thou redeem him not, then shalt thou break his neck. All the firstborn of thy sons thou shalt redeem" (Exod. 34:19–20).

The whole rigor of the claim of the divinity is exposed in the Old Testament by the classic example of Jephthah sacrificing his daughter (Judg. 11).

"And Jephthah vowed a vow" that, should he succeed in defeating the Ammonites, "then it shall be, that whatsoever cometh forth of the doors of my house to meet me, when I return in peace from the children of Ammon, shall surely be the Lord's, and I will offer it up for a burnt offering." When he returned, "behold, his daughter came out to meet him with timbrels and with dances: and she was his only child." Jephthah gave her two months to "bewail her virginity"; when this respite was over, he "did with her according to his vow which he had vowed: and she knew no man." The first-fruit given to the Lord is in this case taken by its primary meaning: the first-fruit (symbolically, who came out first of the door of the house) is sacrificed, i.e., made holy by burnt offering.

306

Truly cruel parents force their love-hungry children into the pathological way of loving through inflicted pain and masochism. Cannibalistic fantasies are always imbued with castration anxieties. It has been pointed out by the analyses of prostitutes that their castration fear of early childhood was not as much a fear of separation from the genitals but a deprivation of the security of a dependable home during the age of dependency. Theirs is an "existential castration fear," the continually pending threat of being cast out from the home, from the family, left without food, shelter, protection. The prehistoric fear of children of being exposed like the infant Oedipus or sacrificed like the innumerable children at the beginning of our history was once a real fear; this fear must have overcome Isaac when he went with Abraham up the mount of Moriah. This fear is still a living element in children's fantasies in our day. The fear of the persecutory parents is also in Freud's terminology a "real fear"; it results necessarily in the "paranoid position" of early childhood.

During the course of cultural development such remnants of prehistoric savagery became transformed, mitigated, or sublimated into various customs. The payment of ransom (Lev. 27) was one way to spare the life of the victims. The Roman historian Festus, for instance, related that since to the Sabine tribe it seemed cruel to slay innocent boys and girls, they were kept until they had grown up, and then they were veiled and driven beyond the boundaries. This driving out of the children from the homeland is one substitute form of the original burnt offering, just as was the custom of dedicating the firstborn for the service as priests to the divinity.

See: ANXIETY, CANNIBALISM.

Initiation

The word *initiation* derives from the symbolic picture of "going in," the Latin *in-īre,* "to go in." The questions raised will ask who is going in and where does he enter. It is one very specific entering into a place characterized by secrecy and mystery and accessible only to the initiated.

Initiation ceremonies as performed all over the world are patristic rituals. They generally act out on preverbal levels unconscious fantasies about birth. If one were to translate the original ritual of initiation into verbal expressions, it would say: the child should be born again, this time by the father. As nonsensical as this idea is, we may understand its intention. It is primarily an attempt to attach the male children to the father. When the age of absolute dependency is over, the boy must be born a second time in order to be able to break away from the mother and to grow fully into the role of being the son of the father.

The classic mythological example of rebirth by the father is the case of Dionysus. Zeus as father carried the fetus in his thigh, as in an incubator, because it was first born prematurely; the second time Dionysus was born by his father Zeus. No wonder he was a favorite son. Pallas Athena is said to have sprung from the head of Zeus. This is unrealistic, too, but says expressively that no motherly element is present in the character of the virgin deity. We all carry the paternal and the maternal inheritance, but to be totally male supposes one, in the language of fantasies, to have had no mother, to have been born by the father. The literary example of such all-male character may be found in Shakespeare's MacDuff, who had been "from his mother's womb untimely ripped."

Transparent as these fantasies seem to be in their final intention, they introduce a strange feminine element into the concept of paternity. Vestiges of such fantasies can be found in the Biblical language. The Hebrew *ōmeneth* means "grandmother." For instance Naomi is called the *ōmeneth* of Ruth's baby, she is the nursing grandmother. The parallel masculine is *ōmen*, "nursing grandfather"; it shows the grandfather in the role of the nurse. Moses says to the Lord: "Have I conceived all this people? have I begotten them, that thou shouldest say unto me, Carry them in thy bosom as a nursing father beareth the sucking child, unto the land which thou swearest unto their fathers" (Num. 11:12). The grandfather as a mother substitute is a familiar picture of Biblical fantasies. It is a promise of the Lord to Israel: that "they [the Gentiles] shall bring thy sons in their arms, and thy daughters shall be carried upon their shoulders. And kings shall be thy nursing fathers, and their queens thy nursing mothers" (Isa. 49:22–23). The nursing grandfather during his earthly presence may already begin his role as the guardian of the child. The Greek called the elderly man who was in trust of the children *paidagogos*. These fantasies may explain the expression *Abraham's bosom,* a Biblical formula difficult to understand otherwise. Jesus says, when the beggar Lazarus died he "was carried by the angels into Abraham's bosom: the rich man also died, and was buried; And in hell he . . . seeth Abraham afar off, and Lazarus in his bosom" (Luke 16:22–23). The Jewish people, being "Abraham's seed" were protected by the ancestral spirit of Abraham, being like the nursing grandfather who is carrying the suckling. This physical relationship between grandfather and grandchild became sublimated in a spiritual sense and expanded upon all believers in Christ: "And if ye be Christ's, then are ye Abraham's seed, and heirs according to the promise" (Gal. 3:29).

The ancestral spirit, out of which the new life should be reborn with the consent of the father, is necessarily invisible and will remain so. Invisibility being its essential characteristic, we should understand the important part that the masks play in initiation ceremonials. The cover-up shows an outside face behind which the ancestral spirit can hide. The masks usually display a terrifying countenance. They inflict horror upon the onlooker. This outward expression impersonates by projection man's inside fear of death. When one deciphers the language of the masks, one of the fantasies expressed by them is bound to be saying that the grandfather is angry. (*Odysseus* means properly "angry"; it is a derivative of the verb *odussomai,* meaning "to be wroth against, to hate." Odysseus received his name by the outspoken request of his maternal grandfather. He is indeed the "little grandfather" and bears his name, because his grandfather was angry.)

A clinical illustration is the case of a boy, Peter, who had lost his father; thus his father became di parentes. *At the age of five, Peter suffered from severe insomnia, and feared that his mother would also die. To these symptoms should be added a complaint that he voiced immediately after his first analytic hour: Thoughts and voices inside his head kept saying, "Daddy angry." In a fuller statement which Peter made when his mother reminded him of pleasant things Daddy had done with him, the boy said, "These people inside tell me about times I didn't like Daddy, times when Daddy was angry with me."*[55]

The grandfather spirit appears in the expressions of

the masks as a revengeful, bloodthirsty enemy of the living family. We shall understand, keeping the senicide in mind, the reason for this anger and hatred expressed in the horrifying masks. Beyond the true psychological reason why the grandfather is supposed to be angry and bloodthirsty, the horrifying masks also serve a practical purpose. They keep away women and children. Those who are not initiated should keep at a proper distance and simply believe in the invisible ancestral spirit. The sad truth, however, is that man's face in the acme of terror or in the hour of death becomes rigid, lifeless as if it were only the *sur-face* of the living *persona*.

The whole complex of mask, death, rebirth, embryo, and fetus can be observed in connection with the Latin *larva*. The Latin *lār, lāris,* mostly in the plural *lāres,* "tutelar deities," is a personification of ancestral spirits. They can belong to the well-attended, good *mānes;* then they are the "tutelar deities of a house, household gods, domestic lares." They may also be roaming, homeless spirits, and then they are worshiped by the roadside, mostly at crossings. The derivative of this name is *larva, larua,* "a ghost, specter," also "a mask, skeleton." The verb *larvō, -āre* means "to bewitch." We observe in this case that the ancestral spirit may appear as a ghost, and that the mask, just as does the skeleton, represents the appearance of the dead. This word, *larva,* however, came to denote in our language, "the earliest stage of certain insects emerging wormlike from the egg, until they become pupae or chrysalises." In the Latin *pūpa* means "little girl, doll, puppet." The *larva* refers thus to the prenatal embryonic and fetal state. The ancestral spirit appears first as a frightening ghost, then as a mask, and finally reaches the stage of rebirth as a new being. The English *bug* also denotes primarily a "bogy, bugbear," an object of superstition, fear; and secondarily, "an insect with a piercing, sucking mouth which creeps and crawls like a beetle." In this case the larval being is once more referred to as a goblin, a specter, an appearance of a spirit, with the implication however that there is nothing real behind it. There exists another Latin term for the malevolent spirits of the dead ones: *lemures,* "shades, ghosts of the departed." This name seems to refer to the "devouring" attributes.

We may ask at this point, Why is the ancestral spirit supposed to be a man-eater, particularly prone to devour children? The ferocity expressed by all the various masks seems to express the rapacious, cannibalistic quality of the ancestral spirit while the spirit of the departed one is also called in Latin *mānes,* which seems to refer rather to the benevolent quality of the spirit. Whether or not this word is coherent with the obsolete Latin *mānus, -a, -um,* "good," is discussed, but even so this supposed "goodness" might be a euphemism and point to the repressed opposite: this is "bad, evil, vicious." The related *mānia* is the "mother of the lares," but it is also a "bugbear for children, bugaboo"; the disbelief of the adults seems to be once more implied. The *māniae* are definitely the frightening spirits of the dead. They are the opposite of those who are *im-mānis.* The Latin *im-mānis* means "monstrous, enormous, frightful, inhuman, fierce, savage"; *im-mānitas* means "monstrous size, hugeness, vastness, excessiveness, enormity, heinousness, savageness, fierceness, cruelty, barbarousness." Thus, by translating the negative forms of the *mānes* complex we can express freely its positive qualities, the attributes of the ancestral spirits. The German *ungeheuer* shows a strictly parallel development.

Summing up these observations, one may state: The ancestral spirit appears by the frightening mask; he threatens to devour children but in it he remains invisible, a mystery, but with a twinkle in the eyes of the adults.

The initiated adults seem to know more about the reality of the spirit than those who are not initiated. One prominent purpose of the initiation ceremonies is just the revealing of the truth concerning the ancestral spirit. The initiation equals a look behind the frightening mask. Then the initiated may have learned something that will remain a secret to the uninitiated.

Initiation was "the central mystery of primitive society."[56] It remained more or less the great motive of religion, especially of mystery religions. The center of all mystery religion is the crucial transit from the outside world to the community of the mystagogues who are in the possession of a secret knowledge that cannot be conveyed to the profane people.[57] It is well known that the religion of the Old Testament as well as that of the New Testament is profoundly influenced by the prehistoric ritual of initiation.

The frightening masks as used at initiation ceremonies expose in rudimentary crudeness the emotional experience which developed during the course of cultural progress into the most sublime moment of all higher religions: this is the event, ineffable by its very nature, when man contacts the sphere of the divine. In the Old Testament the presence of the Lord is still often depicted by the panicky characteristics of the predivine ancestral spirits. Thus it is said about Moses: "And it came to pass by the way to the inn, that the Lord met him, and sought to kill him" (Exod. 4:24). This is still the language which refers to the haunting spirits of the dead. But this crude and primitive fear developed during the long religious maturation into this unique experience which the Romans must have felt when they inscribed on their temples *Numen adest!* "The deity is present." The "fear of God" is in fact the beginning and the center of all religion. The Hebrew word used for denoting this "fear of God" is *yārē;* it is used only in reference to the Lord. The fear of men or objects is denoted by other terms. This means that the "fear of God" is not the same as the fear of men or objects but something specific, a mixture of fear and reverence. The panicky fear that applies rather to the bugbear and to ghosts is also sometimes used in the Old Testament: *ēmāh,* "fright, horror." It also means "idol," as a ghost; thus refers to the spirits. This word is used in this passage: "I will send my fear before thee, and will destroy all the people to whom thou shalt come" (Exod. 23:27). The Greek uses the word *sebar* in this sublime sense; its verbal forms are *sebō* and *sebomai,* "to feel awe or fear before God, especially when one is about to do something disgraceful, to feel shame," also "to honor with pious awe, to worship" and "to pay honor, to respect." The term *sebasma* denoted the object of awe and reverence; *sebastos,* like the Latin *augustus,* became later on the title of the Roman Emperor. The original implication of all these Greek terms is "to avoid, retire from something," which is characteristic of all taboo avoidances. The most appropriate English term for this blending of fear and reverence is *awe,* from an old Germanic word, Old English *age,* Gothic *agis,* "fright, terror." The numinous character of the word is indicated by its repetitious use in modern usage. There must be something uncanny in this word that one feels bound to repeat it frequently without being aware of its proper meaning.

It was a great solemn moment of the Old Testament religion when Moses was called upon to meet the Lord. "And Moses alone shall come near the Lord: but they [who accompanied him] shall not come nigh; neither shall the people go up with him" (*Exod. 24:2*). *This is the dramatic setting for the unique moment when man is confronted with the divine. A cloud covered the mount for six days.* "*And the seventh day he [the Lord] called unto Moses out of the midst of the cloud"* (*Exod. 24:16*). *Yet, the Lord remained invisible to him, even when Moses became initiated into the divine mystery: the people standing and waiting perceived only the outside reflex of the great event:* "*And the sight of the glory of the Lord was like devouring fire on the top of the mount in the eyes of the children of Israel"* (*Exod. 24:17*).

The Lord's presence is felt as a mysterium tremendum, *an event of awe, though no man has ever seen the Lord. The setting was the same when Moses wanted to see the Lord:* "*And he said, I beseech thee, shew me thy glory"* (*Exod. 33:18*). *Moses went to the tabernacle, the dwelling place of the Lord,* "*And it came to pass, when Moses went out unto the tabernacle, that all the people rose up, and stood every man at his tent door, and looked after Moses, until he was gone into the tabernacle"* (*Exod. 33:8*). *This dramatic tension, the expression of wondering and awe, was implied in a crude form in the primitive initiation ceremonies. This "entering" into the domain of the spirit is the decisive moment, the* initiation. "*And it came to pass, as Moses entered into the tabernacle, the cloudy pillar descended, and stood at the door of the tabernacle, and the Lord talked with Moses"* (*Exod. 33:9*). *The people rose up and worshiped.* "*And the Lord spake unto Moses face to face, as a man speaketh unto his friend"* (*Exod. 33:11*). *Moses became thus initiated into the mysteries of religion, but he still did not see the Lord. The Lord said to Moses:* "*Thou canst not see my face: for there shall no man see me and live"* (*Exod. 33:20*). *The Lord remained invisible. He said, I* "*will cover thee with my hand while I pass by. And I will take away mine hand, and thou shalt see my back parts: but my face shall not be seen"* (*Exod. 33:22–23*). *When the Lord spoke first to Moses* "*Moses hid his face; for he was afraid to look upon God"* (*Exod. 3:6*).

This strange hiding of the face is repeated in the relationship between Moses and the people when Moses wants to communicate to the people his personal experience of

God's presence. After returning from Mount Sinai with the two tablets, "the skin of his face shone . . . and till Moses had done speaking with them, he put a vail on his face. But when Moses went in before the Lord to speak with him, he took the vail off, until he came out." But when he was to speak with the people he covered again his shining face (Exod. 34:29–35). Not only his face was covered in the sight of the people, but when he first brought the Ten Commandments, the people were driven away by frightening sounds and signs. "And all the people saw the thunderings, and the lightnings, and the noise of the trumpet, and the mountain smoking: and when the people saw it, they removed, and stood afar off. And they said unto Moses, Speak thou with us, and we will hear: but let not God speak with us, lest we die" (Exod. 20:18–19).

We observe in all these details the effect of the *tremendum,* which is the primary source of religious experience. The elements of these events are present in the initiation ceremonies. The solemn "going in" into the dwelling of the spirit, the covering of the face, hearing but not seeing the spirit, the noises, trumpets driving the uninitiated away—all these are the characteristics of the primitive initiation ceremonies.

The idea underlying the initiation ceremonials can be enacted by many various procedures. The rebirth supposes that the youth first has to die in order to be reborn in the spirit. The killing of the youth in the ceremonials is, of course, not a factual mortification, though the whole procedure often approaches the point of factual death. The killing is performed mostly by a symbolic action. The frightening aspect of the masks serves just this intimidation. One general way of killing is the cannibalistic threat that the spirit may devour the youth. In this case the mask or the appearance of the spirit may be represented as a monster or a rapacious animal; e.g., *bugbear* is a bogy in the appearance of a bear. To be eaten and swallowed up by a monster, as, for example, Jonah was swallowed up by the whale, may be understood according to the general philosophy of digestion and sacrifice as a metabolic transubstantiation of being. But it is equally possible that the motive of cannibalism has grown into a heavy burden upon the conscience of a progressing civilization. If this conscience for one reason or another felt guilty toward the ancestral spirit, it may appear as an act of appeasement or gratification to offer the youth as food.

Initiation ceremonies agree generally on one point: they inflict pain and suffering on the youth. The pain might be physical, and although brutal inventiveness in this respect is almost inexhaustible, the torture might well be a psychological one that leads the youth through an agony of fear and despair. What might be the final intention of those willfully inflicted physical or mental pains? The modern interpretation stating that the "toughening up" of the novices is for their own benefit is only partially true, for torturing in whatever disguise is not simply a benevolent educational procedure, but may be the outlet of deeply repressed sadistic tendencies of those who inflict the pain, in this case the father and other adult men. The father, in the primitive social order, may have reasons to harbor some suspicion or antagonistic feeling toward the growing son. The enactment and ritualization of this usually repressed negative sentiment is at the same time its cure. The open and public expression has a prophylactic preventive effect upon emotions that are harmful to the family.

The effect of pain and suffering upon the novices is indeed the distancing of the spirit from the body, or of the Ego from fear and anxiety with which it may be confronted. The Ego must prevail upon the most adverse situation. The mortification of body and soul, even on the low level of savage rituals, may serve an idealistic spiritual end. The saints of the Church have given innumerable examples of the spiritual victory over the mortal body. All those cutting, wounding, hurting, flogging, hanging, crucifying experiences prove in the end the spiritual supremacy over the flesh. They serve the spiritual rebirth. They enact, perhaps long before it could be properly expressed by words, the idea that the death of the life born of the mother opens the way to the rebirth and resurrection in the spirit of the father. The final verbal formulation of this idea is found in the following words of Paul: "So also is the resurrection of the dead. It is sown in corruption; it is raised in incorruption: it is sown in dishonor; it is raised in glory: it is sown in weakness; it is raised in power: It is sown a natural body; it is raised a spiritual body. There is a natural body, and there is a spiritual body. And so it is written, The first man Adam was made a living soul, the last man Adam was made a quickening spirit" (I Cor. 15:42–45). All initiation ceremonies, however veiled may be their enactment, display in the symbolic language the victory of the resurrection by the spirit over death. Paul says that Christ "entered in once into the holy place, having obtained eternal redemption for us" (Heb. 9:12). This "going in" brought regeneration to all Christian believers.

General psychotherapy as practiced at present, even beyond the techniques of classic psychoanalysis, has inherited some vestiges of the initiation ceremonies. It is mostly a painful experience leading the adept through the "steambath" of his hidden self. In doing so it is imprinted upon his mind that he must be "born again," i.e., must "repattern" the structure of his total personality. At the same time, the therapist as a father-substitute is holding out a reward for all these painful experiences; this is the promise of a greater freedom, creativity and a fullness of life never experienced before.

See: ANCESTOR, CANNIBALISM, INFANTICIDE.

Kinship

It is characteristic for primitive conditions that each human life strictly follows and repeats the common pattern. Individualistic variances seem to be insignificant beside the common features, just as individual animals do not differ much from the over-all characteristics of the species. In a similar way, man raised within a primordial kinship system perceived himself as one of a species, as part of a greater unity. The *I* when still weak feels secure if it is submerged in the *we*. Belonging to a greater unity makes the weak feel stronger.

In case of an offense against one of the group, each member of the group feels offended and is bound to retaliate. Such was even the primeval relationship of man with animals. The animals as a species were thought to react as a clan. If one animal was offended—for instance, if a hunter did not kill it in the prescribed way—the species as a whole was offended and was supposed to retaliate. The difference between our thinking and the primitive logic in respect to animals is linguistically indicated by the use of the definite article with animal names. Whereas the English version of the

Biblical text says, e.g., "there came *a* lion, and *a* bear, and took *a* lamb," the original Hebrew says, "There came *the* lion, and *the* bear" (I Sam. 17:34), because one animal is identical with any other of the same species. Neither animals nor men count as distinct personalities. That which is valid for one applies to the others; therefore ancestry and blood relationship is a matter of common stock.

Traces of common ancestry can be supposed in such instances when a tribe or clan is called by an animal name. In the Anglo-Saxon tradition the Saxon leaders who led the people to Britain were *Hengist* and *Horsa,* both names for the horse, so one may surmise that the horse was considered to be an ancestral animal. The Germanic *Cherusci* derive their name from the Germanic *herūz,* German *Hirsch,* "elk," thus they were called the "Elks"; we surmise because they once considered the elk as their ancestral animal. Such examples can be multiplied. Sometimes trees appear as ancestors. Jeremiah the prophet said about the worshipers of the Baalim in Canaan that they are "saying to a stock, Thou art my father; and to a stone, Thou hast brought me forth" (Jer. 2:27). The creative spirit of the ancestors was venerated in these "stock" or "stone" pillars. If the horse, the elk, or the bull was venerated as an ancestral animal, all members of the clan identified themselves by this name. They were elks, horses, or bulls, or they were, at least, their brothers. They abstained from eating their "ancestral" flesh, except once a year on a sacral occasion.

The members of a kinship were thought to be united through blood; this means the same life substance was flowing in their veins. The original source of this "common blood" might be the common ancestor. Yet the efficacy of this source was evaporating. Because blood changes more than any other body fluid, the original identity in the blood of the ancestor has to be renewed and corroborated by the blood covenant of the members of a kinship. The most primitive way of this participation in the common blood was to eat and drink from the blood substance of the common ancestor, to consume his body and his blood. A derivative form of the blood covenant was that of opening their veins, pouring their blood into a cup, and drinking from this mixed blood; part of it was given to the ancestral spirit. Another derivative form is the animal sacrifice. The animal was obviously the substitute of man. The blood of the victim animal, possibly of the bull or ox, is used for contracting the blood covenant. The same blood consumed by the participant of the sacrifice, and also poured in some way upon the altar, re-establishes the unity of the kinship by participating in the same life substance that unites the ancestral spirit with his worshipers. The smearing of the sacrificial blood upon the altar or upon various objects as upon the threshold of the house or upon persons indicates in symbolic substitution that they were considered as drinking from the same life substance, thus they are of the same kin.

Kinship according to these ideas is not simply a question of common descendance. One may become a "brother" by the ritual of the blood covenant. The "one blood" which carries the substance of kinship might be acquired by drinking it or absorbing it in a more abstract form. In the development of religion the red wine took the place vicariously of the sacrificial blood. The libation of wine upon the altar replaced the original shedding of blood.

This elementary philosophy of kinship was represented primarily by the common sacrifice and the sharing of the sacrificial meal. In further expansion its manifestation became any eating or drinking together. The same food absorbed in two persons establishes a unity, especially if this food carries the meaning of spiritual incorporation and is supposed to be accepted at the same time by the spirit. The kinship is acknowledged in the Old Testament by such formulas as "I am your bone and your flesh" (Judg. 9:2) or "thou art my bone and my flesh" (Gen. 29:14). The full meaning of these formulas will open up if they are taken verbatim. The identity of bones, flesh, and blood is brought about by the same food absorbed. It made each participant of the sacral meal a "brother" of all the others who also ate the same meal.

The primitive kinship is for such reasons not primarily a system of degrees as it is in our society. It is a classificatory system distinguishing one group of families from the others. It is co-ordinate, not subordinate as is our system. We differentiate between nephews, first-degree parallel cousins from second-degree cross-cousins, but for the primitive social order such distinctions appear to be irrelevant, because the individual is bound with each member of his group, equally with the *We*. This was especially important in case the marriage was polygamous.

The kinship in blood was once the only criterion of "friendship." One can even observe that kinship had the decisive part in the development of the concept of "love." No man could exist alone in the desert. The only ones whom he could trust were his own kin. He expanded the generic blood kinship to those with whom he was united by a blood covenant; they became his "brothers" or "friends." Our word *friend* is the present participle of an old verb, Gothic *frijōn*, "to love"; thus the *friend* means properly the "loving one." The same relationship is found in other languages, too. The *fiend*, related German *Feind*, "enemy," properly denotes the "hating one." For the primitive thinking there is nothing in between friend and enemy. But this means, in other words, that one is either kindred or foreigner. The English *kind* and *kindred* still show the same relationship. The German *Kind* is the kindred child. The world, beyond the kinship, was hateful, inimical. The kinship by blood may comprise gods, men, and animals.

The primordial identification of love, friendship, and kinship is borne out also by the various words that denote the "relatives" as "friends." The German *Freundschaft*, "friendship," originally denoted the "in-law" relationship. The same holds true for the Greek *kēdestēs*, denoting "a connection by marriage," thus "a son-in-law," "father-in-law," "brother-in-law"; *kēdeuma* means "connection or alliance by marriage," like the Latin *affinitas*. These words are clearly related to the noun *kēdos*, which means, on the one hand, "care or concern for," especially for the dead, and thus "funeral rites, mourning"; on the other hand, "connection by marriage." The according verb *kēdeuō* means "to take charge of, attend to a corpse (close the eyes, bury, mourn)," and also "to contract a marriage, to make one kinsman by marriage." The adjective *kēdeios* means "cared for, dear, beloved" and "of a funeral, tomb, sepulchral." These words clearly show that the dear and beloved ones belonged to the kinship and marriage, which in turn implied the obligation of the care of the deceased ones. The funeral ritual seems to be the criterion of kinship and love. Other such terms are the Greek *philos;* if from a former *sphilos* it would mean "from the same sib, sibling." The Latin *cīvis* meant also "friend"; this word corresponds phonemically to the Germanic *hiva,* as in the Gothic *heiwa-frauja,* "the master of the household," properly "of the dear ones, the friends." Even the Latin *amicus,* "friend," and *in-imicus,* "enemy," refer to *amō, -āre,* "to love"; moreover, *amicus* meant properly "considering someone as belonging to the household."

Friendship, *kind-ness,* and *kin-ship* were originally identical. It can be well understood that if someone who was not kindred should be accepted as a "friend" he was made symbolically a blood brother by the blood covenant. Brunhild said in one of the Old Icelandic Edda songs: "Rememberest thou that clearly Gunnar? How you both (Sigurd and thyself) did let your blood run together in the footprint (swearing brotherhood)."

The food prohibitions are related to the kinship system, as well as to the specific forms of sacrifice and ancestor worship within this kinship. The animal that represented the kinship or was thought to be related with the kinship became sacrificed on solemn occasions; it was offered as an atonement for the whole community. The animal was consumed in the context of the sacrifice but was strictly forbidden to be consumed like an everyday provision. It was too sacred for daily consumption. We must suppose that the meat of the domesticated animals was originally by no means a daily food for the herdsmen. To "murder" one of those animal members of the household was permissible only as a spiritual act, as a religious ritual. Language preserved this original religious implication of the cattle, e.g., in the Latin *mactō, -āre,* which means "to offer, sacrifice, immolate," "to magnify, extol, glorify, honor," and "to kill, slaughter, put to death." The Greek *hiereion* denotes "a victim, an animal for sacrifice or slaughter," "an offering for the dead" and "cattle slaughtered for food"; the word is a derivative of *hieros,* meaning "sacred, divine." These terms can be understood if one supposes that "cattle slaughtered for food" was originally the victim of sacrifice. The Greek and Roman patristic society venerated the ox and the bull. To kill a sacrosanct animal was a capital offense equal with killing a man. In Greek *phonos* meant "murder, homicide"; *phonē,* "slaughter, murder." The priest who performed the sacrifice at the Athenian festival called

320

bou-phonia, "oxen-murder," was called *bou-phonos,* "oxen-murderer." The whole ritual suggests that this solemn sacrifice reminded one of a murder.

In Egypt where beside Apis-bull the goddess Isis was venerated and matristic ideas influenced the social order, the cow appears as the sacred animal; its meat was prohibited food. Keeping in mind that these animals replaced man as the original sacrificial victim, one can conclude that the primary community of kinship was established through an act that became the primary taboo among all food prohibitions: the eating of human flesh and the drinking of human blood.

See: ANCESTOR, CANNIBALISM.

Matriarchy

The Oedipus trilogy has been interpreted as an illustration of the conflict between the patristic and the matristic social orders.[58] Bachofen disclosed first the new vision of Greek antiquity as seen in the twilight of the waning matriarchy.[59] He found confirmation of his discovery in Sophocles' *Antigone.* He saw in this tragedy a monumental document of the heroic fight of the "Mothers" and their tragic defeat by the new patristic social order. As fascinating as Bachofen's vision is, it still remains an open question whether his interpretation of the Oedipus trilogy hit upon the essential truth. The Oedipus tragedy has its roots, in my understanding, not in the ground of matriarchy, but in polygamous patriarchy. On the surface the family structure is monogamous and patristic in Sophocles' trilogy. Beneath it, one can discover the remnants of an older social order, patriarchal polygamy, which exposes most distinctly the polarity of father and mother. They appear as counteracting forces, and they bring forth tragic conflicts within the extended patriarchal family.

Even in the monogamous unit the child grows up in a psychological matriarchy, which means that during the first years of the infant's life, the mother appears as the all-domineering figure, the child depends on her, belongs to her, and the father remains a stranger, if not an unwanted intruder. In the polygamous family setting the distance and the tension between the figures of the father and the mother is even greater and is felt more intensively by the infantile mind.

His attachment to his mother is greater; therefore, his struggle to free himself is a more tragic one.

Distinct from this psychological matriarchy, through which every child has to grow, are the historical documents that reveal scant indications that at some time the social position of the woman may have been different from that which appears among Indo-European people at the beginning of history. Even in the patristic setting, the situation might have been such as Herodotus described for the Persian children: "Until their fifth year they are not allowed to come into the sight of their father, but pass their lives with the women" (1:136).

Matriarchy, at least matrilineal descent, is reported for various pre-Indo-European inhabitants of Europe and Britain; thus it seems that matriarchy was a prehistoric social institution which was overthrown by the Indo-European invaders. Herodotus tells us, concerning the Lycian people, neighbors of the Greeks, that "something is peculiar with them, they share it with no other people. They call themselves by the name of the mother and not by the father." If asked who he was, a man would tell his name according to his mother and his maternal grandmother. "And if a free woman has children by a slave, the children are considered to be born free, yet if a free citizen, no matter how noble his descent, marries a foreign woman or keeps a concubine, his children never will become free" (1:173). There are other historical descriptions of the Lycian people. They all agree that the Lycians respect the women more than men; they leave their properties as heritage to their daughters and not to their sons. Because this matrilineal social order was once widespread all over the world among non-Indo-European people, one may surmise that it left some vestiges among the colonizers of the Western world. Anthropologists describe this type of family structure as existing in our age in Central Asia, Tibet, and Melanesia.

Even though there are historical evidences depicting matristic social conditions within the Western Hemisphere, I do not want to commit the technical failure of confounding historical realities with psychological facts to which myth, language, and legendary traditions refer. If, for example, various Amazon-like figures appear in the Germanic tradition, this does not prove that a "maiden-land," Old English *Maegde-*

land, factually existed; it may simply indicate that the virginal "tomboy," personifying the rejection of the female role, is an age-old type which is represented all over the world and was also known by our Germanic ancestor people. We should not take the various matristic symptoms in our cultural heritage at their face value either. Matriarchy may have been a psychological reality in the world of fantasies, while the factual reality was ruled by men. Various stories exhibiting women as supreme might have grown up as utopian dreams in an age of female subservience. Observing the symptoms of domineering women who require submissive and domesticated husbands, one will find that these matristic characteristics are rooted not in social realities, but in the depth of ambivalence within the feminine psyche. There, one can discover a stratum where the woman feels misused, abducted, violated in her desire for self-expression and identity. The loss of the maiden name is sometimes characteristic in general for the loss of maiden identity.

The matristic system reverses the patristic social order; it is the fantasy of a revolution, the revolution of the left, against authority, despotism, tyrannism of the domineering father; it implies mostly polyandry, which permits the woman to have many men, none of them being her master. One may observe this compensatory system at work in religion. If the prevailing religion and ritual is patristic, according to the patriarchal social order, female deities grow up to satisfy the popular religious demand which wants to emulate fertility, motherhood, love, and equality. The Mother Earth, *Terra Mater,* is the most general personification of the female chthonian deities; they all dwell under the earth, which means, in psychological language, that they dwell in the unconscious.[60]

The Old Testament depicts Sarah, Rebekah, Rachel, Leah, Bilhah, Zilpah, Keturah, Hagar as distinguished personalities; they are not just items in a household.[61] The Homeric tradition exalted Hecuba, Andromache, Penelope, Nausicaä as highly respected women. Hecuba took part even in the men's council (*Iliad* xxiv. 200). She had borne nineteen sons, among them Hector, Troilus, and Paris, but her lord, Priam, was a notorious polygamist. He had as wife besides Hecuba, Laothoe, who bore him two sons, but he counted in total fifty sons and only twelve daughters. One may suppose he kept a whole harem of women. This means, in other words, that Hecuba, despite her exalted position, still lived under the conditions of polygamy. The proverbial saying, "I don't care for Hecuba," which is still alive in European languages (Hamlet refers to it), does not show any high respect either; yet Hecuba became so exalted among women that she personified to the Greek mind the *Mater Dolorosa*, the Mourning Mother, who bewailed her sons. Penelope, the honored wife of Odysseus, is depicted in the same way, despite evil gossip, as the faithful woman waiting for the return of her husband. These personifications, one may observe, are rather the projection of wishful masculine thinking than the pictures of actually existing social conditions.

The reason for outstanding female personalities growing up must not be sought for in matriarchy, but can be found in the emotional attachment of the son to his mother. A man may have many wives, but can still have only *one* mother. The mother of the master of the house surely held an exalted, sometimes feared, position among the women of the household. The antagonism against the mother-in-law has its emotional roots in the polygamous family and in the fixation of the son's emotion to the mother; it remained distinguished from his relationship to various wives and concubines.

Perhaps more indicative of matrilineal family structure are the cases of the so-called "be'ena marriage" in the Old Testament. In such cases the new husband joined the wife's family instead of introducing the wife to his own paternal family (ba'al marriage). The Old Testament describes such cases (Gen. 29); yet every marriage may raise similar problems of divided loyalties even in our day without matriarchy. The attachment to the wife's family is surely a strange phenomenon within the polygamous family setting. There might be specific reasons for it—e.g., Jacob married two sisters and received their maidservants as concubines (Gen. 29)—but exceptional cases prove little of a general inference of matriarchy.

The emotional climate of the polygamous family is very different from the monogamous unity.

The master of the polygamous family was distant and, therefore, the emotional intimacy and solidarity was restricted to the privacy of the separate tents or houses in which the mother brought up her children. The emotional family is not

324

always identical, especially in the realm of fantasies, with the legal family; the one might be built upon the mother, while the other is ruled by the father. The mother was nurturing and fostering her children during the period of dependency and the following formative years; thus she personified to the children all the emotions invested in the home. The long protracted period of suckling, which was customary in the early ages, made the attachment of the children to the mother even stronger. The closeness to the mother and dissociation from the father does explain that the marriage between the children of the same mother (*adelphoi*) was prohibited, while it was permitted between the children of the same father.

See: INCEST.

Mother

While the father was generally described either as the procreator of children or as the ruler of the house, the woman was perceived primarily in her function as being the *mater-ial* giving birth to the children. A word expressing this function is Greek *gunē*, "wife." Very seldom is the name of the woman derived as a feminine form of the name of the husband. The few cases, however, where the relationship does exist are in the Greek *potnia*, "mistress," and *posis*, "husband"; the Latin *domina*, "mistress," and *dominus*, "master of the house"; the German *Frau*, which means "woman, wife," properly "mistress," and which is the feminine form of an old *frō*, Gothic *frauja*, meaning "lord"; and the Old English *frea* and *freo*.

THE WOMAN The English word *woman* derives from the Old English *wīf-man*, properly "wife-man." The fantasy underlying this word suggests that the female is nothing but an effeminated male. The male represents, according to the patristic philosophy, the true humanity; therefore in many languages, as in English, the *man*, as in *man-kind*, may refer to the total population on earth, on the one hand, and specifically to the male, on the other. All the Germanic languages identify the human with the male. The German word *Mensch* denoting "man" as human being derives from a former *mannishō;* this is an adjectival form of *man*. Thus it points out that the "human" is not simply "man" but "man-ish" indeed. The German language uses *man* even as an indefinite pronoun. This means that when the English says *one* as in *one says,* the French language uses *on* (from the Latin *homo,* "human") as in *on dit,* "one says," and the German language uses *man spricht,* properly "the man is speaking," meaning "one says." If the man represents total humanity, the woman has little to say.

The fact that woman is made out of man not only expresses the thinking of a patristic society, but also corresponds to early infantile fantasies.[62] Eve was made out of the rib of Adam, but the infantile fantasies mostly suppose that the female was made out of man by castration. Because the "woman" does not represent humanity in her own right but is looked upon as a derivation of the male, her name is therefore also mostly derived from the name of the male. For example, in the Hebrew *ish* means "man," and its derivative is *ishshah,* "woman." Thus the Biblical sentence "she shall be called Woman, because she was taken out of Man" (Gen. 2:23) should be understood literally. The English *wo-man* as "wifeman" conveys a fairly accurate translation of the original epicene idea, but Luther's German follows the Hebrew even more closely by translating: *"Man wird sie Männin heissen, darum dass sie vom Manne genommen ist."* Other Indo-European languages also derive the name of the woman from the name of the male, like the Hebrew.

Tacitus related concerning the Germanic people that they venerated Tuisco and his son Mannus as their progenitors.[63] *Mannus* means "man." The Hebrew *Adam* also means "human being, mankind." The Germanic *Mannus* is created by Tuisco, who is a god "out of the earth." It is not clear whether the Father Sky has begotten him with the Mother Earth, in which case his name would mean "sky-son," or whether this name is simply a variant of *two,* denoting the "double," the "wife-man," the bisexual ancestor of all human beings.

The Germanic progenitor reminds one in some way of the case of a schizophrenic child in deep regression. He had a fantasy, with which he lulled himself to sleep, concerning an androgynous figure, a fairy named Mr. and Mrs. Twisky, *who performed good deeds.*[64]

THE OWNED WIFE The many wives necessarily held a subordinate position compared to the authority of the one husband. Man in the patristic society tended everywhere to keep many wives, just as he tended to increase the number of his cattle. The size of his family—women, slaves, concubines, children—displayed his wealth and was also a "proof" of the magic power of his creative capacity. There was not much difference in practice between the slaves, concubines, and wives; they were all bought to serve his concupiscence, so they formed a part of personal properties. In the Old Testament the second wife is often called "maidservant." The difference in social position became apparent rather in the children. The children of the concubines could not inherit as much as the legitimate children, but otherwise they belonged to the household family. Being an object of possession, the women were deprived of the essential attributes of the human personality. This subordinate character of the woman is implied in the Biblical commandment stated thus: "Neither shalt thou desire thy neighbor's wife, neither shalt thou covet thy neighbor's house, his field, or his manservant, or his maidservant, his ox, or his ass, or any thing that is thy neighbor's" (Deut. 5:21). The transgression of this commandment is an offense against the property rights of the neighbor, but not against the person of the wife. "Adultery" was for the Greek mind *gamo-klopia,* properly "marriage-theft"; the adulterer was the *gamo-klepos,* "marriage-thief." The second part of the compound is from the verb *kleptō,* "to steal."

This object character of the woman is expressed in the Germanic languages by the neuter gender of the word "wife," in German *das Weib.* The Old English *wif* is also neuter like any other object. The Latin language expresses even more radically the philosophy of polygamy. A thing is never a unique individual object, but is one of the many, just a singular item of a plurality. In the same way, the ox, for example, that the commandment mentions, is not an individual animal, but just one of a species. The woman, depersonalized and deprived of the attributes of individuality, is also a plural concept; she is only one of the many. There are therefore many wives in the patristic order. The grammatical expression of depersonalized plurality in the Latin ending *-a* characterizes the plural of the neuter, e.g., singular *jument-um,* "draught cattle," plural *jument-a.* The same ending *-a* indicates the singular of the feminine, e.g., *femin-a,* "woman." Cattle breeders are by their occupation patristic minded. In classical Latin "children," *liberi,* is also a plural concept. This word has no singular in classic usage.

PURCHASE MARRIAGE It goes with the depersonalization of the women that the female became an article of purchase. She represented, like other utilities, a specific sales value depending upon supply and demand. Marriage by purchase reflected the economic situation of the buyers and sellers. The father offered his daughter for sale and entered into a commercial dealing with the buyers, often in the form of a marriage contract. Strange as it may seem, this commercializing of marriage opened the way for a gradual improvement of the wife's social position. The seller could impose some obligations upon the buyer. Some languages, like the Hungarian, call the "marriageable" girl *eladó lány,* properly "girl for sale." This original meaning has become completely repressed with the present usage. Aristotle said pointedly concerning the Greek custom (*Politics* ii. 5. 11),* "The pristine customs were very simple and barbarous. The Hellenes carried arms and purchased their wives." Homer called the "maiden" *alphesi-boia,* meaning "yielding oxen"; the first part of this compound derives from the verb *alphanō,* "to bring in, earn, yield." Herodotus attested for the Thracian people that "they sell their children to traders . . . they bought their women from their parents and paid high prices" (v. 6); or it is said by Xenophon (*Anabasis* vii. 2. 38): "I will give you, Xenophon, my daughter as wife, and in case you have a daughter, I will buy her according to the Thracian custom." The sale of women has left some traces in personal names. For example, the Greek *ōpheleia,* "help, aid, assistance," properly meant "utility, profit, advantage," from the verb *ōpheleō,* "to be of use or service."

The trade of women was a general practice with all Indo-European people. The northern neighboring tribes which were engaged in fur trade called the bride not "cattle-yielding" as did Homer, but by the name of the fur for which she was bought. (For example, the Hungarian *meny-assony,* properly

* O. Schrader: *Reallexikon der Indogermanischen Altertumskunde,* 1:61, *s.v. Brautkauf.*

"ermine woman" or "mink woman," means "bride.") The trade of marriageable girls became organized like the fur trade or cattle trade. Some people used the open market for this purpose.

The Old Testament provides us with a full illustration of this trade of women. It was the prerogative of the father to buy a wife for his son or to sell his daughter. "Judah took a wife for Er, his firstborn, whose name was Tamar" (Gen. 38:6). The consent of the persons involved was irrelevant. The bride and the bridegroom often never met one another before their wedding. The motivation behind this blind-marriage custom still persists in our age in the philosophy: the parents know better the conditions of happiness—love comes after marriage anyhow.

The restrictions imposed upon this trade of women were rather insignificant. Most people prohibited the husband from reselling his wife. The father was permitted according to Old Testament law to sell his daughter as "maidservant," in other words, as a concubine, but he was not allowed to trade her abroad to foreigners. The gradual transition of the purchase price of the wife into a "wedding gift" might be illustrated by the Greek term *hednon*, in plural *hedna*, "the word signifying the wedding gifts, presented by the suitor to the bride or her parents after the fashion of Homeric times; the bride received only a portion of it." The phonemically corresponding Old English term is *weotuma*, "a portion, dowry." Thus this word proves the prehistoric origin of the age-old custom of trading women.

THE WIFE AND THE CONTRACT   It is sometimes difficult to draw the borderline between the concept of "wife" and "concubine," between the status of the first wife and the second one, between the handmaid, maidservant, and slave woman. The meanings of the pertinent terms therefore also fluctuate into one another; they include sometimes even the "prostitute," who was also a woman for sale. The common denominator of all these concepts is that they belonged to the family household. They all were servants and sexual partners of the man.

The Old English displays a state in which these concepts were not differentiated within the polygamous order. The verb *haeman* means properly "to cover," thus "to lie with, cohabit, commit fornication or adultery"; *haemed,* "a lying with, cohabiting"; *haemed-gemana,* "marriage"; *haemed-gifta,* "dowry"; *haemed-scipe,* "marriage"; *haemed-ceorl,* "husband"; *haemed-wif,* "matron, wife"; *haemed-thingan,* "cohabit"; *haemere,* "fornicator." Another Old English term for the marital relationship is *ga-maeca,* "an equal companion, a wife," and *ga-maecea,* "wife." These words derive from the verb *ga-macian,* "to make (fire), to fit together, to match"; the adjective *ge-maeclic,* "conjugal, relative to the wife," remains preserved in the German adjective *gemächlich,* which means "cozy, comfortable." All these terms may refer to the wife as well as to the concubine. The Latin term *uxor,* denoting the legal wife, also approaches the idea from the procreative function. The origin of the noun is not completely clear, but relative forms seem to be the Sanskrit *ukshan,* "bull"; English *ox;* the Greek *arsēn,* "male, masculine." All the other related terms refer to "man," "husband," and "bull," and to the verb "to besprinkle, make wet, rain." The Latin *uxor* seems to imply the meaning "who is made wet, besprinkled," while the other forms imply "to emit semen."

The most usual term for wife in Greek, *gunē,* is not transparent etymologically either, but it seems to be related to the Latin *gignō* and the other general terms for procreation. The Greek *gameō,* "to take a wife, to marry," also belongs to this large family of words with the *gen-, gon-, gn-* phonemic pattern. *Gamētēs* means "husband" and *gamētis* or *gamētē,* "wife." *Gamos* means "wedding" and *gamikos,* "of or for marriage, marriageable." The verb *gameō,* considered from the masculine aspect of marriage, can also mean "to have mere sexual intercourse," "to take for a paramour." The same situation is found in the Latin term for marriage. The verb *maritō, -āre* denotes "to wed, to marry, to give in marriage"; *maritus* is "husband," properly the "married man"; and *maritāta,* classic *marita,* the legally "married woman." The English *marry, to get married* derives from this Latin verb.

The idea of "bed-fellow" became expressed in various languages and could mean either "wife" or "concubine." In Greek the "wife" was called *a-lochos,* "partner of one's bed, a bed-fellow"; this is a compound form with the noun *lechos,* "bed." *Alochos* could also mean "concubine." The Latin *con-cubina* derives from the verb *con-cumbō* "to lie together, to lie with." It also refers to the fellowship in bed. The difference in status is indicated linguistically by the fact that the wife shares not only the bed, but the name with the husband, which is a distinction not extended to the concubine. Thus the Greek *a-koitēs* means "husband"; *a-koitis,* "wife." Both refer to the *koitē,* "the marriage bed, the act of going to bed," from the verb *keimai,* "to lie, to be laid." The Old English used a similar term for "wife," which was *ge-bedda,* "bed-fellow, wife"; *ge-bed-scipe,* "bed fellowship, marriage." The German *Bei-schläferin,* properly "by-sleeper," always means "concubine."

The difference between the social position of the "wife" and the "concubine" seems to have been symbolized also by the sleeping position. Whereas the wife was to share the bed, the concubine was allowed to sleep only at the feet of the man, and she therefore was called "foot-wife" in the Slavic and Finnish languages (*jalkavaino*). One can observe the same custom in the Old Testament setting.

> And when Boaz had eaten and drunk, and his heart was merry, he went to lie down at the end of the heap of corn: and she [Ruth] came softly, and uncovered his feet, and laid her down. . . . And he said, Who art thou? And she answered, I am Ruth thine handmaid: spread therefore thy skirt over thine handmaid . . . (Ruth 3:7, 9).

It is a significant symptom that no old genuine term for "marriage" exists. Also none exists for the notion of "wedding." Even for "parents" languages differ widely; they follow their own fantasies and show no common pattern. It was obviously impossible for the prehistoric people who developed the Indo-European stock, to think of marriage as a mutual relationship equally valid for husband and wife. In fact, no such relationship is possible if marriage is polygamous. Even in Greece, where monogamy prevailed, Aristotle pointed out that "the marital connection between husband and wife has no name."* Only the man can "marry" a woman,

---

* "I mean the relation of master and servant, the marriage relation, the conjunction of man and wife, has no name of its own, and the procreative relation, this also has no proper name." *Politics* I. 4. Translated by Benjamin Jowett. (New York: Random House, Inc., The Modern Library, 1943), p. 56.

meaning "to take a wife" (*gameō*). The woman is "taken" in getting married—a passive expression. By the same token, in the Latin the expression *ducere uxōrem*, properly "leading wife," is the term denoting the wedding of the man, while the wedding of the woman is called *nūbō, -ere*, properly "to veil"; thus *nuptiae*, "wedding," applied originally only to the woman. The Latin *maritus* means "husband" and the according verb *maritō, -āre* means "to give in marriage" to a man, "to give to a husband." It could be applied only to the woman as she becomes a *maritata*, "a married woman."

The contractual marriage represented a step ahead in the wife's position as compared with the former purchase marriage. The concubine remained on the purchase level and never achieved this contractual relationship of the first wife. Her position never became as legal and permanent as that of the wife. The marriage contract, originally a mere sales agreement, came to imply moral obligations and to enforce some reciprocity between husband and wife, which justified using the same term for both of them, as, e.g., the Greek *posis*, "lord, master," and *potnia*, an equivalent of "lady." The same holds true for the Old English *frea* and *freo*, Gothic *frauja*, "dominus, lord," and the German *Frau*, "woman," which originally denoted the "lady."

The permanent character of the contractual marriage is indicated by the Old English term *sin-scipe*, properly "a continued or perpetual state," "wedlock." This is a compound form of *sin* and *scipe*, "ever" and "a state, condition," respectively. Yet even this term can mean also "carnal connection, lust." The same association of "marriage" with "law" and "lasting" is present in the Old English term *aew*, meaning "law, wedlock, marriage, marriage vow." It also denotes "a female bound by the law of marriage, a wife, spouse." In the Old English language "law" and "marriage" are inseparable from one another. Therefore the term "in-law" properly means "through marriage."

Adultery was considered as "breaking the law," as Old English *aewbrece*, "marriage breaking, adultery," and *aew-brecca*, "a breaker of the marriage vow." The phonemically corresponding German terms are still *Ehe-brecher*, "adulterer," and *Ehe-bruch*, "adultery." These Old English terms for "law" and "marriage" hang together with the adverb *ever*, with the Greek *aiōn*, the Latin *aevum* and *eternitas*, and it can be discussed whether "marriage" derived its meaning from "law," or whether both derived from the idea of "eternity" or perhaps from "spinal marrow," which was to the Greek mind the seat of generative power. The interrelationship of these ideas is the reason why the German noun *Ehe*, "marriage," has the same phonemic form as the adverb *eher*, "before," in English *ere*.

The gradual desexualization of the pertinent terms and their sublimation, by which they became more and more charged with ethical significance, can be best observed in the relative words in English and German. Starting from the mere biological aspect of procreation implied in the ideas "plow" and "play," which were one-sided masculine concepts, the Greek and Latin monogamies developed the pictogram "to be yoked together." Though this pictogram referred primarily to the "yoked" or "broken in" condition of the female, it implied also the male. Consequently, the Latin *con-jugium* came to denote "connection, union, corporis et animae" and, hence, "connection by marriage, wedlock"; however the idea of wedlock expressed by *conjugium* was from the male's point of view of "plowing," a physical viewpoint. In contrast, *"conu-bium* is regarded as "a civil or political institution" (Harper). Similar fantasies are implied in the Greek *su-dzugos*, meaning "yoked together, paired, united," especially by marriage, and the corresponding verb *su-dzeugnumi*, "to yoke together, couple, or pair together." The noun *dzugon* means "yoke." The same verbal forms are found in Sanskrit and also in the Gothic language, but they refer rather to the comradeship of men and not to marriage. The corresponding Latin terms are *jugum*, "yoke," and *con-iungō, -ere*, "to bind together, connect, join, unite."[65] It is again significant even for the Latin monogamous family that *conjunx* or *conjux* is mostly used in the feminine form *conjuga;* this means that, generally, the wife is considered to be "yoked together," i.e., tied down; not so the husband. It is also "a more honorable designation for concubine"; whereas applied to the man it means fellowship. It was customary in ancient Rome to contract the marriage by an oath upon a yoke.

The English word *plight*, related to "play-plow," and the corresponding German word *Pflicht*, "duty," shows a further step in the institutionalizing of marriage. The Old English *pliht* meant "the danger of forfeiting a pledge," thus English *plight* means "pledge (under penalty), a promise given under pain of forfeit, a duty or solemn engagement for which one has to answer." Because the word developed on the masculine side, "the plight" and "the risk to lose the pledge" obviously had the bridegroom in mind if he did not fulfill his obligation toward the bride.

Which were these marital duties that were supposed to be *ful-filled*, i.e., filled in full? The German verb *pflegen*, the derivative of the old *plegan*, "plow-play" form, is descriptive of the obligations (of the bridegroom). It means "to do something regularly, repeatedly" and "to take care of, to attend someone with care." The procreative function of the male appears in the light of this term as a marital duty. If one considers the various meanings of the German noun *Pflicht*, "duty," the phonemic equivalent of the English *plight*, one will find in medieval usage "intercourse" as the first primary meaning, followed by a fairly elaborate enumeration of various other marital duties.*

The more the primary biological function became repressed, the more clearly emerged the moral qualities of the husband's obligations. Even our word *duty,* from the adjective *due,* derivative of the Latin verb *debeō, -ēre,* "to owe," will lead our fantasies nearer to the primary reference. The word *duty* primarily means a payment, and marriage was not duty free. It also implied moral obligations, as in Nelson's famous command: "England expects that every man will do his duty." This, one may surmise, reflects an already spiritualized concept of marriage. It refers not to the female but primarily to the male. That the male is the repressed point of reference may be illustrated by the symbolic application of the word in agriculture: *duty of water,* meaning "the quantity of water needed to irrigate a given area of a given crop." The Hebrew term used as a circumlocution for the missing word of "marriage" is *ōwnāh,* meaning "to dwell together," like "to cohabit." It also means "duty of marriage." One can observe

---

* "Freundliche Fürsorge, Pflege, Obhut, Aufsicht; Verkehr, Verbindung, Teilnahme, Gemeinschaft, Teil, Dienst, Obliegenheit; Sitte, Art, und Weise, Recht." Matthias Lexer, *Mittelhochdeutsches Taschenwörterbuch* (26th ed., Zürich: Hirzel, 1951), *s.v. Pflicht.*

in these various terms that the unrestricted sexual freedom of the male became more and more tied down by the moral responsibilities of a husband and a father.

The contractual relationship between husband and wife became positively expressed by the Old English verb *weddian,* "to pledge, engage." The phonemically corresponding German term is *wetten,* "to wager." Our *wedding* derives from this idea. The *wed-lock,* Old English *wed-lac,* properly means "wed-gift," "a gift in token of pleasure." It was customary to make a present to the bride on the morning after the marriage had been enacted. This gift, originally denoted *wed-lock,* was called in German *Morgen-gabe,* properly "morning-gift." The position of the wife became established by contract also according to the generally used German terms *Gemahl,* "husband," and *Gemahlin,* "wife." These words derive from the old noun *mahal,* meaning "market, convocation, contract." The term *be-troth, troth,* a variant of *truth,* indicates a further progress in the direction of moral obligation of the contracting parties. The Old English *treow* originally meant "fidelity, faith, truth." The related German *Treue* also refers to "fidelity" and "loyalty." The verb *trauen* means, on the one hand, "to trust" and, on the other, "to wed." These ideas could be implied only in the monogamous conjugal unity of husband and wife.

CONCUBINE AND PROSTITUTE. Not all wives could achieve the distinguished position of the first one. They remained "maidservants" or "concubines" and belonged more or less to the *familia.* This does not mean the "family" in our sense of the term, but the "slaves in a household, a household establishment, family servants, domestics, i.e., wife and children." The wife and the children of the slave were considered like the increase of cattle. After six years of service a Hebrew bondservant "shall go out free for nothing" according to the Old Testament law, but "if his master have given him a wife, and she have born him sons or daughters; the wife and her children shall be her master's, and he shall go out by himself" (Exod. 21:4).

As far as corporal punishment is concerned, the same law sets the limit very low. The slave man or woman has to survive the beating, at least a few days. "And if a man smite his servant, or his maid," and if the servant or maid continues a day or two rather than dying immediately, the master "shall not be punished" because the servant "is his money" (Exod. 21:20–21). Foreigners, especially if they happen to be war prisoners, were the slaves of the slaves. "And seest among the captives a beautiful woman"—says the law—"and hast a desire unto her, that thou wouldest have her to thy wife; Then thou shalt bring her home to thine house; and she shall shave her head, and pare her nails; . . . and shall remain in thine house, and bewail her father and her mother a full month: and after that thou shalt go in unto her, and be her husband, and she shall be thy wife" (Deut. 21:11–13). The same situation is attested for all Indo-European people by various sources. The "free" woman was distinguished from the slave woman by the hairdo. In Old English, as expressed by *fri wīf locbore,* the free wife was called "lock-bearer," while the slave woman's head was shaven. The free woman's head was shaven only if she was found guilty of adultery.

The verbal expressions do not always distinguish between the concubine and the prostitute. This may be an indication that their social standing was not separated much either. Slave women and foreigners were mostly sold for prostitution, and therefore the point of "wage earning" is illustrated in pertinent Greek and Latin terms. The Greek term *pornē* derives from the verb *pernēmi,* "to sell," and thus denotes a woman "sold" for this purpose. The Latin term *merētrix* properly means the "earner," from the verb *mereō, -ēre,* "to deserve, to merit, to be entitled to," "to get by purchase, to buy," "to serve for pay." However, it would be a psychological mistake to derive prostitution simply from commercial motives. It is such an age-old phenomenon familiar to all people that there can be little doubt as to its deep-rooted motivation in human nature. The prostitute is an archetype of female existence, just as is the virgin, the mother, or the wife. The psychological foundations of this existence are exposed by the "sacred prostitution" of the "temple prostitutes," an age-old custom attested to by many sources. The religious meaning of prostitution is also expressed by the Old Testament term *zānāh,* which means "adultery" and "prostitution," on the one hand, and "idolatry," on the other. The covenant between the Lord and Israel is depicted by the prophet in terms of sex relationship (Exod. 16:8). The worship of foreign deities became interpreted accordingly as prostitution. All our languages produced an abundance of verbal expressions related to prostitution—which is a sure symptom of the emotional significance attached to it. The emotions revealed by these denotations may express degradation or debasement, e.g., the Latin *scortum,* the French *peau,* the German *Balg,* all properly mean "skin, hide." Other terms grasp the exhibitionistic impulse. Even the term *pro-stitūta* means literally "someone who is exposed publicly, placed in front," from the verb *statuō, -ere,* "to place." The Biblical account of Israel says: "Behold, therefore I will gather all thy lovers, with whom thou hast taken pleasure, and all them that thou hast loved, with all them that thou hast hated; I will even gather them round about against thee, and will discover thy nakedness unto them, that they may see all thy nakedness" (Ezek. 16:37). It goes with this exhibitionistic tendency that the garment of the prostitute is thought of as checked with loud colors, attracting public attention, and advertising of being free from sexual restrictions. While adultery is mostly "committed" shunning the daylight, prostitution, like other crimes, is characterized by the Biblical formula "to play the whore," i.e., to display and show publicly, being exempt from shame and modesty. Other pertinent terms are symbolic of the instinctual nature, e.g., the Latin *lupa,* the Italian *lupa,* the French *louve,* meaning "she-wolf." Other terms may evoke pictures of tender emotions calling her just a "girl" or "little bride," or may use a pet name, such as the German *Metze,* "prostitute," which is an endearing pet form of *Mechtilde* or *Mathilde.* The Greek *pallakis* or *pallakē* originally meant "girl, maid"; it is implied even in the name of the virgin goddess Pallas Athena. The Greek term *hētaira* properly refers to a good "comrade, companion"; it definitely refers to an appreciated friendly connection. Aphrodite, the goddess of love, was worshiped as Hetaira. *Hētaira* denotes a woman "mostly opposed to a lawful wife, and so with various shades of meaning from a concubine (who might be a wife in all but the legal qualification of citizenship) down to the courtesan, but distinguished from a *pornē.*" The Slavic-Bohemian term *nevestka,* "prostitute," properly means "little bride." It is the diminutive of *nevesta,* "bride." In the same way the French *putain* and the Italian *puttana* derive from the Late Latin *putana,* meaning "little girl." The French *fille* or *fille de joie,* "girl of pleasure," were not derogatory terms either. The German *Dirne,* "prostitute," also originally meant simply "girl," from a former *deo*, "slave," and *deorna*, "maidservant." Luther called his little daughter affectionately in family letters "little whore" (*kleine Hure*). This word is the phonemic equivalent of the Latin adjective *carus, a, -um*, "dear, beloved, loving." Its derivative is *caritas*, "charity."

In order to demonstrate the symbolism that is hidden behind these repressive terms, we choose as example the Greek term *kauka, kaukos* (also the Latin *caucus* or *caucula*), meaning "drinking vessel." This word is continued in the Russian term *kavka*, "prostitute."[*] Why should the woman be called so in reference to a drinking vessel? The answer seems to be suggested because the Greek term also means "vulva," but this does not really solve our problem. We find many instances proving that "vessel" and "jug" are symbolic for the woman, so there seems to be no need for further explanation. The English *loving cup* has nothing in common phonemically with the Greek or Russian terms, yet it will help to understand the repressed fantasies implied in the association of "drinking vessel" and "prostitute." The English word denotes a large drinking vessel of gold or silver with large handles, made for the special purpose of passing it around from one guest to the other at a banquet. It is "a large drinking vessel having two or more outstanding handles (*loving cup ears!*) for convenience in passing from hand to hand." This passing from one guest to the other to drink from it in turn is the point of association between the two disparate concepts. The words *loving* and *cup* are associated on this ground.

The association of "cup" and "concubine" might be the outcome of a hedonistic philosophy; e.g., Shakespeare says: "Have thy drink and thy whore." The connecting link between the two concepts can also be found in the idea of "mixing, blending." It was customary in the Greek and

[*] The old Gothic term *kalkjō*, "prostitute," is of uncertain origin. It might be a loan word, yet it is phonemically related to the Latin *calix, -icis*, "cup, goblet, drinking vessel"; the Greek *kulix*, "cup, wine cup," also the "chalice of the flower"; the German *Kelch*, "chalice." This is perhaps another case of the association of "drinking vessel" with "prostitute." Another interpretation says perhaps it denoted the slave woman working at the megalith stone buildings. Hermann Güntert, *Labyrinth: Eine sprachwissenschaftliche Untersuchung*, Sitzungsberichte der Heidelberger Akademie der Wissenschaften, 1932–33 (Heidelberg: Carl Winter, 1932).

Roman antiquity to mix wine and water in the mixing *kratēr,* "a mixing vessel, especially a large bowl, in which according to the custom of ancients the wine was mixed with water, and from which the cups were filled. It was commonly of silver, sometimes with a brim of gold, sometimes all gilt." The word is the nominal form of the Greek verb *kerannumi,* "to mix, mingle, blend." The Latin verb *adulterō, -āre* (from *ad-alter,* "other, different") preserved its original meaning well in English *adulterate,* "to corrupt, debase, or make impure by a foreign or base admixture." The wine can be "wedded" with another good wine, but will be adulterated by a poor wine according to the English language. The *loving cup* seems to be a late smaller edition of the original huge Greek *kratēr.*

The vicissitudes of the idea of "prostitute" can also be illustrated by the double form of the same English word *queen* and *quean,* a contemptible woman. The differentiation of the two meanings is old. The Plowman said already (C, 9:46) that in the grave all are alike; you cannot there tell "a *knight* from a *knave* or a *queen* from a *quean.*" The original meaning of both forms was "married woman," the same as the Greek *gunē.* Another more recent differentiation can be observed in the word *housewife* which developed the parallel form *hussy,* "a pert girl." A third transitory form of the same compound is *hussif,* "a housewife; a roll of flannel with a pin cushion attached, used for the purpose of holding pins, needles, and thread." One may readily accept the idea that such a pin cushion is symbolic of the good housewife, but why and how did the notion of a pert girl come in? The male organ is termed in vulgar parlance as a pointed object, string, dart, tip, point, pin, pintle; the pin cushion is "a soft pillow or pad into which pins are stuck." This will lead the fantasies to the idea of the pert girl.

JEALOUSY   It goes without saying that the absolute ruler of a large house kept a sharp eye upon his female property. In the Orient, eunuchs were charged with serving as watchmen of the harem. The patristic society which secures almost unrestricted sexual liberty for the man is everywhere characterized by the brutality with which it is ready to retaliate against any sidestep of the woman. The Old Testament law prescribes death by stoning or burning: "the adulterer and

the adulteress shall surely be put to death" (Lev. 20:10). The
Roman law and the Germanic law assert in the same spirit
that the husband is free to kill his wife and her lover if he
happens to surprise them "behind closed doors or under one
blanket." This right of immediate retaliation refers not only
toward the wives but in the Greek laws also toward the
concubines, and the mother, sister, and daughter. When the
immediate hanging, burning, stoning, or stabbing of the wife
caught in adultery became in some way mitigated later on, the
sadistic fantasies of the male found a free outlet by inventing
substitute punishments. We see mostly that the hair of the
woman was shorn; she became exposed publicly and had to
ride on an ass through the city. The husband could flog her in
public, or, as in Russia, harness her together with a horse to a
carriage and flog her out of the community. The Old English
term for the adulteress is *for-legis* or *for-legystre,* from the
verb *for-licgan,* which means properly "to mis-lie, to lie at a
wrong place." "Thou shalt not commit adultery" is properly
a figurative expression; it can refer to the wine as well as to
the woman. A Homeric inprecation says: "Then having
drawn wine from the goblet, they poured it into the cups, and
prayed to the immortal gods . . . so let the brain of themselves and of their children stream upon the ground like this
wine, and let their wives be mingled with other men" (*Iliad* iii.
300). The offense of adultery is committed not against the
person of the woman, as it is not against the wine, but against
the right of ownership of the man who possessed both, wine
and woman.*

Difficult was the position of the woman if the suspicion of unfaithfulness grew up in the mind of her master.
Paranoiac obsessive illusions emerge even in our society of
conjugal monogamy. They were the more dangerous when
adultery was considered the gravest offense against the patristic rule. According to the Mosaic law if "the spirit of jealousy
come upon him, and he be jealous of his wife . . ." (Num.

---

* Aristotle said: "Whereas in a state of having women and
children in common, love will be watery; and the father will certainly
not say my son, or the son my father. As a little sweet wine mingled
with a great deal of water is imperceptible in the mixture, so, in this
sort of community, the idea of relationship which is leased upon these
names will be lost." *Politics* II, 4:15.

5:14), the man is justified to subject his wife to the ordeal of "drinking bitter waters." The elaborate ceremonial of this "jealousy offering" performed before the priest and the altar cannot be understood anymore in its details. The wife was, however, surely obliged to "drink" a bitter potion, and the priest was to say, "This water that causeth the curse shall go into thy bowels, to make thy belly to swell, and thy thigh to rot: And the woman shall say, Amen, amen" (Num. 5:22). It would be a miracle if a woman, tested as to her fidelity by this magic procedure, should not be found guilty.

Such details characterize the emotional situation of the helpless and defenseless woman in the polygamous family setting. The image of the absolute ruler of the house, which is ingrained in all manifestations of family life, became also projected upon Jehovah, the God of the Old Testament. "The fear of the Lord is the beginning of knowledge" (Prov. 1:7); it is, in fact, the foundation of the Old Testament religion. This "fear of the Lord" permeates in every detail the religion of the chosen people and, we may surmise, the fear of the Lord and absolute ruler permeates also every corner of the house. The fear of the Lord may grow into terror. "And thy life shall hang in doubt before thee; and thou shalt fear day and night, and shalt have none assurance of thy life" (Deut. 28:66). This curse of Moses depicts the emotional climate in which the small child had to grow up in the polygamous family setting. "I the Lord thy God am a jealous God" (Deut. 5:9). The man who ruled over his women was a jealous husband.

DIVORCE How could a woman protect herself if trapped by such superior power and delivered to a man who purchased her? The man could divorce her whenever he pleased, but the woman could not divorce him. The Germanic law permits the man to dismiss his wife even if there is no reason for divorce. He simply has to restore the purchase money, not to the wife but to her kin from whom he bought her. The Greek and the Roman laws show somewhat more understanding for the woman's fate, but they are still far from the idea of reciprocity. The Old Testament law also secured the man the right to get rid of his wife if she found "no favour in his eyes . . . let him write her a bill of divorcement, and give it in her hand, and send her out of his house" (Deut. 24:1).

Being imprisoned against her will, delivered to the master who could dispose of her, having no legal resources, the only weapon of self-protection which remained for the woman was the charm of her sexuality. The love of the woman under such conditions cannot develop into a giving and receiving exchange of free partners, but it will become an artifice or ruse to subdue the will of the master. The useful tool of this artifice was the knowledge of aphrodisiac medications, a special female secret science. The borderline between the love potion and poison was not always clear and if the love charm did not work, nothing else remained but poison. One can observe this proximity of love charm and poison in the changing meaning of the words for poison: the Latin *venenum,* "poison," from the former *venes-rom,* "love potion"; *venus,* "love." The Greek noun *philtron,* "love charm, spell to produce love," and the Latin *philtrum* and the English *philter,* "a potion, a drug or charm supposed to have the power to excite sexual love," derive in the final analysis from the Greek verb *philō,* "to love." Shakespeare speaks about the "medicines to make me love him," but the potion was mostly used "to make him love her." The poison turned out to be a dangerous weapon of women. The paranoiac delusion of jealousy appears even in our age mostly associated with the fear of being poisoned. This fear was better motivated in the age of polygamy when the wife had no recourse to divorce. (Illusions of mental patients often fit the ages past better than our present society.) This is the background of the Greek verb *pharmakeuō,* which means, on the one hand, "to administer a drug or medicine" and "to use enchantments, to practice sorcery," on the other. The *pharmakon* means "a healing remedy, medicine" but also "an enchanted potion, philter, and so a charm, spell." Shakespeare still used the English *drug* with the meaning "poison."

Play

The meaning of "play" has been explained with reference to the pleasure principle as opposed to "work"; it has been related to obsessive repetition, to the transformation of passive behavior into active behavior, also to daydreaming and creative imagination. Freud called attention to the linguistic fact that we still speak of "theater play" and "players," and thereby connect this kind of creative activity in verbal fantasies with children's play; the same in German *Schau-spiel* and *Schau-spieler.*[66]

The English verb *to play*, Old English *plegan*, developed a complementary form *plow*, Old English *ploh:* thus *play* and *plow*, being phonemically interrelated must be related in their meaning too. Other phonemically related forms are English *plug* and *plight*, German *Pflock*, "wedge," and *Pflicht*, "duty." The phonemic pattern is of West Germanic origin; it has no parallel forms in other Germanic or Indo-European languages. For this reason it is supposed by Kluge that its origin might be a West Germanic compound *up-legan*, "to lie upon." This "over-lie," as shown by Old High German *ubar-ligan*, is the most common obsolete German term for "coire."[67]

The verbal forms suggest that "play" is founded on a pleasure activity that is libidinous and repetitious by its very nature. The *play-plow* united these motives; they broke under the pressure of reality into the polarity of "play" and "work." The latent fantasies implied in "plowing" are the same as implied in "playing," but they assumed the meaning of "work." Lawson G. Lowrey said about this connection: "Perhaps it is some sort of genius to use a word in an obsolete meaning to express something most important in a technical therapeutic sense."[68] He referred to an obsolete meaning of "play" which was "work"; however, it is evident that "play" appears as a pleasure activity that is opposed to the "work" associated with "labor" and "pain." The interference of the meaning "work" into the meaning "play" can be explained by the splitting of the original *play-plow* complex. The Latin *laborō, -āre*, "to work," also developed into the French *labourer* and the Spanish *labrar*. Both refer specifically to "plowing"; thus "working hard" and "plowing" became identified.

The repressed original meaning of *play*, which is also implied in *plow*, is interfering with the manifest lexical meanings as listed in dictionaries. This interference is obvious in such euphemistic usage as, e.g., in medieval English: "Tristem and Ysaude lay and woke and playden ay between"

(*Oxford New English Dictionary, s.v. play*). In the classic English of Milton, Adam says to Eve: "Now let us play . . . for never did thy beauty so enflame my sense with ardor to enjoy thee" (*Paradise Lost* 9:1027). The original meaning becomes transparent in some compound forms as *play-boy* or *fore-play*. The primary meaning is also present in the German term for "play," *Spiel*, despite the phonemic difference. This demonstrates that the *play-plow* association is not the reason but the consequence of a primary fantasy, e.g., Dutch *over-spel*, properly "over play," means "adultery." The lexical meanings describe the desexualized concepts after repression has wiped out the reprehended fantasy, but in regressed states such as schizophrenia, hypnotic age regression and in dreams, the primary implication may once more interfere with the lexical meaning.

The most general desexualized concept of "play" refers to free motility, which may be rhythmic or "brisk or nimble motion, alternating irregularly, intermittence," in the verbal form "to move rapidly, erratically; to dart to and fro, flutter, vibrate." The German *Spiel*, "play," developed from such original concept that usually became equated with "dancing." The German *Spiel-raum,* properly "play-room," defines the space necessary for uninhibited motion. The obsolete Biblical language regresses to the original meaning: e.g., it is said in the King James Authorized Version that Aaron fashioned in the absence of Moses the golden calf, "the people sat down to eat and to drink, and rose up to play. . . . And when Moses saw that the people were naked . . ." (Exod. 32:6, 25; also I Cor. 10:7). Because the children of Israel "were fruitful, and increased abundantly," the king of Egypt said unto his people: "Come on, let us deal wisely with them, lest they multiply" (Exod. 1:10), but the much older Tindale translation of the same text says: "Let us playe wisely with them." This obsolete meaning of "play" as "dealing" remained preserved in such formulas as *fair play* or *foul play*. The German *Spiel,* though phonemically different, carries the primary implication in the hunter's language; it denotes the "tail of a bird," like *Spiel-hahn,* properly "play-cock," much like our *cocktail* with its repressed meaning similar to *playboy*. In schizophrenic regression this meaning is interfering. A schizophrenic girl, twenty, responded in a word-association test to the stimulus word *Spiel* with the word *Frau,* "woman," and explained in German: *"I am too old still to play, too young for being without the desire."**

A second meaning of "play" refers in a general sense to "sport or lively recreation," "to make love sportively." The word *sport,* however, means in Shakespeare's language "amorous play." In free association a college girl said to her boy friend, who wanted to engage her in such "amorous play": *"No! I wanted it yet I feel just as playing tennis with you. I would not satisfy you. I would be a poor partner." The girl never played tennis and did not know that the zero score in tennis is called "love." (File.)*

A third fully desexualized meaning equates "playing" with "fingering." The point in this meaning is to perform on an instrument of music by touching it lightly, fingering the instrument, also responding to the performer's fingering. *To play with* means "to amuse oneself with, sport with; to touch or finger lightly or to move slightly with the hand by way of frivolous amusement, to dally." In word-association tests frequent responses of students to the stimulus word *play* are *violin* and *piano.* In regressed states the primary fantasies may interfere.

To card number one of the TAT test "the boy with the violin," a girl college student, twenty, in hypnotic age regression to the age of seven responded: *"What is the boy thinking about? He can't decide whether he should play the violin or not. I think he is going to play. Probably thinking . . . if his mother be proud of him? She may not like it. . . . He will play it anyway. . . . Eventually she would not mind it"* (*File*).

A schizophrenic male in a mental hospital said rather angrily to the therapist, who encouraged him to resume playing the violin: *"Why? Do you expect me to masturbate in public?"*[69]

A violinist, an able performer, twenty-four, recognized

* Franz Riklin in Carl Gustav Jung, *Diagnostische Associationsstudien: Beiträge zur experimentellen Psychopathologie* (München: Johann Ambrosius, Barth, 1914), 2:4. The English translation of this book is *Studies in Word Association,* translated by M. D. Eder (New York: Moffat Yard & Co., 1919); by translating the original stimulus word *Spiel* into English *play* the whole verbal situation has changed.

in psychoanalysis that he was not able *"to put real feeling in his play."* Despite many love affairs, he was aware that he had a marked sexual inhibition toward women. . . . A strong urge to attack women with his hands emerged, and he related it to the symptom of numbness in his fingers. This numbness prevented him from playing music with adequate feeling.[70]

As additional interpretation it should be mentioned that there exists, though distant, phonemic relationship between *violin* and *violence.* Also in Old Testament Hebrew *nāgan,* "to beat a tune with the fingers, especially to play on a stringed instrument, hence to make music," hardly can be separated from *naga',* "to touch, i.e., to lay hand upon," a euphemism for "to lie with a woman" and "to strike violently." Similar implications had the Hebrew *chālāl,* "to play the flute" and "to bore, perforate," "to begin as with an opening wedge." I referred to the phonemic relationship that exists between *play-plow* and the German *Pflock,* "opening wedge." The Hebrew term *chālāl* also denotes the "prostitute."

Another group of meanings refers to the behavior in specific games, contests, and various play situations. For example, children *play house* and *play doctor* often in acting out their frustrations. The patient-therapist relationship is also often understood in transference as play. A male patient reported a dream to his therapist two days before the end of his treatment: *"I am playing tennis with a professional. . . . I am losing. . . . He serves in a peculiar way. . . . I miss the ball and the professional wins the game. . . . I say it was a clever game but it was not a fair serve. I say, well, if that is the rule that is all right. But I feel a little mad and funny."*[71]

Another meaning of *play* denoted the stage representation of a drama, referring in general to role playing. This meaning attracted the attention of Freud: in German *Schauspiel,* "drama"; *Lust-spiel,* "comedy," properly "pleasure-play;" *Schau-spieler,* "actor." This denotation suggests the infantile root of acting and role playing.[72] It is a stereotype Old Testament expression "to play the whore" or "to play the harlot" (Deut. 22:21; Hos. 3:3 and 4:10; Jer. 3:1, 6, 8, etc.); the Hebrew term thus translated is the above-mentioned *nāgan,* "to play on a stringed instrument," "to beat the tune with the fingers."

A last desexualized meaning refers "to move or function freely, especially with prescribed limits" and "to discharge, eject, let off (on or upon persons or things), or to be discharged, ejected or fired repeatedly or continuously, as a fountain plays." Spenser said (1590): "Thereby a cristall stream did gently play, which from a sacred fountain welled forth alway." The German *Spiel-raum*, properly "playroom," is illustrative for this meaning. With this in mind it is said "the joints play together." In some Romance languages the "joint" is denoted by the derivative words of the Latin *jocāre*, meaning "to play." The New Testament Greek says for "the joints play together," "they walk together," *sumbibadzō;* the same meaning is present in the Latin *co-ire*, "to walk together." The English *joint* is a derivative of the Latin *jungō, junctum*, meaning "to be yoked together"; the Latin *con-jugium* like the Greek *su-dzux* means "marriage." Thus we arrive again at the complex playing-plowing, from which our investigation started.

See: PLOW.

Pleasure

While "pleasure" has been defined in general usage as the gratification of senses, in more technical terms it has been described as biologically "useful" by Herbert Spencer; as "tension reduction" by dynamic psychologies. Freud saw in pleasure the manifestation of the primary process, the urge for the immediate discharge of accumulated energy and the subsequent reestablishment of equilibrium in the mental apparatus. He distinguished the "fore pleasure" from the "end pleasure" and recognized that fore pleasure if unrelieved turns into unpleasure. He described the primary structure of pleasure in the alimentary process and admitted freely that the tension reduction theory is not comprehensive because there are pleasurable tensions and unpleasurable relaxations. His original idea of "constancy" approached the more flexible principle of "homeostasis,"[73] so he was inclined to consider pleasure not the reduction of absolute tensions but "something in the rhythm of their changes." His last word was still the "we do not know" what is the essence of the sensation of pleasure.[74] Adults still describe their sensation of pleasure chiefly in oral terms as "overflowing," "my cup runneth over," "flowing through my body," etc.[75]

The English *pleasure* as well as *please, pleasant,* or the

French *plaisir* and all the related forms in Romance languages derive in final analysis from the Latin verb *placeō, -ēre,* "to please; to be pleasing"; *placet,* "it pleases." The original concrete meaning is still present in *placidus,* "placid, gentle, quiet, still" but properly "flat, smooth." This basic meaning of "smoothness" is illustrated by the relative Greek term *plax,* "the quiet surface of the sea," also by *plakous,* "a flat cake," thus the Latin term *placenta.*

The psychological theories of pleasure elaborate the unconscious fantasies originally implied in the concept "pleasure." Plato associated already "the stillness of the sea" (*galēnē*) with the serenest calm of the mind. The "tension relief," Freud's "equilibrium," "constancy," and "Nirvana principle" still refer to the "gentle, quiet, calm, mild, peaceful, placid" meanings implied in the Latin *placidus* and the "quiet surface of the sea" of the Greek *plax.* This seems to underline the idea that supposes that the primary object of reference is the flat surface of the quiet sea. However, it is not proven that the calm of the ocean meant "pleasure" to the Greek sailors and fishermen. It meant rather disaster in Homeric ages as described at the beginning of the *Iliad.* The ocean, in Chinese picture writing denoted as "Mother Water," was ever personified by a mother symbol. For example, the name of *Thetis,* Achilles' mother, who dwelt in the sea, is formed from the Greek phoneme *thē-,* referring to the suckling breast. The Greek sea called *Archipelago,* properly the "chief sea," also contains the "flat, smooth" element of *plax* and *placidus.* However, Mother Water, which symbolizes the "equilibrium" and "constancy," is quiet only within the shorelines of the gulfs, called in Greek *kolpos,* "bosom." Our word *gulf* means, on the one hand, the inlets of the sea into the land; on the other hand, it means "an abyss, a deep chasm, hence a wide separation," also "sucking eddy," as in *en-gulf,* "to swallow up." The word *gulf* is a derivative of the Latin-Greek *kolpos.* In Latin, the gulfs are also called *sīnus,* "bosom," so in all Romance languages, so in German *Meer-busen,* "sea-bosom," formerly *Meer-schooss,* "the lap or the womb of the sea." Shakespeare is familiar with these fantasies when he says "in the deep bosom of the ocean." One can observe in these words the fusion of the concepts of "womb, breast, lap" as these concepts are also fused in infantile fantasies. "Pleasure" refers primarily not to the ocean but to the bodily sensation of oral satisfaction. The word is indicative of the regression to the oral stage, the smoothness in pleasure refers to the smooth skin of the breast of the mother. The primary sucking situation is also implied in other terms with similar connotation as *glad, felicity, satisfaction.* Freud's final conclusion is that pleasure refers primarily to a change of the rhythm on a quiet surface; we elaborate and say it refers to the change of rhythm of the waves on the quiet surface of the sea, the change of rhythm of the breath which can be felt on the smooth skin of the breast.

Plow

The idea of the "plow" and of "plowing" may emerge in unconscious fantasies as symbolic for the sex act. Freud interpreted the dream of a young man as an intra-uterine fantasy. The dreamer imagined that while *in utero* he could have observed parental intercourse. Thus in one part of the dream fantasies he saw the picture of "a field which was being ploughed up deeply by some implement."[76] No evidences are given to this interpretation but reference is made to the "plow" as a symbol of the male.

The English word *plow*, like the German *Pflug*, is of West Germanic origin; it replaces the older term, which was in Old English *erian;* "in earing time and in harvest thou shalt rest" (Exod. 34:21). The term *plow* seems to have emerged with the innovation of the wheeled plow with a large plowshare. The word *plow* is significant for its phonemic relationship with *play, plight, plug,* and with the German verb *pflegen*, "to attend someone" and "to do something regularly, repeatedly," also with the German noun *Pflicht*, "duty" (Meringer). English dictionaries do not realize that *plow* and *plowing* refer not to agricultural realities but to fantasies about those realities; thus they discard the phonemic relationship altogether and resort to a questionable supposition by assuming the word must be a loan word from some unknown language, "origin much disputed and quite uncertain" (C. D. Buck, *s.v. plow*). This negative verdict sounds the more strange because the writer does not seem to be aware of the discovery of Rudolf Meringer.[77]

The fantasies implied in "plowing" are of the same order as those implied in "playing." Even though the origin of the English word *plow* might be disputed, it is a fact beyond doubt that the fantasies implied are the same as those implied in "play." These fantasies are prior to and independent of the verbal expression. The fertilization of the soil was perceived as a magic act belonging to the same category as the generation of a new life. The Hebrew Old Testament formula says: "If ye had not plowed with my heifer, ye had not found out my riddle" (Judg. 14:18). The Hebrew term is *charash*, "to scratch, to engrave, to plow." It is understood, without much comment, that the "plowing" and the "riddle" are both related to "genital knowledge." However veiled these words are, there is no doubt what was in Samson's mind when the Philistines learned about his personal secret through his bride. Another example taken from Shakespeare, "She made Caesar lay his sword to bed. He ploughed her, and she' cropt"—or "she shall be ploughed." The meaning of *hus-band* also refers primarily to the "tiller of the soil."

For the Greek antiquity the "plowing" of the Mother Earth was perceived as a magic religious ceremonial equated with the sexual act which had to be performed on the freshly plowed field as sympathetic magic. The phonemic pattern of the Greek *aroō*, "to plow," is utterly different from the English word, yet the fantasies implied are the same. It seems to be significant that the Greek word meaning "to plow" also means "to sow." Plowing and sowing has been perceived as one act, not because the drill plow has been invented and imported from Mesopotamia but because in fertilizing the woman "plowing" and "emitting semen" were inseparable in human experience. The Greek *aroō* means "to plow-sow, to beget" if said of man, "to receive seed, to bear" if said of woman, and in the passive "to be begotten" in speaking of children. The same holds true for the singular *arotron*, "plow"; the plural *arotra*, "genitalia"; also *aroura*, "woman as receiving seed and bearing fruit"; also for *arotros*, which significantly means both "cornfield" and "procreation of children"; and *arosimos*, which means both "arable land" and "fit for engendering," as said of youth in puberty.

It will exclude any misunderstanding of these terms if one observes that some Greek vase paintings depict the plow not as a drill plow but with a huge phallus serving as a plowshare. Aeschylus said about Oedipus in similar context:

his guilt was that he had "plow-sown" into the holy mother's field. About an adulterer it is said: he did not plow his own field. Homer made a similar allusion through the mouth of Calypso by saying that Demeter once had a crush on Iasion and "made her love-bed on the furrows of the plowland" and this plowland was "plowed three times" (*Odyssey* 5. 125). The name *Dē-mētēr*, from *gē-mētēr*, denotes properly the "Earth Mother," and the Greek *arōtē* means the "tiller," who is the plowing-sowing husband-man as well as the "begetter or father." It can be shown that such words as *lord, lady, housewife* carry the same implications. In Dutch the English verb *to till* is the verb *telen*, which means *"coire."* The verb *to cultivate* has kept this double reference to the soil and to the woman until the present usage.

The corresponding Late Greek term for the cultivation of the soil is *kalli-ergō*, properly "to make beautiful." It is consistent with the fantasies implied that the Greek *aroō*, "to plow," also means "to enjoy," which contradicts the concept of "hard work." According to Hesiod the "plowing" of the field has to be carried out in sacral nakedness—the same state in which Moses found the idolaters "playing." How far-reaching and constant these unconscious fantasies are may be illustrated by the Sanskrit terms *langala*, "plow," and *langula*, "penis." It can be also understood in this connection that the *yoke* became a marital symbol: as in the Latin *conjugium*, which means "to be yoked together." To "plow" became also—in opposition to "play"—the equivalent of "hard work"—in French *labourer* and Spanish *labrar*.

See: PLAY.

Senicide

Ancestor worship cannot be separated from the attitude of the head of the house toward his father and toward his children. The feeling of ambivalence is built into their mutual relationship. The commandments of the Mosaic law are not directed against imaginary sins. They reprove with great psychological insight the basic propensities of man. The sixth commandment says "Thou shalt not kill" because, we surmise, people used to kill, properly murder. This commandment is preceded by another somewhat cryptic one: "Honor thy father and thy mother: that thy days may be long upon the land which the Lord thy God giveth thee" (Exod. 20:12–13). The connection between the honor given to the parents and the longevity of the sons is not very clear. It supposes an associative connection between these two. The following "Thou shalt not kill" makes this connection transparent. It is implied that no man has the right to take away life upon the land given by the Lord.

The head of the family ruled with absolute power. He owned the family, women, children, servants; he possessed also the old people who were not able to work any longer. He had the right to dispose of the unwanted children, and he held the same sovereign right with respect to the aged. The disposal of the aged members of the family seems to be complemental to abortion. But while the infant is not aware of the dangers upon which his fate hinges, the old people are exposed, being fully conscious, to the agonies of a situation in which their lives are at the mercy of the head of the house. The fifth commandment, which impressed upon the people the imperative to honor the parents, presupposes that a strong opposite tendency had to be counteracted. The commandment makes a strong appeal to the interests of the sons, in order to protect the parents when they grow old.

The disposal of elderly and sickly people was customary all over the world; it is attested for various cultures. Thus one may infer that it was in primitive family life an original characteristic that was later eliminated or mitigated by the cultural development. This practice is considered by the Greek writers as a horrifying custom of the neighboring non-Greek people. It was observed (by Strabo*) that Alexander the Great tried to suppress a particularly shocking custom of the Persian-Iranian tribes: They used to let the "holy dogs" devour the corpses. Thus, relates Strabo, "those who were worn out by age or sickness were thrown still alive to the dogs kept especially for such purpose, and called 'funeral dogs' in the native language." Strabo also reported about the Caspian tribe: "If the parents reach an age of seventy, they separate them and let them die by hunger." Our expression "to throw to the dogs" is no figure of speech for

* *The Geography*. With English translation by H. L. Jones. (London: Heinemann and New York: G. P. Putnam's Sons, 1923), Ch. 517.

the Iranian culture. This custom is also attested for the Greek antiquity. It was customary among the inhabitants of the island Keos to eliminate people by poison when they reached the age of sixty. They were also forced to commit suicide in this way. Many other indications prove that the senicide had an old venerable tradition in the Greek prehistory. The Romans used the adage *Sexagenarii de ponte*. The original meaning, "off the bridge with the sixty-year-olds," cannot be contested; only the symbolism of the bridge involved might be discussed. Considerable anthropological data, particularly about the Eskimo people, too, prove that this custom still existed in our age. Therefore there is no reason to doubt that it was in even more general practice in prehistoric ages than evidenced by historical relics. The hard reality behind this custom was the pressure of the scarcity of food, particularly in the case of the North Pole Eskimos. Certainly unconscious fantasies, too, were equally effective in its motivation. Paul expressed in classic formulation the principle by which the aged were doomed to starvation: "If any would not work, neither should he eat" (II Thess. 3:10).

The more humane treatment of the elderly supposes a change of the whole cultural climate. It could prevail gradually by introducing a new philosophy of life, a new appreciation of human existence "upon the land which the Lord the God giveth thee." It is obvious that this new aspect could prevail only gradually in opposition to the generally accepted prehistoric tradition of senicide. We can observe only the symptoms of a fight against it, and the fifth commandment is one of them. Negative and positive arguments were used in the fight against it. On the negative side stand all those preventive arrangements, the final intention of which is the protection of the aged.

The Old Testament law imposes a death penalty by stoning upon any man who kills another, but it was thought to be necessary beyond this general rule to point out expressively: "And he that smiteth his father, or his mother, shall be surely put to death. . . . And he that curseth his father, or his mother, shall surely be put to death" (Exod. 21:15, 17). The "cursing" of father or mother was specifically pointed out as an evil; it must have been customary among the people, otherwise the law would not say: "For every one that curseth his father or his mother shall be surely put to death: he that hath cursed his father or his mother; his blood shall be upon him" (*Lev. 20:9*).

It seems to be probable that these penalized "curses" expressed verbally the desire that the parents should die. Such severe punishment as required by the Mosaic law should prevent any attempt on the part of the sons to revolt against the rule of the father. The father was the sovereign lord of the family, even if he had already had great-great-grandchildren; his power and right over the whole household was not restricted by any age limit or retirement policy. On the positive side, the new philosophy is pleading for the "wisdom" of the aged persons. The stress is laid not upon the incapacity to work nor upon senility, but upon the life experience, which outweighs bodily impairments such as blindness. The patriarchs of the Old Testament are such venerated wise men.

In the classic Greek tradition the aged priests, seers, and prophets, by their superior wisdom, plead positively the veneration of the aged. The blind seer Teiresias is one of those superior old men of the Greek tradition. The veneration of the aged is clearly expressed by the word *presbus,* "an old man," then "most august, most honored"; the superlative is often used in the sense of "reverend, honored," from the respect paid to the aged and experienced. At Sparta it was used as a political title, meaning "chief, president." This word was also applied to the "elders" of the church, for the *presbyter.* The Greek *gerōn* denotes "an old man." As early as Homer this word assumed a political sense—the notion of age being merged in that of "dignity." *Gerōntes* are the "elders," or chiefs, who with the king formed the council.

The Latin *sēnex,* "old, aged," displays its implications by the relative verb *seneō, -ēre,* "to be old, weak, feeble"; *senescō, -ere,* "to grow old, become aged, grow hoary," "to linger too long," "to decay or diminish in strength, to grow weak, feeble and powerless, to waste away, to fall off, to wane"; *senilis,* "senile"; *senium,* "the feebleness of age, decline, decay, debility," but also "peevishness, moroseness, vexation, chagrin, mortification, grief, trouble, affliction produced by decay." It becomes obvious by these associations that the Roman mind perceived mainly the negative aspect of *senectūs,* "old age"; yet the *senatus* and the high respect of the *senator* prove that even within this derogatory concept of old age the veneration could break through and could be used as the distinction of political power. The comparative *senior* is continued in the Italian *signore* and the French *seigneur,* meaning "lord."

If the tendency toward senicide was once present, its implications had a strong effect upon the whole structure of the family. No matter how this tendency was condemned by morals or prohibited by the law, its aftereffects, though in humanized or mitigated variations, still persisted at the beginning of historical ages. The concept of "old" is, moreover, a relative one. Some fathers may have been quite young in our estimation when their sons felt that the fathers were "lingering too long," as implied by the Latin verb *senescō,* and acted accordingly on their feelings. Various cultures set different ages for weaning, initiation, and marriage because they had different ideas concerning infancy, puberty, and maturity. So they had also their own ideas about the age when life should come to its end.

We think today about the disposal of elderly people as a repulsive characteristic of prehistoric man. One hardly can believe that such a barbarous custom was familiar, e.g., to the Germanic people. However, there exists an overwhelming bulk of historical and folklore evidences that prove beyond doubt that this practice still persisted at the beginning of history.

For instance, Procopius reported concerning the Germanic tribe of the Eruli. "They do not permit either the aged or the sick to live but, if someone is afflicted by age or sickness, he must ask (himself) his relatives to put him to death." * *Procopius goes on to describe in detail how the killing has to be performed, not by a blood relative but by an agnate member of the family. That the blood relatives were exempt from this murderous act indicates that the conscience was heavily burdened by the feeling of guilt at the time when this custom was reported by the Greek writer.*

The tradition of senicide belonged obviously to the lore of our cultural heritage. The tradition was infested with reverence, awe, and anxiety, as was any other ritual of

---

* *Procopius,* with an English translation by H. B. Dewing, in six volumes, Vol. III. *History of the Wars:* Book V. *The Gothic War.* VI, 14; The Loeb Classical Literary. (London: W. Heinemann and New York: G. P. Putnam's Sons, 1919), pp. 403–04.

ancestral origin. It was an active element of the relationship between father and son as it existed in prehistoric ages. The murderous act itself was not felt to be criminal, because it was in accordance with the religious tradition and with the socially accepted custom. Moreover, the father acted in the same way and also terminated the life of *his* own father. His removal from the family came about in the course of the tradition as a well-deserved retribution on the part of the "little grand-father" upon the father. The departed souls "gathered," according to this primitive philosophy, and met one another. The Germanic people spoke about "death" in the sense of a return to the ancestral community, as a "gathering at the ancestors." So it is promised to Abraham, "And thou shalt go to thy fathers in peace; thou shalt be buried in a good old age" (Gen. 15:15). So it is also said about the old Jacob before his death, "And he charged them, and said unto them, I am to be gathered unto my people: bury me with my fathers in the cave . . ." (Gen. 49:29). "To sleep with his fathers" is the Biblical formula (e.g., I Kings 1:21).

The introduction to and reception of the dead father in the family community of the ancestral spirits has often been celebrated as a special moment in the course of the funeral rituals. Each family kept its own common burial place as a "holy ground," in order that those who lived together should be buried together. Those who were put to death by the family became simply transferred, according to these primitive religious fantasies, from the earthly community to the spiritual one of the ancestors. This may look like a promotion, inasmuch as the ancestors were venerated as semigods; it follows that we may infer from this that the worship of ancestors was complemental to the disposal of the aged ones. It was the compensation of the guilt and shame which the living members of the family must have felt toward those put to death. The spiritual promotion and veneration as well as the almost daily observances of feeding, caring, and attending the spirits of the dead ones strongly indicate that there is something to forget about.

The obsessive repetition of an act may be the outlet of a disturbed conscience. Senicide and ancestor worship thus complete one another. The ancestor worship transforms into a religious performance an act that otherwise would be simply murder. Parricide has become, indeed, the most heinous murder when the belief in the ancestral spirit has lost its power. The general practice of ancestor worship at the beginning of historical ages seems to indicate that senicide was once equally widespread. It can be well understood why ancestor worship persisted even when the practice of senicide had been repressed in the course of cultural development. I do not believe that the scarcity of food was the only or the main motivation of such a deep-rooted prehistoric practice. It was rather the result of the whole philosophy of life and death.

The strongly established authority of the father within the patristic family surely served as a protective shield against the revolution of the sons. The stronger the authority of the head of the family was, the more violent was the resistance against such pressure on the part of the grown-up sons. The turnover from the rule of the father to that of the son became possible within the autocratic family system only through the death of the father. It was especially so when the ruling father was a king. His death or removal meant a revolutionary change in the structure of the family. It is significant that the Greek myth, like other theogonies, depicts such revolutionary removal of the father by the son. This was the case of Ouranos. He had been overcome by his son Kronos. Kronos, in turn, was overcome by his son Zeus. The antagonism between father and son which results in the victory of the son has some specific characteristics in the Greek myth. One is this: the father wants to devour his child. The other: the son wants to castrate the father. A third characteristic is found in the role of the mother: in both cases the mother is plotting with her son against her husband. We may understand this situation by considering the polygamous family. Many wives competed with one another in this family setting, but the one woman whose son succeeded the father was the victor. For this reason the mother is associated with her son against the husband-father in the grasp of power. The revolution of the son which sets an end to the rule of the father appears always as a victory of the mother, too. The revolt of the son is for this reason often blended with the feminine resentment against the head of the household. It strengthens the association between mother and son.

Freud tried to project the Oedipus story into prehistory, thus he arrived, following Darwin's suggestion, at the story of the Cyclopean family in which the sons killed the father. This "family romance" remained a "scientific myth" without plausible evidence of facts. However, apart from such constructive fantasies, ancestor worship and senicide are the well-attested characteristics of the prehistoric family. They are exhibits of the strange, ambivalent relationship between father and sons which often comes to light in history. Senicide derives from the murderous, aggressive part of emotions which becomes expressed on the positive side by the deification and veneration of the ancestral spirit. The antagonism between father and sons results in a closer association of the mother and her sons. This alliance of mother and son in the struggle for power may look like a matristic revolt and the Oedipus tragedy has been indeed understood thus.[78]

See: ANCESTOR, DEATH, GUILT.

Uncle

The family tragedy that engulfed Oedipus casts its shadow also upon the other male figure—this is Creon, the brother of Jocasta. He is properly the uncle of Oedipus, even though Oedipus, in his fatal error, considered him to be his brother-in-law. The brother of the mother held an important legal position within the matriarchal family, but his responsibilities vanished and often turned into a dubious emotional relationship within the patristic family structure.

In the sight of the small child, the maternal uncle may appear in a different light than the brother of the father. The maternal uncle may absorb some of the emotional qualities invested in the mother; the paternal uncle may assume some of the authoritarian characteristics that were the privilege of the father within the polygamous family compound.

The English uncle derives from the Latin avunculus, which, although it properly means "little grandfather," actually denotes the "brother of the mother," never "the brother of the father." He was called "little grandfather," one may surmise, because he assumed the responsibilities of the real maternal grandfather when the latter passed away. If the maternal grandfather was still alive, the maternal uncle was called magnus avunculus, properly "great-little-grandfather."

The diminutive, in both cases, could be the expression of endearment.

The concept of the brother of the mother is also described by the pertinent Germanic terms. The German *Oheim,* "maternal uncle," from a former *awa-haim,* has a parallel form in the Old English *eam,* "uncle," from *ea-ham.* These words describe, properly, the "maternal uncle" as "dwelling in the home" of the grandfather.

Reference is made, in these words, to the "home," Old English *ham,* German *Heim.* This reference indicates that the "uncle" belonged to the "house" of the grandfather, which was also once the home of the mother. One must keep in mind that the nearest "family" circle was called "home," as in the Greek *oikos* and the Latin *domus.* This looks like a Germanic "be'ena marriage," which supposed a line of male succession other than the paternal-grandfather-father-son triumvirate: that is, the unity of the maternal grandfather, brother of the mother, and the son of the mother. This indicates a transitory state in which the female descendant line (maternal-grandmother-mother-daughter) became replaced by their nearest male representatives—maternal grandfather, maternal brother, and son. Such a matrilineal structure seems to contradict the patristic polygamy, which is well attested to for the Germanic ancestor people. It shows that the father figure, however exalted, became distant to the many children and became obscured by the man who was the closest blood relative of the mother—her brother. The image of the father was contested by the ancestral spirit anyway. The spiritual paternity degraded the physical paternity to a sort of adoptive father. No wonder that this marginal paternity became pushed aside finally in favor of the uncle who shared the common ancestry with the mother. Tacitus pointed out expressively (in *Germania,* chap. 20) that the mother's brother held a privileged position within the Germanic family setting. The Germanic heroic legends of the Nibelungen make it abundantly clear that the blood relationships that tie the woman to her brothers are much stronger than her loyalty to her husband. The Latin, Celtic, and Slavic conditions point in the same direction. The only grown-up male person the child could meet within this atmosphere of maternal intimacy was the brother of the mother. The nephew identified himself with his "uncle" because the uncle could give the boy just what the mother could not—the ability to act like a man. The brother-sister tie has deeper roots in the emotional intimacy for the child than the husband-wife relationship. One can still observe that children of divorced mothers tend to replace the distant father with the brother of the mother, as a kind of Uncle Sam. No wonder that the sister's attachment to her brother often appears on the verge of incest, under the pressure of patristic polygyny, just because the omnipotent master of the house was dissociated from tenderness and intimacy. The secret lover may fill an emotional gap. The secret lover is called *Buhle* in German. This is a pet form of the original *Bruder*, "brother."

One can explain that the maternal uncle came to be called "little grandfather" because he substituted for the maternal grandfather. But how should one account for the strange fact that the "grandchild" also came to be called by the same name as "little grandfather" in Germanic and Slavic languages? The ancestral spirit returning into life in the grandchild seems to be the most plausible explanation. The German *Ahn*, former *ano*, denotes the "predecessor." Its diminutive, the noun *Enkel*, "grandchild," properly meant the "little predecessor." The same holds true for the Slavic *vunuku*. These words have a feminine background. The related Latin *anus* means "old woman," and the Greek *annis* means "grandmother." Other languages denote "mother" and "mother-in-law" with the same word. The predecessor in question seems to have originally belonged to the maternal side. Even the English *nephew*, which denotes the child's relationship to the uncle, also referred to the maternal "little grandfather," the equivalent of the "grandchild." The word derives, through the French *neveu*, from the Latin *nepōs*, *-ōtem*, "grandchild." The identification between the little-grandfather-uncle and the little-grandfather-child was surely intensively felt, otherwise both would not have been denoted by the same name.

The Greek, Latin, Slavic, Germanic, and also the Sanskrit languages made a clear distinction between the paternal and the maternal uncle. The names reveal the identification by themselves, since they generally refer either to the father or to the mother. The paternal uncle is called *patrōs* in

Greek, *patrūus* in Latin, and *faedera* in Old English. The accent in all these terms is on the father. The Latin *patrūus* is especially indicative in this respect. It also denotes "a severe reprover as uncles are apt to be toward their nephews," as our excellent lexicographer naïvely says.* This term surely exposes the discrimination between the Greek *patrōs* vs. *mētrōs,* the Latin *patrūus* vs. the *avunculus,* or between the Old English *faedera* vs. the *ēam.* The mother's brother appears as a friend and protector of his nephews. Even in American Indian languages, for instance in the Comanche, the same word is used for the mother's brother and the sister's son (*ara*). This looks like the case of the "little "grandfather." "A boy always looks upon his maternal unicle as a sort of pal, who will back him up if he gets involved in a sexual scrape." Malinowski demonstrated, for the Melanesian people, who live in matristic order, that the brother of the mother is the most important grown-up man in the view of the child. He is more important than the father. He introduces his nephew into the wisdom of magic arts; he also leaves his nephew as heir to his tangible properties, even if he is married and has children of his own, as does the father also. He does not share life with his own children, but leaves everything to the children of his sister. Such strange family arrangements, which are similar to the Trobriand Islanders, may have affected our Western family structure at an early age. Interpreters of our early family history never fail to point out this interference of matrilineal thinking upon the family setting that was polygamous and patristic since the beginning of history.[79] Considering the testimony of our languages, one comes to the conclusion that the uncle-nephew relationship has developed within the patristic, polygamous family compound, in which mother and child are close to one another, and the father is feared, admired, and has remained a distant overlord.†

---

* The Hebrew *dōd,* from an unused root meaning properly "to boil," i.e., figuratively, "to love"; by implication, "a love token," "a lover," "a friend"; specifically, "an uncle"—referring mostly to the "well-beloved father's brother." This seems to contradict everything said about the paternal uncle.

† This is in accordance with A. R. Radcliffe-Brown: "The Mother's Brother in South Africa," *South African Journal of Science* (1924), 21: 542–55.

Virginity

The notion of "virgin" was unknown in prehistoric ages; at least there exists no such term attested for the prehistory of languages. The absence of the word does not prove in itself that the idea was also absent; it rather suggests that this concept underwent a radical change of meaning at the beginning of the historical ages. The Greek and the Roman languages denote the same concept by totally different terms. The Greek word *par-thenos*, "virgin," is, according to our best authorities, unexplained, and so is the Latin *virgo*. Both words are different in their phonemic pattern as well as in the whole realm of associations. These words say no more about the origin of the idea than does the German *Jung-frau*, "virgin," which properly means "young woman." The absence of a prehistoric term is the more indicative because the subordinate situation of the woman seems to preclude all those ethical considerations with which this idea is heavily charged at the beginning of history. In the early prehistoric ages virginity seems to be nothing more than a qualification that made the girl for sale more valuable, but even this consideration is conspicuously absent among many people. Herodotus said about the Thracian people (5:6), "They allow the girls to mix with any man, but they keep carefully their wives." There are many similar data, yet they do not alter the general impression: the great emphasis on the virginity of the bride is a characteristic feature of the patriarchal society. The boundless sexual freedom of the male requires that the female should be intact when entering marriage. Thus the emotional significance attached to virginity is rooted primarily in the male psyche. It exposes that which the male hopes to find in the female.[80]

It was customary not only in Old Testament patriarchy but among Indo-European people that the bride was subjected to a test of virginity. This was not a premarital physical examination, but an important element of the wedding ceremonies. Slavic people, who often preserved age-old customs, arranged the wedding in such a way that the consummation of marriage was to take place in front of the best man and the marriage broker (usually a woman) who traded the girl. After having witnessed the act they took the shirt of the bride and if it was bloodstained they displayed it in great triumph to the guests. Then they started the wedding feast, the celebrating of the successful test of virginity by singing wedding songs and dancing. They also used to break pots and vessels. If, however, no "token of virginity" was found, they presented to the father and the brothers of the bride a vessel with a hole. The Old Testament people went even further. The parents kept the shirt or the linen of the bride as an important legal document. "But if this thing be true, and the tokens of virginity be not found for the damsel: Then they shall bring out the damsel to the door of her father's house, and the men of her city shall stone her with stones that she die" (Deut. 22:20–21). They did not realize that the presence or absence of the *hymen* is a variable anatomical feature.*

These age-old wedding ceremonies help to explain the pertinent Greek terms. It is hard to believe, even though the best authorities try to persuade us, that the Greek *hymen*, "a thin skin, membrane," and *Hymen*, "god of marriage, Hymen," also *hymenaios*, "the wedding or bridal song," "wedding," have nothing in common with one another except the chance homophony. The ancient Greek knew it better and saw the connection of the two words clearly.† The Greek *humnos*, "festive song," is also said to be of unknown origin, but it, too, hardly can be separated from the *humenaios*, the bridal song, and *Humen*, the god addressed in the wedding songs. *Hymeneios* is the attribute of Bacchus-Dionysus.

Ancient and widespread as the celebration of virginity at wedding festivals might be, it has little to do with chastity in the ethical and religious sense.‡ If virginity is regarded as

---

* "The exact importance to be attached to the presence or absence of the *hymen* in medical jurisprudence is still undetermined . . . so that its absence does not prove that coitus had taken place." George A. Piersol, *Human Anatomy* (6th ed., New York: J. B. Lippincott Company, 1926), p. 2020.

† "Some derive the etymology of *hymenaios* from the cohabiting of the bride by the groom; others explain it, however, physically because *hymen* is called the little membrane which is perforated at the defloration of the girl." Quoted by O. Schrader: *Reallexikon der Indogermanischen Altertumskunde.* (Berlin: Walter de Gruyter, 1923), 1:582, *s.v. Keuschkeit.*

‡ "Les anciens médecins ont ignoré ou méconnu l'hymen virginal." (Boisacq, *s.v.*)

just an asset to the sales value of a girl, this fact still begs the question: Why is it so? The answer to this question seems to refer to a paradoxical phenomenon of nature. While the sex drive of the male is blended with aggressiveness, the same drive in the female might be blended with an equally aggressive resistance. The pairing of these two kinds of aggressiveness, one assaulting, the other resisting, has been widely observed in the animal world, so it is probable that the same phenomenon in human relations is more than just a cultural behavior pattern. It may have some instinctual foundations, though it is socially conditioned or even reversed in some cultures. It works, however, once established, in the way of circular causation. The female's resistance, which is accompanied by embarrassment* and shame, may stimulate the aggressive, sadistic impulses of the male, which may, in turn, make the goal more desirable.† The fruits difficult to obtain taste better than the cheap ones. This might be the reason why virginity was an asset to the sale price on the market.‡

It seems to be a significant testimony of our languages that they denote the procreative function not as an expression of love, but from the viewpoint of the male, by terms which appeal to sadistic fantasies. The female organs are perceived by these fantasies as an incision,§ therefore the notion of "blunt knife" is in most of our languages connected with sexual connotations, especially in vulgar and infantile speech.

* The linguistic interdependence of "self-consciousness" and "shame" is evident in the English *self-conscious.* However, this phenomenon has much deeper roots in our languages. The Latin *con-scius* means "that knows something in company with another, privy to," but it also may be used for "knowing something in one's self." The Late Latin continued the word as *coscius,* which spread into the Germanic languages as Old English *cusc,* "chaste, modest, pure, clean," and as the German *keusch,* with the same meaning—all attributes of virginity.

† "Now King David was old and stricken in years; and they covered him with clothes, but he gat no heat. Wherefore his servants said unto him, Let there be sought for my lord the king a young virgin: and let her stand before the king, and let her cherish him, and let her lie in thy bosom, that my lord the king may get heat. . . . And the damsel was very fair, and cherished the king, and ministered to him: but the king knew her not" (I Kings 1:1–2, 4).

‡ Freud supposed that the "dread of what is novel" is present in the taboo of virginity. *Standard Edition* 11:201.

§ The Greek *thelus,* "split," means "female." For this reason the "even" numbers are female.

The most common and vulgar Greek term *bineō,* "to have sexual intercourse," is a derivative of the noun *bia,* meaning "violence," and *biadzō,* "to overpower." The Latin *sexus,* "sex," is the nominal complement to the verb *secō, -āre,* "to cut." The German *Ge-schlecht,* "sex," is in the same way related to the verb *schlagen,* "to beat." The Latin *cauda,* "penis," is a nominal form of *cudō, -ere,* "to beat, strike." Another Latin verb, *stuprō, -āre,* "to defile, dishonor, debauch, deflower, ravish," originally implied the fantasy as "to hit, strike," and therefore it is connected with *stupeō, -ēre,* "to be struck senseless, be stunned, benumbed, be struck aghast." It is also related to *stupe-faciō, -ere,* "to make stupid or senseless, benumb, deaden, stun, stupefy." *Stupor* means "numbness, dullness, insensibility," also "astonishment, wonder, amazement." These words imply a fairly accurate phenomenological description of the psychological shock of the virgin. The Germanic languages elaborate their sadistic fantasies around the concept of "pulling, tearing." For example, Old English *teors* "penis" and Old German *zagal* belong to the verbs *ziehen,* "to pull," and *zerren,* properly "to tear the flesh asunder." The German language may use even without any sexual connotation *bei den Haaren herbeiziehen* "to pull (her) by the hair" (as the English *drag by the hair*).

Sadistic fantasies dictated such words:

> Come down, and sit in the dust, O virgin daughter of Babylon . . . for thou shalt no more be called tender and delicate. Take the millstones: and grind meal; uncover thy locks, make bare the leg, uncover the thigh, pass over the rivers. Thy nakedness shall be uncovered, yea, thy shame shall be seen: I will take vengeance, and I will not meet thee as a man (Isa. 47:1-3).

Terms referring to the sexual encounter expose the different aspects as experienced by the male and by the female. Those verbs describing "beating," "pulling," "violating," "knocking," "striking," "pinching," "scratching," and so on are conceived from the male viewpoint and call accordingly the male organ, like Old English *waēpen,* "weapon," "dagger," "pistol," "sword," "nail," "needle," "rod," "stalk," "sting," etc., always with a strong sadistic component to denote the act as "overpowering" as the Greek *ocheuō,* "entering," "covering," "prevailing," "grasping," "pulling," while the female wants to be "enrapt," "embraced," "enclosed," keeping the mystery of the unknown at the same time, however, that she has the masochistic desire to be unveiled, uncovered and, in the last analysis, to be conquered and defeated. For such reasons marriage is often dreamed and symbolized as a union with death. The transcendental fusion of procreation and death which appears in dreams transforming the wedding night into a funeral, or in the "death-wedding" as practiced in Slavic folklore, is an age-old motive in myth, philosophy, and poetry. The "love-death" (*Liebestod*) fantasies are illustrated by the stories of Amor and Psyche, Tristan and Isolde, Romeo and Juliet, and even by the general Indo-European custom that the wife has to follow the husband in death.

The virginal fear is rape. Because the female may perceive the fight of sexes as a deadly issue of violence, abuse, and defeat, fantasies of vengeance may also grow up. The spider psychology wants to enact the vengeance at the wedding night by beheading, i.e., castrating the male as all Danaïdes did.

The resistance against male violence is not as clearly expressed in our languages as in mythological fantasies. Pallas Athena represented the incarnation of virginity to the Greek mind. Her attribute is *parthenos,* "virgin"; her temple is the *Parthenon.* She seems to be of pre-Greek origin; therefore one may surmise that she personifies well the prehistoric fantasies about virginity. Her attributes are mental power, wisdom, warlike prowess, and skill; she killed a giant named Pallas, but her name *Pallas* seems also to refer to virginity. Why is this virgin goddess equipped with all the wisdom, force, and skill of the fighting men? Virginity implies the eternal struggle of the sexes, aggressiveness and resistance, the readiness to fight. We arrive at the idea of the "male-female," who is the expression of the resistance against the male. Achilles, the Greek ideal of youthful vigor and beauty, was killed by Penthesileia, the virgin Amazon who remained unconquerable. The Latin *virgō,* "virgin," has an alternate form in *viragō,* "a manlike, vigorous, heroic maiden; a female warrior, heroine." This is an epithet of Minerva, Diana, and Amazon. All these goddesses of chastity are at the same time great hunters, handling masterfully the bow and arrow. They are horse-riding, shooting females; they imply a grain of homosexuality.

The German myth elaborated the idea of virgin resistance in the figure of Brunhild. She is the unapproachable maiden living on a secluded island; her castle is encircled by a wall of fire—an adequate symbolization of virginal defense. If an unfit man approached her, according to the Norse tradition of her story, she used to tie his hands to his heels and hang him on the ceiling over her bridal bed. She represents the Germanic picture of the *virago,* burning desire for love, on the one hand, wild resistance on the other. Only a true hero like Siegfried could subdue her. The Old English term *wif-men,* "warlike women, Amazons," is the plural of the singular *wif-man,* "woman," while *waepen-wifestre* means "male-female, Hermaphroditus."

Similar fantasies tuned down to the level of "everyday mythology" became condensed in the verb *to tame* as Shakespeare used it in the *Taming of the Shrew.* This verb belongs to a prehistoric phonemic pattern represented in the Eastern as well as in the Western languages. In the Greek this form appears as *damaō* or *damadzō,* meaning "to overpower; of animals, to tame, break in, bring under the yoke; of maidens, to make subject to a husband, be forced, be seduced, subdue, conquer," also "to strike dead, kill." The corresponding Latin verb, *domō, -āre* carries the same meanings. The Latin word blended its meaning with *domus,* "house," in the noun *dominus,* meaning "master, possessor, ruler, lord, proprietor, owner"; this is also a term of endearment in addressing a lover. The Greek calls the "wife" *damar,* properly "one that is tamed or yoked" (like the Latin *conjux,* properly "wife," "yoked together"); whereas the maiden is called *adamastos* or *adamatos,* "inflexible, untamed, unbroken." The substantive *adamant* denoted the hardest metal, the "unconquerable." This word continued in the French-English *diamond,* "the hardest substance known." It is as a geometrical figure, the pictogram of the female organ since the early Stone Age. The adjective *admētē,* "untamed," is in Homer's language the attribute of "maiden." The Greek noun *damalis* denotes "a young cow, heifer," also "girl." This association of the "heifer" and the "girl" indicates that once again the virginity of the one did not mean more to the *pater familias* than the unbroken neck of the other. We will in the light of these Greek words fully understand the symbolic saying of Samson. "If ye had not plowed with my heifer, ye had not found out my riddle" (Judg. 14:18). Cattle and women belonged to the same category.

Deeply repressed fantasies are implied in the word *subject*. The Latin *sub-iciō, sub-jēci, sub-jectum,* "to throw, lay, place, or bring under or near," is the derivative of *sub-jaceō* with the same meaning. A verb loaded with similar fantasies is *sub-dō,* "to subdue." In the Old English *under-lecgan,* "to lie under," also means "to subject." In German *unter-liegen* means "to be defeated." The modern speaker will perhaps be convinced by common-sense reasoning that one can well understand why the German *unter-liegen,* "to under-lie," came to mean "to be defeated"; yet one will not be as secure in explaining why "to over-lie" as a noun, *Ob-liegenheit,* came to denote "duty." For the complete understanding of the fantasies implied in "over-lie" and "under-lie," one has to visualize the concrete situation to which these meanings refer; it is in this case a wrestling couple. The "over" refers to the masculine "duty," the "under" to the feminine concept. The German *über-legen* as a verb, properly "to over-lay," means "to think it over." This is the sublimation of the original *ubar-ligan,* which was the most general term for the procreative function of the male. In modern Greek the married woman is called *hup-andros gunē,* properly the "woman under man." Aristotle made the *sub-ject,* "thrown-under," a grammatical concept and called the substantive *hupo-keimenon,* "the under-lying."

The sex resistance of the female, which left only few traces in our verbal expressions, can be better identified by its symbolic representations. The undiscovered and unconquered secrets of "virgin islands" or "virgin land" imply the same resistance to the inquisitive desire of knowledge as that which is present when the "bride" is called "the unknown" because she is not discovered by genital knowledge. Cities are always spoken of as "she"; they appear to the fantasies as female symbols. The city might be seen as "Babylon the great, the mother of harlots" (Rev. 17:5), but when the city is enclosed by a wall, or even "fenced till heaven," she may become a symbol of virginity. The besieged city, the fight against the besiegers, was used as a welcome screen upon which the subtle emotions of fear, frustration, embarrassment, and resistance of the female could be projected. Homer set the pattern by depicting Ilium-Troy as an assaulted virgin. The Biblical tradition preserved the Apocryphal book of Judith. Judith is the Jewish virago. She liberated the besieged city Bethulia, whose name means "virgin." Thus Judith liberated the "virgin" city by sleeping with Holophernes, the besieger, and beheading him in her bridal bed. The ambivalent feelings of love and hatred, desire and resistance, pleasure and pain, inquisitiveness and terror, the whole gamut of virginal sensations are implied in the deed of the Jewish heroine.

The Old Testament depicts the *whole Zion* as the bride of Jehovah: "Thou shalt be called *Hephzi-bah* [my delight], and thy land *Beulah* [married]: for the Lord delighteth in thee, and thy land shall be married. For as a young man marrieth a virgin, so shall thy son marry thee; and as the bridegroom rejoiceth over the bride, so shall thy God rejoice over thee" (Isa. 62:4–5).

The meaning of the wall encircling the city became transferred to the bridal girdle, which was supposed to be opened in the bridal bed by the new husband. The opening of the girdle, like the breaking down of the city wall, meant defeat and surrender, the end of the female resistance.

STANDARD REFERENCE SOURCES OF
LINGUISTIC INFORMATION

General introduction:

Carl Darling Buck. *A Dictionary of the Selected Synonyms in the Principal Indo-European Languages: A Contribution to the History of Ideas.* Chicago: University of Chicago Press, 1949 (abbr. Buck). The Preface of this standard work gives a comprehensive introduction to this field of study.

Greek language:

H. G. Liddell and Robert Scott. *Greek-English Lexicon.* New York: Harper & Row, 1889, reprinted 1957 (abbr. Liddell-Scott). The Greek words are quoted according to this dictionary.

Emile Boisacq. *Dictionnaire Etymologique de la Langue Grecque.* 4th ed. Heidelberg: Carl Winter, 1950 (abbr. Boisacq).

J. B. Hofmann. *Etymologisches Wörterbuch des Griechischen.* München: R. Oldenburg Verlag, 1949 (abbr. Hofmann).

Hjalmar Frisk. *Griechisches etymologisches Wörterbuch.* Heidelberg: Carl Winter, 1954– (unfinished; abbr. Frisk).

Latin language:

Harper's Latin Dictionary. New York: American Book Company, 1907 (abbr. Harper). The Latin words are quoted according to this dictionary.

A. Ernout and A. Meillet. *Dictionnaire Etymologique de la Langue Latine.* Paris: Klincksieck, 1932 (abbr. Ernout-Meillet).

A. Walde and J. B. Hofmann. *Lateinisches etymologisches Wörterbuch.* Heidelberg: Carl Winter, 1954 (abbr. Walde-Hofmann).

369

The origin of Latin words—if not pointed out otherwise—is given according to these sources.

Romance languages:

A. Meyer-Lübke. *Romanisches etymologisches Wörterbuch.* 3te Auflage. Heidelberg: Carl Winter, 1935 (abbr. Meyer-Lübke).

French language:

Ernest Gamillscheg. *Etymologisches Wörterbuch der französischen Sprache.* Heidelberg: Carl Winter, 1928 (abbr. Gamillscheg).

German language:

Friedrich Kluge. *Etymologisches Wörterbuch der deutschen Sprache.* 17th ed. revised by W. Mitzka. Berlin: W. de Gruyter, 1957 (abbr. Kluge).
Hermann Paul. *Deutsches Wörterbuch.* 4th ed. revised by Karl Euling. Halle: Niemeyer, 1934 (abbr. H. Paul).

Gothic language:

Sigmund Feist. *Vergleichendes Wörterbuch der gotischen Sprache.* 3te Auflage. Leiden: E. J. Brill, 1939 (abbr. Feist).

Scandinavian languages:

Hjalmar Falk and A. Torp. *Etymologisk Ordbog over det Norske Sprog.* Kristiania, 1906.

English language:

New English Dictionary. Oxford: Clarendon Press (abbr. NED). This classic work of Victorian scholarship, despite its limitations, is the foundation and basic source of all subsequent dictionaries of the English language.
The Shorter Oxford English Dictionary on Historical Principles. Oxford: Clarendon Press, reprinted with corrections, 1964.

Webster's New World Dictionary of the American Language. College Edition. Cleveland and New York: The World Publishing Company.

Funk & Wagnalls Standard College Dictionary. New York: Funk & Wagnalls Company, 1963.

For special cases: *The Oxford Dictionary of English Proverbs.* Oxford: Clarendon Press, 1948.

Specific English dictionaries:

Shakespeare

John Bartlett. *A New and Complete Concordance or Verbal Index to Words, Phrases, and Passages in the Dramatic Work of Shakespeare.* London: The Macmillan Co., 1889.

Bible

James Strong. *The Exhaustive Concordance of the Bible.* Nashville, Tenn.: Abingdon-Cokesbury Press, 1950.

Spenser

Charles Grosvenor Osgood. *A Concordance to the Poems of Edmund Spenser.* New York: Carnegie Foundation, 1915.

Milton

Laura E. Lockwood. *Lexicon to the English Poetical Works of John Milton.* New York: The Macmillan Company, 1907.

John Donne

Homer Caroll Combs and Zay Rusk Sullen. *A Concordance to the English Poems of John Donne.* Chicago: Packard and Co., 1940.

Robert Browning

Leslie N. Broughton and Benjamin F. Stelter. *A Concordance to the Poems of Robert Browning.* 2 vols. New York: G. E. Stechert & Company, 1924.

Old English or Anglo-Saxon language:

Joseph Bothworth and Northcott Toller. *An Anglosaxon Dictionary*. 2 vols. Oxford: Clarendon Press, 1887.

Friedrich Holthausen. *Altenglisches etymologisches Wörterbuch*. Heidelberg: Carl Winter, 1939.

Middle-English language:

Shermann M. Kuhn and John Reidy. *Middle-English Dictionary*. Publication in progress. Michigan University Press.

NOTES
SELECTIVE BIBLIOGRAPHY
INDICES

NOTES FOR PART ONE:

SEPARATION AND REUNIFICATION

1 Sigmund Freud, *The Problem of Anxiety*, translated from the German by Henry Alden Bunker (New York: W. W. Norton & Company, Inc.), p. 15 and chap. X. "The Birth Trauma: A Critique," *Standard Edition*, 20:150–56.

2 *Language* (1952), 28:8.

3 P. Schilder, "Psychoanalysis of Space," *The International Journal of Psycho-Analysis* (1935), 16:274–95.

4 Gisela Pankow, using clay modeling, made extensive research on the distorted body image of schizophrenics: "Dynamic Structurization in Schizophrenia," in *Psychotherapy of the Psychoses*, ed. A. Burton (New York: Basic Books, Inc., 1961), pp. 152–71.

5 Warner Muensterberger, "The Creative Process: Its Relationship to Object Loss and Fetishism," *The Psychoanalytic Study of Society* (1962), 2:161–85.

6 N. van Wijk, "Zur Etymologie einiger Wörter für *leer,*" *Indogermanische Forschungen* (Strassburg: Trübner, 1915), 35:265–68.

7 Paul Schilder, "Psychoanalysis of Space," *The International Journal of Psycho-Analysis* (1935), 16:280. The quotation is from the important paper by L. Binswanger, "Das Raumproblem in der Psychopathologie," *Zeitschrift für die gesamte Neurologie und Psychiatrie* (1933), pp. 598–648. An interesting though not scientific first-hand report is Jane Dunlap, *Exploring Inner Space: Personal Experiences under LSD-25* (New York: Harcourt, Brace & World, Inc., 1961).

8 D. W. Winicott, "The Capacity To Be Alone," *International Journal of Psycho-Analysis* (1958), 39:416–23.

9 R. Kittel, "Holiness," in *Schaff-Herzog Encyclopedia of the Religious Knowledge*, 1953, 5:316–18.

10 Rudolf Otto, *The Idea of the Holy*, translated by J. W. Harvey (London: Oxford University Press, 1925).

11 Rudolf Otto, *op. cit.*, p. 72.

12 *Ellicott's Commentary on the Whole Bible* (Grand Rapids, Mich.: Zondervan, 1954), 6:537. By permission of the publisher.

13 S. Freud, *An Outline of Psychoanalysis* (New York: W. W. Norton & Company, Inc., 1949), pp. 89–90. *Standard Edition*, 23:188.

14 This problem has been approached by the structuralist linguist Roman Jacobson, *Kindersprache, Aphasie, und allgemeine Lautgesetze* (Uppsala, Sweden, 1941). Also, *Lois phonic du language enfantin*, in N. S. Troubetzkoy, *Principes de Phonologie* (Paris: Klincksieck, 1949), pp. 367–79. Rather ridiculing the psychological interpretation of an "oral stage," Roman Jacobson attempts to show that the infant wants to reach the greatest possible phonemic opposites. If this were the case, the infant could achieve this end better by a *ku-ku* or *hi-hi* sound combination.

15 Otto Isakower, "A Contribution to the Pathopsychology of Phenomena Associated with Falling Asleep," *International Journal of Psycho-Analysis* (1938), 19:331–45.

16 See the excellent analysis on the "mother tongue" by Leo Spitzer, *Essays in Historical Semantics* (New York: S. F. Vanni, 1947).

NOTES FOR PART TWO:

OEDIPUS—IDENTITY AND KNOWLEDGE

1 S. Freud, "Infantile Sexuality," 1905, *Standard Edition*, 7:182.

2 S. Freud, "Infantile Sexuality," *Standard Edition*, 7:181. See also David M. Levy, "Fingersucking and Accessory Movements in Early Infancy: An Etiological Study," *American Journal of Psychiatry* (1928), 7:881–918; Harry Stack Sullivan, "The Oral Complex," *Psychoanalytic Review* (1925), 12:31–38, and "Erogenous Maturation," *Psychoanalytic Review* (1926), 13:1–15.

3 Walde-Hofmann, *op. cit.*, 2:255 *s.v. praepūtium*, does not accept this connection because the change of meaning from "little penis" to "child" seems to him to be impossible.

4 Erik H. Erikson, *Identity and the Life Cycle: Selected Papers*, with a historical introduction by David Rapaport in *Psychological Issues* (New York: International University Press, 1959). Edith Jacobson, *The Self and the Object World*. (New York: International University Press, 1964). These excellent studies do not consider the importance of language in the child's discovery of his identity.

5 Kathleen Freeman, *The Pre-Socratic Philosophers: A Companion to Diels:* Fragmente der Vorsokratiker (Cambridge, Mass.: Harvard University Press, 1946), p. 45.

6 Peter Blos, "Comments on the Psychological Consequences of Cryptorchidism: A Clinical Study," *The Psychoanalytical Study of the Child* (1960), 15:395–429, p. 400.

7 Pierre Lacombe, "The Problem of the Identical Twins as Reflected in a Masochistic Compulsion To Cheat," *International Journal of Psycho-Analysis* (1959), 40:6–12. The problems of twins were first analyzed by Otto Rank, "Der Doppelgänger," *Imago* (1914). Reprinted: Internationaler Psychoanalytischer Verlag, Vienna, 1925. See the chapter "The Double as Immortal Self" in *Beyond Psychology* (New York: Dover Publication, 1941), pp. 62–101.

8 "Mourning and Melancholia," 1917, *Collected Papers*, 4:159.

9 Bryce Boyer, "A Hypothesis Regarding the Time of Appearance of the Dream Scene," *International Journal of Psycho-Analysis* (1960), 41:114–22.

10 F. Altheim, *History of Roman Religion* (New York: E. P. Dutton & Co., Inc., 1937), pp. 125, 268.

11 Milton L. Miller, "Ego Functioning in Two Types of Dreams," *Psychoanalytic Quarterly* (1948), 17:346–55.

12 Daniel Paul Schreber, *Mémoires of My Nervous Illness*, translated by Ida Macalpine and Richard A. Hunter (Cambridge, Mass.: Robert Bentley, 1955), p. 137.

13 The exposition of "Gulliver Fantasies" was developed by Norman O. Brown, *Life Against Death* (New York: Random House, Inc., 1959), pp. 179–84, 189–190. A different interpretation by Sándor Ferenczi, "Gulliver Phantasies," *International Journal of Psycho-Analysis* (1928), 9:283–300.

14 Fantasies concerning anal birth were originally formulated by Freud, "On the Transformation of Instincts with Special Reference to Anal Erotism," 1916, *Collected Papers*, 2:164–71.

15 William G. Niederland, "Clinical Observations on the Little Man Phenomenon," *Psychoanalytical Study of the Child* (1956), 2:381–95 (esp. p. 384). Quoted by permission of the author.

16 Victor Tausk, "On the Origin of the Influencing Machine in Schizophrenia," *Psychoanalytic Quarterly* (1933), 2:519–56.

17 Charles Brenner, "A Case of Childhood Hallucinosis," *Psychoanalytical Study of the Child* (1958), 6:235–43 (p. 236).

18 This example, like similar others, raises the psychological problem of derogatory pet names. Marty called them "Koseschimpfwörter." The problem is discussed without psychology by Paul Trost, "Schimpfwörter als Kosenamen," *Indogermanische Forschungen*, 51:101–112.

19 Gregory Zilborg, "The Sense of Reality," *Psychoanalytic Quarterly* (1941), 10:183–210.

20 O. Siebs, "Things und die Alaisiagen," *Zeitschrift für deutsche Philologie* (1891), 24:433–56.

21 Charles Brenner, "A Case of Childhood Hallucinosis," *The Psychoanalytical Study of the Child* (1958), 6:235–43.

22 Clinical instances are reported by Bertram D. Lewin, "The Nature of Reality, the Meaning of Nothing, with an Addendum of Concentration," *Psychoanalytic Quarterly* (1948), 7:524–26. Lewin does not refer to the pertinent verbal expressions.

23 "Negation," 1925, *Standard Edition*, 19:235. See also Julius L. Rowley: "Rumpelstilskin in the Analytical Situation," *International Journal of Psycho-Analysis* (1951), 32:190–95. The linguistic-logistic interpretation of negation in Otto Jespersen, *The Philosophy of Grammar* (New York: Holt, Rinehart & Winston, Inc., 1924), pp. 322–37.

24 S. Freud, *Collected Papers*, 2:246–47. See also *Standard Edition*, 19:143–44. Quoted by permission of the publisher.

25 Martin Heidegger, "Hinein-gehaltenheit in das Nichts," *Existence and Being*, introduction by Werner Brock (Chicago: Henry Regnery Company, 1949), p. 370. Also W. H. Werkmeister, "An Introduction to Heidegger's Existential Philosophy," *Philosophical and Phenomenological Research* (1941), 2:79–87.

378

26 Hegel, *Collected Works*, 7:400.

27 Sigmund Freud, *The Problem of Anxiety*, translated by H. A. Bunker (New York: W. W. Norton & Company, Inc.). "Inhibitions, Symptoms, and Anxiety," 1926 *Standard Edition*, 20:77–175. Also *Collected Papers*, 2:246–47, and "Medusa's Head," *Standard Edition*, 18:273. *New Introductory Lectures on Psycho-Analysis*, Lecture 32, translated by W. J. H. Sprott (New York: W. W. Norton & Company, Inc.), p. 126.

28 Heidegger, *op. cit.*, p. 370.

29 Heinz Werner, *Comparative Psychology of Mental Development* (New York: International University Press, 1957), pp. 172–73.

30 Freud on the "instinct for knowledge," see "Three Essays on Sexuality," 1905, *Standard Edition*, 7:194.

31 Since Freud placed the Oedipus myth at the focal point of psychoanalytical literature, references to it are innumerable, expressing many contradictory views. Freud's classic interpretation is formulated in *A General Introduction to Psychoanalysis*. See also Géza Róheim, *The Gates of the Dream* (New York: International University Press, 1953). Translations: *The Oedipus Cycle of Sophocles*, English versions by Dudley Fitts and Robert Fitzgerald (Harvest Books, Harcourt, Brace & World, Inc.); also *Sophocles: Oedipus King*, translated by Bernard M. W. Knox (New York: Washington Square Press, 1959).

32 The linguistic approach is presented by Theodore Thass-Thienemann, "Oedipus and the Sphinx: The Linguistic Approach to Unconscious Phantasies," *The Psychoanalytic Review* (1957), 44:10–33.

33 S. G. Champion, *Racial Proverbs* (New York: The Macmillan Company, 1938), p. 510.

34 Augustine, *Confessions* (New York: Washington Square Press, 1960), p. 114.

35 K. Abraham's study on the *hodos schistē*, "divided road," in his "Two Contributions to the Study of Symbols," *Selected Papers* (New York: Basic Books, Inc., 1955), 2:84–85.

36 George Devereux, "Why Oedipus Killed Laius," *International Journal of Psycho-Analysis* (1953), 34:132–41.

37 On the Sphinx: J. Ilberg, "Sphinx" in W. H. Roscher, *Ausführliches Lexikon der griechischen und römischen Mythologie* (Stuttgart: Teubner Verlagsgesellschaft, mbH, 1909–1915), 4:1298–1407. Ludwig Laistner, *Das Rätsel der Sphinx: Grundzüge einer Mythengeschichte*, 2 vols. (Berlin: Hertz, 1889). Géza Róheim, *The Riddle of the Sphinx or Human Origins*, International Psycho-Analytical Library, No. 25 (London: Hogarth Press, 1934). Theodor Reik, "Oedipus und die Sphinx," *Imago* (1922), 6:95–131.

38 H. Diels, "Krokodilos," *Indogermanische Forschungen* (1903), 15:1–8.

39 *Beowulf and the Fight at Finnsburg*, ed. by F. Klaeber (3rd ed., Boston: D. C. Heath and Company, 1936), lines 2711–3136.

40 On the "falling dream" see W. v. Siebenthal, *Die Wissen-*

schaft vom Traum. Ergebnisse und Probleme. Eine Einführung in die allgemeinen Grundlagen (Berlin and Göttingen: Springer-Verlag, 1953), chap. "Flug und Fallträume," pp. 383–88.

41 Gustav Bychovski, "Struggle against the Introjects," *International Journal of Psycho-Analysis* (1958), 39:182–87.

42 While Freud himself became more and more convinced of the "enormous energy of the castration fear," his critics, such as A. Kroeber, the outstanding anthropologist, expressed doubts concerning this point: A. Kroeber, *Anthropology, Race, Language, Culture, Psychology, Prehistory* (New York: Harcourt, Brace & World, Inc., 1923), p. 616.

43 Schrader, *Reallexikon*, 2:183.

44 Sir James George Frazer, *The New Golden Bough: A New Abridgment of the Classic Work*, edited, and with notes and foreword by Theodore H. Gaster (New York: Criterion Books, 1959), p. 311.

45 Franz Alexander, *The Medical Value of Psychoanalysis* (New York: W. W. Norton & Company, Inc., 1931), p. 143.

46 Peter Blos, "Comments on the Psychological Consequences of Cryptorchidism: A Clinical Study," *The Psychoanalytical Study of the Child* (1960), 15:395–429 (p. 400).

47 S. Freud, *Collected Papers*, 3:400, 1911, and *Standard Edition*, 12:17.

48 Peter Blos, "Comments on the Psychological Consequences of Cryptorchidism: A Clinical Study," *The Psychoanalytical Study of the Child* (1960), 15:395–429 (p. 400).

49 H. Robert Blank, "Dreams of the Blind," *Psychoanalytic Quarterly* (1958), 27:158–174.

50 Peter Browe, "Zur Geschichte der Entmannung: Eine religions-und rechtsgeschichtliche Studie," *Breslauer Studien zur historischen Theologie*. N. F. Bd. 1. (Breslau: Müller und Seiffert, 1936.)

51 E. Fehrle, *Die kultische Keuschheit im Altertum* (Giessen, 1910).

52 ". . . ipso Domino spadonibus aperiente regna coelorum ut et ipso spadone." Jacques Paul Migne, *Patrologia Latina*, 2:981; quoted by Browe, *op. cit.*, p. 32.

53 Kluge-Goetze, *op. cit.*, *s. v. Zucht.*

NOTES FOR PART THREE:

THE RETURN—CHILDHOOD LOST

1 Hermann Diels, *Fragmente der Vorsokratiker: Griechisch und Deutsch*, 8th ed. by W. Franz (Berlin: Weidmann, 1956), 2:441, 55B, 148.

2 Sándor Ferenczi, *Sex in Psychoanalysis* (New York: Dover Publication, 1956), p. 90, and (New York: Basic Books, Inc., 1950), p.

380

106. Quoted by permission of the publisher. Lawrence D. Trevett, "Origin of the Creation Myth: A Hypothesis," *Journal of the American Psychoanalytic Association* (1957), 5:461–68. Reducing the whole creation cosmogony simply to the Isakower phenomenon of falling asleep or to Lewin's dream screen seems to be a psychological oversimplication and a basic misunderstanding of the abundance of fantasies.

3 Herbert Marcuse, *Eros and Civilization: A Philosophical Inquiry into Freud* (New York: Random House, Inc., 1962).

4 Norman O. Brown, *Life Against Death: The Psychoanalytical Meaning of History* (New York: Random House, Inc., 1959).

5 S. Freud, "Psycho-Analytical Notes upon an Autobiographical Account of a Case of Paranoia," 1911, *Collected Papers,* 3:457. *Standard Edition,* 12:69–70.

6 Our approach is essentially different from that used by J. G. Frazer, "Folklore in the Old Testament" in *Anthropological Essays Presented to E. B. Tylor* (Oxford: Clarendon Press, 1907), pp. 101–174.

7 An excellent exposition of the Greek cosmogonic fantasies is W. K. C. Guthrie, *In the Beginning: Some Greek Views on the Origins of Life and the Early State of Man* (Ithaca, N.Y.: Cornell University Press, 1957). For the Hebrew see the classic work by Hermann Gunkel, *Schöpfung und Chaos in Urzeit und Endzeit: Eine religionsgeschichtliche Untersuchung über Gen I und Ap Jo 12, mit Beiträgen von Heinrich Zimmern* (Göttingen, Germany: Vanderhoeck & Ruprecht, 1895). Also, Richard Reitzenstein, *Weltuntergangsvorstellungen: Eine Studie zur vergleichenden Religionsgeschichte* (Uppsala, Sweden: A. B. Lundequist, 1924).

8 Paul Schilder, "Psycho-Analysis of Space," *International Journal of Psycho-Analysis* (1935), 16:274–95.

9 Berta Bornstein, "Analysis of a Phobic Child," *The Psychoanalytical Study of the Child* (1949), 3–4:181–225.

10 John Arnold Lindon, "Castrophilia as a Character Neurosis," *International Journal of Psycho-Analysis* (1958), 39:525–34.

11 Erich Hofmann, *Ausdrucksverstärkung. Untersuchungen zur etymologischen Verstärkung und zum Gebrauch der Steigerunsadverbia im Balto-Slavischen und in anderen indogermanischen Sprachen* (Göttingen, Germany: Vanderhoeck & Ruprecht, 1930).

12 Merton M. Gill and Margaret Brenman, *Hypnosis and Related States: Psychoanalytic Studies in Regression* (New York: International University Press, 1961), p. 102.

13 Jacob A. Arlow, "Notes on Oral Symbolism," *Psychoanalytic Quarterly* (1955), 24:69.

14 Dorothy W. Baruch and Hyman Miller, "Developmental Needs and Conflicts Revealed in Children's Art," *American Journal of Orthopsychiatry* (1952), 22:186–203.

15 R. Eisler, *Weltenmantel und Himmelszelt* (2 vols., Mün-

chen: Beck, 1910). Three millennia before Christ, the Chinese empire was considered as the country below the canopy of heaven.

16 Reichelt, "Der steinerne Himmel," *Indogermanische Forschungen* (1913), 32:23–57.

17 A. Meillet, "La Religion Indo-Européenne," *Linguistique Historique et Linguistique Générale* (Paris: Champion, 1948), pp. 323–34, pleads for the priority of the day sky.

18 Hjalmar Frisk, *Griechisches etymologisches Wörterbuch* (Heidelberg: Winter, 1954), *s.v. aigis*.

19 A. Meillet, "Le Nom de l'Homme," *Linguistique Historique et Linguistique Générale* (Paris: Champion, 1948), pp. 272–80.

20 H. S. Darlington, "Manufacture of Clay Pots: An Exposition of the Psychology of Pot-making," *Psychoanalytic Review* (1957), 24:392–402. The linguistic evidences are missing.

21 For excellent examples of dynamic structurization of the body image as expressed by modeling-clay technique see Gisela Pankow, "Dynamic Structurization in Schizophrenia," in Arthur Burton, ed., *Psychotherapy of the Psychoses* (New York: Basic Books, Inc., 1961), pp. 152–71.

22 Wilbur Jarvis "When I Grow Big and You Grow Little," *Psychoanalytic Quarterly* (1958), 27:397–99.

23 Such translation of our grammatical categories into the picture language of dreams was first described by Herbert Silberer, "Phantasie und Mythus: Vornehmlich vom Gesichtspunkte der funktionalen Kategorie betrachtet," *Jahrbuch für psychoanalytische und psychopathologische Forschungen* (1910), 2:54–622.

24 S. Freud, *Collected Papers*, 3:392. *Standard Edition*, 12:14.

25 Paul Kramer, "On Discovering One's Identity: A Case Report," *Psychoanalytical Study of the Child* (1955), 10:47–74.

26 *The Zend-Avesta. Part I: The Vendidad*, translated by James Darmestäter (*The Sacred Books of the East*, Vol. IV), (Oxford: Clarendon Press, 1880), 1:17–18. See also R. C. Zaehner, *The Dawn and Twilight of Zoroastrianism* (London: Weidenfeld and Nicolson, 1961).

27 Aurel Kolnai, *Psychoanalysis and Sociology* (New York: Harcourt, Brace & World, Inc., 1922), p. 139, the chapter on "Infantile El Dorado Fantasy of Communism." Ernest Jones on "The Island of Ireland" in his *Essays in Applied Psychoanalysis*, The International Psycho-Analytic Library, No. 40 (London: Hogarth Press, Ltd., 1951), pp. 95–112. Harold Bayley, "The Garden of Allah," *The Lost Language of Symbolism: An Inquiry into the Origin of Certain Letters, Words, Names, Fairy-Tales, Folklore and Mythologies* (New York: Barnes & Noble, Inc., 1951), 2:224–65.

28 Bronislaw Malinowski, *Coral Gardens and Their Magic: A Study of the Methods of Tilling the Soil and of Agricultural Rites in the Trobriand Islands* (2 vols., London: George Allen & Unwin, Ltd., 1935). The "fence" is for the Trobrianders a "magic wall."

382

29 J. Banks, *The Works of Hesiod, Callimachus, and Theognis*, literally translated into English prose (London: H. G. Bohn, 1856).

30 H. S. Darlington, "The Secret of the Birth of Iron," *The International Journal of Psycho-Analysis* (1928), 9:71–95.

31 John Weir Perry, "Image, Complex, and Transference in Schizophrenia," *Psychotherapy of the Psychoses*, ed. Arthur Burton (New York: Basic Books, Inc., 1961), pp. 90–123 (esp. p. 110). Quoted by permission of the publisher.

32 Samuel Noah Kramer, *Sumerian Mythology: A Study of Spiritual and Literary Achievement in the Third Millennium* B.C. (Philadelphia: American Philosophical Society, 1944), p. 107. New Harper Torchbook edition, 1961. Quoted by permission of the publisher.

33 James Darmestater, *op. cit.*, 1:17–18, 2:253–293.

34 J. Banks, *op. cit.*, lines 90–94.

35 Berta Bornstein, "Clinical Notes on Child Analysis," *The Psychoanalytical Study of the Child* (1945), 1:151–66.

36 "Interpretation of Dreams," *Standard Edition*, p. 591.

37 Gregory Zilboorg, "The Sense of Immortality," *Psychoanalytic Quarterly* (1938), 8:171, and Bertram D. Lewin, *The Psychoanalysis of Elation* (New York: W. W. Norton & Company, Inc., 1950), do not refer to the pertinent linguistic material.

38 Calvin Hall, *Empirical Evidence for the Timelessness of the Unconscious*, reprint from the Institute of Dream Research, Miami, 1963.

39 John Weir Perry, "Image, Complex, and Transference in Schizophrenia," *Psychotherapy of the Psychoses*, ed. Arthur Burton (New York: Basic Books, Inc., 1961), p. 112. Quoted by permission of the publisher.

40 Samuel Noah Kramer: *Sumerian Mythology*, quoted by permission of the publisher.

41 *Zend-Avesta*, 1:17–18, 2:253, 293.

42 *Works and Days*, 99–124.

43 On "milk and honey," see Hermann Usener, "Milch und Honig," in *Kleine Schriften* (Stuttgart: Teubner Verlagsgesellschaft, mbH, 1913), 4:398–417. James Hastings, ed., *Encyclopedia of Religion and Ethics*, Vol. II, *s.v. honey*. Martin P. Nilson, *Geschichte der griechischen Religion*, Handbuch der Altertumswissenschaft (München: Beck, 1951), p. 537.

44 Theodore Thass-Thienemann, "Left-handed Writing: A Study in the Psychoanalysis of Language," *The Psychoanalytic Review* (1955), 42:239–61.

45 Vitruvius, *The Ten Books on Architecture*, translated by Morris Hicky Morgan (Cambridge, Mass.: Harvard University Press, 1926), p. 58.

46 S. Freud, *General Introduction*, p. 165.

47 Marguerite Sechehaye, *A New Psychotherapy in Schizo-*

phrenia: Relief of Frustrations by Symbolic Realization (New York: Grune & Stratton, Inc., 1956), pp. 18–19. Also, *Symbolic Realization: A New Method of Psychotherapy Applied to a Case of Schizophrenia* (New York: International University Press, 1951), pp. 48–66.

48 Freud on the apple-tree motive in Goethe's *Faust: Interpretation of Dreams,* p. 287.

49 Helen Merrell Lynd, *On Shame and the Search for Identity* (New York: Harcourt, Brace & World, Inc., 1958).

50 J. G. Frazer, "Dionysus," *Spirits of the Corn and of the Wild* (New York: The Macmillan Company, 1935), pp. 1–34.

51 Richard M. Griffith, "Dreams of Finding Money," *American Journal of Psychotherapy* (1951), 5:521–30.

52 Walter F. Otto, *Die Götter Griechenlandes* (3rd ed., Frankfurt: Schulte-Blumke, 1947). See also Franz Altheim, *Terra Mater: Untersuchungen zur altitalischen Religionsgeschichte, Religionsgeschichtliche Versuche und Vorarbeiten,* vol. 22 (Giessen, Germany: Töpelmann, 1931).

53 Quoted from the famous translation of the *Bacchae* by Gilbert Murray.

54 Hermann Schneider, *Die Götter der Germanen* (Tübingen: Mohr, 1938).

55 Gilbert Gadoffre, "French National Images and the Problem of National Stereotypes," *International Social Science Bulletin* (1951), 3:579–87.

56 About the role of the mother's brother, see Bronislaw Malinowski, *The Father in Primitive Psychology* (New York: W. W. Norton & Company, Inc., 1927).

57 Quoted by permission of the publisher of Marguerite A. Sechehaye, "The Curative Function of Symbols in a Case of Traumatic Neurosis with Psychotic Reactions," in *Psychotherapy of the Psychoses,* ed. Arthur Burton (New York: Basic Books, Inc., 1961), pp. 124–51. Previous publications by the same author: *Symbolic Realization* (New York: International University Press, 1951) and *A New Psychotherapy in Schizophrenia: Relief of Frustrations by Symbolic Realization* (New York: Grune & Stratton, Inc., 1956).

58 Theodore Thass-Thienemann, "Left-handed Writing: A Study in the Psychoanalysis of Language," *The Psychoanalytic Review* (1955), 42:239–61.

NOTES FOR THE ADDENDA

1 Berthold Delbrück, *Die indogermanischen Verwandtschaftsnamen: Ein Beitrag zur vergleichenden Alterthumskunde* (Königl. Sächsiche Gesellschaft der Wissenschaften. Abhandlungen der philologisch-historischen Klasse) (Leipzig: Hirzel, 1889), 9:50.

2 Concerning the "grandfather complex," see Ernest Jones, "The Phantasy of the Reversal of Generations," 1913, *Papers on*

Psychoanalysis (Boston: Beacon Press, 1961), pp. 407–412. Karl Abraham, "Some Remarks on the Role of Grandparents in the Psychology of Neuroses," 1913, *Selected Papers* (New York: Basic Books, Inc., 1961), 2:44–47. Sándor Ferenczi, "The Grandfather Complex," 1913, *Selected Papers* (New York: Basic Books, Inc., 1960), 2:323–24. Ernest A. Rappaport, "The Grandparent Syndrome," *The Psychoanalytic Quarterly* (1958), 17:518–37.

3 Johannes Maringer, *The Gods of Prehistoric Man*, edited and translated from the German by Mary Ilford (New York: Alfred A. Knopf, Inc., 1960), chap. 3, "The Cult of Ancestors and Spirits of the Dead in Western Europe," pp. 176–91.

4 Walter F. Otto, *Die Manen oder von den Urformen des Totenglaubens* (Berlin: Julius Springer, 1923).

5 Schrader, *Reallexikon*, 1:28, *s.v. Ahnenkultus*.

6 Russell E. Mason, *Internal Perception and Bodily Functioning* (New York: International University Press, 1961), p. 386.

7 William F. Murphy, "Character Trauma and Sensory Perception," *International Journal of Psycho-Analysis* (1958), 39:555–68.

8 *The Interpretation of Dreams*, p. 587. *Standard Edition*, 5:584.

9 Elizabeth R. Zetzel, "The Concept of Anxiety in Relation to the Development of Psychoanalysis," *Journal of the American Psychoanalytic Association* (1955), 3:369–87. See also Joachim Flescher, "A Dualistic Viewpoint on Anxiety," *op. cit.*, 3:415–46.

10 See *Standard Edition*, 20:165, footnote.

11 The final formulations of Freud's theory of anxiety are "Inhibitions, Symptoms, and Anxiety," 1926, *Standard Edition*, 20:75–174, and "New Introductory Lectures on Psycho-Analysis," Lecture 32, 1932, *Standard Edition*, 22:81–111.

12 W. J. S. McKay, *Ancient Gynecology* (New York, 1901). Walter Addison Jayne, *The Healing Gods of Ancient Civilization* (New York: University Books, 1962). Hastings, *Encyclopedia of Religion and Ethics* (New York: Charles Scribner's Sons, 1922), Vol. I, *s.v. birth*.

13 F. G. Welcker, "Entbindung," *Kleine Schriften* (Bonn: Weber, 1950), 3:185–208.

14 Otto Rank, *The Myth of the Birth of the Hero and Other Writings* (New York: Alfred A. Knopf, Inc., 1959).

15 Jean Piaget, *The Child's Conception of the World* (Paterson, N.J.: Littlefield, Adams & Co., 1936), pp. 361–69.

16 Gisela Pankow, "Dynamic Structurization in Schizophrenia," in *Psychotherapy of the Psychoses*, ed. Arthur Burton (New York: Basic Books, Inc., 1961), p. 156.

17 A well-documented survey is given by Richard Andree, *Die Anthropophagie: Eine ethnographische Studie* (Leipzig: von Veit, 1887).

18 Hutchison, *Ten Years Wandering among the Ethiopians* (London, 1861), p. 58; quoted by Andree, *op. cit.*, p. 103.

[19] William James, *Memories and Studies*, p. 301.

[20] W. K. C. Guthrie, *In the Beginning: Some Greek Views on the Origins of Life and the Early State of Man* (Ithaca, N.Y.: Cornell University Press, 1957), p. 73.

[21] *Herodotus*, translated by J. Enoch Powell (Oxford: Clarendon Press, 1949), 1:108.

[22] *Herodotus, loc. cit.*, 1:283.

[23] *The Geography of Strabo*, with an English translation by Horace Leonard Jones (London: William Heinemann, Ltd.; and New York: G. P. Putnam's Sons, 1923), 2:259.

[24] R. Andree, "Menschenschädel als Trinkgefässe," *Zeitschrift des Vereins für Volkskunde* (1912), 22:1–12. Clinical material: Theodore Thass-Thienemann, "The Talking Teapot: A Note on Psycho-Linguistics," *Comprehensive Psychiatry* (1960), 1:199–200.

[25] Charton, *Voyageurs Anciens et Modernes* (Paris, 1863), 3:198; quoted by Andree, *op. cit.*, p. 83.

[26] Walter Bromberg and Paul Schilder, "Psychologic Considerations in Alcoholic Castration and Dismembering Motives: Zerstückelungsmotive," *International Journal of Psycho-Analysis* (1933), 14:206–224.

[27] Isador H. Coriat, "The Dynamics of Stammering," *Psychoanalytic Quarterly* (1933), 2:244–59 (esp. p. 248).

[28] Editha Sterba, "Interpretation and Education," *The Psychoanalytical Study of the Child* (1945), 1:309–317 (esp. p. 311).

[29] The basic work was done by Friedrich Reitzenstein, "Der Kausalzusammenhang zwischen Geschlechtsverkehr und Empfängniss im Glaube und Brauch der Natur und Kultur-Völker," *Zeitschrift für Ethnologie* (1909), 41:444–83. The psychological implications of this theory were recognized by Otto Rank, *Psychology and the Soul* (Philadelphia: University of Pennsylvania Press, 1950), pp. 17–20.

[30] Edwin Sidney Hartland, *Primitive Paternity: The Myth of Supernatural Birth in Relation to the History of the Family*, The Folk-Lore Society, Vol. 65 (London: D. Nutt, 1909).

[31] Bronislaw Malinowski, *Magic, Science, and Religion and Other Essays* (New York: Doubleday & Company, Inc., 1948); also *Sex and Repression in Savage Society* (New York: Meridian Books, 1955); also *Crime and Custom in Savage Society* (Paterson, N.J.: Littlefield, Adams & Co., 1959).

[32] Charles Brenner, "A Case Study of Childhood Hallucinosis," *The Psychoanalytical Study of the Child* (1958), 6:235–43.

[33] Harold F. Searles, "The Evolution of the Mother Transference in Psychotherapy with Schizophrenic Patients," in *Psychotherapy of Psychoses*, ed. Arthur Burton (New York: Basic Books, Inc., 1961), p. 262.

[34] Calvin Hall, *Strangers in Dreams: An Empirical Confirmation of the Oedipus Complex* (Miami: Institute of Dream Research, 1963).

386

35 Bronislaw Malinowski, *The Father in Primitive Psychology* (New York: W. W. Norton & Company, Inc., 1927), p. 17.

36 Lauretta Bender and William Q. Wolfson, "The Nautical Theme in the Art and Fantasy of Children," *American Journal of Orthopsychiatry* (1946), 15:462–67.

37 Leon Pierce Clark, *Lincoln: A Psycho-Biography* (New York: Charles Scribner's Sons, 1933).

38 Richard Bronxton Onians, *The Origins of European Thought* (Cambridge, England, University Press, 1954), pp. 254–56, 274.

39 Bronislaw Malinowski, *Sex and Repression in Savage Society* (New York: Meridian Books, 1953), p. 17: "Psychoanalytic doctrine is essentially a theory of the influence of the family on the human mind."

A survey of the pertinent psychoanalytic literature in J. C. Flügel, *The Psychoanalytic Study of the Family*, International Psychoanalytical Library, No. 3 (3rd ed., London: Hogarth Press, Ltd., 1929). A new approach was made by Martin Grotjahn in his *The Psychoanalytic Treatment of the Family* (New York: W. W. Norton & Company, Inc., 1959), and "Analytic Family Therapy: A Survey of Trends in Research and Practice," in *Individual and Familial Dynamics,* ed. Jules H. Masserman (New York: Grune & Stratton, Inc., 1959), pp. 90–104. See also Bronislaw Malinowski, *The Family among the Australian Aborigines* (New York: Schocken Books, 1963).

40 S. Freud, "Family Romance," 1909, *Collected Papers,* 5:74–78.

41 "Leonardo da Vinci and a Memory of His Childhood," 1910, *Standard Edition,* 11:63–137.

42 Hans Kelsen, *Society and Nature: A Sociological Inquiry* (Chicago: University of Chicago Press, 1943). This is an outstanding investigation in the problem of retaliation.

43 An essentially different interpretation is given by Gerhart Piers and Milton B. Singer, *Shame and Guilt: A Psychoanalytic and a Cultural Study* (Springfield, Ill.: Charles C Thomas, Publisher, 1953).

44 Theodore Reik, *Myth and Guilt: The Crime and Punishment of Mankind* (New York: George Braziller, 1957). Also, *The Compulsion To Confess: On the Psychoanalysis of Crime and Punishment* (New York: Evergreen Books, 1961). Different viewpoints are presented by Bronislaw Malinowski, *Crime and Custom in Savage Society* (Paterson, N.J.: Littlefield, Adams & Co., 1959). Helen Merrell Lynd, *On Shame and the Search for Identity* (New York: Harcourt, Brace & World, Inc., 1958).

45 Freud started the discussion of this topic in the first chapter, "The Horror of Incest," of his book *Totem and Tabu.* See also *Standard Edition,* 13:1–17.

46 Otto Rank, *Das Inzestmotive in Dichtung und Sage: Grundzüge einer Psychologie des dichterischen Schaffens* (Leipzig and Wien:

F. Deuticke, 1912). A good review of pertinent theories is given by Leslie A. White, "The Definition and Prohibition of Incest," *American Anthropologist* (1948), 50:416–435, and Otto Klineberg, *Social Psychology* (rev. ed., New York: Holt, Rinehart & Winston, Inc., 1954), pp. 134–47. The classic work is J. G. Frazer, *Totemism and Exogamy: A Treatise of Certain Early Forms of Superstition and Society* (4 vols., London: The Macmillan Company, 1910). S. Kirson Weinberg, *Incest Behavior* (New York: Citadel Press, 1963); this is a comprehensive monograph with extended bibliography and clinical material. Emile Dirkheim, *Incest: The Nature and Origin of the Taboo* (New York: Lyle Stuart, 1964).

47 Irving Kaufman, Alice L. Peck, and Consuelo K. Tagiuri, "The Family Constellation and Overt Incestuous Relations between Father and Daughter," *American Journal of Orthopsychiatry* (1954), 24:266–79. Maurice J. Barry and Adelaide M. Johnson, "The Incest Barrier," *The Psychoanalytic Quarterly* (1958), 27:485–500. Their point is to prove that if the parents condone the incest, the sense of guilt is absent.

48 Karl Abraham, "The Significance of Intermarriage between Close Relatives in the Psychology of the Neuroses," 1909, *Clinical Papers and Essays on Psycho-Analysis* (New York: Basic Books, Inc., 1955), pp. 21–28.

49 Bronislaw Malinowski, *Sex and Repression in Savage Society* (New York: Meridian Books, 1927), p. 99.

50 William Mariner, "The Sacrifice of the Child," in Margaret Mead and Nicolas Callas, *Primitive Heritage: An Anthropological Anthology* (New York: Random House, Inc., 1953), pp. 562–64.

51 On being eaten, see Freud, *Problem of Anxiety* (New York: W. W. Norton & Company, Inc., 1936). J. Fodor, "Nightmares on Cannibalism," *American Journal of Psychotherapy* (1951), 5:225–35. Otto Fenichel, "The Dread of Being Eaten," 1929, in *Collected Papers* (First Series, New York: W. W. Norton & Company, Inc., 1953), pp. 158–59. L. Székely, "Biological Remarks on Fears Originating in Early Childhood," *International Journal of Psycho-Analysis* (1954), 35:57–67. Gert Heilbrunn, "The Basic Fear," *Journal of the American Psychoanalytical Association* (1955), 3:447–66.

52 M. A. Sechehaye, *Symbolic Realization* (New York: International University Press, 1951), pp. 22–23.

53 Bernhard Berliner, "The Role of Object Relations in Moral Masochism," *The Psychoanalytic Quarterly* (1958), 27:38–56 (esp. p. 43).

54 Erich Wellisch, *Isaac and Oedipus: A Study in Biblical Psychology of the Sacrifice of Isaac. The Akedah* (London: Routledge & Kegan Paul, Ltd., 1954).

55 Margaret L. Meiss, "The Oedipal Problem of the Fatherless Child," *The Psychoanalytical Study of the Child* (1952), 7:216–27.

56 J. G. Frazer, *The Golden Bough* (London, 1919), 2:278.

57 Rudolf Otto, *The Idea of the Holy*, translated by J. W. Harvey (2nd ed., Oxford University Press, 1952).

58 Erich Neumann, *The Origin and History of Consciousness* (2 vols., New York: Harper & Row, Publishers, 1962; first in German, 1949). Erich Fromm, *The Forgotten Language: An Introduction to the Understanding of Dreams, Fairy Tales, and Myths* (New York: Holt, Rinehart & Winston, Inc., 1951).

59 J. J. Bachofen, *Der Mythus von Orient und Okzident*, ed. Manfred Schröder (München: Becksche Verlagsbuchhandlung, 1926).

60 Franz Altheim, *Terra Mater: Untersuchungen zur altitalischen Religionsgeschichte, Religionsgeschichtliche* Versuche und Vorarbeiten, Vol. 22 (Giessen: Töpelmann, 1931). Albrecht Dieterich, *Mutter Erde: Ein Versuch über Volksreligion* (Stuttgart: Teubner Verlagagesellschaft, mbH, 1905).

61 Dorothy F. Zelig, "The Role of the Mother in the Development of Hebraic Monotheism as Exemplified in the Life of Abraham," *The Psychoanalytic Study of Society* (1960), 1:287–310.

62 Karl Abraham, "An Infantile Theory of the Origin of the Female Sex," 1923, *Selected Papers* (New York: Basic Books, Inc., 1953), 2:333–69.

63 Tacitus, *Germania*, chap. 2: "celebrant carminibus antiquis . . . Tuisconem deum Terra editum, et filium Mannum, originem gentis conditoremque. . . ." See on this topic the researches of J. Winthuis, *Das Zweigeschlechtwesen*, 1928, and *Die Wahrheit über das Zweigeschlechtwesen*, 1930. The whole controversial question is unfolded by P. Gerhard Pekel: "Das Zweigeschlechtwesen," *Revue Internationale d'Ethnologie et Linguistique* (St. Gabriel: Mödling bei Wien, 1929), 24:1005–72.

64 Alfred M. Freedman and Lauretta Bender, "When the Childhood Schizophrenic Grows Up," *American Journal of Orthopsychiatry* (1957), 27:553–67 (esp. p. 554).

65 On *con-jugium*, see Leopold Wegener, "Sprachforschung und Rechtswissenschaft," *Wörter und Sachen*, (1909), 184–94.

66 Robert Waelder, "The Psychoanalytic Theory of Play," *Psychoanalytic Quarterly* (1933), 2:208–29. Lauretta Bender and Paul Schilder, "Form as a Principle in the Play of Children," *Journal of Genetic Psychology* (1936), 49:254–61. Edward Liss, "Play Techniques in Child Analysis," *American Journal of Orthopsychiatry* (1936), 6:17–22. Paul Holmer, "The Use of Play Situation as an Aid to Diagnosis," *ibid.* (1937), 7:523–31. Maxwell Gitelson, "Clinical Experience with Play Therapy," *ibid.* (1938), 8:466–78. Erik H. Erikson, "Studies in Interpretation of Play," *Genetic Psychological Monograph* (1940), 22:557–671. J. Huizinga, *Homo Ludens* (London: Routledge & Kegan Paul, Ltd., 1949). Lili E. Peller, "Libidinal Phases in Ego Development and Play," *Psychoanalytical Study of the Child* (1954), 9:175–98. "Therapeutic Play Techniques," Symposium, *American Journal of Orthopsychiatry* (1955), 25:575–626, 747–67. Franz Alexander, "A

Contribution to the Theory of Play," *Psychoanalytic Quarterly* (1958), 17:173–93. Phyllis Greenacre, "Play in Relation to Creative Imagination," *Psychoanalytic Study of the Child* (1959), 14:61–80. Eric Berne, *Games People Play* (New York: Grove Press, 1965).

67 Rudolf Meringer, "Wörter und Sachen," *Indogermanische Forschungen* (1904), 16:182–90; also "Pflegen, Pflicht, Pflug," *ibid.* (1904), 17:100–114. Friedrich Kluge and Alfred Goetze, *Etymologisches Wörterbuch der deutschen Sprache* (Berlin: de Gruyter, 1948), *s.v. pflegen.*

68 "Therapeutic Play Techniques," *American Journal of Orthopsychiatry* (1955), 25:574.

69 Hanna Segal, "Notes on Symbol Formation," *International Journal of Psycho-Analysis* (1957), 38:391–97.

70 Milton L. Miller, "Ego Functioning in Two Types of Dreams," *Psychoanalytical Quarterly* (1948), 17:346–55.

71 Hermann Nunberg, "Circumcision and Problems of Bisexuality," *International Journal of Psycho-Analysis* (1957), 28:146.

72 S. Freud, "Writers and Day-dreaming," 1908, *Standard Edition,* 9:144–45, and "Beyond the Pleasure Principle," 1920, *Standard Edition,* 18:23.

73 W. B. Cannon, *The Wisdom of the Body* (New York: W. W. Norton & Company, Inc., 1932).

74 S. Freud, "Introductory Lectures," 1916, *Standard Edition,* 16:356, and "Beyond the Pleasure Principle," 1926, *Standard Edition,* 18:7–64. E. Jacobson, "The Affects and Their Pleasure-Unpleasure Qualities in Relation to the Psychic Discharge Processes," in *Drives, Affects, and Behavior,* ed. R. M. Lowenstein (New York: International University Press, 1953), pp. 38–66. Thomas Szasz, *Pain and Pleasure* (New York: Basic Books, Inc., 1957).

75 Bruce Buchenholz, "Models for Pleasure," *Psychoanalytic Quarterly* (1958), 27:307–326. R. de Saussure: "The Metapsychology of Pleasure," *International Journal of Psycho-Analysis* (1959), 40:81–93. M. Kanzer and I. Eidelberg, "Contribution to the Discussion of the Metapsychology of Pleasure," *International Journal of Psycho-Analysis* (1960), 41:372–74. William Needless, "Comment on the Pleasure-Unpleasure Experience," *Journal of the American Psychoanalytical Association* (1964), 12:300–314.

76 "Interpretation of Dreams," *Standard Edition,* 5:400, and "Introductory Lectures on Psycho-Analysis," 1916, *Standard Edition,* 15:163.

77 Rudolf Meringer, "Wörter und Sachen," *Indogermanische Forschungen* (1904), 16:100–114.

78 Erich Fromm, *The Forgotten Language: An Introduction to the Understanding of Dreams, Fairy Tales, and Myths* (New York: Holt, Rinehart & Winston, Inc., 1951).

79 M. O. Farnsworth, *Uncle and Nephew in the Old French*

Chanson de Geste: A Study in Survival of Matriarchy (New York, 1913).

80 Ottokar Nemecek, *Virginity: Pre-Nuptial Rites and Rituals* (New York: The Citadel Press, 1962). A different interpretation is Freud, "The Taboo of Virginity," 1918, *Standard Edition*, 11:193–208.

A SELECTIVE
BIBLIOGRAPHY

ABRAHAM, KARL. *Selected Papers.* New York: Basic Books, Inc., 1961.

ALEXANDER, FRANZ. *The Medical Value of Psychoanalysis.* New York: W. W. Norton & Company, Inc., 1931, p. 143.

——. "A Contribution to the Theory of Play," *Psychoanalytic Quarterly* (1958), 17:173–93.

ALTHEIM, FRANZ. *Terra Mater: Untersuchungen zur altitalischen Religionsgeschichte.* (Religionsgeschichtliche Versuche und Vorarbeiten, vol. 22.) Giessen, Germany: Töpelmann, 1931.

——. *History of Roman Religion.* New York: E. P. Dutton & Co., Inc., 1937, pp. 125–268.

ARISTOTLE. *Politics.* Translated by Benjamin Jowett. New York: Random House, Inc., The Modern Library, 1943.

——. *Generation of Animals.* With an English translation by A. L. Peck. Cambridge, Mass.: Harvard University Press, The Loeb Classical Library, 1943.

ANDREE, RICHARD. *Die Anthropophagie: Eine ethnographische Studie.* Leipzig: von Veit, 1887.

——. "Menschenschädel als Trinkgefässe," *Zeitschrift des Vereins für Volkskunde* (1912), 22:1–12.

ARLOW, JACOB A. "Notes on Oral Symbolism," *Psychoanalytic Quarterly* (1955), 24:63–74.

AUGUSTINE. *Confessions.* New York: Washington Square Press, 1960, p. 114.

BACHOFEN, J. J. *Der Mythos von Orient and Okzident,* ed. Manfred Schröder. München: Becksche Verlagsbuchhandlung, 1926.

BANKS, JOHN. *The Works of Hesiod, Callimachus, and Theognis.* Literally translated into English prose. London: H. G. Bohm, 1856.

BARUCH, DOROTHY W., and MILLER, HYMAN. "Developmental Needs and Conflicts Revealed in Children's Art," *American Journal of Orthopsychiatry* (1952), 22:186–203.

BAYLEY, HAROLD. "The Garden of Allah," *The Lost Language of*

Symbolism: An Inquiry into the Origin of Certain Letters, Words, Names, Fairy-Tales, Folk-lore, and Mythologies. New York: Barnes & Noble, Inc., 1951, 2:224–65.

BENDER, LAURETTA, and WOLFSON, WILLIAM Q. "The Nautical Theme in the Art and Fantasy of Children," *American Journal of Orthopsychiatry* (1946), 15:462–67.

————, and SCHILDER, PAUL. "Form as a Principle in the Play of Children," *Journal of Genetical Psychology* (1936), 49:254–61.

Beowulf and the Fight at Finnsburg, ed. by F. Klaeber. 3d ed. Boston: D. C. Heath and Company, 1936.

BERLINER, BERNHARD. "The Role of Object Relations in Moral Masochism," *The Psychoanalytic Quarterly* (1958), 27:38–56.

BINSWANGER, LUDWIG. "Das Raumproblem in der Psychopathologie," *Zeitschrift für die gesamte Neurologie und Psychiatrie* (1933), pp. 598–648.

BLANK, H. ROBERT. "Psychoanalysis and Blindness," *Psychoanalytic Quarterly* (1957), 26:1–24.

BLOS, PETER. "Comments on the Psychological Consequences of Cryptorchidism: A Clinical Study," *The Psychoanalytical Study of the Child* (1960), 15:359–429.

BORNSTEIN, BERTA. "Clinical Notes on Child Analysis," *The Psychoanalytical Study of the Child* (1945), 1:151–66.

————. "Analysis of a Phobic Child," *The Psychoanalytical Study of the Child* (1949), 3–4:181–225.

BOYER, BRYCE. "A Hypothesis Regarding the Time of Appearance of the Dream Screen," *International Journal of Psycho-Analysis* (1960), 41:114–22.

BRENNER, CHARLES. "A Case Study of Childhood Hallucinosis," *The Psychoanalytical Study of the Child* (1958), 6:235–43.

BROMBERG, WALTER, and SCHILDER, PAUL. "Psychologic Considerations in Alcoholic Castration and Dismembering Motives: Zerstückungsmotive," *International Journal of Psycho-Analysis* (1933), 14:206–24.

BROWE, PETER. "Zur Geschichte der Entmannung: Eine religions- und rechtsgeschichtliche Studie," *Breslauer Studien zur historischen Theologie.* N.F. Bd. I. Breslau: Müller und Seiffert, 1936.

BROWN, NORMAN O. *Life against Death.* New York: Random House, Inc., 1959.

BUCHENHOLZ, BRUCE. "Models for Pleasure," *Psychoanalytic Quarterly* (1958), 27:307–26.

BYCHOVSKI, GUSTAV. "Struggle against the Introjects," *International Journal of Psycho-Analysis* (1958), 39:182–87.

CALVIN, JOHN. *Commentaries on the First Book of Moses Called Genesis.* Translated by John King. Grand Rapids, Mich.: W. B. Eerdman, 1:73.

CANNON, W. B. *The Wisdom of the Body.* New York: W. W. Norton & Company, Inc., 1932.

CHAMPION, S. G. *Racial Proverbs.* New York: The Macmillan Company, 1938.

CLARK, L. PIERRE. *Lincoln: A Psycho-Biography.* New York: Charles Scribner's Sons, 1933.

COLE, WILLIAM GRAHAM. *Sex and Love in the Bible.* New York: Association Press, 1959.

———. *Sex in Christianity and Psychoanalysis.* New York: Oxford University Press, 1955.

CORIA, ISADOR H. "The Dynamics of Stammering," *Psychoanalytic Quarterly* (1933), 2:244–59.

DARLINGTON, H. S. "The Secret of the Birth of the Iron," *International Journal of Psycho-Analysis* (1928), 9:71–95.

———. "Manufacture of Clay Pots: An Exposition of the Psychology of Pot-making," *Psychoanalytical Review* (1957), 24:392–402.

DELBRÜCK, BERTHOLD. *Die indogermanischen Verwandtschaftsnamen: Ein Beitrag zur vergleichenden Altertumskunde.* Königl. Sächsische Gesellschaft der Wissenschaften. Abhandlungen der philologisch-hist. Klasse. Leipzig: S. Hirzel Verlag, 1889, 9:5.

DEUTSCH, ELINOR. "The Dream Imagery of the Blind," *Psychoanalytical Review* (1928), 15:288–93.

DEVEREUX, GEORGE. "Why Oedipus Killed Laius," *International Journal of Psycho-Analysis* (1953), 34:132–41.

DIELS, HERMANN. *Fragmente der Vorsokratiker: Griechisch und Deutsch.* 8th ed. by W. Franz. Berlin: Weidmann, 1956.

———. "Krokodilos," *Indogermanische Forschungen* (1903), 15:1–8.

DIETERICH, ALBRECHT. *Mutter Erde: Ein Versuch über Volksreligion.* Stuttgart: Teubner Verlagsgesellschaft, mbH, 1905.

DUNLAP, JANE. *Exploring Inner Space: Personal Experiences under LSD–25.* New York: Harcourt, Brace & World, Inc., 1961.

EISLER, R. *Weltenmantel und Himmelszelt.* 2 vols. München: Beck, 1910.

Ellicott's Commentary on the Whole Bible. Grand Rapids, Mich.: Zondervan, 1954, 6:537.

394

ERIKSON, ERIK H. *Identity and the Life Cycle: Selected Papers*, with a historical introduction by David Rapaport, in *Psychological Issues*. New York: International University Press, 1959.
————. "Studies in Interpretation of Play," *Genetic Psychology Monographs* (1940), 22:557–671.

FARNSWORTH, M. O. *Uncle and Nephew in the Old French Chanson de Geste: A Study in Survival of Matriarchy*. New York, 1913.

FEHRLE, E. *Die kultische Keuschheit im Altertum*. Giessen, 1910.

FENICHEL, OTTO. "The Dread of Being Eaten," 1929. *Collected Papers*, First Series. New York: W. W. Norton & Company, Inc., 1953, pp. 158–59.

FERENCZI, SÁNDOR. *Sex in Psychoanalysis*. New York: Dover Publications, Inc., 1956, p. 90.
————. *Sex in Psychoanalysis*. New York: Dover Publications, 1956; the same: New York: Basic Books, Inc., 1950, p. 106.
————. "Gulliver Phantasies," *International Journal of Psycho-Analysis* (1928), 9:283–300.

FLESCHER, JOACHIM. "Dualistic Viewpoint on Anxiety," *Journal of the American Psychoanalytical Association* (1955), 3:415–46.

FLÜGEL, J. C. *The Psycho-Analytic Study of the Family*. 3d ed. (The International Psychoanalytical Library, No. 3.) London: Hogarth Press, Ltd., 1929.

FODOR, J. "Nightmares on Cannibalism," *American Journal of Psychotherapy* (1957), 5:225–35.

FOWLER, WARDE F. *The Roman Festivals of the Period of the Republic*. London: Macmillan & Co., Ltd., 1899.

FRAZER, SIR JAMES GEORGE. *The New Golden Bough: A New Abridgement of the Classic Work*, ed. Theodore H. Gaster. New York: Criterion Books, 1959.
————. "Dionysus," *Spirits of the Corn and of the Wild*. New York: The Macmillan Company, 1935, pp. 1–34.
————. *Totemism and Exogamy: A Treatise of Certain Early Forms of Superstition and Society*. 4 vols. London: Macmillan & Co., Ltd., 1910.
————. "Folk-lore in the Old Testament," *Anthropological Essays Presented to E. B. Tylor*. Oxford: Clarendon Press, 1907, pp. 101–74.

FREEDMAN, ALFRED M., and BENDER, LAURETTA. "When the Childhood Schizophrenic Grows Up," *American Journal of Orthopsychiatry* (1957), 27:553–67.

FREEMAN, KATHLEEN. *The Pre-Socratic Philosophers: A Companion to Diels' Fragmente der Vorsokratiker.* Cambridge, Mass.: Harvard University Press, 1946, p. 45.

FREUD, SIGMUND. *Collected Papers.* Authorized translation under the supervision of Joan Riviere. 5 vols. New York: Basic Books, Inc., 1959.

――――. *The Standard Edition of the Complete Psychological Works of Sigmund Freud.* Translated from the German under the general editorship of James Strachey, in collaboration with Anna Freud. London: Hogarth Press, Ltd., and the Institute of Psycho-Analysis. First published in 1955.

FROMM, ERICH. *The Forgotten Language: An Introduction to the Understanding of Dreams, Fairy Tales, and Myths.* New York: Holt, Rinehart & Winston, Inc., 1957.

GADOFFRE, GILBERT. "French National Images and the Problem of National Stereotypes," *International Social Science Bulletin* (1951), 3:579–87.

GERARD, MARGARET W. "The Psychogenic Tic in Ego Development," *The Psychoanalytical Study of the Child* (1946), 2:133–62.

GILL, MERTON M., and BRENMAN MARGARET. *Hypnosis and Related States: Psychoanalytic Studies in Regression.* New York: International University Press, 1961, p. 102.

GITELSON, MAXWELL. "Clinical Experience with Play Therapy," *American Journal of Orthopsychiatry* (1938), 8:466–78.

GREENACRE, PHYLLIS. "Play in Relation to Creative Imagination," *The Psychoanalytical Study of the Child* (1959), 14:61–81.

GRIFFITH, RICHARD M. "Dreams of Finding Money," *American Journal of Psychotherapy* (1951), 5:521–30.

GRIMM, JACOB LUDWIG CARL. *Teutonic Mythology.* Translated from the fourth edition with notes and appendix by James Steven Stallybrass. 4 vols. London: Sonnenschein and Allen, 1880.

GROTJAHN, MARTIN. *The Psychoanalytic Treatment of the Family.* New York: W. W. Norton & Company, Inc., 1959.

――――. "Analytic Family Therapy: A Survey of Trends in Research and Practice," *Individual and Familial Dynamics,* ed. Jules H. Masserman. New York: Grune & Stratton, Inc., 1959.

GUNKEL, HERMANN. *Schöpfung und Chaos in Urzeit und Endzeit: Eine religionsgeschichtliche Untersuchung über Gen I und Ap Jo 12.* Mit Beiträgen von Heinrich Zimmern. Göttingen, Germany: Vanderhoeck & Ruprecht, 1895.

GÜNTERT, HERMANN. *Labyrinth: Eine sprachwissenschaftliche Untersuchung.* (Sitzungsberichte der Heidelberger Akademie der Wissenschaften, 1932–33.) Heidelberg: Carl Winter, 1932.

GUTHRIE, W. K. C. *In the Beginning: Some Greek Views on the Origins of Life and the Early State of Man.* Ithaca, N.Y.: Cornell University Press, 1957.

HALL, CALVIN. *Strangers in Dreams: An Empirical Confirmation of the Oedipus Complex.* Coral Gables, Florida: Institute of Dream Research, 1963.

————. *Empirical Evidences for the Timelessness of the Unconscious.* Coral Gables, Florida: Institute of Dream Research, 1963.

HARTLAND, EDWIN SIDNEY. *Primitive Paternity: The Myth of Supernatural Birth in Relation to the History of the Family.* (The Folk-Lore Society, Vol. 65.) London: D. Nutt, 1909.

HASTINGS. *Encyclopedia of Religion and Ethics.* New York: Charles Scribner's Sons, 1922.

HEIDEGGER, MARTIN. *Existence and Being.* Introduction by Werner Brock. Chicago: Henry Regnery Company, 1949, pp. 364–72.

HEILBRUNN. "The Basic Fear," *Journal of the American Psychoanalytical Association* (1955), 3:447–66.

HERODOTUS. Translated by J. Enoch Powell. Oxford: Clarendon Press, 1949.

HERODOTUS. *The History of Herodotus.* Translated by George Rawlinson. New York: E. P. Dutton & Co., Inc., 1910.

HOFMANN, ERICH. *Ausdrucksverstärkung. Untersuchungen zur etymologischen Verstärkung und zum Gebrauch der Steigerungsadverbia im Balto-Slavischen und in anderen indogermanischen Sprachen.* Göttingen, Germany: Vanderhoeck & Ruprecht, 1930.

HOLMER, PAUL. "The Use of Play Situation as an Aid to Diagnosis," *American Journal of Orthopsychiatry* (1937), 7:523–31.

HUIZINGA, J. *Homo Ludens.* London: Routledge & Kegan Paul, Ltd., 1949.

ILBERG, J. "Sphinx," *Ausführliches Lexikon der griechischen und römischen Mythologie,* ed. W. H. Roscher. Stuttgart: Teubner Verlagsgesellschaft, mbH, 1909–1915, 4:1293–1407.

ISAKOWER, OTTO. "A Contribution to the Pathopsychology of Phenomena Associated with Falling Asleep," *International Journal of Psycho-Analysis* (1938), 19:331–45.

JACOBSON, E. "The Affects and Their Pleasure-Unpleasure Qualities in Relation to the Psychic Discharge Processes," *Drives,*

Affects, and Behavior, ed. Loewenstein. New York: International University Press, 1953, pp. 38–66.

JACOBSON, ROMAN. *Kindersprache, Aphasie, und allgemeine Lautgesetze.* Uppsala, Sweden: 1941.

———. "Lois phonic du language enfantin," *Principes de Phonologie,* ed. N. S. Troubetzkoy. Paris: Klincksieck, 1949, pp. 367–79.

JARVIS, WILBUR. "When I Grow Big and You Grow Little," *Psychoanalytic Quarterly* (1958), 27:397–399.

JAYNE, WALTER ADDISON. *The Healing Gods of Ancient Civilization.* New York: University Books, 1962.

JESPERSEN, OTTO. *The Philosophy of Grammar.* New York: Holt, Rinehart & Winston, Inc., 1924, pp. 322–37.

JONES, ERNEST. *Papers on Psychoanalysis.* Boston: Beacon Press, 1961.

———. "The Island of Ireland," *Essays in Applied Psychoanalysis.* (The International Psycho-Analytical Library, No. 40.) London: Hogarth Press, Ltd., 1951, pp. 95–112.

JUNG, CARL GUSTAV. *Studies in Word Association.* Translated by M. D. Eder. New York: Moffat Yard & Co., 1919.

———. *Diagnostische Associationsstudien. Beiträge zur experimentellen Psychopathologie.* München: Johann Ambrosius Barth, 1914, 2:4.

KANZER, M., and EIDELBERG, I. "Contribution to the Discussion of the Metapsychology of Pleasure," *International Journal of Psycho-Analysis* (1960), 41:372–74.

KELSEN, HANS. *Society and Nature: A Sociological Inquiry.* Chicago: University of Chicago Press, 1943.

KITTEL, R. "Holiness," *The New Schaff-Herzog Encyclopedia of the Religious Knowledge.* New York and London: Funk & Wagnalls Co., Inc., 1953, 5:316–18.

KLINEBERG, OTTO. *Social Psychology.* Rev. ed. New York: Holt, Rinehart & Winston, Inc., 1954, pp. 134–47.

KOLANSKY, HAROLD. "Treatment of a Three-year-old Girl's Severe Infantile Neurosis," *The Psychoanalytical Study of the Child* (1960), 15:261–85.

KOLNAI, AUREL. *Psychoanalysis and Sociology.* New York: Harcourt, Brace & World, Inc., 1922.

KRAMER, PAUL. "On Discovering One's Identity: A Case Report," *Psychoanalytical Study of the Child* (1955), 10:47–74.

KRAMER, S. V. *Sumerian Mythology: A Study of the Spiritual and Literary Achievement in the Third Millennium B.C.* Philadelphia: American Philosophical Society, 1944, p. 107.

398

KROEBER, A. *Anthropology, Race, Language, Culture Psychology, Prehistory.* New York: Harcourt, Brace & World, Inc., 1923, p. 616.

LACOMBE, PIERRE. "The Problem of the Identical Twins as Reflected in a Masochistic Compulsion to Cheat," *International Journal of Psycho-Analysis* (1959), 40:6–12.

LAISTNER, LUDWIG. *Das Rätsel der Sphinx: Grundzüge einer Mythengeschichte.* 2 vols. Berlin: Hertz, 1889.

LEWIN, BERTRAM D. *The Psychoanalysis of Elation.* New York: W. W. Norton & Company, Inc., 1950.

————. "The Nature of Reality, the Meaning of Nothing with an Addendum of Concentration," *Psychoanalytic Quarterly* (1948), 7:524–26.

————. "Body as Phallus," *Psychoanalytic Quarterly* (1933), 2:24–47.

LEXER, MATTHIAS. *Mittelhochdeutsches Taschenwörterbuch,* 26th ed. Zürich: S. Hirzel Verlag, 1957.

LINDON, JOHN ARNOLD. "Castrophilia as a Character Neurosis," *International Journal of Pyscho-Analysis* (1958), 39:525–34.

LISS, EDWARD. "Play Techniques in Child Analysis," *American Journal of Orthopsychiatry* (1936), 6:17–22.

LUBIN, J. ALBERT. "A Feminine Moses," *International Journal of Psycho-Analysis* (1958), 39:535–46.

LYND, HELEN MERRELL. *On Shame and the Search of Identity.* New York: Harcourt, Brace & World, Inc., 1958.

MALINOWSKI, BRONISLAW. *The Family among the Australian Aborigines.* New York: Schocken Books, 1963.

————. *Crime and Custom in Savage Society.* New York: Littlefield, Adams & Co., 1959.

————. *Sex and Repression in Savage Society.* New York: Meridian Books, 1955.

————. *Magic Science and Religion and Other Essays.* New York: Doubleday & Company, Inc., 1948.

————. *Coral Gardens and Their Magic: A Study of the Methods of Tilling the Soil and of Agricultural Rites in the Trobriand Islands.* 2 vols. London: George Allen & Unwin, Ltd., 1935.

————. *The Father in Primitive Psychology.* New York: W. W. Norton & Company, Inc., 1927, p. 17.

MARCUSE, HERBERT. *Eros and Civilization: A Philosophical Inquiry into Freud.* New York: Random House, Inc., 1962.

MARINER, WILLIAM. "The Sacrifice of the Child," *Primitive Heritage: An Anthropological Anthology,* ed. Margaret Mead and Nicholas Callas. New York: Random House, Inc., 1953, pp. 562–64.

MARINGER, JOHANNES. *The Gods of Prehistoric Man.* Edited and translated from the German by Mary Ilford. New York: Alfred A. Knopf, Inc., 1960.

MASON, RUSSELL E. *Internal Perception and Bodily Functioning.* New York: International University Press, 1961.

MCKAY, W. I. S. *History of Ancient Gynecology.* New York: William Wood & Co., 1901.

MEISS, MARGARET L. "The Oedipal Problem of the Fatherless Child," *The Psychoanalytical Study of the Child* (1952), 7:216–27.

MERINGER, RUDOLF. "Wörter und Sachen," *Indogermanische Forschungen* (1904), 16:182–90; 1904, 17:100–14.

MILLER, MILTON L. "Ego Functioning in Two Types of Dreams," *Psychoanalytic Quarterly* (1948), 17:346–55.

MUENSTERBERGER, WARNER. "The Creative Process: Its Relationship to Object Loss and Fetishism," *The Psychoanalytic Study of Society* (1962), 2:161–85.

NEMECEK, OTTOKAR. *Virginity. Pre-Nuptial Rites and Rituals.* New York: The Citadel Press, 1962.

NEUMANN, ERICH. *The Origin and History of Consciousness.* 2 vols. (The Bollingen Library.) New York: Harper & Row, 1962. First in German, 1949.

NIEDERLAND, WILLIAM G. "The Earliest Dreams of a Young Child," *The Psychoanalytical Study of the Child* (1957), 12:190–208.

———. "Clinical Observations on the 'Little Man' Phenomenon," *The Psychoanalytical Study of the Child* (1956), 2:381–95.

NILSON, MARTIN P. *Geschichte der griechischen Religion, Handbuch der Altertumswissenschaft.* München: Beck, 1951, p. 537.

NUNBERG, HERMANN. "Circumcision and Problems of Bisexuality," *International Journal of Psycho-Analysis* (1957), 28:146.

ONIANS, RICHARD BRONXTON. *The Origins of European Thought.* Cambridge, England, University Press, 1954.

OTTO, RUDOLF. *The Idea of the Holy.* Translated by J. W. Harvey, 2nd ed. New York: Oxford University Press, 1952.

OTTO, WALTER F. *Die Götter Griechenlands.* 3rd ed. Frankfurt: Schulte-Blumke, 1947.

———. *Die Manen oder von den Urformen des Totenglaubens*. Berlin: Julius Springer, 1923.

PANKOW, GISELA. "Dynamic Structurization in Schizophrenia," *Psychotherapy of the Psychoses*, ed. Arthur Burton. New York: Basic Books, Inc., 1961, pp. 152–71.

PEKEL, GERHARD. "Das Zweigeschlechtwesen," *Revue Internationale d'Ethnologie et Linguistique*. St. Gabriel: Mödling bei Wien, 1929, 24:1005–72.

PELLER, LILI E. "Libidinal Phases in Ego Development and Play," *Psychoanalytical Study of the Child* (1954), 9:175–98.

PERRY, JOHN WEIR. "Image, Complex, and Transference in Schizophrenia," *Psychotherapy of the Psychoses*, ed. Arthur Burton. New York: Basic Books, 1961, pp. 90–123.

PIAGET, JEAN. *The Child's Conception of the World*. Paterson, N.J.: Littlefield, Adams & Co., 1913.

PROCOPIUS. With an English translation by H. B. Dewing. 6 vols. London: William Heinemann, and New York: G. P. Putnam's Sons, 1919.

RADCLIFFE-BROWN, A. R. "The Mother's Brother in South Africa," *South African Journal of Science* (1924), 21:542–55.

RANK, OTTO. *The Myth of the Birth of the Hero and Other Writings*. New York: Alfred A. Knopf, Inc., 1959.

———. *Psychology and the Soul*. Philadelphia: University of Pennsylvania Press, 1950.

———. *Die Inzestmotive in Dichtung und Sage: Grundzüge einer Psychologie des dichterischen Schaffens*. Leipzig and Wien: F. Deuticke, 1912.

REICHELT, A. "Der steinerne Himmel," *Indogermanische Forschungen* (1913), 32:23–57.

REIK, THEODORE. *The Compulsion to Confess: On the Psychoanalysis of Crime and Punishment*. New York: Evergreen Books, 1961.

———. *Myth and Guilt: The Crime and Punishment of Mankind*. New York: George Braziller, 1957.

———. "Oedipus und die Sphinx," *Imago* (1922), 6:95–131.

REITZENSTEIN, FRIEDRICH. "Der Kausalzusammenhang zwischen Geschlechtverkehr und Empfängniss im Glaube und Brauch der Natur-und Kultur-Völker," *Zeitschrift für Ethnologie* (1909), 41:444–83.

REITZENSTEIN, RICHARD. *Weltuntergangsvorstellungen: Eine Studie zur vergleichenden Religionsgeschichte*. Uppsala, Sweden: A. B. Lundequist, 1924.

RÓHEIM, GÉZA. *The Gates of the Dream.* New York: International University Press, 1953.

―――. *The Riddle of the Sphinx or Human Origins.* (International Psycho-Analytical Library, No. 25.) London: Hogarth Press, 1934.

ROSCHER, H. *Ephialtes, eine pathologisch-mythologische Abhandlung über die Alpträume und Alpdämonen des klassischen Altertums.* (Sächsische Gesellschaft der Wissenschaften, vol. 20.) Leipzig: S. Hirzel Verlag, 1900.

ROWLEY, JULIUS L. "Rumpelstiltskin in the Analytical Situation," *International Journal of Psycho-Analysis* (1951), 32:190–95.

SAUSSURE, R. DE. "The Metapsychology of Pleasure," *International Journal of Psycho-Analysis* (1959), 40:81–93.

SCHILDER, PAUL. "Psychoanalysis of Space," *International Journal of Psycho-Analysis* (1935), 16:274–95.

―――. "Relation between Clinging and Equilibrium," *International Journal of Psycho-Analysis* (1939), 22:58–63.

SCHNEIDER, HERMANN. *Die Götter der Germanen.* Tübingen: Mohr, 1938.

SCHRADER, O. *Reallexikon der Indogermanischen Altertumskunde.* Zweite, vermehrte und umbearbeitete Auflage. Herausgegeben von A. Nehring. Berlin-Leipzig: Walter de Gruyter, 1917–1923.

SCHREBER, DANIEL PAUL. *Mémoires of My Nervous Illness.* Translated by Ida Macalpine and Richard A. Hunter. Cambridge, Mass.: Robert Bentley, 1955.

SCHULZE, WILHELM. *Der Tod des Kambyses.* Sitzungsberichte der königl. Preussischen Akademie der Wissenschaften. Berlin: 1912, 32–34, pp. 685–703.

SEARLES, HAROLD F. "The Evolution of the Mother Transference in Psychotherapy with Schizophrenic Patients," in *Psychotherapy of Psychoses,* ed. Arthur Burton. New York: Basic Books, Inc., 1961.

SECHEHAYE, MARGUERITE. "The Curative Function of Symbols in a Case of Traumatic Neurosis with Psychotic Reactions," in *Psychotherapy of the Psychoses,* ed. by Arthur Burton. New York: Basic Books, Inc., 1961, pp. 124–51.

―――. *A New Psychotherapy in Schizophrenia: Relief of Frustrations by Symbolic Realization.* New York: Grune & Stratton, Inc., 1956, pp. 18–19.

―――. *Symbolic Realization: A New Method of Psychotherapy*

Applied to a Case of Schizophrenia. New York: International University Press, 1951, pp. 48–66.

SEGAL, HANNA. "Notes on Symbol Formation," *International Journal of Psycho-Analysis* (1957), 38:391–97.

SIEBENTHAL, W. V. *Die Wissenschaft vom Traum. Ergebnisse und Probleme: Eine Einführung in die allgemeinen Grundlagen.* Berlin and Göttingen: Springer-Verlag, 1953, pp. 383–88.

SIEBS, O. "Things and die Alaisiagen," *Zeitschrift für deutsche Philologie* (1891), 24:433–56.

SILBERER, HERBERT. "Phantasie und Mythus: Vornehmlich vom Gesichstpunkte der funktionalen Kategorie betrachtet," *Jahrbuch für psychoanalytische und psychopathologische Forschungen* (1910), 2:540–622.

SINGER, B. *Shame and Guilt: A Psychoanalytic and a Cultural Study.* Springfield, Ill.: Charles C. Thomas, Publisher, 1953.

SITTL. *Gebärden der Griechen und Römer,* p. 103.

SOPHOCLES. *The Oedipus Cycle.* English Versions by Dudley Fitts and Robert Fitzgerald. New York: Harcourt, Brace & World, Inc.

———. *Oedipus King.* Translated by Bernard M. W. Knox. New York: Washington Square Press, Inc., 1959.

SPITZER, LEO. *Essays in Historical Semantics.* New York: S. F. Vanni, 1947.

———. *Classical and Christian Ideas of World Harmony. Prolegomena to an Interpretation of the Word Stimmung.* Edited by Anna Granville Hatcher. Preface by René Welleck. Baltimore: The Johns Hopkins Press, 1963.

STERBA, EDITHA. "Interpretation and Education," *The Psychoanalytical Study of the Child* (1945), 1:309–17.

STERN, WILLIAM. "Cloud Pictures: A New Method of Testing Imagination," *General Psychology from the Personalistic Standpoint.* Translated by H. D. Spoerl. New York: The Macmillan Company, 1938.

Strabo, The Geography of, with an English translation by Horace Leonard Jones. London: Heinemann, and New York: G. P. Putnam's Sons, 1923.

SZÁSZ, THOMAS. *Pain and Pleasure.* New York: Basic Books, Inc., 1957.

SZÉKELY, L. "Biological Remarks on Fears Originating in Early Childhood," *International Journal of Psycho-Analysis,* 35:57–67.

TAUSK, VICTOR. "On the Origin of the Influencing Machine in

Schizophrenia," *Psychoanalytic Quarterly* (1933), 2:519–56.

THASS-THIENEMANN, THEODORE. "The Talking Teapot: A Note on Psycho-Linguistics," *Comprehensive Psychiatry* (1960), 1:199–200.

———. "Oedipus and the Sphinx. The Linguistic Approach to Unconscious Phantasies," *The Psychoanalytical Review* (1957), 44:10–33.

———. "Left-handed Writing: A Study in the Psychoanalysis of Language," *Psychoanalytical Review* (1955), 42:239–61.

TREVETT, LAWRENCE D. "Origin the Creation Myth: A Hypothesis," *Journal of the American Psychoanalytical Association* (1957), 5:461–68.

TROST, PAUL. "Schimpfwörter als Kosenamen," *Indogermanische Forschungen* (1933), 51:101–12.

USENER, HERMANN. "Milch und Honig," *Kleine Schriften*. Stuttgart: Teubner Verlagsgesellschaft, mbH, 1913, 4:398–417.

WAELDER, ROBERT. "The Psychoanalytic Theory of Play," *Psychoanalytic Quarterly* (1933), 2:208–229.

WEGENER, LEOPOLD. "Sprachforschung und Rechtswissenschaft," *Wörter und Sachen* (1909), 1:84–94.

WELCKER, F. G. "Entbindung," *Kleine Schriften*. Bonn: Weber, 1950, 3:185–208.

WELLISCH, ERICH. *Isaac and Oedipus: A Study in Biblical Psychology of the Sacrifice of Isaac. The Akedah*. London: Routledge & Kegan Paul, Ltd., 1954.

WERKMEISTER, W. H. "An Introduction to Heidegger's Existential Philosophy," *Philosophical and Phenomenological Research*, 2:79–87.

WERNER, HEINZ. *Comparative Psychology of Mental Development*. New York: International University Press, 1957, pp. 172–173.

WHITE, LESLIE A. "The Definition and Prohibition of Incest," *American Anthropologist* (1948), 50:416–35.

WIJK, N. VAN. "Zur Etymologie einiger Wörter für leer," *Indogermanische Forschungen*, Strassburg: Trübner (1915), 35:265–68.

WINICOTT, D. W. "The Capacity to Be Alone," *International Journal of Psycho-Analysis* (1958), 39:416–23.

WISSOWA, GEORG. "Religion und Kultus der Römer," *Handbuch der Klass. Altertumswissenschaft*, ed. Iwan Miller. München: Beck (1912), 5:138.

404

WOLBERG, LEWIS R. *Hypnoanalysis*. New York: Grove Press, 1960, p. 181.

ZAEHNER, R. C. *The Dawn and Twilight of Zoroastrianism*. London: Weidenfeld and Nicolson, 1961.

ZELIG, DOROTHY F. "The Role of the Mother in the Development of Hebraic Monotheism, as Exemplified in the Life of Abraham," *The Psychoanalytic Study of Society* (1960), 1:287–310.

Zend-Avesta. Part I: The Vendidad. Translated by James Darmestäter. (*The Sacred Books of the East*, Vol. IV.) Oxford: Clarendon Press, 1880, 1:17–18.

ZETZEL, ELISABETH R. "The Concept of Anxiety in Relation to the Development of Psychoanalysis," *Journal of The American Psychoanalytic Association* (1955), 3:369–87.

ZILBOORG, GREGORY. "The Sense of Reality," *Psychoanalytic Quarterly* (1941), 10:183–210.

———. "The Sense of Immortality," *Psychoanalytic Quarterly* (1938), 7:171–82.

INDEX OF NAMES

(This index consists of proper, place, and mythological names, as well as book titles.)

BIBLICAL REFERENCES

INDEX OF SUBJECTS

412

422

INDEX OF FOREIGN WORDS

FRENCH

GERMAN

GOTHIC

GREEK

In transcription and Latin alphabetical order

428

430

schidzō, 18
skirtaō, 141
skor, skoria, 180
skotos, skotia, 144
Sōkratēs, 124
sōma, sōmatikon, sōtēr, soteira,
  25, 124, 224, 278
Sōphoklēs, 124
spadō, 103
spao, 114
spartos, 245
speirō, 245
sphallō, sphalma, 95
sphilos, 318
sphingō, 87, 237
stoma, stomachos, stomation, 38,
  56, 59
sudzux, sudzeugnumi, 332, 346
sullambanō, 77
sumbibadzō, 346
sunidein, sunoida, 97

teleioō, 28; telelestai, 29
teknon, 30–31
tersomai, 160
tiktō, 31
Thanatos, 277
thēladzō, thēlē, thēlus, thēnion,
  34, 90, 363 fn
theos, theoi patroi, 232, 243
thēsatō, 34
thēsauros, 89–91
thēsthai, 34
Thetis, 347
thlaō, 103
thlibō, 103
thumos, 278
tomias, 103
tromos, 239
tulos, 84
Zeus, Zeus Soter, Zeupatēr, 124,
  159, 233, 265–66; Zeus huei,
  150, 265
Zephyros, 266

HEBREW
In transcription and Latin alphabetical order

Adam, 164, 325
alām, almāh, 79
aphar, 167
bādath, 21
bāth, 18
bethūlāh, 78
Beulah, 368
bhōhū, 20, 143
chābā, chābab, chōb, 32
charash, 349
chālāl, 138, 345
chebyōm, 32
dāgh, 17
dōd, 360 fn
Eden, 176
Elohim, 148, 174, 233
ēmāh, 311
ervāh, 204
ēyshōne, 57
gālāh, 204
Hephzibah, 368
ishshah, 325
Joab, 268, 302
Jahve, 174
kadhash, kadhesh, kadhosh, 26
liwyāthān, 199

mayim, 143
mille yādh, 63
nāgan, 345
nāphach, 203
nephesh, 278
ōmeneth, 307
ōwnāh, 333
pārāh, 201
periy, 201
rēshith, 134, 135
rōsh, 134, 411
ruach, 278
tā'am, tē'em, 74
tappūach, 203
techōm, 143, 144, 146, 152, 160
thōhū, 20, 143
yabbasēth, 160
yādha, 202
yārē, 311
yātsār, yētsēr, 165
Yehonathan, 243
Yiphtāch, Yephtach, 140
yotsēr, 165
zāmar, 201
zānāh, 335
zimrāh, 201

HUNGARIAN

ITALIAN

LATIN

434

tumor, 85
tutō, -āre, tūtus, 270, 288
umbilicus, 224
universum, 160
urina, 150
uterus, 38
ut pote, 80, 284
uxor, 331
vas, vascellum, vasculum, 172
veneris diem, 216
venus, venereus, 210, 341

veniō, -īre, 139
venēnum, 341
verpa, verpus, 101
vertō, -ere, 22, 160
videō, -ēre, 82
virga, 101
virgō, viragō, 361, 365–66
volvō, -ere, 224
volup, voluptas, 189
vortex, 22

OLD ENGLISH

ādiēdan, 271
ae, aew, awa, 192; aewbrecca, 331
age, 311
allne waeg, 191
anlic, 23
aweccan, 242
āwiht, 67–68
baeddel, 113
bancofa, banfaet, banhūs, 276–77
bearn, 31
becuman, 139
beran, 22, 31, 241
besittan, 89
beutan, 23
blodisojan, blōma, blodsung, 184, 245–46
brotherhad, 50
brydguma, 164
cearu, 240
cennan, cenning, 76, 79, 241–42
cild, cildhama, 16, 50
clūd, 155
costian, 73
crocwyrhta, 168
cusc, 363
cwead, 167
cwelan, cwalu, 270
daegee, 285
dagian, dagung, 158
dritan, 167
ealdorgedāl, 273
eam, 358, 360
erian, 348
faedera, 360
faest, 147
feltum, 177
flaeschoma, 277
forlegis, forlegystre, 339
forlicgan, 339

forthfaran, forthfore, 271
forweordhan, 273–74
frea, freo, freobear, 216, 324, 331
frigu, 216
fri wīf locbore, 335
gamaeca, gamaecian, 329
gebedda, gebedscipe, 330
gesceap, gesceapu, 171–72
gestrynan, 243
gierd, 101
ginhan, aginan, onginnan, gin-faest, 146–47
goldhordhūs, 89, 179
gyldan, gylt, gyltend, 291
haelan, 104
haeman, haemed-, haemere, 77, 328–29
had, 50
hāl, hālic, 25
ham, 358
Hengist, 316
heofen hwealf, 157; heofonrōf, 158
hlaefdige, 285
hlāf, hlāford, 285
hord, hordweard, 91–92, 285
Horsa, 316
hūsheofan, 157
hyd, 92
invit, 81
jobbe (Middle-English), 209
laewede, 116
lamwyrhta, 168
leas, 19
līc, līcian, 169
macian, 166
Maegdeland, 321–22
manhad, 50
meltan, 276

OLD HIGH GERMAN

OLD NORSE

SANSKRIT

In transcription and Latin alphabetical order

aham, 53
astam, 123
dampati, 279, 284
durvana, 180 fn
Dyaush, dyū, div, 159
kapāla, 254
kōsthah, 91, 92
langala, langula, 350
nasatē, 123

pairidaēza, 176
pitar, 159
ragatam heranyan, 180 fn
savarna, 180 fn
sunyam, sunyata, 27
ukshan, 329
Ushas, 158
vanas, 210
varsati, 150

SLAVIC

In transcription and Latin alphabetical order

atyuska, 36
baba, 35
gonchar, 167
gospodi, 284
grunici, grinicari, 167
jalkavaino, 330
kavka, 337
matka, 37
nevesta, nevestka, 336
neprazdinu, 19

niemowle, 30
niewasta, 78
ogni, ogniste, ogniscaninu, 285
pats, 80, 284
prazdinu, 19
rabu, rabota, robota, 197
samo, 284
svetu, 162
vunuku, 359

SPANISH

alba, 158
caribe, 249
comenzar, 139
cumplitudo está, 29
labrar, 342, 350
mondo, 162
niña, ninnolo, 58

ollero, 167
principio, 138
puto, 100
saber, 74
seno, 32
trabajo, 197